Competitive Government: Public Private Partnerships

Series Editors
Simon Hakim, Center for Competitive Government, Temple University, Philadelphia, PA, USA

Adrian Moore, Reason Foundation, Los Angeles, CA, USA

Robert M. Clark, University of Cincinnati, Cincinnati, OH, USA

More information about this series at http://www.springer.com/series/16085

Robert M. Clark • Simon Hakim
Editors

Public Private Partnerships

Construction, Protection, and Rehabilitation of Critical Infrastructure

Springer

Editors
Robert M. Clark
Environmental Engineering and Public Health Consultant
Cincinnati, OH, USA

Simon Hakim
Center for Competitive Government
Temple University
Philadelphia, PA, USA

ISSN 2524-4183 ISSN 2524-4191 (electronic)
Competitive Government: Public Private Partnerships
ISBN 978-3-030-24599-3 ISBN 978-3-030-24600-6 (eBook)
https://doi.org/10.1007/978-3-030-24600-6

This Springer imprint is published by the registered company Springer Nature Switzerland AG
The registered company address is: Gewerbestrasse 11, 6330 Cham, Switzerland

Contents

About the Authors

P. O. Achard is an Associate Professor of Economics and Business Management at the University of L'Aquila (Italy). She is currently teaching Economics and Business Management to graduate students and Management and Governance of International Business to postgraduate students. She is component of the Scientific Board of the MS on Health Care Management of University of L'Aquila, and local referent of the Italian Society of Management. She teaches Healthcare Strategic Management and Organizational Design and Behavior and Strategic Human Resource Management to healthcare professionals. She collaborates with the Italian School of Finance Police teaching Economics and Business Management. Her special area of research and teaching is Public Management, with emphasis on healthcare sector. She published several papers and leading books on the topic, mainly referring to the Italian system. She was member of the Control and Evaluation Unit at the University of L'Aquila, for almost 8 years. She was also a member of Ph.D. Committee at the University of L'Aquila and at the Guido Carli Free International University for Social Studies (LUISS) in Rome, member of the Scientific Committee of Inter-departmental Unit of Epidemiology and Health Care Planning, and Scientific Referee for Health Care Education, at the University of L'Aquila, from 2006 to 2009. She had several Visiting Chairs at LUISS since 2001, teaching Management and Organization Behavior, Economics and Management of Public Utilities, and Human Resource Management. She also taught Behavior and Healthcare Management at the Catholic University of the Sacred Heart in Rome from 1997 to 2006, and she was charged of teaching in several undergraduate, graduate, and postgraduate classes for students, professionals, and managers (university and professional posts). She was component and leader of researcher teams for the development of theoretical and applied studies funded by public and private organizations. She had a long time experience (more than ten years) as Manager of a Private Company working in the field of high education in Italy. She earned an M.S. in Economics at LUISS, a Professional Qualification as Chattered Accountant at the University of L'Aquila, and a cooperation Ph.D. program in Management at the University of Cassino, LUISS, University of L'Aquila, and University of Rome "La Sapienza."

James Barlow has been a Professor of Technology and Innovation Management at Imperial College Business School since 2003. He previously worked at the Science Policy Research Unit (SPRU), University of Sussex, and the Policy Studies Institute, London. James' work focuses on innovation in healthcare from creation to adoption. He is particularly interested in the complex relationship between innovation in health technologies, services, and infrastructure. From 2006 to 2013, he was principal investigator of a multi-university research center focusing on innovation in healthcare infrastructure. James has led or been involved in many research projects and has extensive experience advising and consulting for government and industry. His work includes research on the development and operation of Public-Private Partnerships (PPP) in the health sector. James' research on the implications of the UK's health PPP program for innovation helped inform a House of Commons Treasury Committee inquiry into their effectiveness. His current research focuses on a range of health technology innovation issues. James has a number of advisory roles, including Associate Director of Research for Imperial College Health Partners, President of the International Academy for Design and Health, and membership of Deloitte's health innovation advisory board. He has published widely in journals including *Organization Science*, *Research Policy*, *Health Affairs*, *Social Science & Medicine*, *California Management Review*, and the *Bulletin of the WHO*. His latest book *Managing Innovation in Healthcare* was published in 2017 by World Scientific.

Eddie W. L. Cheng is an Assistant Professor in the Department of Social Sciences at the Education University of Hong Kong. He earned his first Ph.D. in Project Management from Hong Kong Polytechnic University and his second Ph.D. in Business Management from the University of New South Wales. He also completed postgraduate programs from several well-known universities, including University of London, The University of Hong Kong, University of Leicester, and Griffith University. He has got more than 15 years' working experience in the education sector. He has served as a researcher at Hong Kong Polytechnic University and The University of Hong Kong. He has also worked in Australia as a lecturer at School of Management, Queensland University of Technology, and a senior lecturer at Southern Cross Business School, Southern Cross University. He is an active researcher and has published more than 70 papers in mainstream journals. He has presented in international conferences and is well received by colleagues in the field of construction economics and project management. He is currently a member of the Editorial Advisory Board of the journal *Information and Learning Sciences* (Emerald Publishing; listed in Emerging Sources Citation Index).

Robert M. Clark is currently an independent consultant in environmental engineering and public health. He is an Adjunct Professor in Civil and Environmental Engineering at the University of Cincinnati and was a member of the National Research Council's Committee on "Public Water Distribution Systems: Assessing and Reducing Risks." As a consultant, Dr. Clark's work includes research on homeland security and protection of critical infrastructure in collaboration with Sandia National Laboratories, the US Environmental Protection Agency (USEPA), Rutgers

University (Newark Campus), and the University of Cincinnati, among others. He served as an environmental engineer in the US Public Health Service and the US EPA from 1961 to August 2002 and was Director of the USEPA's Water Supply and Water Resources Division (WSWRD) for 14 years (1985–1999). In 1999, he was appointed to a Senior Expert Position in the USEPA with the title Senior Research Engineering Advisor and retired from the USEPA in August 2002. Dr. Clark was a member of USEPA's Water Protection Task Force and was USEPA's liaison for homeland security research. Dr. Clark has published over 415 papers and 6 books and has edited 6 volumes and has been professionally active in several organizations where he served in numerous leadership positions. He is a lifetime member of both the American Water Works Association (AWWA) and the American Society of Civil Engineers (ASCE). Dr. Clark is recognized both nationally and internationally and has received numerous awards for his work. Dr. Clark holds B.S. degrees in Civil Engineering from Oregon State University (1960) and in Mathematics from Portland State University (1961), M.S. degrees in Mathematics from Xavier University (1964) and Civil Engineering from Cornell University (1968), and a Ph.D. in Environmental Engineering from the University of Cincinnati (1976). He is a registered engineer in the State of Ohio.

Baruch Feigenbaum is Assistant Director of Transportation Policy at Reason Foundation a nonprofit think-tank advancing free minds and free markets. He earned his Master's degree in City and Regional Planning (Transportation) with a focus in Engineering from the Georgia Institute of Technology. Prior to joining Reason, Feigenbaum handled transportation issues on Capitol Hill for Representative Lynn Westmoreland. Feigenbaum has a diverse background researching and implementing transportation issues including revenue and finance, public-private partnerships, roadway pricing, highways, transit, intelligent transportation systems, land use, and local policymaking. Feigenbaum is involved with various transportation organizations. He is a member of the Transportation Research Board Intelligent Transportation Systems Committee, Secretary of the Bus Transit Committee, and chairs the Bus Transit Conference Subcommittee. He is President of the Transportation and Research Forum Washington Chapter, a reviewer for the *Journal of the American Planning Association* (JAPA), and a contributor to Planetizen. He has appeared on NBC Nightly News and CNBC. His work has been featured in the *Washington Post* and *Wall Street Journal*. Feigenbaum has testified in front of the Senate Finance and House Oversight Committee on transportation matters.

Michael J. Garvin is an Associate Professor in the Via Department of Civil and Environmental Engineering and a principal faculty member in the Myers-Lawson School of Construction at Virginia Tech. His research and teaching focus on infrastructure development strategies, project delivery methods, and contract design and administration. He has a particular interest in the structure and effectiveness of Public-Private Partnerships (P3s). He has led or participated in a variety of research projects including ones funded by the National Science Foundation, the Federal Highway Administration (FHWA), the Virginia Department of Transportation, and several private organizations. Dr. Garvin served as an advisor to the Eno Transportation Foundation on its P3 policy initiative, and he is a member of the Advisory Board of the Association for the Improvement of American Infrastructure (AIAI), which was formed to help shape the direction of the US P3 marketplace. Since 2012, he has served as an expert advisor to FHWA's Office of Innovative Program Delivery, providing input to multiple P3 initiatives by the Office. Dr. Garvin has authored or coauthored over 100 journal articles, book chapters, conference papers, and technical reports. He received a B.S. in Civil Engineering from the United States Military Academy and M.S. and Ph.D. degrees from the Massachusetts Institute of Technology. He is a registered professional engineer in the State of Georgia.

Tristan P. Gleeson is an Associate Director in Ernst & Young's, Transaction Advisory Services, and Infrastructure team. He has provided commercial and financial advisory services on PPPs and other infrastructure projects in Victoria and Australia in this capacity and prior to this worked for Transurban Group, a private toll road investor and operator, for 8 years. He is a Senior Associate of the Financial Services Institute of Australasia (Finsia). Mr. Gleeson has contributed toward a number of thought leadership pieces published by Ernst & Young. He holds a B.A. majoring in Economics, a Diploma in Modern Languages majoring in Indonesian, and a Postgraduate Diploma in Planning and Design majoring in Urban Planning, all from the University of Melbourne. He also holds a Graduate Diploma of Applied Finance majoring in Corporate Finance from Finsia/Kaplan.

Darrin Grimsey is Partner with Ernst & Young's, Transaction Advisory Services, and Infrastructure team, based in Melbourne, Australia. He has 30 years' experience working on infrastructure projects as an engineer, project manager, and financial adviser. He specializes in commercial, strategic, and financial advice, project structuring, risk identification, procurement, and contract negotiations. He has extensive experience advising governments on PPP policy and guidelines as well as delivering PPP projects in health, education, corrections, light rail, roads, justice, events, and water. Mr Grimsey's publications include 3 books, 16 journal articles, and 6 book chapters. A special area of interest has been PPPs, with 3 books and numerous articles coauthored with Professor Mervyn K. Lewis. Their book, *Public Private Partnerships: the Worldwide Revolution in Infrastructure Provision and Project Finance* (Elgar, 2004), won the $30,000 Blake Dawson Waldron Prize for Business Literature in 2005, and a Chinese language edition was published in Shanghai in 2008. The other two books published on PPPs and related topics are *The Economics of Public Private Partnerships: The International Library of Critical Writings in Economics* (Elgar, 2005) and *Global Developments in Public Infrastructure Procurement: Evaluating Public Private Partnerships and Other Procurement Options* (Elgar, 2017). He holds a B.Eng. (Hons) in Civil Engineering and an M.Sc. in Management and the Implementation of Development Projects. He regularly conducts lectures, training, and presentations on infrastructure-related topics.

Simon Hakim is a Professor of Economics and Director of the Center for Competitive Government at Temple University. He is currently editing a book series on Protecting Critical Infrastructures with Springer Publisher. He earned an M.A. and Ph.D. degrees in Regional Science from the University of Pennsylvania. He also holds an M.Sc. degree in City and Regional Planning from the Technion, Israel Institute of Technology, and a B.A. in Economics at Hebrew University in Jerusalem. His special areas of research and teaching are privatization, public policy, private/public police, and homeland security. Dr. Hakim has published 58 scientific articles in leading economic, criminal justice, security, and public policy journals. He has written over 40 professional articles and edited 14 books. He collaborated with Professor Blackstone on a major textbook dealing with the security industry. He is constantly invited to teach classes on privatization, and international economics in M.B.A. programs worldwide. Dr. Hakim has conducted several funded research and consulting projects for the US Departments of Justice and Labor, the Commonwealth Foundation, the Independent Institute, the Alarm Industry Research and Education Foundation, the City of Philadelphia, the Philadelphia International Airport, ADT, Vector Security, and other leading security companies.

I. M. Korayem Ph.D. is a licensed Professional Engineer and Project Management Consultant. His international experience includes almost 20 years of completed projects in Canada and the Middle East. Since 2012, he has worked for ASTAD Project Management as the Project Manager for the Qatar Foundation Tram, the first hybrid energy battery-powered tram system and first rail project of its kind in Qatar. This $600M endeavor is pivotal to Qatar's goal of transforming Education City into an environmentally friendly "smart-city" and is a model for sustainable rail rapid transit. The two-person team formed to manage the project has grown by Dr. Korayem to 55. He was instrumental in its becoming the basis for ASTAD's new rail division of 100 employees, which has secured subsequent projects in Qatar. Prior to that, between 2006 and 2012, Dr. Korayem worked for Jacques Whitford AXYS (now Stantec) and AMEC, providing civil design and construction services for numerous projects in Western Canada, ranging from oil and gas facilities and pipelines to transportation projects including railways, highways, and bridges, as well as several commercial and residential developments. Dr. Korayem has explored his long-standing interest in infrastructure project finance both practically and theoretically. He is committed to ongoing research and has taken public-private partnerships, risk management, and decision-making theories as applied to infrastructure projects as his subjects of particular study. He is the author of a number of articles and presents at academic conferences on these topics, activities that have brought him two nominations and, in 2017, the honor of being named "Project Manager of the Year in Qatar" by Construction Week. Dr. Korayem earned his Ph.D. in Construction Management and Economics from Heriot-Watt University, UK, and holds a B.Sc. degree in Civil Engineering from Alexandria University, Egypt.

Patrick T. I. Lam is a Professor in the Department of Building and Real Estate at the Hong Kong Polytechnic University. He has had rich professional and academic experiences. On the professional side, he practiced for 10 years in multidisciplinary design office, consultant quantity surveyors, and contractor/developer both in Hong Kong and Singapore. On the academic side, he has had substantial experience lecturing on undergraduate and postgraduate programs in universities and polytechnics. Patrick is active in research and consultancy projects related to the business management aspects of construction, including contracts, financing, PPP, etc. Recently, he has been engaged in research on the business models of renewable energy and smart cities. He is a Certified Cost Professional with AACE International and a Certified Data Centre Specialist (Operations).

Mervyn K. Lewis was appointed Emeritus Professor of the University of South Australia in 2016. He is also Emeritus Fellow of the Academy of Social Sciences in Australia. Until his retirement he was Professor of Banking and Finance at the University of South Australia. Previously, he was for 12 years Midland Bank Professor of Money and Banking at the University of Nottingham, UK. Elected a Fellow of the Academy of the Social Sciences in Australia in 1986, Professor Lewis' publications include 28 books, 72 journal articles, and 94 book chapters. A special area of interest has been PPPs, with three books and numerous articles coauthored with Darrin Grimsey. Their book, *Public Private Partnerships: the Worldwide Revolution in Infrastructure Provision and Project Finance* (Elgar, 2004), won the $30,000 Blake Dawson Waldron Prize for Business Literature in 2005, and a Chinese language edition was published in Shanghai in 2008. The other two books published on PPPs and related topics are *The Economics of Public Private Partnerships: The International Library of Critical Writings in Economics* (Elgar, 2005) and *Global Developments in Public Infrastructure Procurement: Evaluating Public Private Partnerships and Other Procurement Options* (Elgar, 2017).

Lawrence L. Martin is Professor of Public Affairs at the University of Central Florida in Orlando. He earned his M.B.A. from the American Graduate School of International Management (Thunderbird) and his Ph.D. in Political Science from Arizona State University. He has taught at Arizona State University (Tempe) and Columbia University (New York City). Prior to his academic career he worked for 15 years in state and local government in Arizona. He has published 45 books and major monographs and over 100 professional papers. Two of his most recent publications are *Private Financing of Public Transportation Infrastructure Utilizing Public-Private Partnerships* (Lexington Books, 2015) and *Public-Private Partnerships: What Local Government Managers Need to Know* (International City/County Management Association [ICMA], 2018). Dr. Martin has provided consultation, training, and technical assistance on public procurement and service contracting to government and nongovernmental organizations (NGOs) domestically and internationally. He served on the task force that developed the "Public-Private Partnership (P3) Facilities & Infrastructure" guidelines for the National Institute of Governmental Purchasing (NIGP). He currently serves on the "Public-Private

Partnership Task Force" of the Governmental Accounting Standards Board (GASB). He is a member of the International Public-Private Partnership Scholars Network (IP3SN).

S. O. Ogunlana is currently the Chair of Construction Project Management at the School of Energy, Geo-Science, Infrastructure and Society at Heriot-Watt University, Scotland. He has an international reputation for research in the application of system dynamics simulation to construction projects and organizations. He is the author of over 200 scholarly publications in top-tier journals and refereed conferences. He is also the editor of the book *Profitable Partnering for Construction Procurement* published by Taylor and Francis and *Training for Construction Industry Development* published by the CIB/AIT and coeditor of *Joint Ventures in Construction* (Thomas Telford) and *Public-Private Partnership in Infrastructure Development – Case Studies from Asia and Europe* (Bauhaus Universitat Weimar). He is also the coauthor of the book, *Megaprojects Risk Analysis and Simulation: A Dynamic Systems Approach* (Emerald). His research work has been funded by the Canadian International Development Agency, European Union, Thai National Housing Authority, UNOCAL, Japanese Government, The British Council, Thailand Research Fund, etc. His works on leadership were awarded Emerald Literati Award for two consecutive years (2009 and 2010) for the most outstanding paper in the journal *Engineering Construction and Architectural Management.* Professor Ogunlana is the joint coordinator of CIB W107 Commission on Construction in Developing Economies and a member of the Editorial Board for over 10 internationally refereed academic journals. He has continuing interest in technology innovation for project management and in public-private partnerships for infrastructure delivery.

Seung-Kuk Paik is a Professor and a Department Chair of Systems and Operations Management in the David Nazarian College of Business and Economics at California State University, Northridge. He received his Ph.D. and M.B.A. from the George Washington University, Washington, DC. He also holds a B.A. from Sogang University in Seoul, South Korea. His recent research interests include supply chain management in small and medium sized enterprises, the bullwhip effects in supply chains, and the impacts of the elements of manufacturing excellence on supply chain performance. He has published a number of his scholarly articles in several leading international journals in operations management and supply chain management, including *European Journal of Operational Research* and *International Journal of Logistics Management.* He has also completed several funded research projects in logistics and supply chain management in developing countries for the World Bank and the USAID.

Robert W. Poole Jr. was among the first to propose the commercialization of the US air traffic control system, and his work in this field has helped shape proposals for a US ATC corporation. A version of his nonprofit corporation concept was implemented in Canada in 1996. He has advised the Office of the Secretary of

Transportation, the White House Office of Policy Development, the National Performance Review, the National Economic Council, and the National Civil Aviation Review Commission on ATC commercialization. He is a member of the Air Traffic Control Association and of the GAO's National Aviation Studies Advisory Panel. In 2012–2013, he was a member of the Business Roundtable task force on ATC reform, and in 2014–2015 he was part of the Eno Center for Transportation working group on ATC reform. In 2018, he received the Eno Center's Thought Leader Award for his work on ATC corporatization. Poole's Reason studies helped launch a national debate on airport privatization in the United States. He advised both the FAA and local officials during the 1989–1990 controversy over the proposed privatization of Albany (NY) Airport. His policy research on this issue helped inspire the privatization of Indianapolis airport management under Mayor Steve Goldsmith and Congress's 1996 enactment of the Airport Investment Partnership Program. In aviation security, Poole advised the White House and House Republican leaders on what became the Aviation & Transportation Security Act of 2001, enacted in response to the 9/11 attacks. He has authored a number of Reason policy studies on aviation security and is the author of a paper on risk-based aviation security for the OECD's International Transport Forum. Poole has testified on airports, aviation security, and air traffic control on a number of occasions before House and Senate aviation and homeland security subcommittees, and he has spoken on these subjects before numerous conferences. He has also done consulting work on several airport privatization feasibility studies. Poole also edits a monthly Reason Foundation e-newsletter on aviation policy issues. He received his B.S. and M.S. in Mechanical Engineering at MIT and did graduate work in Operations Research at NYU.

Jens K. Roehrich is the HPC Chair in Supply Chain Innovation and the Director of the HPC Supply Chain Innovation Lab at the School of Management, University of Bath, UK. Before joining Bath, Jens was a researcher at Imperial College London, UK. Individual and collaborative research activities have emphasized a research focus on long-term inter-organizational relationship management across public and private organizations. Within this agenda, significant strands of research explore: (1) the interplay of contractual and relational governance mechanisms; (2) procuring and managing complex capital projects such as public-private partnerships; (3) the dark side of relationships such as conflicts, trust breaches, and opportunism; and (4) sustainable supply chain management. His research is multidisciplinary, drawing theoretical inspiration and methodological support from operations management, economics, strategy, innovation management, healthcare, and policy management. Jens's research has been published in journals such as *Journal of Management Studies*, *International Journal of Operations & Production Management*, *British Journal of Management*, *Social Science & Medicine*, and *Industrial Marketing Management*. Jens has also written for leading news outlets and trade journals such as *The Conversation*, *Retail Gazette*, and *Supply Management - CIPS*. His research and expert insights have also been profiled in the media including *Forbes*, *The Times – Raconteur*, *The Epoch Times*, and *South West Business Insider*.

Stephen Wright is based in the UK. He began his professional career in resource and energy industry issues—university research, consultancy, and then an energy investing holding company. He joined the European Investment Bank in 1987 to work on arranging the finance for projects in energy, and later industrial sectors, transport, mining, economic development in emerging countries, and solid waste. From 1997, he initiated, and then ran until 2007, the Bank's project techno-economic and sector role in the health and education sectors. EIB clients were and are entities in the public and private sectors, and public-private partnerships. He has been the coeditor and coauthor of a number of books, including particularly *Investing in Hospitals of the Future* (2009) with an accompanying case studies volume, *Capital Investment in Health*; a book on modern hospitals is forthcoming in 2019. He has written many papers in peer-reviewed and professional journals on healthcare planning, finance, and PPP, and speaks regularly at conferences in Europe and further afield. From 2009, Stephen has set up two research and strategic advisory organizations, focused on the interface between the built environment and delivery of healthcare, and social investment in the wider sense. Stephen carries out multiple consulting assignments annually, mostly in the health sector, for a variety of clients including the European Commission, EIB, World Bank, World Health Organization, and multiple governments (Hungary, Slovakia, Ireland, and others). Much of his work is in emerging markets, in Europe or beyond, and covers macroeconomics, trade impact, health policy, finance, and PPP. Stephen has a joint Geography and Economics B.Sc. (Econ.) from University College London (1974) and an M.Litt. in the Economics of Natural Resources from Kings College Aberdeen (1975).

Frank Vram Zerunyan is a Professor of the Practice of Governance at the University of Southern California Sol Price School of Public Policy and Director of Executive Education at USC Price Bedrosian Center on Governance and The Neely Center for Ethical Leadership and Decision Making, an Interdisciplinary Center USC Marshall USC Viterbi and USC Price (DECIDE). His key areas of expertise include local governments, public-private partnerships, civic and ethical leadership, land use, regulation, negotiation, and executive education. Frank earned his Doctor of Jurisprudence (Doctor of Laws) degree from Western State University College of Law and his Bachelor of Arts degree from California State University Long Beach. He also completed his advanced legal studies in Corporate Taxation at the University of Southern California Law Center (USC Gould). He is a graduate of California League of Cities' Civic Leadership Institute, an educational forum for the state's rising leaders. He teaches graduate courses on intersectoral leadership (collaborative governance), business and public policy, international issues in public policy, negotiation, place institutions, and governance, as well as international laboratory. Frank also lectures locally and globally to build capacity and foster leadership among public executives worldwide. In his capacity as an honorary instructor colonel in the Armenian Army and Air Force, he lectures, coaches, and advises on academic affairs at the Vazgen Sargsyan Military University in Armenia. For his influential work over the past five years at American University of Armenia, Yerevan State University, and Public Administration Academy in Armenia, he was awarded

LL.D. Doctor of Laws—Honoris Causa by the Public Administration Academy of the Republic of Armenia. Frank is a three-term Mayor and still serving Council member in the City of Rolling Hills Estates, California. As a gubernatorial appointee under Governor Schwarzenegger, Frank was a state regulator serving on the Medical Board of California in the Department of Consumer Affairs. Frank has more than 30 years of comprehensive and multi-sectorial experience as a lawyer, judge pro tem, author, consultant, director, board member, professor, and public servant. Frank has been honored as one of Southern California Magazine's Super Lawyers since 2004, The Legal Network's Top Lawyers in California, Marquis' Who's Who in America and American Law and Government institutions like the California Assembly, the California Senate, the County of Los Angeles, and various city governments for his leadership in the public sector.

Chapter 1
Public–Private Partnerships and Their Use in Protecting Critical Infrastructure

Robert M. Clark and Simon Hakim

Abbreviations

ASCE	American Society of Civil Engineers
DHS	Department of Homeland Security
EPCIP	European Program for Critical Infrastructure Protection
GAO	Government Accountability Office
IMF	International Monetary Fund
LLB	Lease and Lease Back
NCPPP	National Council for Public–Private Partnerships
OECD	Organization for Economic Cooperation and Development
PFI	Performance-based initiatives
PPP	Public–Private Partnership
US	United States

Introduction

Critical infrastructure is defined as the essential service or services that underpin and support the backbone of a nation's economy, security, and health, according to the United States (US) Department of Homeland Security (DHS) (Homeland Security 2013). These services include the power used by homes and businesses, drinking water, transportation, stores and shops, and communications. Sixteen

R. M. Clark (✉)
Environmental Engineering and Public Health Consultant, Cincinnati, OH, USA

S. Hakim
Center for Competitive Government, Professor of Economics, Temple University, Philadelphia, PA, USA
e-mail: simon.hakim@temple.edu

R. M. Clark, S. Hakim (eds.), *Public Private Partnerships*, Competitive Government: Public Private Partnerships, https://doi.org/10.1007/978-3-030-24600-6_1

critical infrastructure sectors have been identified that compose the assets, systems, and networks, physical or virtual that are vital to physical security, economic security, and national public health and safety including the following:

- Banking and finance.
- Transportation including road, rail, air, and water transportation infrastructure.
- Power including electricity, oil, and gas.
- Information and communications.
- Federal and municipal services.
- Emergency services.
- Fire departments.
- Law enforcement agencies.
- Public works including safe water systems and drainage.
- Agriculture and food.
- National monuments and icons.

In May 1998, an American Presidential Directive set up a national program of "Critical Infrastructure Protection" Homeland Security Presidential Directive 7: Critical Infrastructure Identification, Prioritization, and Protection (Homeland Security 2003), which was updated on December 17, 2013 (The White House 2013). In Europe, the European Program for Critical Infrastructure Protection (EPCIP) was established as a result of the European Commission's directive (European Commission and Mitigation and Home Affairs 2008). The EPCIP resulted in an agreement in 2004 by the European Council, to establish a program to protect critical infrastructure.

Critical infrastructure in urban areas is particularly important and difficult to protect and maintain. According to Liu et al. (2007), cities and municipalities are complex systems of social, economic, and ecological factors and are at the heart of infrastructure protection. They become very vulnerable when any of their subsystems are destroyed or fail to adapt to new challenges (Coaffee 2010). Critical infrastructure plays a role in protecting against natural disasters, climate change, energy crises, political instability, financial crises, food security, and terrorist attacks and plays an important role in the stability of urban areas. Infrastructure is the backbone of urban economic activity and a necessary input to every economic output. It is critical to every nation's prosperity and its public's health and welfare.

An important constraint on providing critical infrastructure for urban areas is the lack of available financial resources; however, a solution often suggested to help provide these resources is the use of public–private partnerships (PPPs). PPPs have the potential to fill the void between typical annual government accounting and capital budgeting. PPPs include both existing facilities and new-capacity facilities, and a commonality among the different types of PPPs is the need for a dedicated revenue stream.

This book will discuss the objectives and legal requirements associated with PPPs. Experts will discuss the elements that make up a successful PPP as well as provide examples where PPPs have failed. These examples will include the application of the PPP concept in the United States, as well as in Europe, the UK, China, South Korea, and in Australia for a wide variety of infrastructure investment.

Need to Protect, Repair, and Rehabilitate Urban Infrastructure

Poor infrastructure adversely affects public health and social service systems as well as business productivity in urban areas. For example, when one part of the infrastructure system fails, the impact can spread throughout the system and economy (ASCE 2016). The US economy relies on low transportation costs. Business costs and, therefore, prices will generally increase if surface transportation systems and ports, airports, and inland waterways become outdated or congested. Deteriorating infrastructure has the potential to take a toll on families' disposable household income and can impact the quality and quantity of jobs in the economy. Travel times will lengthen with inefficient roadways and congested airports and airspace. Greater costs to transport imported goods that supply domestic manufacturers will affect a nation's ability to compete in global markets for goods.

In another example, the reliable delivery of clean water and electricity to businesses and households in urban areas is important to a community's public health in addition to its economic viability. It is a serious problem if water, wastewater, and electricity infrastructure systems deteriorate or fail to keep up with changing demand. Irregular delivery of water and wastewater services and electricity will make production processes more expensive and divert household disposable income to these basic necessities and adversely affect public health. Increased reliance on electricity to support modern data-driven systems and industries is particularly important when the cost of service outages and interruptions is considered.

Every 4 years, the American Society of Civil Engineers (ASCE) (2017) publishes "The Report Card for America's Infrastructure," which grades the current state of national infrastructure categories on a scale of A through F. Since 1998, America's infrastructure has earned persistent D averages, and the failure to close the investment gap with needed maintenance and improvements has continued. The Report Card for America's Infrastructure released in 2017, grades the US infrastructure as D+. As has been discussed, a mechanism that might be useful in order to enhance both the construction and rehabilitation of urban infrastructure is the use of public–private partnerships or PPPs.

Key Characteristics of Public–Private Partnerships (PPPs)

There is no single definition of a P3. The US Government Accountability Office (GAO) defines a public–private partnership as "a contractual arrangement that is formed between public and private sector partners" (GAO 1999). These arrangements typically involve a government agency contracting with a private partner to renovate, construct, operate, maintain, and/or manage a facility or system, in whole or in part, that provides a public service. Under such arrangements, the agency may retain ownership of the public facility or system, but the private party generally invests its own capital to design and develop the properties. Typically, each partner shares in income resulting from the partnership. Such a venture, although a contractual arrangement, differs from typical service contracting in that the private sector partner usually makes a substantial cash, at-risk, equity investment in the project, and the public sector gains access to new revenue or service delivery capacity without having to pay the private sector partner.

The National Council for Public–Private Partnerships (NCPPP) (United States Department of Transportation 2017) defines a public–private partnership as “a contractual agreement between a public agency (federal, state, or local) and a private sector entity.” Through this agreement, the skills and assets of each sector (public and private) are shared in delivering a service or facility for the use of the general public. In addition to the sharing of resources, each party shares in the risks and rewards potential in the delivery of the service and/or facility.

Well-Designed Public–Private Partnerships

Zerunyan (Chap. 2, this volume) argues that the infrastructure in the US is increasingly vulnerable. His argument is supported by the American Society of Civil Engineers (2016), who report that the US infrastructure has suffered years of neglect and needs significant investment. According to Zerunyan (Chap. 2, this volume), this need creates unique opportunities for collaboration between the private and public sectors through the use of procurement and contracting arrangements commonly known as public–private partnerships (PPPs) or alternatively performance-based initiatives (PFIs). A variation on the PPP concept is the Lease and Lease Back (LLB) concept. These approaches can potentially provide a range of benefits or meet major policy objectives for growing cities, counties, and states. Projects can range from forestry and agriculture to transportation and water infrastructures. The World Economic Forum estimates the global infrastructure deficit as $5 trillion a year. Zerunyan (Chap. 2, this volume) discusses the variations in both PPPs and LLBs, and the range of services they provide.

PPPs have been used for a range of projects in transportation, solid waste disposal, water and sewer services, and more recently parking. These projects are generally fee-generating in nature, for example, actual use of a toll road, water service, and parking. “Social” infrastructures, on the other hand, do not generate revenues, but PPPs may also be used for schools, hospitals, court houses, police and fire stations, prisons, and other public buildings. An attractive feature of PPPs is their ability to save time, money, and effort in the government procurement process.

A key feature of implementing a PPP is the importance of managing risk. If risk is not managed properly, the cost of the project will increase. For example, political risks associated with changes in government, laws or regulations, unanticipated tax increases, or fee impositions are best managed by the government. However, construction risks, such as faulty design, delays in construction, poor performance, and poor quality are all within the control of the private sector and can be properly managed or insured by it.

Zerunyan (Chap. 2, this volume) presents two very detailed case studies of the use of PPPs in providing government services. The first is the Oxnard Fire Station 8 which is an innovative example of an LLB social infrastructure project, located in Oxnard, California, and is one of the most advanced fire stations in the state. A second case study is the Long Beach, California Courthouse, which is a PPP concession model and the most commonly used and studied PPP methodology. The Long Beach Courthouse is the first social infrastructure of its kind using this methodology in California.

Public–Private Partnerships for Transportation

According to Feigenbaum (Chap. 3, this volume), the private provision of transit services comes in the following three forms:

- Privately financed, operated, and maintained services which are limited to locations in which operating transit services can turn a profit.
- Private service in which the public sector procures a contract with the private sector to design, build, finance, operate, and maintain service.
- The private sector plans and operates transit service via a competitive service contract, often called tendered service.

Fixed-route transit service ranges from heavy rail to other types of fixed route service including local bus service, vanpool, jitney, and ride sharing. Funding for transit is challenging in most countries, and in Europe, Canada, and Japan, public transit is considered an essential government service and supported for economic development in dense, urban areas. Tokyo, Hong Kong, and Singapore have very large private transit systems that are proven to be very successful. High population and employment density and a positive attitude by the government toward the private sector have contributed to this success. Where private provision of service and public–private partnerships are not feasible, contracting-out can deliver lower cost and higher quality than conventional transit operations.

For the future, the combination of ridesharing companies such as Uber and Lyft is going to substantially change transit service over the next 20 years, and some experts believe that automated ridesharing vehicles may be <10 years away. Transit agencies will need to transition from being bus and train operators to mobility providers. It is clear that transportation in the US in 2030 will be very different than it is now.

Financially Distressed Highway Public–Private Partnerships in the USA

Garvin (Chap. 4, this volume) discusses the increased interest in the US in private involvement in transportation infrastructure investment, development, and management. He examines financial distress and bankruptcy in highway P3s by presenting four case studies of the US highway P3 projects employing the revenue risk model: (1) South Bay Expressway, (2) Indiana Toll Road, (3) SH 130 Segments 5 & 6, and (4) Capital Beltway Express. Each project experienced financial distress, and three of the four ultimately declared bankruptcy. All of the projects received loans, a federal loan under the Transportation Infrastructure Finance and Innovation Act (TIFIA) program. The South Bay Expressway is a toll road and is an extension of SR 125 near San Diego, California. Construction was initiated in 2003 and was completed in 2007. Traffic fell far short of expectations, so the concession company filed for bankruptcy in 2010. The San Diego Associations of Governments now operate the toll road. The Indiana Toll Road serving northern Indiana has been fully operational since November 1956. In 2008 the economic recession hurt toll road traffic so that by 2010 average traffic was 35% lower than expectations. The concession company filed for bankruptcy in 2014. SH 130 is located south of Austin, Texas, and the toll road traffic was roughly 60% below forecasts. The concession company filed for bankruptcy in 2016, but the project emerged from bankruptcy in 2017. The Capital Beltway Express serves as a perimeter highway circling Washington DC. As with the other case studies, actual traffic flows were below expectations. The construction was accomplished with an agreement between the Virginia Department of Transportation and the private sector. Although the project had some initial financial difficulties, it appears to have solved them.

It is unclear how these experiences will impact equity investors, commercial lenders, and TIFIA in future P3 transactions. It is very clear that in the future the involved partners will likely exercise greater due diligence when considering such opportunities.

Public–Private Partnerships (P3S) for Social Infrastructure

Martin (Chap. 5, this volume) discusses the use of public–private partnerships (P3s) for "social infrastructure" projects in contrast to the traditional use of P3s for transportation. The use of social infrastructure P3s is discussed, in particular their use in public universities, and recommendations on how state and local governments can make greater use of social infrastructure P3s are made.

Examples of social infrastructure are as follows:

- Schools (elementary and high school)
- Universities (dorms, classrooms)

- Libraries
- Parks and recreation facilities
- Housing
- Conventions centers
- Sports facilities
- Correctional facilities (jails, prisons)
- Museums
- Government buildings (all types)
- Others

As with other types of infrastructure, the financing and funding of social infrastructure P3s, it is assumed that the private partner delivers the social infrastructure project and may provide or arrange the financing.

Financing covers the upfront design, construction, and operating costs and funding to pay for the design, construction, and operating costs comes from user fees or availability payments which generally take the form of dedicated revenue streams such as: (1) admission fees to parks, recreation facilities, museums, art galleries, sports facilities, health care facilities, etc. or (2) utilization fees tied to, college and university dorms, housing, etc. If user fees are insufficient to cover the total operating costs of a social infrastructure project (e.g., museum or park), so the government covers the deficit via availability payments.

In the absence of alternative methods to finance and deliver the facility needs of universities, schools, libraries, and government buildings, social infrastructure P3s provide an attractive alternative. However, the use of social infrastructure P3s by state and local governments appears poised to expand dramatically.

The Potential for PPPs in Air Traffic Control

According to Poole (Chap. 6, this volume), most developed countries have converted their air traffic control system from a government organization to a public utility-like organization. These organizations are generally paid for directly by the aviation customers. This approach has produced a number of improvements in performance, productivity, and customer-responsiveness with no adverse impact on aviation safety. However, the United States, which has the world's largest air traffic system, has resisted this trend. He explores the reasons for these changes in other countries and the resistance to this change in the United States.

Air traffic control (ATC) is a critical part of the infrastructure needed for air travel. Prior to 1987 when New Zealand separated its ATC system from the transport ministry, most ATC was operated as part of the national government transport agency. At that point aircraft operators began paying their ATC fees to Airways Corporation of New Zealand, rather than to the government.

In 1938, Congress converted the Bureau of Air Commerce into the Civil Aeronautics Authority (CAA). In 1940, the CAA was split into the Civil Aeronautics

Board (CAB) for economic regulation and subsidy, and the Civil Aviation Authority (CAA), responsible for air safety regulation and operating the ATC system. Both agencies were funded out of general federal tax revenues. In 1958, the CAA became the Federal Aviation Administration (FAA), which remained an independent agency until 1967, when it was folded into the newly created U.S. Department of Transportation (DOT).

Analysts at the federal Government Accountability Office (GAO) and the DOT's Office of Inspector General have documented numerous ongoing problems with the FAA's air traffic system, including:

- ATC Funding Problems include reliance on a set of aviation excise taxes that bear no direct relationship to the cost of ATC services. A second aspect of the funding problem is the FAA's reliance on uncertain annual appropriations from Congress. A third aspect of the funding problem is the inability of FAA to issue *long-term bonds* to finance large capital improvements.
- Governance because the FAA must respond to multiple masters.
- Organizational Culture because despite FAA operating the world's largest ATC system by far, it lags well behind many other developed countries in applying new technology and management methods.

Efforts to corporatize the US ATC system date back to at least 1975 and were attempted in the Reagan, Clinton, the George W. Bush, and Obama Administration. Efforts to reorganize the ATC have been minimal under the Trump Administration.

PPPs for Critical Healthcare Infrastructure in Europe

In the health sector, P3s represent part of the continuum between having the state provide services or the private or commercial provision of services. PPPs are not limited by economic sector, by country, by size, or by timescale. Wright et al. (Chap. 7, this volume) focus on healthcare PPPs in Europe which have been deployed to improve patients' experience through the provision of new infrastructure and innovative services. For purposes of this discussion, the authors have a relatively restrictive definition of what counts as a PPP. They rely primarily on European PPP experience, and therefore that of relatively rich countries and in these countries the state dominates health policy and healthcare finance. A lesson to be drawn is that the decision to deliver services by the private sector actors using PPPs should be done on a case by case basis and should be based on whether or not finance could be accessed on acceptable terms or the services could be supplied better through this mechanism. The decision should not be based on an ideological basis. The authors believe that in a European context, there will inevitability be a stable or increasing role for PPPs and the private sector generally. The heart of a PPP relationship in health is the existence of a scalable, replicable, and sustainable business model.

This PPP model has been most completely developed in the UK, where it is called the Private Finance Initiative (PFI), and has been used to construct more than a hundred healthcare facilities—with individual projects of up to USD3 billion. The model has been copied in many countries—France, Italy, Portugal, Spain, Sweden in Europe, and Canada and Australia outside Europe, among many others. However, as will be discussed healthcare PPP programs in Europe have proven politically controversial.

In considering PPPs, there are two important dimensions. One is the conversion of services from public to private, and to a lesser degree of the "bundling" of services into a contract. The prospects for PPPs in the European health sector will be based on cost, performance, funding, and political acceptability.

PPPs for Fire, Police, and Ambulance Services

As an extension of the discussion of PPPs for health care, Lam (Chap. 8, this volume) discusses the use of public–private partnerships for fire, police, and ambulance services. There is a growing trend for the private sector to provide emergency services to the public, and this idea has spread to include fire, police, and patient transport. Instead of outright privatization, an option is for emergency services is to be supported by public–private partnership (PPP) projects. The United Kingdom has had a number of PPP projects under the umbrella of Private Finance Initiatives (PFI).

As public budgets have become increasingly strained in many countries, some forms of public–private partnerships have been considered as an alternative for emergency services including police, fire rescue, and ambulance services.

Contracting out has always been used to supplement public disciplinary and emergency-relief forces; however, controversy has resulted when governments made it standing policy to outsource the majority of emergency services to the private sector. Examples from the UK, and to a lesser extent, the US, are evaluated.

Lam (this volume) discusses both successful and unsuccessful examples of the application of this concept. According to Lam (this volume) to ensure success, a public body must put maximum effort into the selection of the contractors, their governance, and their monitoring, once the decision to go down the private path is made. Prior to this, the need to consult and engage the public and concerned stakeholders is greater than ever in the modern social-political atmosphere.

The PPP Model in Australia

Australia has initiated approximately 80 PPP projects over the last 18 years, and nearly every political jurisdiction in Australia has developed PPP policies and programs. There is a perception that the PPP concept in Australia has been a success. Grimsey et al. (Chap. 9, this volume) examine the failures and successes of the public–private partnership (PPP) model in Australia since the year 2000. These programs include roads, water, energy, hospitals, prisons, courts, schools, social housing, and convention centers.

There is considerable support for PPPs in Australia; however, problems have arisen. The authors assess the successes (and failures) of this approach and make an evaluation as to what type of model and size of project seems best suited to the use of PPPs.

At a practical level, a PPP can bring private sector efficiency, regulation through competition, economic pricing of services, filter out "white elephants," and free up public services. PPPs cannot, however, bring in additional funding for infrastructure except in the case of tolls and charges. Other than toll roads, nearly all PPP projects in Australia are fully funded by Government out of budget appropriations.

Hospitals were among the first PPP projects delivered in Australia. There is also a long history of privately run prisons. Toll roads appeared in Australia in the 1990s and 2000s. A number of lessons learned from the Australian experience with PPPs are as follows: political support is critical and should come from the highest positions in government; PPPs core purpose is to deliver value for money to the tax payer; a core policy statement needs to be supported by clear guidelines that articulate the rules; training the workforce is essential and this applies equally to the private sector as it does to the public sector; having a pipeline of projects to support investment in the market place. The Australian experience has also shown that not all projects are suited to the PPP model.

PPPs for the Development of Port IT Infrastructure

Paik in Chap. 10 (this volume) discusses the use of public–private partnerships (PPPs) for the development of port information technology infrastructure. He uses the Pusan port in South Korea to examine the major problems and challenges faced by the port and discusses how the establishment of a public–private partnership resolved them. Ports are critical to the flow of goods and services, both within and between countries, and as such provide a critical infrastructure that is essential to economic development and national security. Since globalization is expected to continue, a port is increasingly considered the most critical gateway in a national supply chain through which materials and finished goods are transferred among countries. Construction and effective management of ports often involve many participants and enormous resource investments that neither the public sector nor the private sector could do alone.

In the mid-1990s, large trade volumes, coupled with insufficient port capacity, caused frequent freight and ship congestion at the port. Realizing these challenges and issues, the South Korean government concluded that an efficient and accurate information flow would be the key to achieving material velocity and that the use of information technology could enhance the overall operations. The Pusan port community used various strategies and actions in setting up and implementing its information systems. Clearly it was the successful partnership involving the South

Korean government, the data processing specialist, and commercial shipping entities, which made it possible. The IT system developed at the Pusan port further strengthened the linkage of South Korea's national supply chain to the global marketplace. Port decision makers in other countries should be able to benefit from this case study as a successful example of the use of a PPP for enhancing port operations.

PPPs for Critical Infrastructure Development in Hong Kong

The PPP concept has been applied to many different kinds of projects in Hong Kong including infrastructure development, hospital services, and tourism-related preservation. Although there are several successful PPP infrastructure projects in Hong Kong, including the Tsing Ma Control Area, the Chemical Waste Treatment Plant, and the Asia World-Expo (AWE), other projects are quite controversial. These include the Western Harbor Crossing and the West Kowloon Cultural District. Cheng in Chap. 11 (this volume) presents a general background on PPP establishment in Hong Kong and identifies the trends and lessons learned from these applications. He explores opportunities for expanding PPP services such as China's One Belt One Road initiative which encourages infrastructure development partnerships along the "new" Silk Road. He also discusses how the government would increase the use of PPPs to facilitate public housing projects in Hong Kong.

Hong Kong is one of the world's most expensive housing markets. To deal with the climbing rents in Hong Kong's private property market, the government has attempted to increase the provision of subsidized housing. Several policies have been introduced such as the Home Ownership Scheme and Hong Kong Property for Hong Kong People Scheme. However, these policies have yet to solve the housing problem. To address this issue, the new chief executive of the Hong Kong Special Administrative Region has pledged to launch a starter home program. These units will be constructed using a PPP approach in which the government invites private developers instead of the Housing Authority to develop and construct subsidized homes. The use of PPPs for housing projects has been proposed in other countries. For example, the Thai government is considering collaborating with domestic and foreign investors to develop housing projects through a PPP scheme for low-income earners and the lower-middle class under the Pracha Rat Home project.

The "Water-Specific PPP Risk Model"

Korayem and Ogunlana, Chap. 12 (this volume), have proposed a model to incorporate tangible and intangible variables into a risk assessment process for water infrastructure projects. In the 1990s, market-driven approaches for water resources management were gaining acceptance. The World Bank, International Monetary Fund (IMF), and the Organization for Economic Cooperation and

Development (OECD) introduced privatization as one of their major reform policies. Water became recognized as an economic good or a commodity that should be priced at its cost of provision and its true value to society. However, the water sector has many characteristics that make it challenging for private sector investment. One of these characteristics is the large initial fixed cost capital investment. These high fixed costs lead to economies of scale that contribute to conditions of a natural monopoly. Because of the importance of water supply to society, governments are typically heavily involved in regulating water services, which increases the regulatory and political risks to private companies. Therefore, interest in water infrastructure for investment has been low when compared to other types of infrastructure but nevertheless the Egyptian Government decided to construct a waste water treatment plant in New Cairo. New Cairo is a city that was created in 2000 in the southeastern part of Cairo, in a former desert area, to ease problems deriving from an overcrowded capital. New Cairo covers an area of about 30,000 hectares with a presumed plan to host a population of five million.

In earlier research, the authors had developed the so-called Water-Specific PPP Risk Model. The authors' application of their research to the Cairo WWTP case study is described in this chapter. The model utilizes the Analytical Network Process (ANP) methodology, which contemplates the interdependency between the risk elements.

Strategic Management of Public–Private Partnerships

PPPs have often been used as a financial instrument for a construction or rehabilitation project and are generally structured so that the capital invested in a project is recovered through the cash flows generated by the project itself. Achard in Chap. 13 (this volume) discusses the wide application of public–private partnerships throughout the world, especially for public utility services. Based on this approach, a PPP is characterized by the structure of the project, and the specifics which specify the recovery of the investment by the private partner. In many cases, the cooperation between the public and private parties at both the local and national levels for the provision of important public services is required, as well as the satisfaction of the stakeholders' interests. Typical examples and applications of PPPs in the last 20 years include the construction or rehabilitation of infrastructure all over the world. Other examples include the construction of the tunnel under the English Channel and other important infrastructure in Canada, India, Japan, China, Taiwan, Russia, Brazil, the EU, and the US. The phenomena that has led to the widespread use of PPPs, even though application has been uneven, is related to globalization, the recent financial crises, and the wide spread application and development of the knowledge economy. All of these effects have profoundly modified views about competition in the public sector.

This diffusion of knowledge has led to the introduction of tools, values, and business logic into the public sector, known as New Public Management (NPM). NPM is based on four main principles: the use of private sector approaches in the public sector; the change from centralized and bureaucratic organizational models to more flexible management systems; the importance of culture in the innovation processes, in terms of both the base of the change process and the role of management; and the need to combine private management tools with the mission and values of public services. The Chinese government has been a strong advocate for using the PPP approach.

Public–Private Partnerships in the US Drinking Water Supply

There are more than 160,000 public drinking water systems in the United States (US), but most Americans receive their drinking water from one of the nation's over 50,000 community water systems (CWS). Three hundred and sixty-one CWSs serve more than 45% of the total population, or approximately 120 million people. The passage of the US Safe Drinking Water Act (SDWA) has been very effective in protecting the public health of American drinking water consumers. It has resulted in the reduction or elimination of exposure from drinking water contaminants ranging from potentially carcinogenic disinfection byproducts to neurotoxic contaminants such as lead. The SDWA provides an outstanding example of the successful collaboration of local authorities (drinking water utilities), state agencies, and the Federal government in protecting the health and welfare of the American public (Allen et al. 2018). Despite the US success in operating and managing water systems, there has been much concern expressed over the state of the nation's infrastructure in general and water supply in particular. Organizations such as the American Society of Civil Engineers (ASCE), the American Water Works Association (AWWA), and the US Environmental Protection Agency (EPA) have estimated that billions of dollars will be needed to rehabilitate and repair US drinking water systems. Clark and Hakim (Chap. 14, this volume) explore the potential use of PPPs for making these investments. They conclude that there are no advantages for water systems to be privatized and that for large water systems there is adequate capital available for infrastructure investment and there are standard mechanisms for acquiring these funds. However, there are thousands of systems that will need major investments for infrastructure investments. They conclude that the PPP concept could be used at the state or regional level to provide the needed drinking infrastructure investments.

Summary and Conclusions

Critical infrastructure is defined as the essential services that underpin and serve as the backbone of a nation's economy, security, and health. These services include the power used by homes and businesses, drinking water, transportation, stores and shops, and communications. In urban areas, critical infrastructure is particularly important and is difficult to protect and maintain. An important constraint on providing critical infrastructure is the lack of available financial resources, and a solution often suggested to help provide these resources, and as discussed in this book, is the use of public–private partnerships (PPPs).

There is, however, no single definition of a P3. The US Government Accountability Office (GAO) defines a public–private partnership as “a contractual arrangement that is formed between public and private-sector partners” (GAO 1999). These arrangements typically involve a government agency contracting with a private partner to renovate, construct, operate, maintain, and/or manage a facility or system, in whole or in part, that provides a public service. Under such arrangements, the agency may retain ownership of the public facility or system, but the private party generally invests its own capital to design and develop the properties. Typically, each partner shares in income resulting from the partnership. Such a venture, although a contractual arrangement, differs from typical service contracting in that the private sector partner usually makes a substantial cash, at-risk, equity investment in the project, and the public sector gains access to new revenue or service delivery capacity. Public–private partnerships can help fill the void between typical annual government accounting and capital budgeting. PPPs include both existing facilities and new-capacity facilities, and a commonality among the different types of PPPs is the need for a dedicated revenue stream.

The goal of this book is to discuss the potential for the use of PPPs for encouraging major infrastructure investment throughout the world. Clearly, there is great potential for PPPs to help achieve this goal. It makes an attempt to “demystify” the PPP concept and to discuss both the successes and failures associated with PPPs. Hopefully the information presented in this book will assist decision makers in making these important decisions.

References

Allen, Martin, Clark, Robert M., Cotruvo, Joseph A., Grigg, Neil. (2018) Drinking Water and Public Health in an Era of Aging Distribution Infrastructure. *Public Works Management & Policy 23*(4), 301–309.

ASCE. (2016). *Failure to act: Closing the infrastructure investment gap for America’s economic future*. Reston, VA: American Society of Civil Engineers.

ASCE. (2017). *American Society of Civil Engineers 2017 infrastructure report card*. Retrieved May 24, 2019, from https://www.infrastructurereportcard.org/

Coaffee, J. (2010). Protecting vulnerable cities: The UK’s resilience response to defending every day urban infrastructure. *International Affairs, 86*(4), 939.

European Commission, Mitigation and Home Affairs. (2008). *Critical infrastructure*. Retrieved December 21, 2019, from https://ec.europa.eu/home-affairs/what-we-do/policies/crisis-and-terrorism/critical-infrastructure

GAO. (1999). In United States Government Accountability Office (Ed.), *Public-private partnerships terms related to building and facility partnerships*. Washington, DC.

Homeland Security. (2003). *Homeland security presidential directive 7: Critical infrastructure identification, prioritization, and protection*. Retrieved May 24, 2019, from https://www.dhs.gov/homeland-security-presidential-directive-7

Homeland Security. (2013). *Supporting policy and doctrine*. Retrieved October 20, 2018, from https://www.dhs.gov/what-critical-infrastructure

Liu, J., Dietz, T., Carpenter, S. R., Alberti, M., Folke, C., Moran, E., … Taylor, W. W. (2007). Complexity of coupled human and natural systems. *Science, 317*(5844), 1513–1516.

The White House. (2013). *Presidential policy directive – Critical infrastructure security and resilience*. PRESIDENTIAL POLICY DIRECTIVE/PPD-21. Retrieved May 24, 2019, from https://obamawhitehouse.archives.gov/the-press-office/2013/02/12/presidential-policy-directive-critical-infrastructure-security-and-resil

United States Department of Transportation. (2017). *Public private partnerships*. Retrieved May 24, 2019, from https://www.transit.dot.gov/funding/funding-finance-resources/private-sector-participation/national-council-public-private

Chapter 2
Well-Designed Public Private Partnerships

Frank Vram Zerunyan

Abbreviations

ADA	American's with Disability Act
AOC	Administrative Offices of the Courts
ASCE	American Society of Civil Engineers
DB	Design build
DBF	Design build finance
DBFO	Design build finance operate
DBFOM	Design build finance operate and maintain
DOF	Department of Finance
LLB	Lease lease back
NCPPP	National Council for Public Private Partnerships
OFS	Oxnard fire station
PBI	Performance-based initiatives
PPP or P3	Public Private Partnerships
RDA	Redevelopment agency
RFP	Request for proposal
RFQ	Request for qualification
ULI	Urban Land Institute

Introduction

Our country's aging infrastructure is increasingly vulnerable due to impacts of severe weather, growing population in cities, and technology-driven, land-use patterns. According to the American Society of Civil Engineers (ASCE), years of

F. V. Zerunyan (✉)
Professor of the Practice of Governance at the University of Southern California Sol Price School of Public Policy (USC Price), Los Angeles, CA, USA
e-mail: frank.zerunyan@usc.edu

R. M. Clark, S. Hakim (eds.), *Public Private Partnerships*, Competitive Government: Public Private Partnerships, https://doi.org/10.1007/978-3-030-24600-6_2

neglect and systemic infrastructure deficits present significant challenges for both the public as well as the private sectors today.[1] On the other hand, such significant challenges represent unprecedented opportunities for leadership and investment of greater proportions for these sectors. Never have the public and private sectors been so interdependent, creating unique opportunities for intersectoral relationships or collaborations to deliver important public infrastructures. Arguably, the public policy and financial interests of these sectors have never been so clearly aligned for what could be the greatest social good since the Progressive Era ushered in by the strong voice of President Theodore Roosevelt's White House[2] or the New Deal proposed by President Franklin D. Roosevelt[3] immediately after the Great Depression of 1929–1939. While several procurement methodologies have brought the sectors together over the last century, none could have a more profound impact on our economy today than well-structured involvement of the private sector in the delivery of public infrastructures through the use of procurement and contracting arrangements broadly known as public private partnerships or technically referred to as performance-based initiatives or infrastructures.

Shortened to PPP, P3, or PBI for brevity, these arrangements are not business as usual. Individual variations of PPPs, including arrangements known as lease and lease back (LLB), can potentially provide a range of benefits or meet major policy objectives for growing cities, counties, and states, while placing private human capital and private financial capital into a historically secure sector, employing millions of Americans. Recognizing these benefits, governments worldwide and in the USA are increasingly considering PPPs or LLBs over traditional procurement and delivery methodologies to hire, integrate, maximize expertise, reduce risk, and tap into special resources for the planning, financing, designing, and building public infrastructure projects (Zerunyan and Meyers 2010). These projects range from forestry and agriculture to transportation and water infrastructures (Fig. 2.1).[4] According to the World Economic Forum, the global infrastructure deficit is $5 trillion a year.

In this chapter, I discuss the variations of PPPs and LLBs, the range of services they provide, as well as the risks they distribute to be effective and efficient for the shared interest and value system that makes them attractive. I also provide examples of successful as well as some failed projects. PPPs are not magic bullets. While they have significant and transformational advantages to uplift more than one sector, not every public project is a candidate to use the methodology.

---

[1] The 2017 Report Card found that the national grade for infrastructure remains at a "D+"—the same grade the USA received in 2013—suggesting that only incremental progress was made over the last four years toward restoring America's infrastructure. http://www.asce.org/infrastructure/.

[2] https://www.gilderlehrman.org/history-now/2008-09/theodore-roosevelt-and-progressive-era.

[3] http://www.loc.gov/teachers/classroommaterials/presentationsandactivities/presentations/timeline/depwwii/newdeal/.

[4] The Organization for Economic Co-operation and development (OECD)-World Economic Forum.

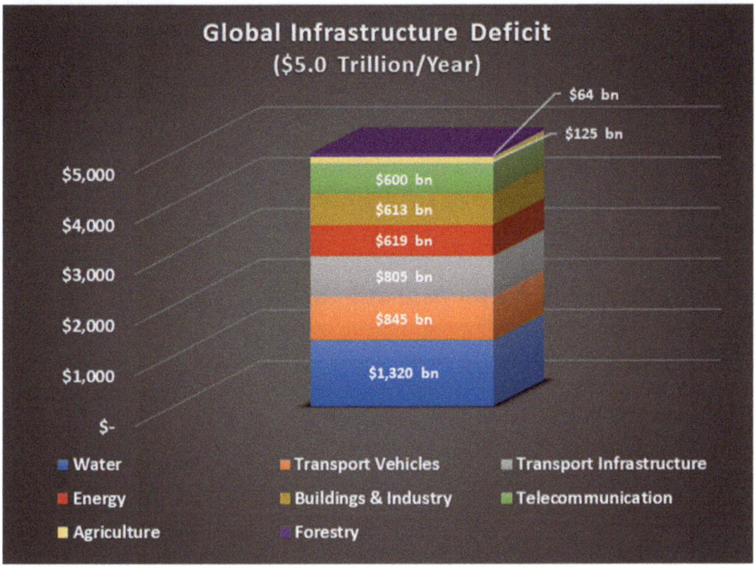

Fig. 2.1 Global infrastructure deficit

Public Private Partnerships as an Infrastructure Delivery Methodology

PPPs are legal fictions. They are typically contractual arrangements between the public, the private, and sometimes the not-for-profit sectors. The National Council for PPPs (NCPPP) developed a useful definition:

> A Public Private Partnership (P3) is a contractual agreement between a public agency and a private sector entity. Through this agreement, the skills and assets of each sector (public and private) are shared in delivering a service or facility for the use of the general public. Each party shares in the risks and rewards potential in the delivery of the service and/or facility.[5]

In exchange for a fee, typically the private sector delivers built infrastructures, facilities, and services. Leveraging the private sector to economically or socially benefit the public sector is a fairly new phenomenon in governance. PPPs have been used for a range of "economic" infrastructures in transportation, solid waste disposal, water and sewer services, and more recently parking. These "economic" infrastructures are generally fee-generating in nature, based for example, on actual use of a toll road, water service, parking, etc. "Social" infrastructures, on the other hand, do not generate revenues per use but are also attractive for PPPs. Schools, hospitals, court houses, police and fire stations, prisons, and other public buildings have used this methodology to benefit from PPP efficiencies. According to the NCPPP, 37 states enable PPPs by statute, most in economic infrastructures and

[5] http://www.ncppp.org/ppp-basics/7-keys/.

more specifically in transportation.[6] Some are more structured and helpful than others. Only Arkansas, Indiana, Maryland, New Jersey, North Carolina, and Virginia provide statutory help in social infrastructures, except that California does have education code sections to facilitate schools, which I will discuss specifically in this chapter as a concept of PPP that we, in practice, label LLB.

One of the many fundamentally attractive features of PPPs is their ability to save time, money, and effort in the government procurement process. Governments seeking to use the methodology may consolidate many otherwise significant and time-consuming activities into a single solicitation. In other words, instead of hiring a designer (architect), arranging for financing, soliciting bids for construction, overseeing construction, and ensuring maintenance and repair over the life cycle of the infrastructure, governments may hire a competent group or a qualified "concessionaire" to perform all or some of these activities. Using this methodology, governments can focus on their core business of public safety and delivery of quality of life. Other potential benefits to governments include greater price and schedule certainty, innovations available in the private sector, and higher levels of maintenance, all of which I discuss in this chapter through specific examples.

PPPs are generally grouped by the range of services they provide. A well-informed and advised government, depending on its appetite for risk, may select one of several recognized PPP methods of delivering an infrastructure. This process may begin with government's request for qualifications (RFQ) or similar procurement process to identify one or more suitable government partner. Typically, once several suitable partners are selected through the RFQ process, a request for proposal (RFP) follows to complete the solicitation. While the benefits of the methodology are remarkable for governments, some of its limitations may arise early in the process. Unless governments employ in-house or hire the necessary human capital to confront risks with a more complex procurement process or meet unforeseen challenges in the structuring of the methodology, PPPs may limit government flexibilities and increase costs.

An RFQ or an RFP is as good as the quality of the specifications and levels of sophistications written in the solicitations. In a 2012 report, the California Legislative Analyst's Office,[7] based on expert input to which I participated, recommended that the state establishes an overall PPP policy to implement a transparent process. This requires government expertise in the methodology to precisely adopt criteria in the evaluation of good partner candidates and conduct rigorous value-for-money analysis. California still lags behind states like Indiana and Virginia in relevant policy, regulation, or laws guiding PPPs. For example, Virginia established an Office of Transportation PPPs[8] to institutionalize the procurement process by attracting qualified developers and builders transparent to stakeholders and the public. I advocated and continue to recommend PPP procurement policy be written in statutes to make the process more transparent and usable by various levels of governments in the

[6] http://www.ncppp.org/resources/research-information/state-legislation/.

[7] http://www.lao.ca.gov/reports/2012/trns/partnerships/P3_110712.pdf.

[8] http://www.p3virginia.org.

state of California. For example, NCPPP developed 7 keys to success in PPP development. Among them is the requirement of a favorable statutory environment to implement each partnership. Transparency and the competitive proposal process written in statute only enhance the ability of each sector to participate to successful PPPs. An organized structure with a dedicated team can help each government in the procurement and implementation of each project. It is inefficient and too expensive for some levels of government (e.g., state, county, or city) to invent the wheel or reinvent the wheel so to speak to structure PPPs.

Greatest Challenges in Designing Effective Public Private Partnerships

PPPs are mostly long-term and performance-based initiatives. Like good governance, they are also based on accountability, efficiency, and results. Every stakeholder's interest in the partnership is to be fully informed and to know the parameters of the project. Contrary to the claims of some of the opponents of the methodology, no one in the partnership has the motivation to be misinformed or to misinform another partner. Therefore, PPP fluency in communication is paramount to the success of each project for both the public and private sectors. A common vision and a shared set of goals by both sectors, public and private, are paramount to the success of a PPP project.

Most known failures in this methodology come from optimistic data collection, lack of communication, and a blurred framework for project goals. For example, the initial failure of the 91 Express Lanes, a toll road in Southern California, came as a result of erroneous traffic counts, misinformation about alternative roads, and legal shortcomings in the contract, which were more positional rather than interest-based for the benefit of the project goals. Lessons learned from this project include complete transparency and the understanding by each partner that any substantial advantage or legal loophole created for one is a disadvantage to all and potentially may lead to the demise of the long-term relationship. My parents will celebrate their 60th wedding anniversary next year. They say that the success to their long-term relationship is transparency, communication, and care for the purpose of the union rather than self-interest. A 30-year PPP is no different. Entering into a PPP solely for self-interest is misguided and will prove to be fatal to the project. As a result, while PPPs are not a magic bullet to solve our infrastructure shortcomings, it is also not for every government, developer, contractor, financier, or designer to use as a methodology. In *Anna Karenina*, Tolstoy observed that "happy families are all alike; every unhappy family is unhappy in its own way." In short, to succeed, PPPs must be organized for success with full appreciation of the business model of the private sector, which values risk and life cycle costs of the asset for a sustainable future in earnings. PPPs must also be organized to benefit municipalities in long-term cost sharing, infrastructure maintenance, and delivery of other public services.

In the private sector, both risk and continued maintenance of capital facilities play a direct role in the profitability of the enterprise. Arguably, a Class A office building is predisposed to retain a proactive investment program for maintenance, repair, and refurbishment of its building to retain the levels of rent charged in similar Class A buildings. In other words, the motivation to maintain a building as a decision directly correlates to economics. Governments are not structured with this motivation. They are in the business of public safety, education, transportation, and generally, quality of life. These are very important for governance including economic development in the private sector, where real estate values for example directly correlate to public safety. In turn, vacant and abandoned real property increases crime, health risks, and therefore, the cost of municipal governance.[9] However, when the physical condition of courts, schools, fire stations, or city halls declines, there is no corresponding direct loss of revenue to signal unacceptability. As a result, government investments in maintenance and repairs either fall woefully short or are not provided at all. Many studies, including those by the Urban Land Institute (ULI), seem to correctly conclude that the integrated use of PPPs in economic and social infrastructure development may be a better way to design, build, finance, operate, and maintain public infrastructures if in fact the purpose for the use of the methodology is to save on life cycle costs, reduce risk to government, and maintain optimal standards of the capital asset during its long life cycle.[10]

Before examining the range of services PPPs provide, it is important to examine how to manage risk in the structuring of a successful PPP. In fact, one of the other attractive features of this delivery method is the proper allocation of risk to the party in the partnership most equipped to manage it (Fig. 2.2). If risk is not managed properly from the inception of the project, the cost of the project will increase. This allocation of risk across a continuum is rooted in full, open, and honest cooperation between the partners. If the objective for each party is to simply shift risk to the other, the PPP will be much less efficient or effective. The goal here is to transparently identify and equitably allocate risk to reduce cost. For example, political risks associated with changes in government, laws or regulations, unanticipated tax increases, or fee impositions are best managed by the government, which is responsible for them. If government asks the private sector to absorb these risks, the private sector may choose to do so in return for a fee, which unnecessarily increases the price of the project. On the other hand, construction risks, such as faulty design, delays in construction, poor performance, and poor quality, are all within the control of the private sector and can be properly managed or insured by it. Governments taking on these risks typically deliver projects of lesser quality teeming with cost overruns, schedule delays, and missed budgets. Other risks to be allocated include legal and contractual risks, which may be mitigated by proper representation. As is the case with the highly specialized pool of PPP partners, specialized law firms or professional consultants also create value in structuring these PPPs. Income risks based on faulty data, such as inaccurate traffic volumes for a toll road or the construction of a

[9] https://www.huduser.gov/portal/periodicals/em/winter14/highlight1.html.

[10] https://uli.org/wp-content/uploads/ULI-Documents/Successful-Public-Private-Partnerships.pdf.

Fig. 2.2 Risk continuum (DBFOM versus DB)

competing infrastructure, may reduce the effectiveness of the PPP. Financial risks and force majeure such as natural disasters, terrorism, or war may also affect the structuring of a PPP. While the private sector, for the right price, can deliver whatever governments want, as a matter of prudent policy, governments must assess these risks and costs. They must retain those that they may be able to control or manage to reduce the cost of the project.

In short, to achieve success in PPP procurement, risks must match the expertise and objectives of each participant to optimize implementation. Governments look for infrastructure to support public safety, economic development, and quality of life for their constituents. Governments also desire lower life cycle costs, timely repairs, quality products, and the ability to focus on their core functions. The private sector aims for a steady and most secure return on its investment. It wants the ability to use innovation to improve productivity to meet performance goals. The proper alignment of these objectives creates successful PPP projects. These constitute common goals that governments and private sector participants must discuss and achieve to see improvements in PPP arrangements.

Crafting effective PPPs requires skills for both the public and private sectors. The Urban Land Institute (ULI) describes these skills with "ten principals for successful public private partnerships." The "ten principles include the following:

- Prepare properly for a public/private partnership
- Create a shared vision
- Understand your partners and key players
- Be clear on the risks and rewards for all parties
- Establish a clear and rational decision-making process
- Make sure all parties do their homework
- Secure consistent and coordinated leadership
- Communicate early and often
- Negotiate a fair deal structure
- Build trust as a core value (Corrigan et al. 2005)."

Fig. 2.3 ULI's public private partnership council survey results

In 2016, ULI's Public Private Partnership Council ran an informal survey of its membership. The survey identified 13 significant challenges in crafting effective PPPs (Fig. 2.3) (Long 2016). The top 3 survey responses ranging from 48.78% to a very significant 60.98% response rate clearly describe the importance of the "ten principals" in the implementation process. My experiences that I share in the case studies described in this chapter are not different.

From a very modest risk allocation to the private sector to a full transfer of risk, PPPs range in services to governments. The Public Contracting Code in California traditionally describes a design-bid-build process whereby the public agency describes in a solicitation its specific needs and awards separate contracts to architects, engineers, and construction firms. There is not much room for negotiations, and most risks remain with the public sector, except of course the specific costs associated with services sought and provided. The law requires the public agency to award the contracts to the lowest responsible bidder who submits a responsive bid.[11] A responsible bidder is typically a licensed contractor in good standing. In addition, a responsible bidder is deemed to have the equipment and skills necessary to perform the work described in the bidding documents. If the bidder does not fit this criterion, the public agency need not award the contract to the lowest bidder. The second requirement is that the bid be responsive. Quite simply, the bid must be an unconditional offer to provide all the goods and services that are being solicited. For example, a bid which excludes a portion of the work or fails to follow procedures set forth in the bid document is deemed non-responsive. This methodology is quite rigid and hardly a partnership.

[11] Public Contracting Code Sections (20161 and 20162).

Fig. 2.4 Risk continuum (DBFOM, DBFO, DBF, and DB)

The alternative project delivery methodology of Design–Build (DB) combines the design and construction phases of the project into one fixed-fee contract. The private sector designs and builds the infrastructure to specifications for a fixed fee. In the DB methodology, the risk of cost overruns is transferred to the private sector. Design–Build and Finance (DBF), Design–Build–Finance and Operate (DBFO) and Design–Build–Finance–Operate and Maintain (DBFOM) are all various iterations of PPP methodology describing private sector's responsibilities and assumption of risks (Fig. 2.4). Depending on the needs of the public sector, procurement may take different forms for best results. While different factors such as value for money, risk, life cycle costs influence the successful implementation of procurement, there is considerable literature and studies focusing what amounts to be the strong motivation of the private sector to act responsibly when it must design, build, finance, operate, and maintain an infrastructure. This, of course, is because of the assumption that the private sector has a greater incentive to innovate along with maximizing profits.[12]

Lease and Lease Back as a Methodology

While PPPs have a long-proven record internationally, leveraging the private sector to socially benefit the public sector is a fairly new phenomenon in the USA, especially in the context of social public spaces. PPP or LLB can provide a range of benefits or meet major policy objectives for municipalities if competently and appropriately applied. LLBs like PPPs are not magic bullets in building public spaces, but they come with very attractive advantages. They are typically "turnkey

[12] https://www.nao.org.uk/report/good-practice-briefing-for-pfi-ppp/.

delivery" projects where the private sector assumes at least construction and delivery risks. The construction price is guaranteed, and no payment is due until occupancy is delivered to the municipality based on a measurable outcome.

California's Education Code contains a well-designed statutory scheme to permit public private partnerships using the LLB methodology.[13] Section 17406 of the Code permits the governing board of a school district to let, "for a minimum rental of one dollar ($1) a year, to a person, firm, or corporation real property that belongs to the school district if the instrument by which this property is let requires the lessee therein to construct on the demised premises, or provide for the construction thereon of, a building or buildings for the use of the school district during the term of the lease, and provides that title to that building shall vest in the school district at the expiration of that term."[14] Section 17406 requires a "competitive solicitation process to the proposer providing the best value to the school district." The Code defines best value based on an "objective criteria for evaluating the qualifications of proposers with the resulting selection representing the best combination of price and qualifications." This of course differs from the requirement of the Public Contracting Code to award the project to the lowest responsible bidder who submits a responsive bid.[15]

The California Education Code on LLB is quite prescriptive. It requires a lease document, also referred to as the "Site Lease," from the school district to the private entity, which typically is a single-purpose entity organized to specifically build and deliver the school project in question. This is the first document that the Code refers to for a minimum rental amount of $1 per year. This Site Lease simply defines the property, the landlord (school district), the tenant (single-purpose entity), the rent (typically $1 per year), and the term, which cannot exceed 40 years.[16] This Site Lease must also vest title in the school district at the expiration of its term.[17]

The second document in the LLB methodology is the "Sublease or Master Lease." The Sublease, aside from similar provisions of the Site Lease, is the document that leases back the property to the school district with the completed school project on the site. The Sublease also defines the maximum guaranteed price for the project, and the lease payments to fully pay the cost of the project over the course of the term, not to exceed 40 years.[18]

The third document in the LLB transaction is the "Construction Services Agreement or Development Agreement," which is entered into between the single-

[13] California Education Code—EDC Title 1 General Education Code Provisions [1. - 32500] (Title 1 enacted by Stats. 1976, Ch. 1010.) Division 1 General Education Code Provisions [1. - 32500] (Division 1 enacted by Stats. 1976, Ch. 1010.) Part 10.5. School Facilities [17210–17653] (Part 10.5 repealed (by Sec. 4) and added by Stats. 1996, Ch. 277, Sec. 3.) Chapter 4. Property: Sale, Lease, Exchange [17385–17561] (Chapter 4 added by Stats. 1996, Ch. 277, Sec. 3.)

[14] Education Code Section 17406.

[15] Public Contracting Code Sections (20161 and 20162).

[16] Education Code Section 17403.

[17] Education Code Section 17406.

[18] Education Code Section 17403.

purpose entity and the designers, engineers, and builders. This Construction Services Agreement binds the entire development team to construct the school project according to plans and specifications approved by the school district, and in California, the State Architect's Office.[19] The Construction Services Agreement in California provides for prevailing wages to be paid in accordance with the California Labor Code.[20] As a public works project, the Construction Services Agreement, among other legal requirements, also includes requirements regarding the payment of bonds used to finance the project, compliance with seismic specifications, indemnifications, use of payment and performance bonds, and insurance. In some municipalities, especially in California, a project labor agreement may also be required to satisfy collective bargaining laws.

The Code permits LLBs to be financed by bonds, notes, warrants, or "other evidences of indebtedness." The interest on these financial instruments is exempt from all taxation except from inheritance, gift, or franchise taxes.[21] Depending on the credit quality of the school district, these bonds can be very attractive in terms of rates and conditions. The final technical piece in the methodology is an "in rem" legal action to validate the transaction. The California Code of Civil Procedure authorizes a civil action by the school district or any interested party to validate the actions of the school district. This action, filed in the trial courts of the state, validates conclusively the LLB transaction and all documentation used to document the transaction, against any persons or litigants, who might challenge it.[22] The California Government Code is the broadest authorization for validation actions, and it allows a plaintiff to bring a validation action to determine the validity of any local agency's bonds, warrants, contracts, obligations, or "evidences of indebtedness."[23] Given LLBs are performance-based initiatives, all up-front costs are the responsibility of the private sector. No payment is due from the school district on the sublease until the project is completely delivered to the school district for occupancy.

Case Study: The Oxnard Fire Station 8

Building schools under the prescription of the Education Code is well-established in California. Other social infrastructures, however, are not as well-recognized. One innovative example of an LLB social infrastructure project is Oxnard Fire Station 8, in Oxnard, California. Perhaps among the most advanced fire stations in the state, Oxnard Fire Station 8, the first of its kind using this methodology, was built and

[19] Education Code Section 17406(b)(1).

[20] Labor Code Section 1720 et seq.

[21] Education Code Sections 17419 and 17420.

[22] Code of Civil Procedure Sections 860–870—http://www.dailybreeze.com/2013/08/15/torrance-unified-wins-lawsuit-challenging-no-bid-construction-contracts/.

[23] Government Code Section 53511.

delivered on-time and on-budget.[24] An incredibly experienced team of professionals in collaboration with city of Oxnard leaders pioneered the LLB model for a fire station, borrowing key components from the well-established concept codified in Education Code Section 17406. Subject matter experts on both sides openly collaborated to design an efficient methodology focusing on mutual benefits. The entire LLB transaction was carefully and transparently structured from its inception.

The Site Lease

Oxnard Fire Station 8 is designed as a 13,956-square-foot fire station and training complex constructed on city-owned property. Oxnard Fire Station 8, including its associated training building, occupies approximately 2.46 acres of a larger 70-acre site. These 2.46 acres are leased under a Site Lease to Oxnard Fire Station, LLC (OFS), a single-purpose entity fully owned by a non-profit organization. At the time of the transaction, OFS had no operating history, no historical earnings, and no assets or liabilities other than the bonds sold and borrowed to finance Oxnard Fire Station 8. OFS' sole member, however, is an experienced property management nonprofit specifically qualified to "lessen the burdens of government" with a portfolio of approximately $1 billion in real estate assets under management. The Site Lease is $1 dollar per year for 15 years, which is tied to a city revenue stream known as measure O. Measure O is a half-cent sales tax previously approved by the voters to finance city infrastructures in general. At the end of the 15 years, OFS will dissolve, and title will vest fully onto the City of Oxnard (Fig. 2.6). While a specific revenue stream like Measure O in Oxnard is not necessary for the LLB, it is helpful in underwriting the transaction for the bond market.

One complication with a Site Lease of this type of infrastructure is the trigger of property tax obligation because the tenant is a non-governmental organization. California has dealt with this issue in the Revenue and Taxation Code.[25] A claim for organizational clearance for a "Welfare Exemption" is filed with the Board of Equalization. The Board on a case-by-case basis reviews these claims to determine compliance with the Revenue and Taxation Code's welfare or public purpose requirements.[26] Once the requirements are met, the certificate is issued for the assessor and/or tax collector of the county in which the property is located to exempt the property from the collection of property tax. The Site Lease for Oxnard Fire Station 8 is exempt from property taxation for the duration of its lease term.

---

[24] (a) http://archive.vcstar.com/news/local/oxnard/oxnards-new-fire-station-8-open-for-tours-thursday-at-formal-unveiling-ep-1246424339-351143351.html.
(b) http://www.bernards.com/portfolio/civic/oxnard-fire-station-8/.
(c) http://hmcarchitects.com/solutions/civic/oxnard-fire-station-no-8/.

[25] Revenue and Taxation Code Section 254.6.

[26] Revenue and Taxation Code Section 214.

The Sub or Master Lease

The Master Lease is between OFS, as the lessor, and the City of Oxnard as the lessee. The amenities and improvements under the Master Lease include the following: (a) four emergency vehicle apparatus bays; (b) ten dormitory living quarters with individual, private restrooms; (c) public lobby and ADA compliant public restroom; (d) administrative offices; (e) public lobby area; (f) firemen day room, kitchen, and dining facilities; (g) physical fitness gym; (h) paramedic emergency medical supply unit; (i) workshop, hose storage, oxygen supply, "Turn-Out" and storage rooms; (j) ancillary building equipment and support spaces; (k) naturally ventilated and day-lighted apparatus bays; and (l) conference and library room. In short, it is a fully built out and turnkey fire station in the city of Oxnard (Fig. 2.5).

The Master Lease is for 15 years with an option to purchase. Title of the fire station will vest onto the City of Oxnard at the end of the 15-year term (2031) free and clear or sooner if the City of Oxnard elects to purchase the balance of the Master Lease obligation. According to the Master Lease, the City is required, subject to its abatement rights, to pay "Base Rental" and "Additional Rental" of any taxes, assessments, and insurance premiums with respect to the Oxnard Fire Station and the fees, costs, and expenses incurred by OFS for developing and financing the project (collectively "Rental"). Rental payments are payable five business days prior to each June 1 and December 1, commencing on the "Commencement Date," which is defined in the Master Lease to mean the date upon which the certificate of occupancy is issued with respect to Oxnard Fire Station 8. Rental payments are subject to abatement during any period in which, by reason of material damage, destruction, or failure of any warranted condition, there is substantial interference with the City's

Fig. 2.5 Oxnard Fire Station 8 (Source for picture HMC Architects. Used with permission from HMC)

right to use and occupy Oxnard Fire Station 8 or any portion thereof. These provisions protect the city in case of a private sector failure.

Under the Master Lease, at all times following the Commencement Date, the City is required to maintain rental interruption insurance covering a period of 24 months, in an amount equal to two times the maximum annual Rental payments. In addition, Oxnard Fire Station 8 is insured, through insurers meeting certain requirements set forth in the Master Lease, against loss or damage. Any net insurance proceeds and condemnation awards are agreed to be applied to repair or replace Oxnard Fire Station 8 or to redeem all or a portion of the Bonds. The City has covenanted in the Master Lease to take such action as may be necessary to include and maintain all Rental payments due under the Master Lease in its annual budget and to make the necessary annual appropriations for all such payments. All Base Rental payments are pledged by OFS to pay off the bonds. OFS, in return for a small predetermined fee, manages and properly maintains the structures of the building as a lessor (landlord) for the duration of the Master Lease. These provisions protect the investors in case of public sector failure.

The Construction Services or Development Agreement

The Development Agreement is between OFS (the nonprofit) and a team of private sector organizations as the developer, designer, engineer, builder, and special-related-service professionals. Under the Development Agreement, the developer is obligated to cause all service providers (e.g., designers and builders) to perform services necessary to achieve the completion of Oxnard Fire Station 8 within 24 months from the delivery date of the bonds necessary to finance the project. While all legal requirements are spelled out in this Agreement, the most important provision that is particular to the LBB methodology is the guaranteed maximum price also known as the "Contract Price." The Contract Price covers from excavation to the delivery of Oxnard Fire Station 8 with its occupancy permit. While unusual, the Development Agreement in Oxnard also required the developer to procure all machinery, equipment (including fire trucks), and other furnishings (beds, televisions) and fixtures (hoses) related to the operation, maintenance, and administration of the fire station.

The Bonds and the Loan Agreement

The Bonds to finance the entire project were issued by the California Municipal Finance Authority ("Authority"), which loaned all of the proceeds to OFS, under a "Loan Agreement," for the purpose of financing the design, construction, and equipping of a "turnkey" fire station in the City of Oxnard. The Loan Agreement also funded 24 months of capitalized interest on the Bonds and initial debt service on the bonds until the commencement of the Master Lease, which provides for the payment of Base Rental as discussed in the previous section. The Bonds are issued according the provisions of the Joint Exercise Powers Act in California, which enables the Authority to issue bonds based on the credit rating of the member municipality.[27]

The Bonds are limited obligations of the Authority, payable solely from and secured by the pledge of revenues (Base Rental). Neither the Authority, its members, the State, nor any of its political subdivisions are directly, indirectly, or contingently obligated to use any other moneys or assets to pay all or any portion of the debt service due on the Bonds, to levy or to pledge any form of taxation whatsoever, or to make any appropriation for their payment. The Authority has no taxing power. OFS as the Borrower executed and delivered a Leasehold Deed of Trust, Assignment of Rents and Leases, and a Security Agreement and Fixture Filing, for the benefit of a designated trustee, as trustee for the owners of the Bonds. In other words, the loan to OFS is solely secured by the Master Lease revenue or the Base Rental.

Finally, these Bonds to design and build a public fire station are tax exempt under federal income tax law. While the credit rating of the City of Oxnard was used to issue these Bonds, the underwriting of the Bonds was based on the City's ability to pay the Base Rental, which is necessary to retire the Bonds. These Bonds, unlike General Obligation Bonds, did not require the vote of the people of Oxnard for issuance. Technically, the obligation on the Bonds is that of OFS', and the City of Oxnard is simply the lessee with an obligation to make Rental payments. The City in its financial statements simply records this transaction as any other lease that the City may enter into for the necessary use of public facilities (Fig. 2.6).

The PPP Concession Model—Long Beach Courthouse

The PPP concession model is the most used and studied PPP methodology of all time. Most of the available literature on the topic describes this methodology especially for economic infrastructures going back to the fifteenth century. The French nobleman Luis de Bernam was granted a river concession on the Rhine in 1438. The Perrier brothers operated a water distribution concession in 1792. It was not until the 1970s that the methodology became part of the market-oriented economy especially in transportation projects as in toll roads.[28] Today, we experience the expansion of the methodology into both economic as well as social infrastructures. The Long Beach Courthouse is the first social infrastructure of its kind using the methodology in California.

In June of 2007, the Administrative Offices of the Courts (AOC), which is the staff agency for the Judicial Council of California, chaired by the Chief Justice of the California Supreme Court, completed its review of a potential project to replace the then existing and dangerously dilapidated Long Beach Courthouse. The AOC

[27] Government Code Sections 6500 et seq.

[28] http://ppp4krakow.net/About_PPP/Definition,_origin_and_evolution/

LLB MAIN FEATURES

TURN-KEY DELIVERY
- Private sector designs, builds, then leases public space to the public agency
- Construction and delivery risks shifted to development and financing team

NO DELIVERY = NO LEASE PAYMENTS DUE
- Guaranteed construction price and no payments during construction
- Public agency makes lease payments after completion of project

LEASE TO OWN
- 100% amortizing lease with terms up to 40 years
- After lease term, public space is owned by the public agency

TAX-EXCEMPT FINANCING
- Same credit rating and interest rates as public agency's tax-exempt bonds
- Covenants similar to lease revenue bonds and certificates of participation

EFFECTIVE TEAM SELECTION PROCESS
- Merit-based bidding requirements for public agencies (not just lowest cost)
- Prevailing wage and local sub-contractors

Fig. 2.6 LLB main features

recommended the construction of a new courthouse. As part of the review, the AOC also considered alternative project delivery methods and developed a proposal to construct the courthouse utilizing the concession model of PPP. While Governor Schwarzenegger was supportive of this PBI methodology, no legal structure existed empowering the State of California to consider this procurement method.

Through language in the Budget Act of 2007, the Legislature directed and authorized the Judicial Council to enter into an agreement for a PBI project, subject to both notice to the Legislature as well as approval from the State's Department of Finance (DOF) that the project agreements met "established performance expectations."[29] The Legislature also amended the Trial Court Facilities Act[30] to add a process for the Judicial Council, the DOF, and the Legislature to evaluate facility proposals that included a public private partnership component.[31]

The AOC and the City of Long Beach reached an agreement in early 2007, whereby the AOC agreed to acquire the pre-selected site from the Redevelopment Agency (RDA) of the City, which owned the land bounded by West Broadway, Maine Avenue, West 3rd Street, and Magnolia Avenue in the City of Long Beach.[32]

[29] California Stats. 2007, ch.171.

[30] Government Code Sections 70301 et seq.

[31] Government Code, Section 70391.5, added by Statutes 2007, chapter 176.

[32] I was personally involved in this project starting late 2006 and in early 2007 I, on behalf of a private consortium, proposed to the RDA an Exclusive Negotiating Agreement for this site. Figure 2.7 represents our concept for the site. AOC wanted to take control, so instead I made my first presentation about the concept and the methodology to the AOC in April of 2007.

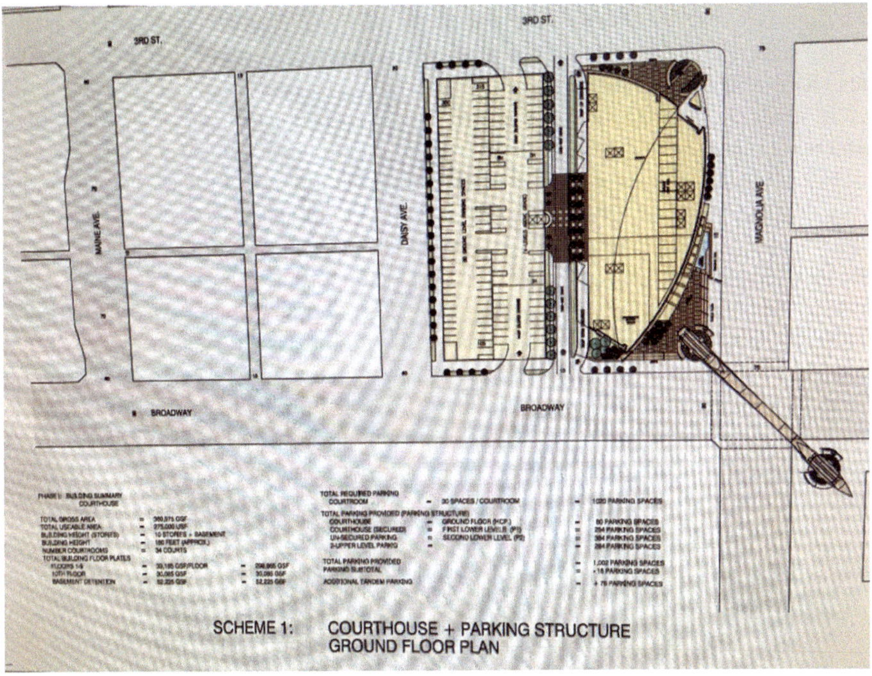

Fig. 2.7 Long beach courthouse floorplan

The site is about 6 acres, one block north from Ocean Avenue, where the former courthouse was located. After the AOC took control of the site from the RDA, it agreed to follow the PBI methodology by issuing a Request for Qualifications (RFQ) to potential proposers for the Long Beach Courthouse Project.

The AOC defined the project as a design, build, finance, operate, and maintain (DBFOM). It expected any proposer to be responsible for the design, construction, and financing of the project, including any risks associated with them. More importantly and different than any other procurement methodology, the AOC expected the proposer to be responsible for life cycle maintenance, repairs, and capital replacements to sustain the courthouse to expectations specified by the AOC. This included all interior and exterior, custodial, site maintenance, and all other operational services necessary to operate a courthouse building. For the first time in California, the maintenance and management of a public building is tied to economics. In other words, the agreement between the AOC and the proposer allows for the AOC to deduct payments if the building fails expectations outlined in that agreement. The proposer has a monetary incentive to keep the property in the condition promised for the duration of the term of the agreement, which in Long Beach Courthouse's case is 35 years.[33] The people of California are at least assured a "Class A" courthouse for 35 years.

[33] http://www.designbuilddoneright.com/long-beach-courthouse/.

Approximately 12 proposers responded to the RFQ, from which, based on established selection criteria, the AOC interviewed 5 and short-listed 3 to request proposals (RFP). To incentivize participation to a relatively expensive RFP process, the AOC made available technical reports on the site like geotechnical, environmental, and other planning documents, along with $500,000 to each unsuccessful RFP participant.[34] While this amount seems substantial, in a project of this size, responding to a detailed RFP may cost more than double the amount. However, proposers in this "league" know the losses and the rewards of their participation. At the AOC, the RFPs were evaluated based on cost, quality, and appropriateness of design, performance potential, and financial strength of the proposer to name a few important criteria. Both the process and the outcome in building a quality courthouse named after California Governor George Deukmejian served the needs of the AOC and the state of California.[35] While the price tag of $490 million seemed high for some observers (over $1100 per square foot),[36] 31 courtrooms, 100,000 square feet of office space leased to Los Angeles County Agencies, and more than 10,000 square feet of supporting retail uses serve more than 4000 visitors per day.[37]

Conclusion

The 2017 report card issued by the ASCE still grades our national infrastructure at a D+. This is the grade that the same infrastructure earned in 2013.[38] Not much progress to report in 4 years. The infrastructure challenge before governments seems overwhelming. The economic booms and busts along with the lack of political will have created significant deficits in the USA and around the world. Slowly but surely, at least out of necessity, governments are realizing that inaction is not an option. While PPPs are not a panacea, they are a very important tool for governments to have and use with careful application. As discussed in this chapter, PPPs are collaborative intersectoral processes. Participants to these collaborations work to redistribute power and control from a central authority to many vested individuals and groups. This sharing of power leads to innovation, cooperation, coordination, and partnership on a higher level than is possible in a typical hierarchical system. Each sector participating to the collaboration has a different challenge and motivation. Therefore, PPP policies, rules, and laws must be tailored to the specific needs of each participating sector. Properly incentivizing each sector is key for the success of this infrastructure development tool.

---

[34] http://www.courts.ca.gov/documents/newlbcourt-rfq2.pdf?1511988880319.

[35] https://www.lacourt.org/courthouse/info/LB (note from the author. Well-deserved honor for Governor Deukmejian, a friend and a personal mentor of mine.)

[36] http://www.presstelegram.com/2016/05/28/judges-say-high-cost-of-long-beach-courthouse-is-depriving-other-areas-of-courtrooms/.

[37] http://www.designbuilddoneright.com/long-beach-courthouse/.

[38] See footnote 2.

Governments must welcome these collaborations by creating clear rules and key attributes also defined in "good governance" such as transparency, efficiency, effectiveness, participation, accountability, and results. Learning from successes and past failures, instead of retreating from the challenges, governments must use these alternative methodologies to maximize their potential to meet their infrastructure objectives. In this endeavor, governments must define their goals and objectives to develop the legal framework and processes to qualify partners in the private sector. As in California's Long Beach Courthouse example, establishing the necessary legislative and regulatory framework for PPPs might be necessary to ensure implementation. Starting 2018, governments worldwide will compete to attract private capital. In fact, in the USA, infrastructure finance and development may be the only bipartisan issue on the political agenda before the 2018 elections. A poor legislative and regulatory environment will stymie any government's efforts to engage the private sector.

Finally, the role of relationships and trust in organizational and/or individual leadership is not to be underestimated in designing and implementing a successful PPP. We would not have been successful in our design and delivery of Oxnard Fire Station 8 if we did not forge a relationship with all participants and did not align the interests of all participants, taking the longer view for all negotiations in life cycle considerations of the project. Interest-based and integrative negotiations for PPPs are keys to their success. I discuss this concept in greater detail in our book "Newgotiation for Public Leaders Duzert and Zerunyan 2019." After all, the Oxnard collaboration is designed to be successful for all participants for at least 15 years. It is a well-designed PPP aligning a shared vision followed by shared and achievable goals throughout the life cycle of the project. This alignment does not occur on its own. At every stage of the process, from the initiation of the procurement through the implementation phase, government officials must protect the public interest through core values. Public and private sectors together must work through important issues, such as cost-to-benefit analysis, access to services, fairness and equity, conflicts of interest, financial accountability, stability, and quality. Working through these issues, together, guarantees the longevity of the relationship building the trust necessary to forge the long-term partnership. True and meaningful "partnership" is the most important concept in the methodology known as PPP

References

Corrigan, M. B., Hambene, J., Hudnut, W., III, Levitt, R. L., Stainback, J., Ward, R., & Witenstein, N. (2005). *Ten principles for successful public/private partnerships* (p. 1). Washington, DC: Urban Land Institute.

Duzert, Y., & Zerunyan, F. (2019). *Newgotiation for public administration professionals*. Vandeplas Publishing.

Long, C. A. (2016). Public private sector survey. Successful public/private partnerships. In S. B. Friedman (Ed.), *Successful public/private partnerships: From principles to practices*. Washington, DC: Urban Land Institute.

Zerunyan, F., & Meyers, S. (2010). *The use of public private partnership for special districts and all levels of governments*. California Special District-May-June 2010.

Chapter 3
Summary of Transit Public–Private Partnerships

Baruch Feigenbaum

Abbreviations

AP	Availability Payment
BRT	Bus Rapid Transit
CDOT	Colorado Department of Transportation
CRMF	Commuter Railroad Maintenance Facility
DBFOM	Design, Build, Finance, Operate, Maintain
DC	District of Columbia
JR	Japanese Railways
LTA	Land Transport Association (Singapore)
MDOT	Maryland Department of Transportation
MTA	Maryland Transit Administration
MTR	Mass Transit Railroad Corporation (Hong Kong)
NCPPP	National Center for Public–Private Partnerships
P3	Public–Private Partnership
PAB	Private Activity Bond
RTD	Regional Transit District
TfL	Transport for London
TIFIA	Transportation Infrastructure Finance Innovation Act

Introduction

Private provision of transit services comes in one of three forms. The purest provision—privately financed, operated, and maintained services—is limited to locations in which operating transit services can turn a profit. Thus far that has been limited

B. Feigenbaum (✉)
Reason Foundation, M.C.R.P. Transportation Planning, Georgia Institute of Technology, Great Falls, VA, USA
e-mail: baruch.feigenbaum@reason.org

R. M. Clark, S. Hakim (eds.), *Public Private Partnerships*, Competitive Government: Public Private Partnerships, https://doi.org/10.1007/978-3-030-24600-6_3

to cities with a population density of 10,000 people or more per square mile. These include dense Asian cities such as Hong Kong and Tokyo, as well as other densely populated cities such as Mexico City and Cairo. As these are the only places in the world where transit systems can be operated profitably, there are a limited number of truly private services.

In a second type of private service, the public sector procures a contract with the private sector to design, build, finance, operate, and maintain service. These public–private partnerships (P3) are becoming an increasingly popular method of building new rail lines. Some experts believe that they could be used for bus rapid transit lines as well. P3s have a track record of producing a higher-quality, lower-cost transit solution compared with public management. Most popular in parts of Europe and Latin America, P3s for transit are now being used in Canada, the United States, and the Middle East. Most transit P3s use some amount of public funding to help build and/or operate the service.

A third option is for the private sector to plan and operate transit service via a competitive service contract, often called tendered service. Public entities will choose to contract different service provisions including operations, service planning, and maintenance to a private entity. These public agencies seek requests for qualifications and requests for proposals from several consortiums. They select between three and five finalists and award service to the team that offers taxpayers the best overall value. Paratransit service for the disabled is the most frequently contracted service, but some agencies contract all of their operations to the private sector.

This chapter summarizes the three ways that the private sector is involved in transit service by explaining different types of transit service, the history of transit privatization/P3s, privatization/P3s around the world, the political realities, as well as the advantages and disadvantages of using private service models. It closes with recommendations on future private provision of service.

Transit Service Basics

Fixed-Route Transit Technologies

Fixed-route transit service is provided in many different forms. It is important to understand all of the different types of transit services to better understand which types of privatization work best for each mode. The largest, profitable heavy rail systems are the systems that could benefit most from true privatization. One example is the Seoul Metro system. Large, but not super large, transit lines alongside property that generates tax revenue through value capture are the ideal P3 candidates. From a modal perspective, these are typically heavy rail, light rail, and bus rapid transit lines. Finally, smaller, local bus lines can benefit from contracting out service.

The following paragraphs include a definition of all of the traditional and emerging transit modes. These include heavy rail, light rail, commuter rail, bus rapid transit, express bus, limited stop bus, local bus, vanpools, jitneys, and rideshare services.

Heavy Rail

An electric railway with the capacity for a "heavy volume" of traffic and characterized by exclusive rights-of-way, multi-car trains, high speed, and rapid acceleration. Heavy rail vehicles typically receive their power from an electrified third rail (American Public Transportation Association 1994). International heavy rail systems in Hong Kong and Tokyo are privately operated.

Light Rail

An electric railway with a "light volume" of traffic capacity compared to heavy rail. Light rail may operate using shared or exclusive rights-of-way, in trains ranging from two to four cars.[1] Many Canadian light rail lines and the Denver's A Line (connecting downtown with the airport) were built and are operated using P3s.

Commuter Rail

Regional passenger train operations between a central city, its suburbs, and/or another central city.[2] It may be either locomotive-hauled or self-propelled, and is characterized by multi-trip tickets, specific station-to-station fares, railroad employment practices, and typically one or two stations in the central business district. Many commuter rail lines are privately operated, typically though tendered service.

Bus Rapid Transit

A high capacity, low-cost compared to rail, transit technology using high-quality buses to improve mobility. Buses typically rely on traffic signal priority that provides special green time to the buses not provided to automobiles. Buses may use a dedicated lane or travel in mixed traffic (National BRT Institute 2016). Most BRT lines are publicly operated, but some are contracted out. BRT routes with daily ridership forecast above 10,000 are good candidates for P3s.

---

[1] Ibid.

[2] Ibid.

Express Bus

A bus that operates a portion of the route without stops or with a limited number of stops. Express bus typically operates on freeways, expressways, or arterials with traffic signal priority. Express bus service is often contracted out.

Limited-Stop Bus

A bus that stops less frequently than local service. Limited-stop service typically supplements local bus service often in the peak service direction. Limited stop bus service can be contracted out as well.

Local Bus

A rubber-tired, self-propelled, manually steered vehicle. Local bus service is the backbone of all transit agencies. Some local bus services are contracted out.

Vanpool

An informal type of transit in which commuters traveling from an origin in one general area and a destination in another general area share the ride. Vanpools typically have 7–15 passengers. Riders pay a small charge to cover gasoline and insurance of the vehicle. Many vanpools receive financial assistance from a local government. They are popular in areas lacking the density for fixed-route transit.

Jitney

Privately operated small buses or cars transporting passengers on a fixed-route. Jitneys thrive in many developing countries including India. However, they are illegal in most US cities since they compete with municipal transit systems.

Ridesharing

Private companies providing single-person or carpool rides through technology platforms. Examples include Uber, Lyft, Grab, EasyTaxi, Hitch-a-ride, and Didi.

Other Transit Technologies and Transit Integration

Transit service today is undergoing multiple changes. And most new transit service is not fixed-route. Ridesharing companies such as Uber and Lyft are expanding beyond point-to-point single passenger service into carpool service. Private, microtransit providers are offering supplementary transit service to public agencies in major metro areas such as San Francisco. In addition, these microtransit providers are contracting with public transit agencies to offer variable service in low-density areas.

Most public, private, and microtransit providers seldom work together to create seamless travel. Traditional transit services such as rail and bus often feel threatened by ridesharing services such as Lyft and flexible on-demand transit services such as Chariot. Public agencies have had a de facto transit monopoly for the past 50 years and are just now adapting to new service. Private transit services are banned in most US metro areas. However, enforcement including the will of the public agency to enforce bans on private transit varies immensely. In the USA, every major transit agency lost ridership between 2017 and 2018; while this ridership may simply have switched from public transit to private transit, public agencies are under pressure to cut costs, reduce service, or sometimes both.

Leading transit agencies work with the Lyfts and Chariots of the world to provide better service. For example, a public transit agency may partner with Lyft to offer first-mile and last-mile rides to transit agency stops, particularly in low-density areas. Other agencies are locked in a more adversarial relationship. This harms transit riders the most.

For our purposes, it is important to understand how these new transit services work and what privatization opportunities are available. There are three basic types of service: fixed-route, paratransit, and micro transit.

Fixed-Route

Service which is provided on a consistent, fixed-schedule basis along a specific route with vehicles stopping to pick up and deliver passengers at specific destinations. Section 1A details the types of fixed-route transit.

Paratransit

Transit service required by the Americans with Disabilities Act in areas in which fixed-route transit service is available for disabled individuals who are unable to use fixed-route transit service (American Public Transportation Association n.d.). Paratransit services are contracted out more than any other type of transit service. In a recent National Academy of Sciences study, only four transit agencies did not contract out paratransit service.

Micro-Transit

Complementary, public or private, transit service using jitneys or small buses that provide reliever service in highly trafficked routes or service in low-density areas not served by fixed-route service (Westervelt et al. 2018). Microtransit is often privately operated. In cases where microtransit is publicly operated, it is typically contracted out. Chariot is a US microtransit provider.

How Countries Fund Transit and the Need for Taxpayer Support

In many European countries as well as in Canada and Japan, public transit is considered an essential government service. Funding for transit is widely supported to promote economic development in dense, urban areas and to provide mobility for the elderly and disabled community. There is also wider support for private provision of transit in these countries. One reason for increased support may be the lack of a users-pay/users-benefit funding model. Although all European countries have a gas tax, the gas tax is used for general expenditures (Pomerleau 2015). Both roadway and transit funding are disbursed with no relationship to how they were collected.

In the United States, most transportation services operate on the users-pay/users-benefit principle. Modes such as highways, aviation, and ports have their own dedicated user fees. Since transit does not have a user fee that supports it, transit is funded from other sources. On the national level and in some states, transit receives gas tax funding. Transit is also funded through general funds, property taxes, and sales taxes.

The level of transit funding per capita varies from country to country based on several factors: population and employment density, transit usage, parking availability and pricing and car ownership. More urbanized countries, with 70% or more of their population in metro areas, tend to fund transit at a higher per capital level (Porjani and Stead 2015). Traditionally, countries with higher per capita levels of taxpayer funding have less need to use P3s. However, transit privatization is about far more than funding. Some of the most-extensive systems in Europe have used forms of transit privatization to improve service. Further, countries with more funding per capita have found a way to use P3s to increase the speed and quality with which transit projects are built. The usage and familiarity with private provision of services is a much bigger factor than the available revenue.

Transit service provides different benefits to different groups. First, transit service provides mobility for citizens without an automobile, including transit-dependent riders such as the low-income, elderly, and disabled. Transit enhances mobility by providing a choice for those who could drive a car but prefer to take rail or bus. Second, transit service improves economic opportunities, particularly in dense city centers by providing access. If roadways are congested during rush hour, transit service can increase the number of commuters who can reach a given area. Third, transit service in combination with targeted municipal spending can be a positive influence on neighborhood rejuvenation. These gentrification projects must be analyzed for their tendency to force out low-income residents and the potential misuse of tax dollars to attract certain "types" of residents. Regardless, many cities throughout the world have gentrified around rail transit lines over the past 15 years (Dong 2017).

Transit funding is provided by all levels of governments (federal, state/provincial, and local governments) with smaller countries and those with a stronger federal government providing a larger federal share compared to larger countries or those with weaker federal governments. Some countries such as France provide 50% of more funding at the federal level. Others such as the USA provide a smaller share, typically less than 33% (O'Sullivan 2018). Unlike, highways, which receive most of their funding from user fees such as the gas tax, transit fares (commonly known as the farebox) commonly cover 25–50% of the costs of building and operating transit systems. Other revenue sources such as advertising, bond proceeds, and value capture provide additional revenue. However, finding the revenue to build transit lines is challenging.

Private Provision of Service

Several very large cities have excelled at true transit privatization. Tokyo is the most famous, but Hong Kong and Singapore also have large systems. There are two reasons that these regions have such extensive private transit systems. The first is the urban spatial structure (the arrangement of space in cities) and the second is government attitude toward the private sector. With more than 35 million people, the megacity of Tokyo is the largest in the world (http://www.newgeography.com/content/005593-the-largest-cities-demographia-world-urban-areas-2017). Tokyo also has a very high population density of 11,500 people per square mile. These factors create the population and employment density necessary for rail transit to succeed. Hong Kong's population density of 67,100 people per square mile is even more impressive as is Singapore's at 29,700. But more important are the decisions that Japanese government made in the Post-World War II period.

After World War II transit came under state control in Europe and North America. Starting with railroad regulation in the pre-war era and continuing with local transit service in the post-war period, transit service was nationalized.

Japan

In Japan, the private railway industry continued to flourish. The public entities continued to lose significant amounts of money, so in 1987 the government privatized the Japanese National Railways (Wakuda et al. 2000) (Many of the longer rail lines outside Tokyo are still owned by the Japanese government. Shorter, regional rail service was spun off to local governments or the private sector). JR East, JR Central, and JR West, the three railroads that spun off around Tokyo, Nagoya, and Osaka, respectively, were healthy and profitable. JR East was able to pay back its construction debt and make capital improvements, reversing the stagnation and decline under the government-operated service. Based on the success of JR, the Tokyo Metro was also privatized. Currently, Japan is planning to privatize, Toei, the other local rail service provider. The remaining public Japanese railways strive to emulate the private firms. Japanese firms do rely on minor government assistance. They receive low interest construction loans and are subject to price controls and rolling stock protectionism.

Figure 3.1 is a map of the Greater Tokyo area and rail system.

Hong Kong

The Mass Transit Railroad (MTR) Corporation was established in 1975 with the mission of constructing and operating Hong Kong's urban transport system (Cervero and Murakani 2008). The for-profit stock company is overseen by a chief executive officer and an executive committee. The two report to a board made up of a non-executive chairman and of local business and community leaders and government representatives.

In 2012 the corporation reported revenue of $36 billion Hong Kong dollars with a $2 billion profit. The farebox recovery ratio (the percentage of operational costs covered by fares) was 185%, the highest in the world. However, most of MTR's profit does not come from operating a railroad but rather from the profit the company makes on value capture. Transit boosts land values within ¼–½ mile of the transit station. Value capture dedicates this increase in land value to building or operating the transit line. In Hong Kong, MTR offers commercial property owners a choice among three options. In exchange for building the line, the MTR receives a cut of the mall's profits, signs a co-ownership agreement, or accepts a percentage of property development fees. In some cases, the MTR owns the land. The metro functions as a transit line and real estate developer by controlling both the means of transit and the location where customers depart the train. Many of the subway stations have large amounts of retail, which are leased from MTR itself.

Fig. 3.1 Tokyo Metro Area Transit Services

The profits from real estate and a farebox surplus of 85% subsidize transit development: proceeds are plowed back into new capital projects. Fares are kept relatively cheap from about \$0.50 to \$3 depending on distance. Low-income households receive a signficant stipend.

Hong Kong's geographic structure help the line succeed. The rail lines are a closed system. There are no suburbs from which people can commute by car. Car ownership is low: six out of every 100 vehicles are for personal use compared to 70 out of every 100 in the USA.[3]

Figure 3.2 provides an overview of Hong Kong's geography. Note that the transit system serves all three islands.

[3] http://faculty.fiu.edu/~revellk/pad3800/Cullinane.pdf, 12 June 2018.

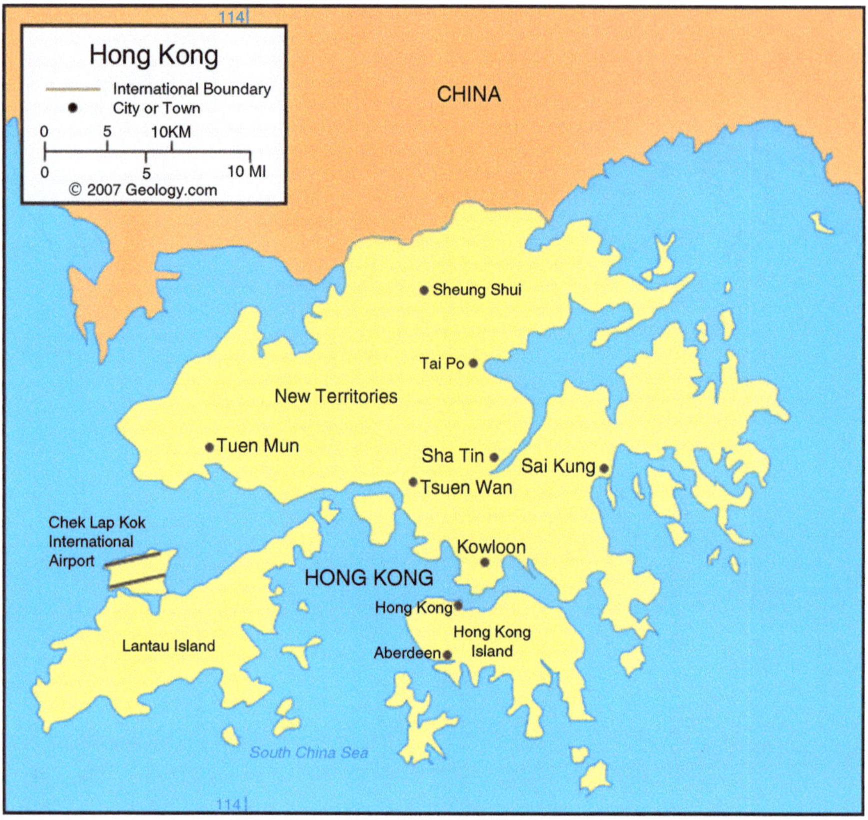

Fig. 3.2 Hong Kong

Singapore

The Land Transport Association (LTA) of Singapore is managed by the government and was established by combining the road, transit, and waterway divisions (Land Transport Authority 2012). The system includes a comprehensive heavy rail, light rail, and bus-based operations.

In 2014, the government made significant changes to the model switching from a privatized model to a contracted model (LTA to Buy SBS Buses Take Over Contracts 2015). Previously, the bus companies owned their capital equipment and offered services with input from the LTA. The government began taking over all of the assets including buses, bus stops, bus depots, and fleet management systems. Under the new arrangement, operators bid to run the bus routes for a fixed fee and the government collects all of the revenue.

The government promised shorter headways and better overalls service, but results have been uneven. All bus routes will be bundled into 14 packages. Thus far four of the 14 packages have been put up for competitive bid and

Fig. 3.3 Singapore

awarded. The remaining bus service is still operated by the private sector. However, as those contracts expire in two–10 years, those contracts will be put up for bid as well. Currently Del Gro Transit, SMRT, SBS Transit, and Tower Transit operate bus service. Combined, there are 3.9 million daily riders on 4,600 daily buses. While buses currently carry 1 million more passengers than rail, there are plans to replace many of the bus lines with rail lines over the next 30 years.

In 2016, the government made a similar switch for rail operations.[4] It reached a deal to acquire the North-South, East-West, and Circle Lines as well as the Buket-Panjing Circle Line. Singapore has a 123-mile heavy rail system with five main lines and 119 stations. Light rail in Singapore is similarly designed to bus, in that its main purpose is to serve heavy rail lines. The city-country has three light rail lines. SMRT will continue to operate the lines, but it will pay the government a licensing charge. SMRT Corporation and SBS Transit operate all the passenger rail lines in Singapore. Unlike the bus service, there are no plans to competitively bid the rail lines.

Figure 3.3 shows a map of Singapore. Note that the transit system serves most parts of the island.

[4]LTA to https://www.straitstimes.com/singapore/transport/lta-to-take-over-sbs-transit-rail-assets-worth-308m.

Public–Private Partnerships

Due to many factors including the limited availability of public funding, the preference to finance, not fund, major capital projects, and the desire to bring a more business-like approach to operating transit, many agencies have explored using public–private partnerships (P3s). The (U.S.) National Council for Public Private Partnerships defines a P3 as "… (A) contractual arrangement between a public agency (federal, state or local) and a private sector entity (Abdullah 2018). Through this agreement, the skills and assets of each sector (public and private) are shared in delivering a service or facility for the use of the general public. In addition to the sharing of resources, each party shares in the risks and rewards potential in the delivery of the service and/or facility."

P3s have been used throughout the world for all transportation modes including highways, airports, and transit systems. In 2017, there was more than $15 billion in worldwide P3 surface transportation activity (Feigenbaum 2018). In 2017, three of the four most valuable surface transportation P3s were transit projects. These projects included a commuter rail project in Italy and light rail projects in suburban Washington DC and Edmonton, Alberta.

Typically, transit P3s are composed of at least three or four of the five P3 elements. Common P3 elements include designing the system, building the system, financing the system, operating the system, and maintaining the system. Similar to roadways, there are two major types of contracts: traffic-based concessions and availability-based concessions. In traffic-based concessions, the concessionaire receives farebox revenue and/or access fees; it does not receive payment from the public authority in the years that it operates the service. Because most transit lines that are built and operated using P3s are not profitable, demand-based concessions are not a good investment for the private partner. For this reason, over the past 20 years, there has been a large increase in availability payments (APs) and a decrease in traffic-based concessions in transit. In APs, the transit operator pays a fee to the private sector for the project's construction or operation; the success of both the Eagle P3 Project in Colorado and the Purple Line in Maryland has caused APs to surge in popularity in North America. Transit P3s cannot be easily copied or duplicated. Each project has unique ridership numbers and risk allocation.

History of Transit P3s

Most transit P3s have been used for rail projects. Over the past 35+ years, there have been three waves of P3s (Engel and Galetovic 2014). The first was during the 1980s in England, in large part due to Margaret Thatcher desire to privatize certain services. The Eurotunnel was one of the first P3 projects developed. The second wave came in the 1990s and focused on highways connecting airports to central city links.

On example is the Sydney airport link. The third wave came between 2006 and 2012; many of these projects were complex endeavors that were part of a larger transit system. The best example is the development of the Eagle P3 project in Denver that included remaking Union Station and adding a light rail line connecting downtown with the airport.

One of the major changes between the 2nd and 3rd rounds was the use of availability payments. Prior to 2001 not a single P3 transit project used an availability payment structure. Yet from 2010 to 2012, 64% of rail P3s used availability payments.

Many experts are expecting a fourth wave to develop in the next few years that focuses on existing infrastructure (brownfield concessions). Continuing population growth and infrastructure reaching its original design life is expected to provide multiple P3 opportunities particularly in Europe, Australia, Canada, and the United States.

The profitability struggles of traffic-based projects are one reason that availability payments have become more popular and more successful (Mallett 2017). Of the 11 existing traffic-based concessions, including nine with more than 2 years of operation, six have had to receive public support or have most of their debt written off and two benefit from very extensive public guarantees; of these eleven, eight received federal support (Sydney-airport rail link, Channel tunnel rail link, Seoul-airport express, Eurotunnel, Adelaide-Darwin railway, Brisbane AirTrain, Kuala Lumpur airport rail link, and the Arlanda Express).

Rail projects as a whole are particularly prone to having lower ridership and higher costs than projected. However, P3 projects were far more likely to be on time and within budget than projects using convention design and build methods. In Great Britain, 69% of P3 projects were delivered on time and 65% were delivered at budget (European Court of Auditors 2018). A 2003 National Center for Public Private Partnerships (NCPPP) survey found that governments experienced a 10–40% cost savings and service quality improvements through P3s (P3 Digest 2017).

Sometimes P3 projects are rebid. There are two types of rebidding: scheduled reconcession and unscheduled reconcession. Scheduled reconcession is planned and used for projects that will last an exceptionally long period of time. Unscheduled reconcession is for projects that reverted to government control because the private sector failed to execute the terms of the contract.

Reconcession is controversial because it is unclear if it benefits taxpayers. If a company thinks that it may lose the concession in the upcoming rebidding, it will skimp on capital investment and maintenance toward the end of the original concession. However, many favor reconcession because it allows the government to reassess the contractor's performance. If a different contractor offers a better overall value, then the project can be rebid. Reconcessions also provide governments with better pricing information. Further, reconcessions increase competition, often netting a more favorable deal for the taxpayer than a monopoly concession.

Advantages and Disadvantages of P3s

Public–private partnerships for transit have five major advantages compared to convention construction and operations (Feigenbaum 2011).

1. Delivery of needed additional transportation infrastructure PPPs offers a way to fund the construction of transit lines that otherwise would not be built. Many regions are facing a "perfect storm" of growing demand for transit systems and declining funding from conventional sources. Further, most heavy rail and many of the early light rail systems have unmet maintenance needs. With long-term PPPs, the private sector takes on much or all of the responsibility for financing new highways, enabling governments to use the funds generated through upfront concession fees or revenue-sharing agreements to invest in the maintenance of existing roads.
2. Ability to raise large, new sources of capital for projects: Construction and operation of transit lines are very costly. Further, many lines have not been adequately maintained. The long-term concession model can raise significant investment capital for new and reconstructed transportation infrastructure because it is attractive to many different types of investors, including private investors, pension funds, banks, and other lenders.
3. Shifting risk from taxpayers to investors: PPPs involve parceling out duties and risks to the parties best able to handle them. The state remains responsible for public rights-of-way and environmental permitting. Private companies typically assume the risks associated with construction cost overruns and possible ridership and revenue shortfalls. Shifting these risks to parties that have strong financial incentives to contain costs increases the likelihood that the project will be completed on time and costs will be kept down.
4. Providing a more business-like approach: Compared with government-run transit lines, privately operated lines are less susceptible to pressure from narrow political interests and tend to be more customer-service oriented. They are quicker to adopt cost saving and customer-service oriented technology, products, and services.
5. Enabling major innovations: Another important advantage is the motivation to innovate to solve difficult problems or improve service. One major innovation in the Eagle P3 project was the ability of the private sector to build the line considerably cheaper. Private sector construction saved Denver's Regional Transit District (RTD) approximately $300 million.

P3s can have potential downsides. Formulating and navigating a public–private contract can increase exploratory and legal expenses. To balance the costs, a P3 must provide a significantly better value over the long-term than public financing. P3s also take some control and decision-making away from politicians and government officials. Highly charged political projects may not be appropriate as P3s.

For example, if a country plans to build a light rail line with a P3 but a political leader insists on building a second light rail line nearby, the private sector may not be able to provide good value on the first line. Private companies would worry that the second line would steal traffic from the first, undermining the ability to use ticket revenue to pay back the bonds. Building two light rail lines close together is typically a bad idea. But if the country wanted to do so, it would have to fund the projects through conventional means.

Politics can be the biggest challenge to P3s. Some local officials may want to have intimate control over a project and fight private sector decision-making. Public employee unions may resent P3s as a threat to their survival. A lack of information may lead to irrational fears about using P3s. Some officials may feel that building transit projects is an inherent task for government.

The following section provides details for three transit P3 projects.

Eagle P3 Project

The Eagle P3 project was part of the RTD FasTracks Initiative, a voter approved program to expand rail and bus transit in metro Denver (Federal Highway Administration Center for Innovative Financial Support 2018a). The Eagle P3 project consists of the following elements:

- University of Colorado A Line: 22.8-mile commuter rail line from Union Station to the Denver International Airport with 5 stations;
- Northwest Rail B Line Westminster segment: A 6.2-mile commuter rail line segment from Union Station to South Westminster;
- Gold (G) Line: An 11.2 mile commuter rail line from Denver Union Station to Wheat Ridge; and
- Commuter Rail Maintenance Facility (CRMF): Adjacent to the Gold and Northwest B Lines, the center includes a control center, maintenance shop, and rail storage yard.

Different project elements are funded from various sources. The University of Colorado A Line, Gold Line, and CRMF are financed with a Transportation Infrastructure Finance and Innovation Act (TIFIA) loan. The B Line is locally funded.

The project is being procured through a concession agreement between RTD and Denver Transit Partners to design, build, finance, operate, and maintain the rail line's components for 34 years. The P3 revenue model is an availability payment. RTD retains ownership, sets fares and fare policies, and keeps all project revenues. RTD makes availability payments to the concessionaire based on performance metrics.

The project has a variety of different funding sources:

- FTA New Starts Full Funding Grant Agreement $1,030.4 million
- Private Activity Bonds: $396.1 million
- TIFIA Loan: $280 million

- Other Federal Grants: $57 million
- RTD Sales Tax Revenue: $128.1 million
- Revenue Bond Proceeds: $56.8 million
- Local/CDOT Contributions: $40.3 million
- Equity: $54.3 million

RTD built the line using a P3, in part because it was required to by law. However, the use of a P3 proved so successful that RTD plans to build future rail expansions via P3s.

Figures 3.4, 3.5, and 3.6 show maps of the Eagle P3 project components. Figure 3.4 shows the A Line connecting downtown with Denver International Airport. Figure 3.5 shows the B Line connecting downtown Denver with the northern suburb of Westminster. Figure 3.6 shows the Gold Line connecting downtown with the western suburb of Wheat Ridge.

The Canada Line

Canada has an extensive history with transit P3s. The Canada Line, the first line constructed using P3s, connects Vancouver with Richmond, a suburb (Bian 2016). The line carries 112,000 riders per day or 40 million riders per year. The project used a DBFOM availability payment P3 structure. The line is connected to the other two rail lines run by the local government agency, Translink.

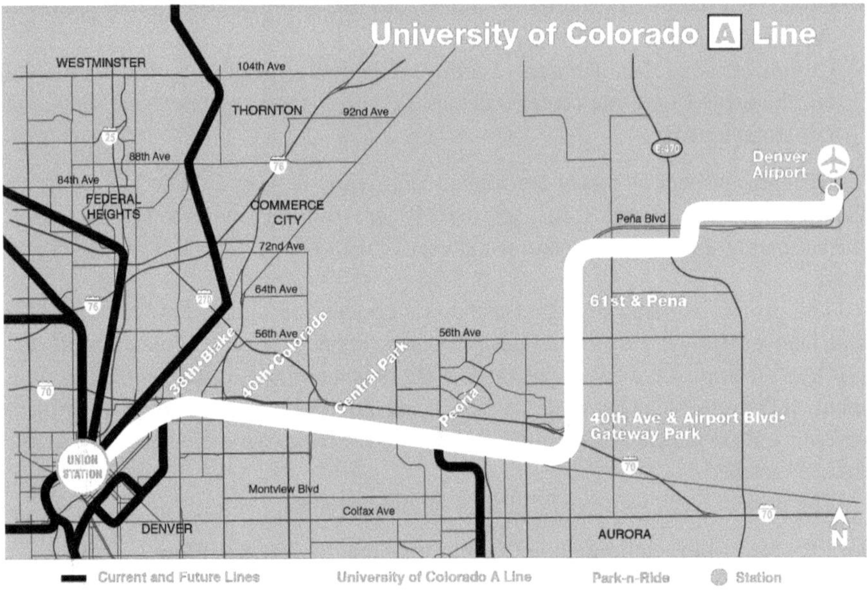

Fig. 3.4 Denver's A Line

Fig. 3.5 Denver's B Line

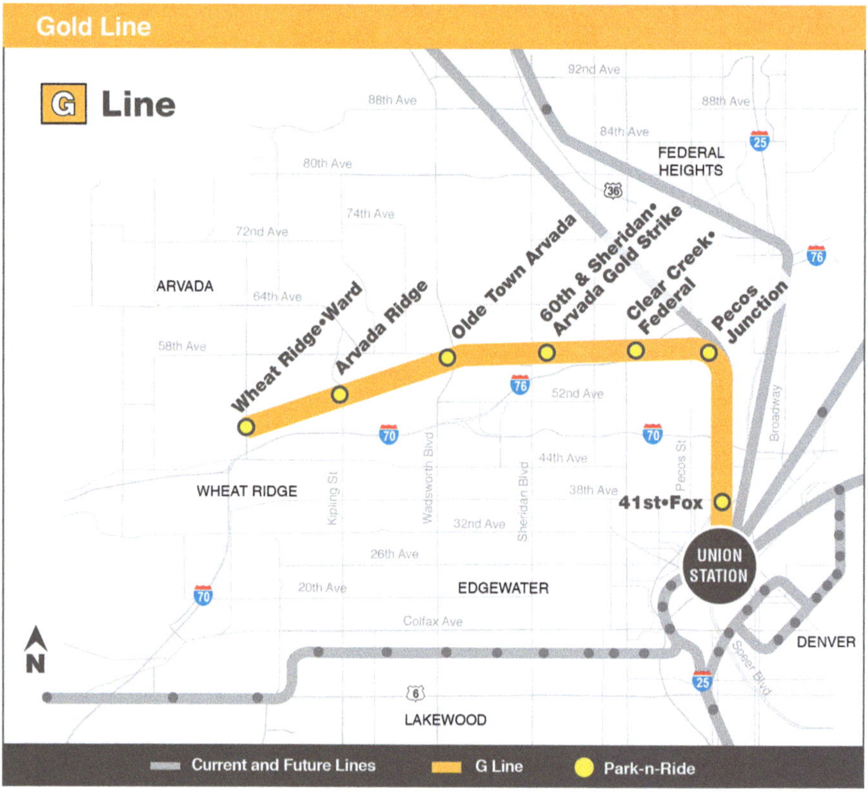

Fig. 3.6 Denver's Gold Line

The private sector consortium is called InTransitBC. The consortium's partners are SNC-Lavalin (engineering and construction company), the Caise de Depot et Placement du Quebec (a credit union), and B.C. Investment Management Corporation (pension manager). A subcontractor ProTrans BC (a subsidiary of SNC-Lavalin) operates the trains and handles maintenance tasks.

InTransit invested \$720 million Canadian in the deal. That equates to 40% of the project's total price tag of \$2.05 billion Canadian. The remaining funds came from a mix of government entities: the federal, provincial, and city governments each contributed as did Translink (the transit agency) and the Vancouver Airport Authority. In exchange for TransitBC's upfront investment, Transit Link pays the consortium monthly payments to cover the debt repayment as well as money for maintenance and operations. The payments are calculated based on InTransitBC meeting certain performance goals. Seventy percent of the payment is based on successfully running 40 trains per hour. Another 20% of the payment is based on maintaining general repair and cleanliness.

Passengers report strong satisfaction with the service. The Canada Line ranks higher than the other lines on a number of measures: service frequency, safety, reliability, and absence of graffiti and litter. It did score worse than the publicly operated lines in staff courtesy.

There were several factors that led Vancouver to build the line as a P3. First, transferring risk was very important to the government. There are risks at every stage of a rail project. For example, a design flaw can cause problems during construction. A construction flaw can cause problems during operations (The one risk that the government did not transfer in this project was ridership). In other Canadian non-P3 transit projects, the government has been responsible for all of the risk and often received an over-budget, late project. Second, the project needed to be finished by the Olympics. Sharing responsibilities with the private sector sped up the project timeline. Additionally, the ability to share risks protected political leadership if the project would fell behind schedule.

Figure 3.7 shows the routing of the Canada Line.

Purple Line

The Purple Line is the second transit P3 project to be built in the United States. The 16-mile, 21-station light rail line connects communities in the suburban DC counties of Montgomery and Prince Georges (Federal Highway Administration Center for Innovative Financial Support 2018b). The line will connect with two MARC rail

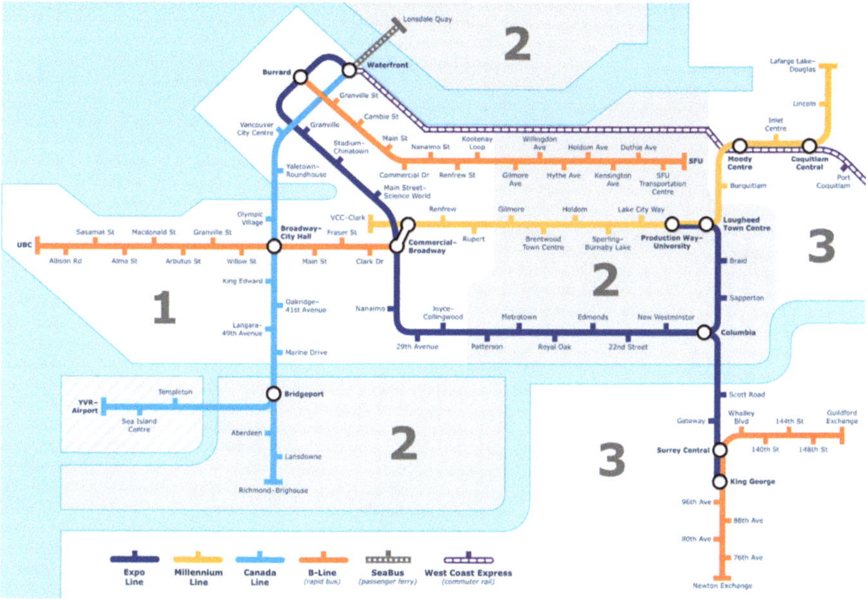

Fig. 3.7 Canada Line (in light blue)

commuter rail lines and four Washington Metro Area Transit Authority (WMATA) heavy rail lines.

In April of 2016, the Maryland Department of Transportation (MDOT) and the Maryland Transit Authority (MTA) entered into a DBFOM availability payment agreement with the Purple Line Transit Partners. A large part of the project is accepting the risk transferred. The Purple Line Transit Partners will also complete five additional partners that will complement the Purple Line.

The total project cost is $2.65 billion. Funding comes from 10 different sources:

- Progress Payments: $860 million
- Revenue Service Availability Payment: $100 million
- Final Completion Payment: $30 million
- Short-term PABs: $100 million
- Long-term PABs: $213 million
- PABs Premium: $54.3 million
- TIFIA Loan: $874.6 million
- Equity: $138.5 million
- Interest Income: $6.8 million
- Maryland Transit Authority Funds: $609 million

Project completion is expected in 2022. The project has been held up due to environmental lawsuits, but the lawsuits have been resolved and construction has begun.

Figure 3.8 shows a map of the Purple Line in suburban DC

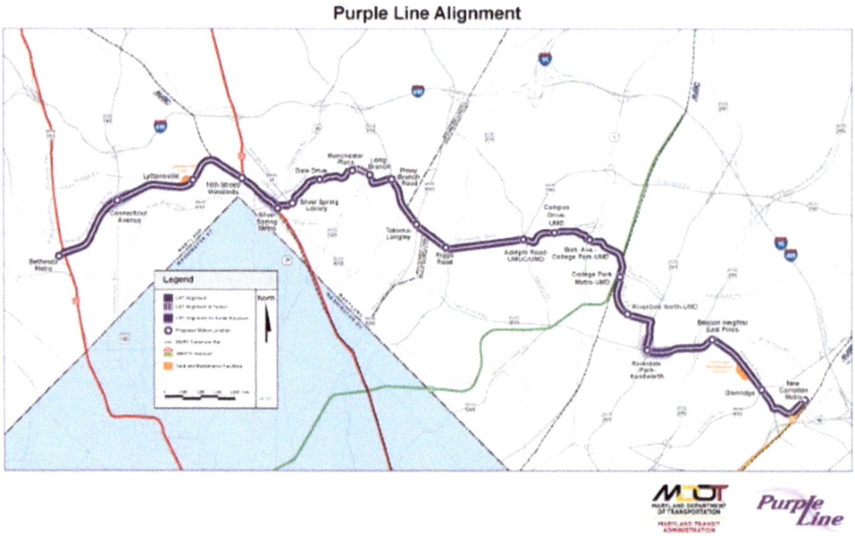

Fig. 3.8 Purple Line

Contracting Out Service

In regions where private provision of service and public–private partnerships are not feasible, contracting out can deliver lower cost and higher quality than conventional transit operations.

Around the world, the use of contracting has grown significantly over the last 10 years (Bucher 2016). Contracting occurs when a private entity provides some or all services that a public entity traditionally manages. Successful contracting needs public sector and private entity agreement on a series of performance measures.

Contracting out by itself will not lead to better or worse service. Contracting can do more than increase service quality or reduce costs. It presents an opportunity to rethink the responsibilities of the transit agency itself. Contracting can allow agencies to better respond to changing demographics, new technologies, and challenging politics. The emergence of the new ridesharing providers Lyft and Uber is providing a challenge to transit agencies around the world.

There are several factors that can encourage contracting service. Financial incentives and competition in the bidding process can provide better overall service and/or lower prices. Contracting allows an agency to focus on policy and planning rather than operations. Similar to a roadway public–private partnership, a new contractor can bring innovation and a new way of looking at the business. Well-written contracts can bring accountability into the operator–management relationship.

Some systems contract out some of the services such as operations. In this model the private carrier provides the vehicles and the drivers, but the bus routes and the frequency of service are dictated by the public agency. Other systems contract out all aspects of transit including operations and planning. In this model the private carrier provides the vehicles, the drivers, the route planning, and bus maintenance. The public entity still determines the amount of funding to spend on transit. Additionally, the public sector still has a vital role monitoring and reviewing service quality.

Contracting service started with Great Britain in the mid-1980s (Ball 2013). Sweden pursued contracting in 1988, Denmark in 1990, and Norway in 1994. Countries contract service for different reasons. Initially, Great Britain under Margaret Thatcher contracted service to reduce government costs. Later, British authorities used contracting to improve service quality. Further, different countries prefer differently sized contracts. Great Britain contracts each route individually. Norway contracts out a number of routes at a time.

There are five different types of transit contracting discussed below (Transit Center and Eno Center for Transportation 2017):

Net-cost contracts allow the private contractor to manage most aspects of transit delivery, including service planning, operation, and fare collection. The public agency focuses on general management and oversight and allows the private contractor to collect the fares. Then, the public agency provides a subsidy to the contractor in order to preserve relatively low fare prices and high service quality. Rio de Janeiro and Amsterdam employ this kind of contract to shift the financial risks of revenue collection to the private sector and to stimulate consumer demand.

Delegated management contracts are very similar to net-cost contracts, but the private contractor also handles the general management of the transit system. The public agency is therefore free to concentrate on oversight. In addition to collected service fares, the private contractor receives a fixed fee per each service provided from the public agency. When cities lack adequate expertise and need to develop transit capacity quickly, they use this type of contract. Due to Hurricane Katrina, New Orleans used a delegated management contract to quickly rebuild its public transit capacity.

In comparison, *cost-plus contracts* vary considerably from net-cost and delegated management contracts. The public agency retains authority over service planning, general management, and fare collection. Only responsible for the service operations, the private contractor is fully reimbursed for its operating costs and rewarded with a fixed management fee. Contracts like this allow the transit agencies in Dallas and Pensacola a significant degree of control over the prices and service levels, while enabling contractors to focus on quality.

The only difference between cost-plus and *gross-cost contracts* is the payment to the private contractor. Although the public agency still controls service planning and fare collection, it compensates only the private contractor with a fixed fee rather than covering all operating costs. Of the five contract types, gross-cost contracts minimize the public's costs most effectively but also drive down service quality as the contractor attempts to shed costs as well. Singapore, Mexico City, and Las Vegas are cities that take advantage of this type of contract.

The final contract type available to public transit agencies is the *quality incentive model*. Developed in response to private contractors lowering both costs and standards, quality incentive contracts improve service reliability and quality by instituting bonuses and penalties in gross-cost contracts. By authorizing increased or reduced payoffs based on certain quality and performance guidelines, the public sector can counteract the private contractor's incentive to cut costs. Therefore, quality incentive contracts still effectively control the cost to public agencies without risking the quality of the transit services. After initially selecting net-cost or gross-cost contracts, cities such as London and Stockholm made periodic adjustments to the structures of their agreements and eventually developed quality incentive models.

The following section details competitive contracting in London and Los Angeles.

London

Great Britain has engaged in a number of types of contract tendering.[5] While costs have increased over time, both quality and service offered have increased. This is the likely reason for increased costs. Compared to most US regions that have been losing service for years, London has increased its bus ridership by 69% since 2000.

[5] Ibid.

Margaret Thatcher introduced the Land Regional Transport Act as a part of a plan to increase private sector involvement in the provision of transportation services. The concern over public finances at London Transport was the motivating factor for the change. (The public contribution to transit services increased from 6.5 million pounds in 1972 to 370 million pounds in 1982). The early contract focused on cost savings; London Transport paid private providers to run the service for a fixed fee. This saved the agency 16% on bus operations. However, labor was unhappy and the contracts did not establish financial incentives so service quality decreased.

In 1993, London switched to net-cost contracts to provide better service with more opportunities for financial gain. However, the contracts were not structured well. Rather than rewarding high quality service, the contracts rewarded low costs so contractors focused on service costs only.

London Transport underwent significant internal restructuring due to government reforms. Now known as Transport for London (TfL), the agency continues to value quality factors over cost factors. Every year about 20% of the network is tendered. Operators bid on multiple routes. There are currently 16 different private entities running bus service. Bonus payments are awarded for exceeding targets. Reliability indicators are excess wait times for high frequency routes and on-time performance for low frequency routes. TfL uses performance metrics to decide whether to extend contracts. TfL uses its purchasing power to its benefits and those of its concessionaires. For example, TfL purchased double decker buses. While the contractor was required to maintain the bus, it was not charged for the vehicle.

Los Angeles

US cities have been far less likely to contract transit service. Austin, Los Angeles, and New Orleans have considerable experience with contracting. Los Angeles' experience is the most significant.[6] In the region, several agencies have used contracting for decades to provide about 15% of transit trips in the region. The city of Los Angeles used outside contracted, unionized workers in lieu of service cuts. This focused agency staff on management and allowed the agency to add bus service. Metrolink, which provides commuter rail service, contracts out its operations. Foothill transit previously used contracted drivers and management for all of its operations but switched to in-house personnel to gain more control. The county agency, L.A. Metro, uses contractors to supplement its core network.

The city of L.A. used contractors for operations. The city of L.A. started providing transit service because the county canceled low-ridership routes in downtown L.A. Originally, the contracts were 3-year gross-cost contracts paid by revenue hours of bus service. Contracts have evolved as the agency's service has grown. Today's contracts are 5 years with no renewals and require the contractor to provide

[6] Ibid.

bus operations and maintenance. The city has added specific service benchmarks: road-safety financial incentives to support the Vision Zero safety goals, 85% on-time performance, no late preventive maintenance, and completion of 99% of scheduled service hours. Contractors are penalized if they do not provide this level of service. The city of L.A. plans, designs, and contracts out service by geographic area. The county has two private operators that meet with city officials every two weeks to discuss problems.

Most of the existing research focuses on cost savings from labor. And the savings can be substantial, up to 50% of total costs. The San Diego Metropolitan Transit System decreased costs between 30 and 60% when it contracted its bus routes in 1991. However, costs are not always lower. After initially declining in Norway and Finland, costs increased in later rounds. And correcting contracting service is not as easy as issuing a request for proposals and selecting the cheapest bidder.

Contracting requires the transit agency to have knowledgeable staff and a supportive political climate. Contracting out service has provided several important lessons. First, contracted service must provide quality service at a realistic price.[7] Some agencies focus only on cost savings in contracting. These agencies may achieve significant savings, but if the transit service has significantly deteriorated to the point that riders quit using it, transit is no longer meeting its goals. Other agencies add numerous routes that cannot be financially supported over the long-term. This approach is unsustainable and will lead to service cutbacks.

Second, clear contracts align contractors' profit motive with agency goals.[8] The private sector contracts transit service with the public agency because there is a profit potential. If the goal is to improve on-time service, public agencies can offer penalties and/or bonuses for meeting a certain on-time threshold, such as 95%. If the goal is to offer better technology to riders, the agency can offer penalties/bonuses for implementing Wi-Fi on a certain number of buses during rush hour. At the same time, many of the advantages of highway and aviation P3s have resulted from private sector innovation. For example, the private sector was able to rebuild and widen the I-495 Beltway outside Washington DC several years quicker and for 25% less funding due to private sector innovations. Similar innovations come from transit sector contracting. It is important that contracts include quantitative benchmarks but are flexible enough to allow innovation.

Finally, constructive agency/contractor relationships can improve operations and foster innovation.[9] Contractors improve transit service by bringing experiences from other transit agencies. A good relationship with open dialog is critical to a successful contract. Agencies should not use contracts to unfairly penalize the private sector for trivial matters such as minor uniform violations. Contractors should be encouraged to report customer feedback to management since contractors may often be on the front lines.

---

[7] "A Bid for Better Transit," Transit Center and Eno Center for Transportation.

[8] Ibid.

[9] Ibid.

Conclusions

Some countries have had more experience with private sector transit, P3s, and contracting service. But the combination of ridesharing companies such as Uber and Lyft, evolving development patterns and automated vehicles is going to substantially change transit service over the next 20 years. Many experts believe that automated ridesharing vehicles may be less than 10 years away. Due to their high costs, they will primarily be used by fleet owners. These services will essentially function as microtransit in low-density areas. These services may decrease traditional fixed-route transit ridership, allowing providers to switch from traditional service using 60-foot buses to smaller microtransit vehicles in these low-density areas.

While rail lines and bus rapid transit will remain vital services for regions, the local bus may be limited to dense central cities, busy commercial corridors, and select high ridership routes. The pace and extent of this change is unknown, but now is the time for many transit agencies to start preparing.

Many agencies are losing riders to Uber and Lyft. While some agencies have reacted to this change by building partnerships with ridesharing entities, others have bitterly fought new entrants threatening legal action. Ridesharing agencies can be real threats, and they may not be pleasant to interact with, but creative transit agencies can benefit by contracting their low-density, low-ridership routes that lose the most money to ridesharing companies.

Further, transit agencies need to transition from being bus and train operators to mobility providers. America in 2030 will be very different from America in 1950. The traditional mobility choices will expand beyond car or bus to include microtransit, work-at-home, and more. The private sector may be able to provide better transit service at a similar price; with more options, contracting service out will be a better option for most transit agencies. Commuters are not interested in who operates the bus service. They want a range of transit options. Transit agencies that coordinate mobility and provide choice, by overseeing different providers and contracting out service, are going to be in better position than agencies that operate their own service.

References

Abdullah, Z. (2018, February 15). LTA to take over SBS transit rail assets worth $30.8 million. *The Straits Times*, straitstimes.com. Retrieved April 24, 2018, from https://www.straitstimes.com/singapore/transport/lta-to-take-over-sbs-transit-rail-assets-worth-308m; News. (2014, April 4). NCPPP.org. www.ncppp.org. Retrieved April 24, 2018, from https://ncppp.org/news/

American Public Transportation Association. (1994). *Transit glossary fact book*, apta.com. Retrieved September 7, 2018, from http://www.apta.com/resources/reportsandpublications/Documents/Transit_Glossary_1994.pdf

American Public Transportation Association. Transit glossary fact book.

Ball, J. (2013, April 12). The Thatcher Effect: What changed and what stayed the same. *The Guardian*, theguardian.com. Retrieved from April 12, 2018, from https://www.theguardian.com/politics/2013/apr/12/thatcher-britain

Bian, J. (2016, July). *The effectiveness of using a public private partnership model for urban rail transit: The Vancouver Case*. Western University. http://localgovernment.uwo.ca. Retrieved April 12, 2018, from http://localgovernment.uwo.ca/resources/docs/research_papers/2016/Bian,%20Jie%20-%202016%20-%20PUBLIC.pdf

Bucher, M. (2016, June 9). *Contracting pros and cons, global trend becoming more national*, masstransitmag.com. Retrieved from April 4, 2018, from http://www.masstransitmag.com/article/12210235/contracting-pros-and-cons-global-trend-becoming-more-national.

Cervero, R., & Murakani, J. (2008, May). *Rail and property development: A model of sustainable transit finance and urbanism* (Working Paper). Retrieved from http://citeseerx.ist.psu.edu/viewdoc/download?doi=10.1.1.232.7439&rep=rep1&type=pdf

Dong, H. (2017, July). Rail transit induced gentrification and the affordability paradox of TOD. *Journal of Transport Geography, 63*, 1–10. doi:10.1016/j.jtrangeo.2017.07.001. 7 September 2018.

Engel, E., & Galetovic, A. (2014, May). Urban transport: Can public private partnerships work. *World Bank*. Retrieved August 28, 2018, from http://documents.worldbank.org/curated/en/566251468153289708/pdf/WPS6873.pdf

European Court of Auditors. (2018, September). *Public private partnerships in the EU: Widespread shortcoming and limited benefits*. Retrieved September 8, 2018, from http://publications.europa.eu/webpub/eca/special-reports/ppp-9-2018/en/

Federal Highway Administration Center for Innovative Financial Support. (2018a). *Project profile: Eagle project*. fhwa.dot.gov. Retrieved May 24, 2018, from https://www.fhwa.dot.gov/ipd/project_profiles/co_eagle_project.aspx

Federal Highway Administration Center for Innovative Financial Support. (2018b). *Project profile: Purple Line Project*. fhwa.dot.gov. Retrieved April 12, 2018, from https://www.fhwa.dot.gov/ipd/project_profiles/md_purple_line.aspx

Feigenbaum, B. (2011). *Risks and rewards of public-private partnerships for highways*. Reason Foundation. Retrieved April 12, 2018, from https://reason.org/policy-brief/public-private-partnerships-highway/

Feigenbaum, B. (2018, August). *2018 Annual privatization report surface transportation chapter*. Reason Foundation. Retrieved May 24, 2018, from https://reason.org/wp-content/uploads/2018/08/annual-privatization-report-2018-surface-transportation.pdf

Land Transport Authority. (2012, October). *Our history*. Retrieved September 26, 2013, from https://www.lta.gov.sg/content/ltaweb/en/about-lta/our-history.html

LTA to Buy SBS Buses Take Over Contracts. (2015, December 30). *The Straits Times*, straitstimes.com. Retrieved April 28, 2018, from https://www.straitstimes.com/singapore/transport/lta-to-buy-sbs-buses-take-over-contracts

Mallett, W. (2017, November 2). *Public private partnerships*. Congressional Research Service. Retrieved May 14, 2018, from https://fas.org/sgp/crs/misc/R45010.pdf

National BRT Institute. (2016). *BRT basics*. Retrieved September 7, 2018, from https://nbrti.org

O'Sullivan, F. (2018, May 16). *Paris gets serious about free transit*, citylab.com. Retrieved September 7, 2018, from https://www.citylab.com/transportation/2018/05/paris-ponders-an-audacious-idea-free-transit-for-all/560522/

P3 Digest. (2017, October 17). https://ncppp.org. Retrieved April 12, 2018, from https://ncppp.org/news/page/2/ss

Pomerleau, K. (2015, March 3). *How high are other nations' gas taxes*. Washington, DC: Tax Foundation. Retrieved September 7, 2018, from https://taxfoundation.org/how-high-are-other-nations-gas-taxes/

Porjani, D., & Stead, D. (2015). Sustainable urban transport in the developing world: Beyond megacities, *Sustainability, 7*(6), 7784–7805. Retrieved September 7, 2018, from http://www.mdpi.com/2071-1050/7/6/7784

Transit Center and Eno Center for Transportation. (2017). *A bid for better transit*. Retrieved April 12, 2018, from http://transitcenter.org/wp-content/uploads/2017/10/TC-A-Bid-For-Better-Transit-Publication-20170925-Digital.pdf
Wakuda, Y., Aoki, E., et al. (2000). *A history of Japanese railways, 1872–1999*. Tokyo: East Japan Railway Culture Foundation. Retrieved June 12, 2018, from https://www.deepdyve.com/lp/elsevier/a-history-of-japanese-railways-1872-1999-eiichi-aoki-mitsuhide-KLnccBQuCh
Westervelt, M., Huang, E., & Schank, J. (2018, January). *UpRouted exploring microtransit in the U.S.* Washington, DC: Eno Center for Transportation. Retrieved September 7, 2018, from https://www.enotrans.org/wp-content/uploads/2018/01/UpRouted-18.pdf?x43122

Chapter 4
Case Studies of Financially Distressed Highway Public–Private Partnerships in the United States

Michael J. Garvin

Abbreviations

AB 680	Assembly Bill 680 in California
CDA	Comprehensive Development Agreement
CTV	California Transportation Ventures (an SPC in SBX case)
HOT	High-occupancy toll
HOV	High-occupancy vehicle
IFA	Indiana Finance Authority
IRR	Internal rate of return
ITR	Indiana Toll Road
ITRCC	Indiana Toll Road Concession Company (an SPC in ITR case)
LBJ Express	Lyndon Baines Johnson Express Lanes in Texas
NAFTA	North American Free Trade Agreement
ORC	Otay River Constructors (design & construction consortium in SBX case)
P3	Public–Private Partnerships
PAB	Private activity bond
PPTA	Public–Private Transportation Act in Virginia
SANDAG	San Diego Association of Governments
SBX LLC	South Bay Expressway Limited Liability Company (an SPC in SBX case)
SBX	South Bay Expressway
SBXLP	South Bay Expressway Limited Partnership (an SPC in SBX case)
SPC	Special Purpose Company
TIFIA	Transportation Infrastructure Finance & Innovation Act

M. J. Garvin (✉)
Department of Civil and Environmental Engineering, Virginia Tech, Blacksburg, VA, USA
e-mail: garvin@vt.edu

R. M. Clark, S. Hakim (eds.), *Public Private Partnerships*, Competitive Government: Public Private Partnerships, https://doi.org/10.1007/978-3-030-24600-6_4

Introduction

Over the last several decades, the United States has experienced increased private involvement in infrastructure investment, development, and management—particularly in the transportation sector. This contemporary activity has rekindled interest in public–private arrangements for infrastructure that were common in the nineteenth and early twentieth centuries but fell dormant until the 1990s.

Today, these arrangements are typically called public–private partnerships (P3s or PPPs in short). Most P3s:

- Involve a contract, or concession agreement, between a governmental agency and a single private entity to design, build, finance, operate, and/or maintain a facility;
- Where the private entity is often a special purpose company (SPC) established exclusively for the intended functions and a number of private firms provide funds or services to the company;
- Typically have contract durations of 30 years or more;
- Include a financing package that the SPC puts together comprised of equity from the company's sponsors and debt provided by bonds or commercial loans; and
- Equity and debt are secured solely by the revenue stream that the SPC receives from the facility/project.

In such arrangements, the SPC receives payments in the form of user fees (tolls) or budgetary disbursements over time (or sometimes a combination of the two) from the government *in return for* providing the services and the financing associated with the facility/project; moreover, these payments are the primary or exclusive means for repaying up-front equity and debt investments. Consequently, the structure of these payments to the SPC dictates associated risks, and governments have various ways of structuring them. Three structures have become most prevalent in the United States and elsewhere. Table 4.1 depicts the basic characteristics of these three common structures.

1. In Structure 1, tolls are imposed on a transportation facility and collected by the SPC, and an up-front budgetary payment may (or may not) be made to help fund design and construction; this is referred to as the *revenue risk* or *toll concession* P3 model.
2. In Structure 2, tolls are also imposed on a facility, but they are collected by a public agency, and periodic "availability" payments are made to the SPC from public budgetary sources; this is referred to as the *availability payment plus public sector toll collection* P3 model (or *availability payment plus toll* model in short).
3. In Structure 3, tolls are not imposed on a facility, and periodic "availability" payments are made to the SPC; this is referred to as the *availability payment* P3 model (or it may be referred to as a "pure" availability payment model).

The *revenue risk* structure transfers toll collection rights to the SPC; this gives the company the ability to set toll rates in accordance with the conditions set in the P3 agreement over its duration. Generally, this structure relieves the government of

Table 4.1 Alternative payment structures in P3s

Structure	Tolls imposed?	Tolls collected by:	Budgetary payments made?	Typical form of budgetary payment[a]	P3 payment model
1	Yes	Private entity (SPC)	Maybe	Up-front contribution to fund design and construction	Revenue risk or toll concession
2	Yes	Public agency	Yes	Periodic availability payments over the duration of the agreement	Availability payment plus public sector toll collection
3	No	Not applicable	Yes	Periodic availability payments over the duration of the agreement	Availability payment

[a]Typical forms of government budgetary payments are shown; a government may make various modifications such as extending an up-front payment over time, making additional payments for the completion of project milestones or offering other forms of support such as subordinated loans or credit enhancements

the project's demand and revenue risk and provides incentives to the SPC to seek facility investment opportunities that may enhance access and connectivity as well as lifecycle cost reduction strategies. Conversely, affordable toll rates in this structure may be more difficult to achieve without public monetary contributions, and agreement on a strategy for handling competing routes is usually necessary.

The *availability payment with toll* structure keeps control of toll rates in the hands of the government but obligates it to pay an SPC over an agreement's duration as long as the company meets specified requirements for performance or progress. Consequently, the government can defer short-term budgetary requirements while project development takes place and gain significant certainty over the timing and amount of its long-term payments to the SPC. Further, the SPC company is incentivized to reduce project lifecycle costs. On the other hand, the government's promised payments to the SPC have created a financial liability, which can prove problematic in many jurisdictions. Plus, the government is holding the demand and revenue risk associated with the project.

The *availability payment* structure eliminates tolls from a project, which takes these challenges out of the equation altogether. However, a government must now come up with the budgetary funds needed to make all promised payments to an SPC. In summary, the payment structure ultimately chosen for a project will depend on the government's goals, the legal and commercial conditions in a jurisdiction, the prevailing market situation, and the characteristics of each project.

When the contemporary movement toward utilizing P3s for transportation projects began in the 1990s in the USA, the *revenue risk payment* structure (Structure 1) was used almost exclusively. Over the past several years, however, the use of the *availability payment plus toll* (Structure 2) and the *availability payment* (Structure 3) structures has increased. A touted benefit of the *revenue risk* structure is the transfer of the market/demand risk to the SPC. If financial issues arise, such as actual demand is less than expected, then financial distress occurs and the SPC bears this burden; if the distress is prolonged, the SPC can go bankrupt and administration proceedings may follow. In such cases, the public sector is likely insulated from the financial failure. Yet, a financial failure of this sort is hardly a "win-win" outcome since investors, debt providers, and even governmental agencies may lose money or experience financial restructuring. This circumstance, among others, partly explains the increased use of other payment structures.

However, the *revenue risk* structure should remain an option for P3s since its track record includes successful projects such as the LBJ Express Toll Lanes in Texas (Reinhardt 2016a). Accordingly, this chapter examines financial distress and bankruptcy in highway P3s by presenting four case studies of US highway P3 projects employing the revenue risk model: (1) South Bay Expressway; (2) Indiana Toll Road; (3) SH 130 Segments 5 & 6; and (4) Capital Beltway Express. Each project experienced financial distress, and three of the four ultimately declared bankruptcy. The cases provide the basis for explaining the causes of financial distress and examining the outcomes as well as implications for the US market.

South Bay Expressway

Project Overview

The South Bay Expressway (SBX) project (originally called the SR 125 Toll Road) was developed pursuant to California Assembly Bill 680 (AB 680), which was passed in 1989. AB 680 authorized Caltrans to solicit proposals from private entities and then enter into contracts to finance, build, lease, operate, and maintain four transportation projects in California (Miller 2000). The other three projects that were selected under AB 680 were SR 91, SR 57, and the Mid-State Tollway (Eno Center for Transportation 2014). Caltrans pre-qualified 10 consortiums based on their skills, experience, and background, and invited "Conceptual Proposals" from the consortiums for any transportation project in the state which met qualifying criteria set by Caltrans.

In response to Caltrans' solicitation, California Transportation Ventures or CTV, an equal partnership among Parsons Brinckerhoff Inc., Transroute International S.A., Fluor Daniel Corporation, and Prudential Bache Capital, proposed to develop the long-planned southern extension of SR 125 as a toll road. Caltrans selected CTV's proposal as one of the four projects recommended for development. In January 1991, Caltrans and CTV signed a franchise agreement sanctioning CTV to finance and build the roadway, transferring title to Caltrans on completion. In exchange, CTV would get operational rights for a 35-year concession period, during which the concessionaire could set toll rates, subject to a cap on its rate of return. Caltrans also agreed to a non-compete clause, which essentially prohibited Caltrans from building any other competing routes that would divert traffic away from SBX during the concession period (USDOT 2014).

Under the agreement, CTV was to develop and submit final environmental documentation for the project by December 1997. CTV faced many challenges ranging from public opposition to environmental permitting delays. The SBX project faced strong opposition from local residents, especially from Bonita along the highly developed northern end. Near the Otay Mesa River at the southern end of the proposed road, it also faced numerous endangered species problems and wildlife issues (Samuel 2007; AECOM Consult Team 2007). To reduce impacts on established local communities at the northern end, the road alignment was changed several times and CTV had to implement major efforts to conceal the highway and contain traffic noise by sinking the roadway below natural grade and bounding it with berms and sound walls. Extensive landscaping and high quality architectural finishes were also incorporated, in response to local concerns (Guiliano et al. 2012). These issues and legal challenges, among other factors, delayed the final environmental approval from the US Environmental Protection Agency (USEPA) and US Fish and Wildlife Services, to mid-2000 and expected capital costs escalated from $400 million to $635 million (Samuel 2005).

Due to these delays and increased costs, CTV began exploring a variety of ownership models, including formation of a non-profit corporation, but the franchise agreement with Caltrans was not conducive to non-profit ownership since the government wanted to demonstrate that privately developed projects were profitable ventures. In September 2002, Macquarie Infrastructure Group and Macquarie Infrastructure Partners based out of Australia acquired a majority 81.6% stake in CTV for an undisclosed amount. Shortly thereafter, Otay River Constructors (ORC), a joint venture of Fluor and URS, was awarded the project's design-build contract. In May 2003, Macquarie acquired the remaining 18.4% stake from various minority interests (Guiliano et al. 2012). A new company, South Bay Expressway Limited Partnership (SBXLP), was formed to implement the project. Construction for the project began in May 2003 and was completed in November 2007, a delay of roughly 13 months from the contractual completion date (Samuel 2010). The road was opened to the public on November 19, 2007, and tolling began about two months later.

The project was financed by a syndicate of 10 international banks with BBVA as administrative agent and Depfa Bank as co-lead for the term loan that was arranged in 2003 and set to mature by 2021. The other lenders included Allied Irish, Bank of Ireland, BNP Paribas, Commonwealth Bank, DVB Bank, DZ Bank, and HSH Nordbank. Wells Fargo acted as collateral agent on behalf of various lenders, including Banco Bilbao Vizcaya Argentaria, S.A. and Depfa Bank at a later stage of the project (Fretz 2010). The project also received a federal loan under the Transportation Infrastructure Finance and Innovation Act (TIFIA) program. South Bay Expressway was one of the first five projects selected for credit assistance through TIFIA. The total funds required for development was projected at $658 million. Table 4.2 summarizes the overall financial structure.

Table 4.2 Financial structure of South Bay Expressway project

Bank debt	$340 million
TIFIA loan	$140 million
Donated right-of-way	$48 million
Investor equity	$130 million
Total	$658 million

Financial Challenges

As mentioned, construction of the project was delayed by over 13 months, and the roadway opened for public use in November 2007, with two months of non-tolled usage to promote patronage. From the onset, actual traffic fell short of projections. The Traffic and Revenue studies completed by Wilbur Smith and Associates (WSA) in 2003 for the concessionaire indicated average daily traffic of roughly 60,000 vehicles/day by 2009. Actual traffic was 22,600 vehicles/day. In addition, average daily revenue collections were $58,341—well short of the daily expectation of $102,000 (Reston Citizens Association 2012).

On March 22, 2010, SBXLP filed for a reorganization under Chap. 11 US bankruptcy writing off the private equity. The equity holder Macquarie Infrastructure Group had already written down the project's value shortly after opening in 2007 and had valued it at zero ($0.00) in its financial report from June 2009 onwards (Samuel 2010).

The primary cause for the project to file for bankruptcy as stated in the bankruptcy proceedings (Case No. 10-04516-A11) was ongoing litigation with the project's contractors, ORC. ORC filed multiple claims for cost overruns and delays, but SBXLP had rejected these claims. Consequently, ORC took SBXLP to court, and the private concessionaire incurred $40 million in legal defense fees (Allen 2010) against these claims, which at one point totaled $740 million (Allen 2010; Eno Center for Transportation 2014). SBXLP requested that US bankruptcy courts address both: (1) the reorganization and write-off of debts and (2) the ORC claims. ORC also filed a first priority "mechanics lien" over other creditors when settling debts under the bankruptcy case (US Bankruptcy Court 2010). The court ruled against ORC denying them any settlement for their claims.

Another major cause for the bankruptcy was lower traffic than projected. Only about 38% of the traffic forecasted by SBXLP materialized (Samuel 2010). Toll revenues in 2008 were $22 million, or 70% of the projected $31 million and in 2009 toll revenues dropped to $21 million, about 50% of the $42 million projected (Reston Citizens Association 2012). The project simply did not have enough revenue to fulfill its debt obligations. A deeper look, however, suggests underlying factors that contributed to the aggressive projections. When Macquarie Infrastructure Group decided to acquire a majority stake of CTV in 2002, the population in Chula Vista and neighboring areas in San Diego County was increasing, and Otay Mesa was a growing industrial zoned area and the only commercial port of entry in United States in San Diego County. Further, enactment of the North American Free Trade

Agreement (NAFTA) in 1994 heightened the potential strategic importance of this new route, given its proximity to US/Mexico border and the Otay Mesa Port of Entry. This Act was expected to increase trade between the two countries, and generate higher truck traffic on this route. However, political wrangling between the United States and Mexico has mitigated cross-border freight movement; the US has blocked truckers from entering the United States, and Mexico has imposed trade tariffs (Guiliano et al. 2012).

Additionally, the project opened to the public just before the burst of the housing bubble in 2008 and an economic recession, the worst since the Great Depression. Prior to the recession, regional demand for housing and economic development was strong. San Diego's population was expected to grow from 2.5 million in 1990 (actual) to 3.6 million in 2015, a 44% increase. Actually, the population of San Diego in 2015 was 3.1 million, only a 25% increase (Guiliano et al. 2012). As trouble in US housing market began and a series of high profile banks were impacted, consumer spending dropped and unemployment increased. The fall in housing prices resulted in home ownership decreases in areas around SBX. The economic crisis impacted traveler behavior; many preferred driving less or only on non-tolled routes. Especially during and after the recession, travelers preferred to use I-805 and I-5, which ran north–south parallel to SBX (Guiliano et al. 2012). Cross border traffic, specifically trucks, dropped significantly. Such drastic changes in the economy from project conception to actual operations certainly exacerbated the difference between forecast and actual demand by the private concessionaire.

Resolution and Aftermath

The US Bankruptcy Court confirmed the bankruptcy in April 2011 and established a new concession company, SBX LLC, under the ownership of the project's secured lenders. Thus, TIFIA and the project's commercial lenders were given control of the road allowing them to collect tolls to recover their share of investment. Under the reorganization plan as illustrated in Table 4.3, about half of the debts were written off for secured lenders while unsecured debtors (Otay River Constructors) and equity providers lost their entire investment.

TIFIA had initially issued $140 million in 2003 with payments scheduled from 2010 to 2040. When the project applied for bankruptcy in 2010, the outstanding balance for TIFIA with accrued interest was $172 million. After reorganization, TIFIA's debt came on par with that of the commercial lenders. The "springing lien" of TIFIA's loan agreement allowed TIFIA to be in a junior or subordinated debt position to senior lenders during investment, but in case of insolvency or bankruptcy, the TIFIA lien would create parity with senior creditors (FHWA 2001).

The project's commercial lenders (a consortium of 10 banks) had loaned $340 million for a term period of 18 years (until 2021). The outstanding balance for commercial lenders before bankruptcy was $363 million; after restructuring, the bankruptcy

Table 4.3 Pre-bankruptcy and post-bankruptcy loans (adapted from Oakley and Farrell 2017)

Party	Type	Pre-bankruptcy	Post-bankruptcy	% Loss
US DOT (TIFIA)	Springing lien	$172 million	$6.9 million (equity) + $92.5 million (secured loans)	42%
Private bank (consortium of 10 banks)	Senior lien	$363.3 million	$14.6 million (equity) + $195.5 million (secured loans)	58%
Otay River Constructors	Unsecured; mechanics lien	$95 million	$0	100%
Macquarie Infrastructure Group	Private equity	$200 million	$0	100%

courts heavily wrote off the lenders debt to $195 million (Guiliano et al. 2012). In addition, residual equity was apportioned between the banks and TIFIA. With the control of the new company, SBX LLC, in the hands of TIFIA and the commercial lenders, all the future toll revenues were shared pro-rata between TIFIA (32%) and the commercial lenders (68%). The reorganized company emerged from bankruptcy on April 28, 2011 (Samuel 2011a).

Shortly after the bankruptcy proceedings, the San Diego Association of Governments (SANDAG) board had a closed meeting where it decided to pursue purchase of the toll road franchise. It appointed Barclays to establish a purchase price for buying the facility; Barclays viewed SANDAG as a "strategic investor" that would likely place a higher value on the asset (Guiliano et al. 2012). On July 22, 2011, SANDAG approached TIFIA and the commercial lenders about purchasing the toll road for $344.5 million. On December 21, 2011, SANDAG closed the deal and purchased SBX for the proposed price. The lenders received 100% of their portion of the sales price in cash, allowing them a full exit from the project; TIFIA received a cash distribution of $15.4 million, but reinstated $94.1 million of its debt (Oakley and Farrell 2017). SANDAG funded the purchase using TIFIA's reinstated debt, $247.5 million from its TransNet program,[1] and around $4 million by issuing toll revenue bonds. SANDAG would repay TIFIA and its revenue bond holders from SBX's toll revenues.

In June 2012, SANDAG lowered tolls to maximize traffic throughput and relieve congestion on I-805. Toll rates were reduced by up to 40% depending on the length of travel. Between 2013 and 2017, annual revenue grew from $26 million to $37 million (Oakley and Farrell 2017). Consequently, SANDAG issued $194 million in A/A-rated revenue bonds in November 2017 and used the proceeds to refinance its acquisition debt, and TIFIA received a prepayment total of $168.1 million; this amount combined with the $15.4 million cash distribution and 6 years of principal and interest payments from SANDAG gave USDOT nearly a full recovery of its initial investment in the project (Oakley and

[1] TransNet is a regional half-cent sales tax fund for transportation administered by SANDAG.

Farrell 2017). Currently, SBX is operational, and SANDAG staff, augmented by private contractors, operate and maintain the facility. Control of SBX is scheduled to revert back to Caltrans in 2042 under the terms of the original franchise agreement.

Indiana Toll Road

Project Overview

In 1951, the Indiana General Assembly passed legislation creating the Indiana Toll Road Commission. Construction of the Indiana Toll Road (ITR) began in September 1954. The project was valued at $280 million; it was opened in sections beginning in August 1956 with the final section opening in November 1956 (Wensits 2006). The road has been operational since. Several additional interchanges were built between 1980 and 1985, financed by bonds sold in October 1980.

ITR's vehicular volume followed an overall increasing trend, with minor fluctuations attributable to construction activities. Even after a toll increase in October 1985, transactions rose by 5.1% with a 15.7% annual increase in revenue. The tolls remained stagnant after 1985, though, and were eventually among the lowest per-mile rates in the country. Contributing about 60% of the traffic on the toll road, commercial trucks are a substantial portion of the traffic volume and toll revenue (Table 4.4). Given the road's nature as a cross-state thoroughfare, the majority of tolls are collected from non-Indiana drivers (Samuel 2006).

After his election in 2004, Governor Mitch Daniels began exploring avenues for funding transportation investments within the state; he recognized that leasing the toll road could enable a substantial contribution toward a 10-year, $10.6 billion "Major Moves" investment in statewide transportation infrastructure (Samuel 2006). To enhance ITR's attractiveness to prospective concessionaires, he announced a toll increase in 2005, which was designed to double toll revenues to $170 million annually, raising rates 72% for passenger vehicles (from $0.03/mile to $0.05/mile) and 122% for trucks—still lower than the per-mile rates in Pennsylvania and Illinois (Samuel 2006). Consequently, he directed the Indiana Finance Authority (IFA), which was formed in 2005, to consolidate all debt issuance by state building agencies, to manage leasing ITR through a competitive procurement.

After deciding to seek bids from interested private companies to lease the toll road, the state developed a fast-track procurement process in which binding offers

Table 4.4 ITR's toll revenues in 2004

	Western section (barrier system, 24 miles) (m)	Eastern section (ticket system, 133 miles) (m)	Total (m)
Passenger	$10.7	$24.7	$35.3
Commercial	$4.4	$45.2	$49.6

were submitted only 117 days from solicitation. The goal was to have bids in hand by the end of the General Assembly session in March 2006 for a vote on HEA 1008 (the "Major Moves" legislation), which would authorize the lease. Ultimately, the bill was passed by a single vote.

The procurement was done in phases. Nine qualified bidders were invited to participate in the final process of evaluation by early January 2006, and four groups submitted offers. Statewide Mobility Partners, a team formed by Macquarie and Cintra, the equity concessionaire partners in the Chicago Skyway lease, won the bid for $3.8 billion obtaining the right to operate the toll road for a 75-year lease period. Other bidders, in the order of decreasing bids, were a group led by Babcock & Brown at $2.84 billion, an all-Spanish group at $2.52 billion, and Kwame Parker at $1.9 billion. Financial close was achieved in June 2006. The winning consortium planned an initial 80/20 debt-equity financing to fund the deal. ITR's equity risk premium was 8–9%, resulting in an equity internal rate of return between 12.5% and 13.5% (Samuel 2006). The concession agreement permitted annual toll increases starting in 2011 at the highest of three factors: (1) 2.00%; (2) increase in the Consumer Price Index (CPI); or (3) increase in nominal Gross Domestic Product (GDP) per capita.

Governor Daniels issued Executive Order 06-10 on June 7, 2006, authorizing a seven-member citizen's board to oversee lease operations and compliance (ITR Concession Company, LLC 2015). Upon receipt of $3.8 billion, IFA transferred the operation and management of ITR to the Indiana Toll Road Concession Company (ITRCC) on June 29, 2006. The proceeds were subsequently used to defease $225 million in state debt on the toll road while $2.6 billion of funding was provided to the Major Moves program. Indiana not only benefited from the concessionaire's up-front payment, but the state's credit rating also increased from AA to AA+ (Nickerson 2006).

To obtain the $3.8 billion bid, ITRCC arranged contributions from its equity partners, Cintra and Macquarie, of $374 million each and borrowed over $3 billion from a syndicate of international banks. The debt was arranged in three tranches; series A was a $3.25 billion term loan, series B was a $150 million liquidity facility to fund certain early period interest payments, and series C was a $665 million liquidity facility to fund capital improvements through 2014; all tranches were due in 2015 (Healey 2014). As part of the debt arrangements, ITRCC utilized accreting interest rate swaps. ITRCC agreed to make fixed interest payments to its counterparty, whereas the counterparty's interest payments to ITRCC were floating; according to ITRCC Chief Executive Officer Fernando Redondo, the swaps at inception were "at the money"—in other words, the total value of the expected fixed interest payments was essentially equal to the expected floating interest payments (Healey 2014).

Financial Challenges

ITRCC assumed operation of the toll road in June 2006. The concession agreement committed ITRCC to a long-term capital program of roughly $4 billion over the 75-year lease period. By 2009, the company invested $191 million in upgrades, adding fully electronic tolling and widening congested stretches, with another $157 million in projects scheduled by the end of 2010 (Schnitzler 2009).

The onset of the economic recession in 2008 hurt US toll roads. A June 2009 report from Moody's gave the toll road industry a negative outlook for the coming year to 18 months, indicating that traffic growth had flattened due to weak economic conditions. ITR was no exception. While ITRCC had boosted revenues from pre-lease amounts, traffic and revenue projections were not meeting expectations. These circumstances fueled speculation about what ITRCC might do—from selling the asset to failing to meet its contractual obligations (Schnitzler 2009). In 2010, average traffic transactions were 74,600/day, which was 35% lower than expected and revenues were about 17% lower than forecasts (Samuel 2011b). Toll revenues were $164.2 million and non-toll revenues were $9 million while toll collection expenses were $9.6 million, routine maintenance and repair expenses were $8.7 million and other operating costs were $16.3 million. With $79.7 million in depreciation and amortization deductions, profit before interest was $59.1 million (Samuel 2011b). Yet, interest was $268 million while losses from the interest rate swaps were $51.9 million; consequently, the total loss was $260.8 million (Samuel 2011b).

In 2012, ITRCC retained Morgan Stanley and Moelis & Co. to address its outstanding debt of roughly $3.7 billion that was set to mature in 2015; Morgan Stanley was charged with exploring capital raising options, while Moelis & Co. was to explore liability management scenarios, including restructuring (Berke et al. 2012). The interest facility funded at $150 million was down to $40 million; further, the series A term loan's interest rate was set to jump from Libor + 110 bps to Libor + 125 bps in 2014, and the swap fixed interest rate would increase from 3.65% to 4.15% in June 2013 until June 2015. Concurrently, ITRCC's creditors interviewed financial advisors for a potential mandate (Berke et al. 2012). As interest rates continued to fall, ITRCC's interest rate swaps had become a $2.15 billion liability by 2014; this liability came due and payable after early termination of the swaps when ITRCC could not make a $102 million payment in June 2014 (Healey 2014).

Resolution and Aftermath

On September 22, 2014, ITRCC filed for Chap. 11 bankruptcy in Illinois Bankruptcy court, eight years after it first started operations. The company had about $6.3 billion in obligations to secured lenders (Bathon 2014). The project company presented a pre-packaged proposal, which was the result of over 2 years of work with creditors. The proposal sought an early exit from Chap. 11 requesting that the court allow a post-bankruptcy approval of an asset sale by August 2015 with proceeds distributed among its creditors, OR if the asset sale was unsuccessful its creditors could buy a 95.75% stake in the restructured company, using proceeds from a $2.75 billion additional borrowing to restructure its debt (Randazzo and Fitzgerald 2014). The plan had support from more than 87% of senior secured debtholders and 100% support from equity owners (IBJ 2014). Given this, ITRCC asked the courts to approve the plan within a month. The sale or restructuring process was expected to take until the summer of 2015. Shortly after filing, the courts approved the plan.

ITRCC CEO Redondo stated to the bankruptcy court that "the global economic recession stifled interstate commerce, which depressed the interstate trucking activity that accounts for a significant part of the toll road's revenues." He commented further that "even though earnings increased every year between 2008 and 2013, they were lower than projected, forcing the company to devote an ever-greater share of operating income to debt service" (Bathon 2014). For instance, in 2013, ITRCC had $193 million in debt service while revenue was only $158 million (Randazzo and Fitzgerald 2014). Further, actual traffic was 11% lower in 2013 than it was in 2007 (Mallett 2014).

As soon as news regarding ITR's auction spread, some of the world's leading pension funds and infrastructure investors formed consortia to bid. Teams reported to have an interest were (Roumeliotis and Stone 2014) as follows:

1. A consortium of Canada Pension Plan Investment Board (CPPIB) with Ferrovial SA's toll road operator Cintra and Canadian investment manager Brookfield Asset Management;
2. Australia's Hastings Funds Management who partnered with the California Public Employees' Retirement System (Calpers) and Italian toll road operator Autostrade Meridionali SpA;
3. Spanish infrastructure operator Abertis Infraestructuras SA with Borealis, which is the infrastructure investment arm of the Ontario Municipal Employees Retirement System;
4. Alberta Investment Management Corporation (AIMCo) and Abu Dhabi Investment Authority (ADIA); and
5. Australian infrastructure fund manager IFM Investors, which is owned by 30 Australian pension funds.

In May 2015, Australia's IFM Investors reached a $5.73 billion agreement to purchase ITRCC's lease of ITR for 66 years until 2081; subsequently, the road would revert back to IFA/INDOT. IFM must follow the guidelines and performance standards set in the initial lease agreement. IFM contributed $3.2 billion in equity, expecting yields ranging from 8 to 9%; the balance of the funds came from $2.5 billion in senior debt financing from nine banks and three institutional investors (Reinhardt 2015a). IFM also secured a $328.5 million capital expense facility and plans to spend $260 million in the next five years (Reinhardt 2015a). Michael Kulper, former president of Transurban USA and new board member of ITRCC, indicated that current traffic levels will generate revenues sufficient to repay the new senior debt, so IFM's large equity contribution was critical (Reinhardt 2015a). ITR is IFM's first toll road in the United States; it holds other infrastructure assets mainly in Europe. With the closing of the IFM deal, ITRCC's creditors recovered 95 cents on the dollar (Fitzgerald 2015). By July 2015, IFM had refinanced a portion of the bank debt through the issue of over $1 billion of senior secured revenue bonds by ITRCC; the notes were rated BBB and applied to a $551 million bridge loan and a portion of a $1.27 billion term loan (Reinhardt 2015b).

In February 2016, ITRCC awarded a $200 million contract to Reith-Riley Construction to repave and rehabilitate a 70-mile segment of the 157-mile ITR, which was completed in late 2017; this was the largest capital investment in the roadway since its original construction (Reinhardt 2016b). In September 2018, Indiana Governor Eric Holcomb announced a deal between the state and ITRCC where the state would receive $1 billion over three years from ITRCC in exchange for a one-time 35% toll increase on commercial trucks; the Indiana Finance Authority (IFA) subsequently approved the arrangement (Carden 2018). On October 5th, the rate increase on commercial trucks took effect, and the state received $400 million; subsequent payments of $300 million each are due in October 2019 and 2020 and are secured by a letter of credit (Carden 2018). Holcomb plans to use the proceeds to fund his "Next Level Connections" program, which will accelerate completion of I-69 while funding broadband access to underserved regions, a grant program for local/regional trails and other transportation infrastructure improvements (Kelly 2018a). The deal, however, caught legislators by surprise, and several voiced concerns about the transparency of the arrangement and their lack of involvement (Kelly 2018b). Not surprisingly, the trucking industry took issue with the deal, but the governor's office countered that the rate per mile after the increase remains lower than many other similar roads across the country; for Class 5 vehicles, rates in Indiana will be higher than Ohio and New York but lower than Illinois and Pennsylvania (Kelly 2018a).

SH 130 Sections 5 & 6

Project Overview

SH 130 was built in six different segments from 2003 to 2012. Segments 1–4 were delivered by design-build (DB), and this roadway forms the Central Texas Turnpike System. Segments 5 & 6 were developed through a public–private partnership arrangement by the SH 130 Concession Company.

In the early 2000s, TxDOT was exploring the feasibility of developing a new long-distance route parallel to I-35 called the Trans-Texas Corridor 35 (TTC-35), which was part of a proposed network of super-corridors across the state. In September 2003, TxDOT received three competing proposals from Fluor, Trans Texas Express LLC (a Skanska led consortium), and the consortium of Cintra and Zachry American Infrastructure (Cintra-Zachry) to prepare a master plan for TTC-35 (AECOM 2007). On December 16, 2004, the Texas Transportation Commission unanimously voted for the Cintra-Zachry proposal, and a Comprehensive Development Agreement (CDA) was established in March 2005 (AECOM 2007). The master plan CDA also sought to identify specific projects in the corridor which were ready to advance and gave the Cintra-Zachry team the right to negotiate separate CDAs for these projects (Build America Bureau 2015).

Consequently, the Cintra-Zachry team proposed to develop segments 5 & 6 of SH 130 as a part of TTC-35, and formed SH 130 Concession Company (65% Cintra and 35% Zachry) for the project (Build America Bureau 2015). Following negotiations, TxDOT and the Concession Company executed a CDA in March 2007 to develop segments 5 & 6 of SH 130 as Texas' first DBFOM P3 project; the term of the agreement was 50 years from opening. Under the CDA, the Concession Company would collect tolls from users of the road but would also share revenues with TxDOT based on a predetermined schedule. Moreover, the concessionaire would also make a minimum up-front payment of $25 million to TxDOT when the roadway opened. To increase the attractiveness of the facility compared to parallel free routes, the concessionaire could offer $100 million in the form of a concession fee, if TxDOT authorized a maximum speed limit of 85 mph, the highest legal speed limit in the USA.

A year after signing the agreement, SH 130 Concession Company was able to reach financial close in March 2008 with project funding of $1327.9 million. A syndicate of European banks loaned $685.6 million in the form of long-term senior debt and the TIFIA program loaned another $430 million as subordinate debt. The equity partners contributed $209.8 million and made additional commitments for a $35 million "liquidity facility" that could support debt service obligations for the first five years of operations. Construction began in April 2009 and opened to traffic in October 2012; toll collection began in November 2012. The Concession Company opted to pay the full concession fee of $125 million to have the right to raise the speed limit to 85 mph.

Financial Challenges

Once opened in 2012, traffic fluctuated and grew slowly, but never met expectations with reports that demand was 60% below forecasts. A year after the road operations began, Moody's downgraded the credit rating due to lower than expected traffic projections; eight months later it released another report that warned of SH 130 Concession Company's near default situation and downgraded the ratings on the outstanding debt from B1 to Caa3 with the outlook as negative (Moody's 2013). The rationale for downgrading the rating was the increased chances of the SH 130 Concession Company to default on its loan repayment because of its substantially weaker and falling revenue performance compared to its forecast. It had also used up its "liquidity facility" for debt service, and Moody's expected that the SH 130 Concession Company would not have enough cash to meet its debt service payment of June 2014 (Moody's 2013). The Concession Company renegotiated with the banks to postpone its June 2014 debt service payment to January 2016 to avoid default (Build America Bureau 2015).

Resolution and Aftermath

Unable to ramp up the traffic on its road, SH 130 Concession Company filed for Chap. 11 Bankruptcy on March 2, 2016, in the US bankruptcy courts in Austin, Texas. When it filed for bankruptcy, the Company had late payments on about $1.7 billion of debt, including the principal and accrued interest on the project's TIFIA loan; consequently, USDOT was the project's largest creditor (Reinhardt 2017). On August 12, 2016, the Company submitted its reorganization plan to the courts and agreed to continue to operate the road for at least 18 months.

In June 2017, the Concession Company emerged from bankruptcy protection with new ownership, new senior management and $260 million in new financing in the form of a three-year debt facility for working capital and other needs (Reinhardt 2017). The reorganization removed $1.4 billion in debt from the Company's balance sheet; Strategic Value Investors (SVI) took ownership of over half of the reorganized company while the lending banks and TIFIA owned the balance. SVI contracted Louis Berger to operate and maintain the roadway. Estimates indicated that TIFIA's ownership share was roughly 34%, and it was expected to sell its stake as soon as possible (Reinhardt 2017). Prospects for the project had improved as annual toll transactions increased by 11% in 2016 (Morton 2017). However, pavement flaws that first appeared along the roadway's shoulders before the roadway's construction was completed had spread to about 5% of its travel lanes; these flaws became the subject of a lawsuit filed by the new owners of SH 130 Concession Company against Cintra and 13 others (Reinhardt 2018). This action has slowed TIFIA's ability to put its ownership stake up for sale.

Capital Beltway Express

Project Overview

The Capital Beltway (I-495) was initially constructed in 1956 and completed in 1964. It serves as a perimeter highway circling Washington, D.C. In 1977, four additional lanes were added to the existing four lanes; this was its last major improvement. Originally designed to serve through traffic bypassing Washington, D.C., the primary use has shifted toward local traffic with more than 75% of the current travelers along the Virginia section of the Beltway beginning or ending their trips in Fairfax County. The Beltway totals 3% of the lane miles in Northern Virginia while carrying nearly 11% of all daily regional trips. Without improvements, future growth would lengthen periods of severe congestion.

Realizing that the congestion issue along the Beltway required action, the Virginia Department of Transportation (VDOT) completed a Major Investment Study in 1994, concluding that highway improvements on the Beltway should promote high-occupancy vehicle (HOV) and bus travel in the region to address the area's congestion problems. In 1998, VDOT and the Federal Highway Administration

(FHWA) began an Environmental Impact Study (EIS) to examine various improvement alternatives.

During this period, the state of Virginia passed the Public–Private Transportation Act (PPTA) in 1995 that enabled state and local authorities to enter into agreements with the private sector to provide needed transportation infrastructure that could not be funded out of the state budget. PPTA is the legislative framework enabling VDOT to enter into agreements with private entities to construct, improve, maintain, and operate transportation facilities. The act allowed for both solicited and unsolicited proposals. Amendments have also granted VDOT the right to solicit competing proposals when an unsolicited proposal is received in order to promote competition and improve the value for money of the proposed project.

In 2002, FHWA approved the EIS that included several HOV lane alternatives for the Beltway. In the same year, VDOT received an unsolicited PPTA conceptual proposal from Fluor Daniel to develop, finance, design, and construct high-occupancy toll (HOT) lanes on the Capital Beltway. Although VDOT advertised for competing proposals, none were received. In the spring of 2003, VDOT submitted a grant application to FHWA to study HOT lanes and other "value pricing" applications in Northern Virginia; it also held several public input meetings to solicit input regarding HOV versus HOT lane alternatives. A strong majority of the public feedback supported the HOT lanes concept. Early in 2005, the state's Commonwealth Transportation Board selected the HOT lanes plan as the preferred alternative. By 2006, FHWA gave its final approval of the HOT lanes plan. In September 2007, Capital Beltway Express LLC, a joint venture between Fluor and Transurban, and VDOT reached an agreement in principle for the design, construction, operations, and maintenance of the Capital Beltway HOT Lanes. This comprehensive agreement was finalized on December 20, 2007. Under this agreement, VDOT owns and oversees the HOT lanes, and the Concessionaire will construct and operate them. The total length of the concession is 80 years—5 years of construction and 75 years of operation.

The project adds fourteen miles of new HOT lanes (two in each direction) on I-495 between the Springfield Interchange and north of the Dulles Toll Road in Northern Virginia in the United States. Tolls for the HOT lanes will change according to traffic conditions, which will regulate demand for the lanes and keep them congestion free. The project is electronically tolled using transponder technology. This project also makes a contribution to the Beltway's 45-year-old infrastructure, replacing more than 50 aging bridges and overpasses, upgrading 10 interchanges and enhancing bike and pedestrian access.

Construction began in the summer of 2008, and the HOT Lanes opened for service in November 2012, ahead of schedule. A key aspect of the project was the effort to gain public support. The promise of the HOT Lanes is the trip reliability it will allow to both public transit and commuters along this highly congested corridor; both have access to traveling lanes that are expected to provide an average travel speed (55 mph) with the latter paying a toll for use if a vehicle has less than 3 travelers. Capital Beltway Express and VDOT made a concerted effort to assure the public of these anticipated benefits.

The total $1.93 billion in costs were financed through:

- $587 million senior debt in private-activity bonds (PABs)
- $587 million in Transportation Infrastructure Finance and Innovation Act (TIFIA) loans
- $350 million in equity (Transurban 90% and Fluor 10%)
- $409 million of VDOT funds

The internal rate of return (IRR) was projected at 13% once operations commenced, and the concession includes a revenue-sharing agreement with VDOT where the Department will receive a portion of the gross revenue once certain levels of return are met. VDOT's entitlement starts at 5% when IRR is over 12.98%, rising to 15% when IRR is over 14.5%, and 40% when the IRR exceeds 16%. Transurban also receives 1% of the net asset value of the concession as a base management fee.

Financial Challenges

Development of the HOT Lanes took place amidst the economic recession that hit in 2008. Consequently, Capital Beltway Express had revised down its traffic and revenue forecasts from 2007. After opening in late 2012, initial traffic numbers were still disappointing—average daily traffic during the first quarter of 2013 was running at only 21,000 vehicles; experts, however, pointed out that traffic on SR 91 Express in California took up to three years to stabilize while project company personnel indicated that savings during the project's design-build phase were used to bolster reserve accounts (Reinhardt 2013).

By early 2014, traffic was still below expectations, so revenues were insufficient to meet all of the project company's liabilities. Transurban decided in February 2014 to pay down $430 million in variable rate PABs by liquidating $150 million in reserves and contributing $280 million in corporate equity; the strength of its asset portfolio, particularly the performance of its toll roads in Sydney, Australia, provided Transurban the capacity to restructure the project (Reinhardt 2014a). Transurban CEO Scott Charlton commented, "We put it on a long-term sustainable footing" (Reinhardt 2014a). In the process, Transurban also bought out Fluor's stake in the project, so it now had 94% ownership of the asset. Second quarter 2014 traffic figures showed some promise as volume increased by 20% (Reinhardt 2014b). By the end of 2014, revenues were sufficient to cover all of the company's operating expenses.

Resolution and Aftermath

At the end of the first quarter of 2016, average daily traffic in the HOT Lanes was approximately 36,000 vehicles—a 71% increase from first quarter of 2013 (Reinhardt 2016c). Further, the maximum toll for an end to end trip had climbed to $19.50 from $6.35 over the same timeframe. The addition of nearly thirty miles of

HOT Lanes along I-95, which opened in late 2014, as well as planned future expansions of HOT Lanes throughout northern Virginia will create a network of managed lanes in the region. In 2018, VDOT began planning an extension of the I-495 HOT Lanes from its current northern terminus to the state line with Maryland; an environmental study of the 495 Express Lanes Northern Extension (495 NEXT) began in April and is expected to be completed in Spring 2019. Hence, the Capital Beltway Express appears that it has weathered its financial troubles.

Discussion

Table 4.5 summarizes pertinent information from the four case studies.

Indeed, the four cases provide several insights about revenue risk P3s that experience financial distress.

Traffic Forecasts and Aggressive Financing

Chief among the lessons in the cases is the challenge of forecasting traffic demand; the literature has documented this phenomenon and generally characterized it as "optimism bias" where traffic forecasters overestimate traveler demand and willingness to pay (Bain 2009). In particular, two of the cases, SBX and SH 130 Segments 5 & 6, were arterial type Greenfield routes that relied on expected sources of traffic that did not materialize. Further, both were affected by non-tolled parallel routes. The ITR case, in particular, demonstrated the susceptibility of such routes to economic cycles especially when roadway users are non-local; in these circumstances, freight movement and transient travelers tend to decrease. However, while the economic recession of 2008 certainly hit ITR's traffic hard, ITRCC put together an aggressive financing plan through senior commercial loan arrangements with tenors of less than 10 years. Moreover, the company employed an accreting interest rate swap where it fixed its interest rates, and its counterparty took a floating interest rate. In 2006, ITRCC's CEO indicated that the expected value of each party's position offset each other. With the onset of the recession, prevailing interest rates reached historic lows. Consequently, ITRCC found itself on the wrong side of the swap, so its liability ballooned to over $2 billion. When it could not make its payment to its counterparty in June 2014, bankruptcy was triggered.

Legal and Market Remedies

As financial distress mounted, the SPCs in SBX, ITR, and SH 130 made the logical decision to file for Chap. 11 bankruptcy. The courts oversaw the reorganization of the companies and the write-down of debts while equity providers lost their

Table 4.5 Summary of case studies

Project	Overview	Financial issues	Current status
South Bay Expressway (SBX)	One of four projects authorized by AB 680 in California 35-year franchise awarded to concession company in 1991 to develop southern extension of SR 125 in the San Diego region as a toll road alternative to I-805 and I-5 Construction did not commence until 2003 and was completed in 2007	Construction costs escalated from $400 million to $635 million Traffic fell short of expectations, so revenues were roughly half of forecasts Concession company, SBXLP, filed for bankruptcy in 2010 Emerged from bankruptcy in April 2011 under new concession company, SBX LLC, under ownership of project's secured lenders	SANDAG purchased franchise from SBX LLC for $344.5 million in December 2011; however, TIFIA reinstated $94.1 million SANDAG lowered tolls in 2012 and annual revenue grew; SANDAG issued $194 million in revenue bonds in 2017 to refinance its acquisition debt and pay off TIFIA SANDAG operates and maintains toll road until franchise ends in 2042
Indiana Toll Road (ITR)	Lease of ITR was part of governor's Major Moves program to fund transportation infrastructure throughout Indiana HEA 1008 authorized the 75-year lease, and following a competitive procurement the state received $3.8 billion payment from a concession company, ITRCC, in 2006	2008 economic recession hurt toll road traffic so by 2010 average traffic was 35% lower than expectations ITRCC's use of interest rate swaps in its financing was also detrimental to its situation ITRCC filed for bankruptcy in 2014 with a pre-packaged proposal to sell or restructure the project company IFM purchased ITRCC in 2015 for $5.73 billion with a mix of equity and debt	ITRCC refinanced a portion of its bank debt soon after IFM's purchase In 2016, ITRCC awarded a repaving contract for a 70-mile segment of ITR In fall 2018, Governor Holcomb reached a deal with ITRCC for state to receive $1 billion in installments in exchange for a one-time 35% toll rate increase on commercial trucks; Holcomb plans to use proceeds to fund other infrastructure investments

Table 4.5 (continued)

Project	Overview	Financial issues	Current status
SH 130 Segments 5 & 6	Cintra-Zachry team selected to support TxDOT's TTC-35 proposed developing Segments 5 & 6 of SH 130 south of Austin, TX, as DBFOM project In 2007, TxDOT and SH 130 Concession Company executed a 50-year CDA to develop segments that parallel I-35 as a toll road Construction of $1.3 billion roadway commenced in 2009 and was completed in 2012	Once opened, traffic was far short of expectations, roughly 60% below forecasts Concession Company renegotiated with banks to postpone June 2014 debt payments to January 2016 Concession Company filed for bankruptcy in 2016 Emerged from bankruptcy in 2017 under ownership of SVI as well as TIFIA and lending banks	Louis Berger is contracted to operate and maintain the roadway Pavement flaws that appeared during the roadway's construction are subject of a lawsuit filed by new owners against Cintra and others Lawsuit has hampered TIFIA's prospects for selling its stake in Concession Company
Capital Beltway Express	In 2002, Fluor submitted unsolicited proposal authorized by state's PPTA legislation to VDOT to develop 14 miles of HOT lanes in median of Capital Beltway in region northwest of DC In 2007, joint venture of Fluor and Transurban reached agreement with VDOT to develop project with 5-year construction and 75-year operating period Construction of the $1.9 billion project was completed in 2012	Once opened, traffic numbers were short of expectations; by 2014, traffic was still lower than anticipated Transurban chose to pay down debt by liquidating reserve funds and contributing $280 million in additional equity; in the process, it also bought out Fluor's stake	By 2016, traffic had increased by 71% from 2013 and maximum price for an end to end trip on lanes had risen substantially By 2014, similar lanes were opened on I-95 at the southern end of the project. In 2018, planning began to extend the lanes to the state border with Maryland

investment. In SBX, the commercial lenders and TIFIA emerged as the owners of the project; subsequently, SANDAG initiated negotiations to purchase the SBX franchise, which it successfully completed in 2011. It will operate the facility until it reverts to Caltrans in 2042. In ITR, IFM Investors purchased ITRCC's lease of ITR for 66 years until 2081 when the toll road will revert back to IFA/INDOT. In SH 130, SVI, the commercial lenders and TIFIA became owners of the concession. In each case, neither the state nor its executive agency had to step in to facilitate these remedies; the legal system, not surprisingly, handled the proceedings as they would any other filing, but reorganizations and purchase arrangements demonstrate the emerging market for infrastructure assets, albeit distressed. In Capital Beltway Express, Transurban elected to reinvest in the project to mitigate its financial troubles; to date, this corporate remedy appears to have solved this project's challenges.

Commercial Lending

Interestingly, each of the bankruptcy cases acquired debt through commercial loans; this circumstance afforded the SPC's some flexibility to renegotiate their debt when financial distress occurred as illustrated in the SH 130 case. Comparable flexibility is not likely with bond issues (Yescombe 2007); PABs were issued in the Capital Beltway Express, so Transurban's options to mitigate its financial troubles were likely constrained by the project's financial structure—which may have partially influenced their decision to recapitalize the project. While the cases provide no hard evidence of a connection between P3 bankruptcies and commercial lending, this is potentially an area for further inquiry and research. In each of these cases, however, the commercial lenders suffered losses, so how this impacts their appetite for similar arrangements in the future remains to be seen.

TIFIA's Springing Lien and Patience

TIFIA funds were provided in three of the four cases (SBX, SH 130 Segments 5 & 6, and Capital Beltway Express), and these loans were certainly important to their financial structure. The TIFIA program is known as a "patient" lender since it takes a subordinate position, and it often will provide flexible repayment terms. When SBX and SH 130 went bankrupt, however, the "springing lien" of TIFIA functioned generally as intended. TIFIA was brought on par with other senior debt providers during bankruptcy proceedings. Like other providers, TIFIA was given an ownership stake in the reorganized companies. In SBX, it committed funds to the project in 2003 and received the vast majority of it back in 2017. In SH 130, it is currently the project's largest creditor. While it is expected to sell its ownership, legal issues arising from pavement flaws have delayed such a transaction; here, its "patience" is certainly being tested.

Other Issues

An issue that warrants further investigation and future observation is the provision of toll road services by a P3 concession company during financial distress or bankruptcy proceedings. The P3 concession company remains under contract to operate and maintain its project regardless of the financial situation, so financial distress and bankruptcy cases could impact the quality of these services. While the cases did not delve into this issue, it is certainly worth additional consideration.

In addition, P3 equity investors certainly lost significant sums of money in each case; however, some were not complete losses—at least from a parent organization perspective. For instance, in the SH 130 Concession, the Central Texas Highway Constructors joint venture was formed to design and construct the roadway; Ferrovial Agroman (a sister company of Cintra in Ferrovial) and Zachry (the parent of Zachry American Infrastructure and among the companies in the Zachry Group) were lead organizations in the joint venture engaged by the SH 130 Concession Company for such services. Hence, they received payments to complete design and construction services. So, equity dollars can indeed be lost but often sister organizations receive compensation for services rendered. This is not necessarily inappropriate, but it tempers financial losses by the private sector.

Finally, Indiana has continued to find ways to tap into ITR's revenue potential to fund other infrastructure requirements, albeit toll rate increases on commercial trucks were necessary to exchange longer-term revenues for short-term payments from ITRCC. The Governor's 2018 deal with the new owners is resourceful, but it did break precedent with the legislative oversight present in the original deal. Whether this causes any sociopolitical backlash bears monitoring.

Conclusion

Four P3 highway projects that have experienced financial distress or bankruptcy were examined to explore the causes and outcomes. The evidence from case studies illustrated that the legal system and the market can handle bankrupt P3s, so the public sector is not significantly affected when these conditions occur. Moreover, the transfer of the revenue risk to the private sector is generally sustained. However, commercial lenders did experience sizeable losses, and the TIFIA program had to bear the transaction costs of the bankruptcy proceedings and aftermath. Further, it is still awaiting the opportunity to sell its stake in one of the cases. How these experiences will impact equity investors, commercial lenders, and TIFIA in future P3 transactions is not entirely clear. At the very least, these players will likely exercise greater due diligence when considering such opportunities.

References

AECOM. (2007). *Case studies of transportation public-private partnerships in the United States*. Washington, DC: Federal Highway Administration.

Allen, M. (2010, March 29). Expressway builders file for bankruptcy protection in S.D. *San Diego Business Journal* (on-line at www.sdbj.com).

Bain, R. (2009). Error and optimism bias in toll road forecasts. *Transportation, 36*(5), 469–482.

Bathon, M. (2014). Indiana Toll Road seeks bankruptcy as traffic declines. *Bloomberg* (on-line at www.bloomberg.com).

Berke, J., Brumby, S. and Gilligan, E. (2012, November 7). Indiana Toll Road paves the way for restructuring with advisors, Debtwire.

Build America Bureau. (2015). *SH 130 (Segments 5-6)*, Austin, TX (on-line at www.transportation.gov/policy-initiatives/build-america).

Carden, D. (2018, September 20). State board approves deal hiking toll road truck rates in exchange for Indiana getting $1 billion. *NWI Times* (on-line at www.nwitimes.com).

Eno Center for Transportation. (2014). *Partnership financing: Improving transportation infrastructure through public private partnerships*. Washington, DC: Author.

Federal Highway Administration (FHWA). (2001). TIFIA non-subordination: Where are we now? *FHWA's Innovative Finance Quarterly, 7*(2).

Fitzgerald, P. (2015). Indiana Toll Road exits bankruptcy protection. *The Wall Street Journal* (on-line at www.wsj.com).

Guiliano, G., Schweitzer, L., Holliday, K., Minch, T., & Kuhn, M. (2012). *Public private partnerships in California – Phase II report section VII: California political environment*. Los Angeles, CA: METRANS Transportation Center, Sol Price School of Public Policy, University of Southern California.

Healey, A. (2014, October 8). ITR expected to ignite interest. *Project Finance International*.

Indianapolis Business Journal (IBJ). (2014, October 28). Indiana Toll Road operator wins approval of bankruptcy plan (on-line at www.ibj.com).

ITR Concession Company LLC. (2015). United States Bankruptcy Court Northern District of Illinois, Case No. 14 B 34284.

Kelly, N. (2018a, September 4). Indiana Toll Road rates going up. *The Journal Gazette* (on-line at www.journalgazette.net).

Kelly, N. (2018b, September 16). Toll Road move surprises: Holcomb's $1 billion deal skipped legislators. *The Journal Gazette* (on-line at www.journalgazette.net).

Mallett, W. J. (2014, September 29). Indiana Toll Road bankruptcy chills climate for public-private partnerships. *CRS Insights*.

Miller, J. B. (2000). *Principles of public and private infrastructure delivery*. New York, NY: Springer Science & Business.

Moody's Investor Service. (2013, October 15). Moody's downgrades SH 130 Concession Company to Caa3 from B1; Outlook negative (on-line at www.moodys.com).

Morton, K. M. (2017, June 28). SH 130 emerges from bankruptcy protection with new leadership and new financing. *TollRoads News* (on-line at tollroadsnews.com).

Nickerson, S. (2006). *State of Indiana east-west toll road financial analysis*. Indianapolis, IN: Crowe Chizek and Company.

Oakley, B., & Farrell, J. (2017). Ultimate recoveries – Patience pays off for USDOT on South Bay expressway bankruptcy. *Public Works Financing, 332*, 18–19.

Randazzo, S., & Fitzgerald, P. (2014, September 22). Indiana Toll Road operator files for bankruptcy. *Wall Street Journal* (on-line at www.wsj.com).

Reinhardt, W. (2013). Concern grows over 495 express forecast optimism. *Public Works Financing, 283*.

Reinhardt, W. (2014a). 495 express lanes restructured. *Public Works Financing, 290*.

Reinhardt, W. (2014b). Transurban's I-495 traffic up 20%. *Public Works Financing, 295*.

Reinhardt, W. (2015a). Indiana Toll Road lease now worth $5.7 billion to pension fund investors. *Public Works Financing, 304.*
Reinhardt, W. (2015b). IFM refinances ITR bank loans with toll revenue bonds. *Public Works Financing, 306.*
Reinhardt, W. (2016a). LBJ lanes best transportation project in US? *Public Works Financing, 318.*
Reinhardt, W. (2016b). Indiana Toll Road rebuild wins governor's praise. *Public Works Financing, 312.*
Reinhardt, W. (2016c). 495 express traffic recovering. *Public Works Financing, 316.*
Reinhardt, W. (2017). SH 130 refinancing leaves TIFIA with $600m equity stake. *Public Works Financing, 328.*
Reinhardt, W. (2018). More trouble on SH 130 toll concession. *Public Works Financing, 334–335.*
Reston Citizens Association. (2012). *Wilbur Smith Associates' traffic and revenue forecasts: Plenty of room for error*. Reston, VA: Author.
Fretz, D. (2010, March 24). PFI - First US TIFIA road files for protection. *Reuters* (on-line at www.reuters.com).
Roumeliotis, G., & Stone, M. (2014). Exclusive: Infrastructure investors line up for Indiana Toll Road. *Reuters* (on-line at www.reuters.com).
Samuel, P. (2005). 125 South going for ten more years – for 45-year franchise. *TollRoads News* (on-line at tollroadsnews.com).
Samuel, P. (2006, January 23). Cintra-Macquarie bid of $3.85b for Indiana TR accepted. *TollRoads News* (on-line at tollroadsnews.com).
Samuel, P. (2007). South Bay Expressway to open Nov 19 - tenacity pays off. *TollRoads News* (on-line at tollroadsnews.com).
Samuel, P. (2010). South Bay Expressway company files for bankruptcy in San Diego. *TollRoads News* (on-line at tollroadsnews.com).
Samuel, P. (2011a). South Bay Expressway reorganized out of bankruptcy. *TollRoads News* (on-line at tollroadsnews.com).
Samuel, P. (2011b). London news wire says Indiana TR concession in financial trouble. *TollRoads News* (on-line at tollroadsnews.com).
Schnitzler, P. (2009, August 3). Toll-road lease tumbles in value. *Indianapolis Business Journal* (on-line at www.ibj.com).
US Bankruptcy Court. (2010). South Bay Expressway LP and California Transportation Ventures, Inc. v. Otay River Constructors, Wells Fargo Bank and Intrans Group, Inc. Case No. 10-04516-A11.
US Department of Transportation. (2014). "South Bay Expressway (SR-125), San Diego, CA," Build America Bureau, Washington, DC (on-line at: https://www.transportation.gov/policy-initiatives/build-america/south-bay-expressway-sr-125-san-diego-ca)
Wensits, J. (2006, January 22). Indiana's Toll Road seen as link in a chain. *South Bend Tribune* (on-line at www.southbendtribune.com).
Yescombe, E. (2007). *Principles of project finance*. New York: Elsevier.

Chapter 5
Air Traffic Control as a Quasi-Private Corporation

Robert W. Poole Jr.

Introduction

Air traffic control (ATC) is part of the infrastructure needed for air travel, along with airports. ATC requires facilities, operators, technology, and procedures, all of which must be vetted for safety on an ongoing basis. For most of the twentieth century, ATC was operated as part of the national government transport agency. This began to change in 1987 when New Zealand separated its ATC system from the transport ministry and incorporated it as a utility corporation, with the government as its sole shareholder. From that point forward, aircraft operators paid the already existing ATC fees to Airways Corporation of New Zealand, rather than to the government, which made Airways self-supporting like most other utilities.

The USA actually started out with a private model for ATC: a not-for-profit user cooperative setup by the fledgling airlines in 1929. The Commerce Department took over this function in 1936, and it has remained in the federal government ever since. Yet since 1987, more than 60 other countries have followed New Zealand's lead and "corporatized" their ATC systems.

This chapter reviews the history of the US ATC system, discusses the problems that have been well-documented by external audit agencies, summarizes the global move toward corporatized ATC systems, reviews the changes resulting from corporatization, and then summarizes nearly four decades of attempts to corporatize the US system. It concludes with some lessons learned from these efforts.

R. W. Poole Jr. (✉)
Director of Transportation Policy, Reason Foundation, Los Angeles, CA, USA
e-mail: bob.poole@reason.org

R. M. Clark, S. Hakim (eds.), *Public Private Partnerships*, Competitive Government: Public Private Partnerships, https://doi.org/10.1007/978-3-030-24600-6_5

What Is Air Traffic Control?

Surface transportation vehicles operate on physical infrastructure, such as rails or roadways, and various traffic control systems seek to keep them from colliding with one another. For aircraft, the airspace is three-dimensional, so it takes a combination of communications, navigation, and surveillance systems to keep track of where planes are and to keep them safely separated. This is the task of the air traffic control (ATC) system.

Historically, ATC began with air-ground radio communications between airline dispatchers and pilots, supplemented by lighted beacons along various defined air routes. Lighted beacons were later replaced by omnidirectional radio beacons, and instrument landing systems (ILSs) were installed at airports to guide planes to a safer landing. Radar, developed during World War II, enabled "controllers" on the ground to see where planes are during their flights. This basic system was in place by the early post-World War II era, when airlines were becoming commercially viable businesses.

Organizationally, the earliest US ATC system was developed by Aeronautical Radio, Inc. (ARINC), a nonprofit co-op setup by the extant airlines in 1929 (Goldsborough 1951). ARINC set up the first two staffed ATC facilities in 1935–36, to serve the air route linking Newark, Cleveland, and Chicago. In 1936, in the depths of the Depression, the Bureau of Air Commerce (in the Department of Commerce) took over this service from ARINC, relieving the struggling airlines of this expense.

In 1938 Congress converted the Bureau of Air Commerce into the Civil Aeronautics Authority. Its duties included not only developing and operating the ATC system but also issuing pilots' licenses and regulating and subsidizing the young airline industry. In 1940, the CAA was split into two agencies, the Civil Aeronautics Board (CAB) for economic regulation and subsidy and the Civil Aviation Authority (CAA), responsible for air safety regulation and operating the ATC system. Both agencies were funded out of general federal tax revenues. In 1958 the CAA became the Federal Aviation Administration (FAA), which remained an independent agency until 1967, when it was folded into the newly created U.S. Department of Transportation (DOT). In 1970 Congress authorized various aviation excise taxes and a new Airports & Airways Trust Fund, from which the new tax revenues could be allocated by Congress to airports and air traffic control improvements. Thereafter, aviation tax revenue funded the majority of FAA's budget.

Organizationally, operation of the ATC system was handled by one branch of the FAA, with a different branch responsible for ATC facilities and equipment. By the 1960s, FAA operated four types of staffed facilities:

1. Control towers, located at airports, to control landings and take-offs;
2. Terminal radar approach control facilities (TRACONs), to handle arrivals and departures between airports and high-altitude airspace;
3. Air route traffic control centers (Centers), to manage large blocks of high-altitude airspace across the country; and

4. Flight Service Stations (FSS), to assist pilots of small private planes (known as general aviation) with filing flight plans, obtaining weather forecasts, and other services.

These functions remain the same today, but with three organizational changes. In the aftermath of the illegal 1981 strike by air traffic controllers (nearly all of whom were fired), the Reagan Administration launched a federal contract tower program in which small (non-radar) control towers are put out to bid, with operating contracts awarded to commercial control-tower companies. (As of 2018, some 236 out of 521 control towers are operated as federal contact towers.) In 2005, FAA contracted out the operation of FSSs under which the winning bidder was authorized to consolidate their numbers (from 61 to 5) and significantly automate their operation (Office of Inspector General 2016). Most significantly, in 2003, following a Clinton Executive Order and congressional authorization, FAA brought together the ATC operations and the ATC facilities and equipment branches into a consolidated entity called the Air Traffic Organization (ATO).

Several key ATC technology upgrades took place in the post-war decades. In the 1950s, following two serious mid-air collisions of airliners, radar surveillance became mandatory in all airspace used by airlines and other high-performance aircraft. In the 1960s, the FAA installed mainframe computers in each of the 20 domestic high-altitude centers to manage real-time flight data. Also in that decade, all planes in controlled airspace were required to install transponders, which are interrogated by a separate kind of radar (secondary surveillance). Whereas the original (primary) radar simply shows a blip on the controller's screen, the transponder provides the aircraft ID and altitude. In the 1980s, a collision-avoidance system called TCAS became mandatory for all passenger aircraft, and by 1991 for all jet and turboprop aircraft with ten or more seats.

It became clear as early as the Reagan Administration that it was not necessary to have 20 separate centers, each located physically beneath a geographical region of airspace. FAA Administrator Lynn Helms' 1981 ATC modernization plan called for significantly reducing their number, but Congress took no action to authorize the spending that would have been needed for consolidation. In more-recent decades, text-messaging has been developed to provide more-accurate messages between controllers and pilots—but as of 2018 is still not in routine use in most of US airspace. Other technology innovations include using a single GPS installation to replace aging instrument landing systems (ILSs) at the end of each runway, but FAA has not opted to install this newer technology. A number of other countries are replacing staffed control-tower structures with a set of cameras and other instruments monitored by controllers in a less-costly ground-level facility, but FAA has not embraced this lower-cost "remote tower" concept. A group of overseas ATC providers, working with satellite provider Iridium, has invested in a global satellite-based ATC surveillance system using GPS that will make possible radar-like separation of planes over the 70% of earth's surface where there is no radar (oceans, polar regions, mountains). Service will begin by 2019, but as of this writing, FAA has not signed up.

Problems with the US ATC Status Quo

Over several decades, analysts at the federal Government Accountability Office (GAO) and the DOT's Office of Inspector General have documented numerous ongoing problems with the FAA's air traffic system. These problems have also been documented in reports by federal commissions, such as the Baliles Commission (Baliles et al. 1993) and the Mineta Commission (Mineta et al. 1997), as well as in reports from think tanks such as the Brookings Institution (Robyn 2008), Heritage Foundation (Poole 2007), and the Reason Foundation (Poole and Butler 2001). Broadly speaking, these problems can be separated into three categories: funding, governance, and organizational culture.

ATC Funding Problems

The *funding* problem has several dimensions. The first is reliance on a set of aviation excise taxes that bear no direct relationship to either the cost of ATC provision or individual aircraft use of such services. As economist Dorothy Robyn pointed out in a Brookings Institution policy paper (Robyn 2008), when (for example) airline passengers are taxed to provide the largest portion of the funds that support ATC, airlines themselves have less incentive to be concerned about high costs and low productivity of the ATC system. And the miniscule tax revenue generated by business jets bears very little relationship to their extensive use of ATC services. As Robyn pointed out in this study:

> The current system of tax financing encourages commercial airlines to overuse scarce air traffic control capacity because they pay for that capacity indirectly through passenger taxes, rather than directly for each use. Moreover, because the taxes collected are linked to the number of passengers (and the price of their tickets), a small aircraft contributes significantly less than a large one, even though it costs the air traffic control system about the same amount to serve .... In short, because they impose a disproportionate burden on large aircraft, passenger taxes have the perverse effect of encouraging airlines to use smaller planes.

A second aspect of the funding problem is the FAA's reliance on uncertain annual appropriations from Congress. The revenues from aviation excise taxes (on passenger tickets, cargo waybills, fuel, and several other minor sources) are accounted for in the Airports and Airways Trust Fund. FAA makes an annual budget request to Congress, but that request needs to be cleared by the White House Office of Management & Budget (OMB), which generally has a focus on limiting federal spending. So FAA may well have needs that it knows OMB will not approve; hence, Congress may start with an incorrect view of ATC needs.

The FAA budget is also subject to problems affecting the entire government, such as the 2013 federal budget sequester, whose budget reductions forced FAA to furlough controllers and threatened to shut down most of the contract towers for the second half of the fiscal year. The aviation excise taxes have to be "reauthorized" every 3, 4, or 5 years (depending on the length of the previous reauthorization Congress enacted). Usually, the reauthorizations are delayed, sometimes for several years, and in one or two cases, the authority to continue collecting the aviation taxes has lapsed altogether. This funding uncertainty plays havoc with long-term modernization planning.

A third aspect of the funding problem is the inability of FAA to issue *long-term bonds* to finance large capital improvements (such as replacing 20 aging centers with a small number of consolidated centers). The U.S. Treasury is generally opposed to allowing federal entities to issue bonds, and FAA has only once sought to overcome this de facto policy. Yet it makes sense for multi-billion-dollar technology and facility modernization to be *financed*, rather than having to be paid for out of (uncertain) annual appropriations. Other transportation infrastructure is often financed via revenue bonds—toll roads, some non-toll roads, railroads, pipelines, seaports, etc. This problem is not unique to the FAA in the federal government; there is no overall federal capital budget; hence, many other agencies are also not allowed to finance major capital projects.

Governance

The second ATC problem is *governance*. Put simply, the FAA has far too many masters. The Air Traffic Organization itself reports directly to the FAA Administrator, who is the aviation safety regulator. This means that while FAA regulates airlines, pilots, mechanics, aircraft and engine manufacturers, airports, repair stations, etc. *at arm's length*, when it comes to ATC the practice is self-regulation. This was officially judged to be a conflict of interest by the International Civil Aviation Organization (ICAO), which in 2001 called for functional and organizational separation between aviation safety regulation and the provision of services such as airports and air traffic control (ICAO 2001).

The FAA Administrator reports to the Secretary of Transportation, and as noted previously, all budgets from all federal entities must be submitted in advance to OMB review, before they can be transmitted to congress as funding requests. FAA is also subject to outside audits and critiques by GAO and DOT's own Inspector General. If these oversight bodies were not enough to keep senior FAA and DOT officials busy, there is also congressional oversight. For FAA's budget and programs to be approved by congress, they must be reviewed, questioned, and modified by three separate kinds of committee in each house. First, an *authorizing* committee holds hearings and decides what amounts of funds it will approve for the coming year's (or years') budget. But actual spending for each fiscal year is decided by the *appropriations* committee in each house, which may well disagree with the authorizing committee's decisions. And if the proposed spending is more than will be generated by current aviation excise taxes, the relevant *taxation* committee (Ways & Means in the House) must also weigh in to adjust tax rates. When each house has completed this process, the two resulting FAA bills almost always differ, so the differences must be worked out in a conference committee.

All of the above offers Members of Congress opportunities to micromanage the FAA and hence ATC, such as forbidding a proposed consolidation of facilities (jobs in members' districts), requiring the purchase of certain equipment not requested by FAA, and numerous other changes that may or may not reflect the judgment of aviation experts or ATC system customers.

Organizational Culture

The third problem is the ATO's *organizational culture*. As noted in the previous section, despite FAA operating the world's largest ATC system by far, it lags well behind many other developed countries in applying new technology and management methods. In a policy study commissioned by the Hudson Institute's Initiative on Future Innovation, the author of this chapter concluded that the ATO has a risk-averse and status-quo-oriented culture (Poole 2014). The report used case studies of seven technology and organizational innovations that were being implemented by ATC providers in other countries:

- Digital communications between pilots and controllers;
- Replacing ILS with GPS-based landing systems (GBAS);
- Using GPS technology for surveillance (ADS-B);
- Performance-based navigation (PBN);
- Real-time weather data;
- Remote towers; and
- Large-scale facility consolidation.

While FAA had made some progress with some of these innovations, even in those it has been years behind ATC providers in other developed countries. The study identified five factors that may have led to this status-quo orientation, as follows:

1. Self-identity as a safety agency, rather than as a technology-enabled service provider;
2. Loss of technical expertise, due to civil service constraints and other factors;
3. Loss of management expertise, for the same reasons;
4. Excessive oversight (as discussed above); and
5. Lack of customer focus—i.e., focusing on pleasing Congress rather than those who use its ATC services.

The hypothesis that the risk-averse culture stemmed from the above factors was subjected to review by a set of two dozen peer reviewers with extensive aviation experience. They judged this hypothesis to be valid.

What Other Countries Have Done (1987–2018)

In 1987 the reformist government of New Zealand separated its ATC system from its transport ministry and converted it to a government corporation, expected to support itself via charges for its services. At that point in time, nearly all national governments (except Canada and the USA) charged aircraft operators ATC fees generally based on aircraft gross weight and distance flown. Those charges are based on worldwide airport and ATC charging principles promulgated by ICAO (ICAO 2012). By "corporatizing" the ATC function, New Zealand made the ATC charges payable to the new Airways New Zealand corporation, rather than to the government.

New Zealand's reform created a more business-like approach to the provision of ATC services. Freed of the constraints of being a government department, Airways could manage its own personnel, procure new systems free of government procurement rules, and potentially issue revenue bonds backed by its stream of ATC fee revenue. In effect, New Zealand converted a government agency into a public utility company. The reform succeeded, and by 1993 four other governments (Austria, Germany, Netherlands, and South Africa) had followed suit, with a number of others, including Canada, planning to do likewise. By 1996, with the number of corporatized ATC providers in the low double digits, Airways NZ and the other pioneers created an international organization to represent such companies, the Civil Air Navigation Services Organization (CANSO). By 2017, CANSO had a total of 88 full members (ATC providers) and 77 associate members (aerospace companies with an interest in ATC). Of the 88 full members, 62 are self-supporting corporations, with the balance being more traditional government agencies (like the FAA's ATO) that provide ATC in those jurisdictions.

Air traffic control at a national scale is a de facto (or de jure) utility monopoly. In principle, there are three ways to protect airspace customers from monopoly pricing. These are the same three alternatives for dealing with any utility monopoly:

- Government ownership and operation, with a presumption that government would not exploit its utility customers;
- Investor-owned utility, with external rate regulation;
- Nonprofit user co-op, in which the governing body represents the customers of the utility's services, and therefore has an inherent interest in the lowest prices consistent with good service.

In air traffic control's three-decade history of corporatization, all three models have appeared. By far the most common is a government corporation. There is one current example of the nonprofit user co-op: Nav Canada, which began operations in 1996. And there are now two examples of for-profit, partially investor-owned ATC corporations: Italy's ENAV and Britain's NATS (in both cases, the government holds approximately one-half of the shares). Another form of investor ownership can be seen in the US and European examples of the operation of control towers by investor-owned contract firms.

It is also important to note the difference in meaning of the term "government corporation" in the USA and in other countries. There are many federal government corporations, including the Amtrak, the Overseas Private Investment Corporation (OPIC), the Export-Import Bank, and the U.S. Postal Service (General Accounting Office 1995). Most of these corporations receive some degree of federal funding, which means they are subject to micromanagement by Congress as well as numerous regulatory requirements. They also generally have politically appointed boards. By contrast, government corporations in most of Europe, Australia, New Zealand, and elsewhere are entities that are incorporated under commercial corporation law, usually with government as the sole shareholder. In its shareholder role (usually filled by a transport or treasury minister), the government can protect the public interest as well as the well-being of the corporation's customers.

Key Features of ATC Corporations

Five features are common to nearly all the ATC providers that have been corporatized. They directly address the kinds of underlying problems afflicting the FAA's Air Traffic Organization, which were also present in most of these overseas ATC providers, prior to corporatization.

Separation of Safety Regulation from ATC Operations

It is now widely recognized that self-regulation (which is inherent in having air safety regulation as part of the same organization that provides ATC) is a conflict of interest. It potentially treats that one segment of aviation (ATC) differently from all the others—airports, airlines, manufacturers, pilots, mechanics, etc.—which are regulated at arm's-length.

One US example is the difference in FAA's response to pilot fatigue and controller fatigue. Former FAA Administrator Langhorne Bond (Bond and Poole 2010) pointed out that FAA's treatment of pilot fatigue in two 2009 instances (a Colgan Air crash and a Northwest airliner overflying Minneapolis/St. Paul Airport) was far harsher and more decisive than its response to controller fatigue in the 2007 Comair crash at Lexington, KY. Another example in the same article concerned controversies over issues such as ATC facilities consolidation, in which opponents often raise safety concerns. In such cases, "because the ATO is embedded within it, [FAA] is not in a clear-cut position to act as the neutral safety arbitrator."

In 2007, eight former senior FAA officials and former CAB chairman Alfred Kahn issued a public statement that,

> As the ATO moves forward to implement the dramatic changes in technology and procedures inherent in the NextGen concept … many decisions about increasing capacity by reducing aircraft spacing have important safety consequences and should be arrived at in a

> transparent manner. Arm's length separation cannot be accomplished as long as ATO operations and aviation safety regulation remain in the same governmental unit. (Former DOT Officials 2007)

Clinton Oster, who served as research director of the Aviation Safety Commission in 1987–88, elaborated on this point in a book co-authored with John S. Strong. They wrote the following:

> Trade-offs between safety and capacity would remain and be just as technically difficult [after separation of regulation from ATC provision] but the regulatory tensions that are now internal to one organization would become external .... Decisions that are now made internally within FAA would become external in a manner similar to safety regulatory decisions in other aviation sectors. The debate about trade-offs between safety and capacity would be more public and open to outside scrutiny.... The regulatory organization would have to consider, specify, and defend the criteria it used for selecting one standard over another, and for accepting or rejecting any proposed changes [by the ATC provider]. (Oster and Strong 2007)

As noted previously, ICAO since 2001 has urged governments to separate the provision of air safety regulation from the provision of air traffic control, and all corporatizations of ATC have followed this recommendation.

Self-Funding from Fees and Charges

As noted previously, nearly all governments charge fees for the use of their airspace, and nearly all follow ICAO charging principles which call for en-route and overflight charges to be paid by aircraft operators based on the plane's gross weight and distance flown, and for terminal-area charges based only on gross weight. A 2005 review of ICAO data by this author found that out of 180 countries listed in an ICAO document on ATC charging, only 21 didn't charge for ATC (Cordle and Poole 2005). Apart from the USA, the non-chargers were all island mini-states (Bahamas, Comoros, Samoa) or very poor developing countries (Gambia, Namibia, Somalia). Corporatization changes the recipient of the ATC user-fee revenues from the national government to the ATC corporation. This converts the ATC system into a customer-supported utility.

The change to self-support has several important implications. First, it creates a customer/provider relationship between the ATC corporation and those who use its services. When an ATC provider receives its revenue from the national government, management's focus invariably is on pleasing the government (which, in practice, may mean some combination of the transport ministry and the national legislative body). By contrast, when the revenues are paid directly to the ATC corporation, management focus changes to satisfying those paying customers. Over time, this can be expected to generate increased attention to improving the productivity of ATC services, via some combination of investing in better technology, gaining regulatory approval for changes in ATC flight procedures, and potentially reforming labor practices.

One example of the latter is AENA, the ATC provider in Spain. Prior to corporatization, it had the highest costs of any developed-country provider in Europe, due in significant part to labor practices that included among the lowest scheduled controller hours worked per year, massive overtime expenses, and among the highest rates of pay. Post-corporatization reforms included shifting smaller control towers to contract operators, increasing scheduled hours to reduce overtime hours, and moderating rates of pay. AENA is no longer the most-costly ATC provider in Europe (Poole 2012a).

A second benefit of self-support via user-fee revenues is the potential to use long-term financing for major capital modernization (such as major technology programs and facility consolidation). Like other utilities, ATC is well-suited to using revenue bonds to finance such investments. Aviation is a growing field, and for the foreseeable future, ATC will remain a monopoly. Those factors make ATC revenue bonds attractive to bond-buyers. Larger ATC corporations (such as Nav Canada and UK provider NATS) had no trouble obtaining investment-grade credit ratings on their financing.

One concern raised in debates over corporatization is the cost of collecting ATC user fees. The good news for a government considering corporatization is that global ATC billing and collection services are available to handle this function, providing economies of scale that keep collection costs low. In Europe, the agency called Eurocontrol offers such a service via its Central Route Charging office (CRCO). According to Oster and Strong, its administrative costs are typically 0.5% of the amounts collected, and its recovery rate for 1996–1999 was 99.48% (Oster and Strong 2007). CANSO (in cooperation with SITA) in 2014 began offering a system known as FlightYield, originally developed by Airways New Zealand. In 2015 COMSOFT began offering its CAB billing system. Many developing countries use a billing system offered by IATA, called Enhancement & Financing Services, that has been in operation since 1992 (Poole 2015).

Elimination of Political Micromanagement

Micromanagement can arise from at least two different sources—the executive branch of government and the legislative branch. Corporatization generally eliminates the latter by essentially removing the ATC provider from the government's budget, which is the primary means by which legislators try to intervene in what should be management decisions by the ATC provider. The former might still be a problem, to the extent that the transport or finance ministry in most cases will have some degree of oversight of the ATC corporation, especially its rates and charges. In the 30-plus years of corporatization experience, this has not emerged as a significant problem.

In the USA, examples of political decisions that over-ride ATO management decisions are numerous. One example is the case of "zombie towers." An internal

FAA study from 2010–2011 identified 102 control towers that had so few flights at night that—per long-standing criteria—they should shut down at night, but *none had been*. Bloomberg reporter Alan Levin found at least 26 cases where members of Congress "pressured [FAA] regarding controller staffing issues" at such towers (Poole 2012b). Since FAA's de facto customer is Congress, FAA chose not to rock the boat. There are many other examples, including a number of proposed consolidations of TRACONs and towers that have been blocked by congressional action or threats of action.

Streamlined Procurement of New Technology

The FAA has a long track record, documented by GAO and Inspector General reports, of developing new systems that are delivered months or years late, with significant cost overruns, and sometimes with less than the promised capabilities. These problems stem directly from the agency's nature as a government agency funded via annual appropriations, unable to do long-term financing, and constrained by civil service regulations and pay scales. Congress in prior decades legislated reforms of both procurement and personnel at FAA, but the problems persist. By contrast, the record of large ATC providers that have been corporatized is considerably better.

Uncertain funding and inability to issue bonds are only part of the problem. More fundamental is the bureaucratic nature of FAA's ATO and its need to satisfy the government rather than its aviation customers. The lack of a direct customer/provider relationship means there is very little focus on reducing unit costs or increasing productivity. The FAA's cost per unit of ATC service increased by 66% between 1997 and 2016 (Robyn 2017). During that same period, corporatized Nav Canada's unit cost decreased. Despite the economies of scale inherent in ATC, the smaller Nav Canada is significantly more cost-effective. The cost per flight hour (domestic) in controlled airspace in 2016 was $453 for FAA's ATO but only $335 for Nav Canada (CANSO 2016).

Civil service pay scales and bureaucratic constraints make it difficult for a provider like the ATO to attract and retain highly skilled technical and managerial people. This leads, over time, to insufficient internal knowledge about new technology and how to define what the ATC system needs. In turn, that leads to aerospace contractors gaining a dominant role, via contracts under which they "define" in detail what a new system should do, and are then in the best position to win the contract to produce it. On average, the ATO program managers tend to be less capable than is desirable to drive hard bargains and hold the contractors accountable for delivering systems on time and on budget. The superior performance of advanced technology implementation in corporatized ATC providers demonstrates the advantages of this model.

Entrepreneurial Organizational Culture

Poole (2015) documented, via seven case studies, that a less-cautious, more-entrepreneurial corporate culture is developing in ATC providers that have been corporatized. That report found that:

- Digital communications between controllers and pilots is many years ahead of ATO's efforts in providers such as NATS and Nav Canada.
- Providers such as Germany's DFS and Airservices Australia have implemented GPS-based landing systems, while the ATO has not (and has no plans to).
- A group of corporatized providers, led by Nav Canada, created a company with satellite operator Iridium which is launching a 66-satellite system, including payloads that will provide global radar-like surveillance beginning in 2019; the ATO has not signed up for this.
- The ATO has lagged behind a number of other ATC providers in making effective use of very precise Required Navigation Performance (RNP) procedures.
- Corporatized providers are pioneering the use of less-costly remote towers in Europe and New Zealand; Congress finally provided a token amount of funding in 2018 for the ATO to begin exploring this.
- Corporatized providers in Australia, Germany, and the UK have accomplished large-scale consolidation of centers, whereas the ATO has done nothing comparable.

What Other Research on Corporatized ATC Has Found

The most-detailed, quantitative study on the impact of corporatization was carried out in 2005 by MBS Ottawa, with assistance from the School of Public Policy at George Mason University, the Maxwell School at Syracuse University, and the Centre for Research on Air & Space Law at McGill University (MBS Ottawa 2006). The study identified key performance indicators (KPIs) and applied them to ten commercialized ATC providers, along with the ATO for comparison. The time period for comparison was from 1997 to 2004. Here is a brief summary of the results.

- *Safety*: Serious safety incidents per instrument flight movements showed a downward trend for most of the providers (though no comparable data were available for Switzerland's Skyguide or FAA's ATO).
- *Capital Spending* (larger providers only): The corporatized providers exhibited a downward trend, despite significant modernization; only the ATO showed an increasing trend of capital spending.
- *Unit Rate Charged* (to Aircraft Operators): The general pattern was downward, in inflation-adjusted terms, but with an uptrend in the first years following the 2001 terrorist attacks.

- *Productivity*: As measured by cost per instrument flight movement, six of the commercialized providers showed a downward trend (between 5% and 15% over the time period), while three experienced an uptrend. The largest increase in unit cost, 23%, was reported by FAA's ATO.
- *Controller Pay, Including Overtime*: The ATO's payroll cost increased by 40% over this time period, compared with 20% for four providers and a flat trend for the others.
- *Reduced Overhead*: As measured by the ratio of all staff to controller staff, Airservices Australia and Nav Canada achieved significant reductions, reducing that ratio by 30% and 20%, respectively. One showed a slight increase, while the others—including the ATO—showed around a 5% decrease.
- *ATC-Related Delays* (Minutes/Flight): Figures from four providers in Europe showed modest decreases, but the ATO showed a significant increase; data were not available for the others.

There is a great deal of more discussion and lessons learned in this important (though now somewhat dated) empirical study. One paragraph from the Executive Summary provides a useful overview of the findings:

> The major finding is that commercialization [corporatization] models that provide the right balance of incentives have resulted in significant cost reductions, dramatic improvements in modernization, and major improvements in service quality, while improving safety. Commercialized [ATC providers] exhibit three main strengths—sensitivity to customer needs, agility in reaching a decision, and ability to carry it through. These characteristics have led to continuous improvements in efficiency, business discipline that delivers projects on schedule and on budget, and rapid deployment of modern technology to enhance service quality.

Two book-length studies provide considerably more detail on the evolution of ATC corporatization and deal with various policy questions. The longer of the two is the previously mentioned volume by Oster and Strong, *Managing the Skies* (Oster and Strong 2007). The second volume, by policy analyst Rui Neiva, is more recent (Neiva 2015). It is narrower and somewhat more technical than the other book, focusing more on regulatory impacts and the extent of efficiency improvements. It finds that rate-of-return regulation of [many] ATC providers in Europe has had the perverse effect of permitting rising costs to be passed along to customers, an outcome not seen in Canada, Australia, or New Zealand. Despite that caveat, Neiva concludes overall as follows:

> Canada, Germany, and New Zealand, among others, have shown how commercialized systems are able to depart from the old ways. From government agencies used to serving their political overlords, they became independent entities that serve the interests of their customers, the airspace users, first. They are now also able to be self-sufficient financially, not requiring any taxpayer subsidies: a must in fiscally constrained times. Commercialization has created leaner, more-focused organizations that are able to adapt more swiftly to rapidly changing operational and technological environments.

US ATC Reform Efforts

The history of efforts to corporatize the US ATC system dates back to at least 1975. In that year, Glen A. Gilbert, popularly known as the "father of U.S. air traffic control" due to having been the first controller hired by the Bureau of Air Commerce in 1936, released a two-volume report, proposing to shift ATC from the FAA to a "Comsat-type corporation" funded half by ATC user fees and half by federal taxes (Gilbert 1975). That same year, the U.S. Special Air Services Advisory Group issued a report recommending that a study be conducted "to determine whether the air traffic system would be operated more efficiently with advanced technology as an independent public company" (U.S. Special Air Safety Advisory Group 1975).

Reagan Administration

In the immediate aftermath of the Reagan Administration's firing of all the controllers who refused to return to work after their illegal strike in 1981, the White House invited this author to give a briefing to DOT Secretary Drew Lewis and FAA Administrator Lynn Helms on the potential of an ATC corporation to rebuild and modernize the system. Although Helms rejected that approach, it led to the author presenting a paper on this subject at the 1982 annual meeting of the Transportation Research Board. The paper was subsequently published in TRB's journal, *Transportation Research Record* (Poole 1983). In 1985, the Air Transport Association released a paper calling for ATC to be removed from FAA and set up as a user-funded government corporation, the National Aviation Authority (Air Transport Association 1985). TRB returned to the issue in 1990, creating a special committee to study policy changes to help the aviation system cope better with airline deregulation. Its report compared an ATC corporation and an FAA corporation, and judged the latter to be preferable, ignoring the conflict of interest problem (Transportation Research Board 1991).

Clinton Administration

ATC reform moved to the front burner in the mid-1990s. The Clinton Administration's special committee on ensuring a competitive airline industry, headed by former Virginia Gov. Gerald Baliles, in 1993 recommended corporatization of the ATC system (Baliles et al. 1993). At the same time, Vice President Gore's National Performance Review team had identified Airways New Zealand as its model for a self-supporting government ATC corporation. Its report led to a detailed study by the Office of the Secretary of Transportation. The resulting two-volume study laid out a detailed proposal to move the ATC function out of FAA and set it up as a self-supporting, nonprofit U.S. Air Traffic Services (USATS) corporation (Kruesi et al. 1994). The Clinton Administration's USATS would have been a government corporation, governed by a board of directors representing users of ATC services and USATS employees, with ATC fees paid only by commercial aviation. DOT Secretary Federico Pena and FAA Administrator David Hinson strongly supported enactment of legislation to set up the corporation, but there was not a critical mass of aviation stakeholder support. In addition, the chairman of the House Aviation Subcommittee strongly opposed any such change, so the legislation never made it out of that subcommittee.

The Clinton Administration made another reform attempt in 1997 by appointing the National Civil Aviation Review Commission, chaired by former Congressman Norm Mineta. Its report called for setting up a "performance-based organization" within FAA that would combine all FAA's ATC-related activities into a single unit, would charge ATC fees to commercial aviation only, and would be able to issue revenue bonds based on its user-fee revenue (Mineta et al. 1997). In the FAA reauthorization bill passed in April 2000, Congress authorized the creation of a Chief Operating Officer for ATC, as called for in the Mineta Commission report, but ignored all the other ATC recommendations. So in December, President Clinton issued an executive order going further, directing FAA to create a performance-based organization for ATC within FAA (the ATO). But the order did not include any of the funding and financing changes urged by the Mineta Commission, which would have required legislation.

George W. Bush Administration

During this Administration, the FAA began experiencing funding problems, due partly to reduced flight activity in the several years following the 2001 terrorist attacks, but also due to decreasing air fares which meant lower ticket-tax revenues than had been projected. The Air Transport Association began talking about shifting from aviation excise taxes to ATC user fees, like the rest of the world. FAA Administrator Marion Blakey was interested, and in the years leading up to the 2007 reauthorization, the agency commissioned studies of the possible impact of ATC fees on various categories of aircraft users. The ATO itself did studies using data from the greatly improved FAA accounting system to identify possible cost savings. FAA also held a Trust Fund Forum in April 2005, getting pro and con inputs from various interest groups (pro, from the airlines, but anti, from general aviation groups AOPA and NBAA).

Unfortunately, instead of arguing for ICAO-type weight-distance fees, which give a break to smaller planes by including weight in the formula, the Air Transport Association seized on the user-fee idea as a way to level the playing field between airlines and business jets, which ATA saw as siphoning off a growing share of its first-class customers. Using the mantra of "a blip is a blip," it argued for charging all jet aircraft the same user fee. It also paid for a large-scale media campaign, characterizing business jets as free riders. This led NBAA in particular to raise large sums to lobby Congress against any move toward user fees. The FAA stuck to its guns, issuing a detailed ICAO-type ATC user-fee proposal in February 2007 (but exempting business jets altogether). The proposal also included the ability to issue revenue bonds, backed by the user-fee revenue stream. But the FAA proposal was dead on arrival in Congress. After all those efforts, Congress passed a business-as-usual reauthorization.

Obama Administration

Things picked up again in 2011, when the CEO of the Business Roundtable, former Michigan governor John Engler, decided that a poorly run ATC system was a drag on business growth and created a working group of experts to develop a business plan for an ATC corporation. The author was a member of this group, which included former U.S. DOT and FAA officials and several aviation consultants. It held regular working sessions in 2011 and 2012, drawing on knowledge of both the Clinton Administration's USATS proposal and the (by-then) 16-year-old Nav Canada. In spring 2012, the BRT group made an initial proposal to the leadership staff of Airlines for America (A4A, the new name of the former ATA), but received only a lukewarm initial response.

A catalytic event for ATC reform was the March 2013 federal budget sequester, which went into effect automatically under the Budget Control Act because Congress had failed to agree on other spending limits. It required cuts in all non-entitlement spending, and since the sequester took place nearly half-way into the government's fiscal year (which runs from October 1st to September 30th), the reduced spending all had to occur in the remaining 6 months of the fiscal year. FAA's way of coping was to require employees, including controllers, to take 1 day off without pay every 2 weeks, and to shut down up to 100 contract towers. This generated intense concerns within controllers' union NATCA, and their briefing by the BRT working group got a positive response. A4A and AOPA leadership were also very concerned, and became more favorable to reform.

At a meeting in the BRT boardroom in May 2013, the leaders of A4A, private plane group AOPA (which had also had a BRT briefing) and NATCA reviewed the then-current BRT "term sheet" for ATC corporatization. It presented two options, either a USATS-type government corporation or a Nav Canada-type nonprofit private corporation—either with a board representing a cross-section of aviation stakeholders. After some discussion of the pros and cons, the consensus of that meeting was that the nonprofit, private model was likely to work better in the US context. By the end of the year, BRT had found a congressional champion in Rep. Bill Shuster (R, PA), who chaired the House Transportation & Infrastructure (T & I) Committee.

In the summer of 2013, another working group on ATC reform was convened by the Eno Center for Transportation, a DC-based think tank with a bipartisan focus on transportation. Its plan (unrelated to the BRT effort, which was not yet public knowledge) was to convene all the relevant ATC stakeholders in a series of monthly meetings to work out how best to reform the ATC system. After the first few meetings, the focus shifted to corporatization, and the group's monthly meetings continued through the end of 2014, concluding with a day-long visit to Nav Canada's headquarters in Ottawa. The group's final report, reflecting division among the stakeholders, suggested that Congress considers either the USATS or the Nav Canada model (Eno Center for Transportation 2016). By that point in time, it appeared that the most aviation stakeholders were on board with corporatization, except for business jet group NBAA.

Sessions on ATC corporatization took place at the TRB annual meeting in 2014 and at the US Chamber of Commerce's annual aviation summit. In addition, that January the FAA's outgoing Management Advisory Council issued its final report, calling for sweeping reform, including ATC corporatization (Van Beek 2014). The House T & I Committee held its first briefing session on ATC reform in November 2014, with BRT's John Engler among the witnesses. BRT commissioned quantitative studies by the same firm that had analyzed both USATS and the previous decade's FAA user-fee studies. Those results were presented at briefings to which all major aviation stakeholders were invited, in fall 2014 and early 2015.

In early 2015, the House T & I Committee held two more events: a private briefing for Ranking Member Peter DeFazio (D, OR) and a roundtable discussion session for Committee members. In March, the Committee held a formal hearing on corporatization, with testimony from stakeholders including American Airlines CEO Doug Parker, NATCA president Paul Rinaldi, and this author. In May, the Senate Commerce Committee held its first hearing on ATC reform, with NATCA's Rinaldi again testifying in favor. TRB convened an all-day session on ATC corporatization in July 2015, keynoted by former senior DOT policy chief Jeff Shane (who had also been a member of the BRT group). However, by fall 2015, there were warning signs. Former AOPA CEO Craig Fuller was no longer supporting corporatization. As a member of the new FAA Management Advisory Council, he circulated a concept paper calling for converting the entire FAA into a corporation. And Rep. DeFazio made some comments along the same lines.

When Shuster's corporatization bill was finally introduced in February 2016, DeFazio was no longer interested in reform; he attacked the bill across the board as far worse than the status quo. In this he was joined by the leadership of the two main general aviation groups, AOPA and NBAA. After only a few weeks, the House bill was passed by the T & I Committee on a party-line vote—but went no further.

Attacks by AOPA and NBAA went public, aided by an NBAA-funded group called the Alliance for Aviation Across America (AAAA). These groups characterized Shuster's bill as handing control of US airspace and the ATC system to a "private board dominated by the big airlines." That was their rendition of a 13-member stakeholder board, to which airlines would nominate four seats and general aviation groups three seats, with others nominated by pilot and controller unions as well as members appointed by the DOT Secretary to represent the flying public. AAAA's rhetoric aimed especially at rural America, arguing that the "big-airline-dominated board" would redirect ATC resources away from small airports and toward major hubs. The campaign succeeded in creating fear, uncertainty, and doubt among small-town mayors, directors of small airports, and elected officials in rural states.

One result was that the draft bill to reauthorize FAA in the Senate Commerce Committee did not address ATC at all.

Advocates of corporatization pointed out flaws in Shuster's bill that played into the hands of opponents. The stakeholder board did not include airports, or regional airlines (which serve the smaller airports and account for about 50% of all daily airline take-offs). It also included no provisions aimed at safeguarding small airports from possible reductions in ATC services, though it did include a statutory ban on charging ATC user fees to both small private planes and business jets—except for commercial air taxi service using similarly small planes.

Trump Administration

The overall FAA reauthorization bill failed to gain floor time in either house of Congress during the remainder of 2016, and since a new Congress had been elected that November, all previous legislation had to start over in 2017. The co-chairman of the House General Aviation Caucus, Rep. Sam Graves (R, MO), worked with Shuster on a revised bill that would correct the flaws of the 2016 version. Graves was pleased that the new bill revamped the stakeholder board, with only one seat nominated by the major airlines, another by regional airlines, and a third by cargo airlines. General aviation groups would nominate two seats, and airports would also nominate a board member. This was a better cross-section of aviation than in the 2016 bill. The 2017 bill also included a whole new section of protections for smaller airports, as well as a guarantee that the contract tower program would be continued. The bill banned ATC user fees for any category of GA—even commercial air taxi companies (a key AOPA demand). Graves believed that these changes would win over at least AOPA, if not NBAA.

However, the day the new bill was introduced, AOPA and NBAA made a joint declaration of war. Attempting to justify its new stance despite being given everything it had asked for (via Graves' changes), AOPA issued a statement saying, "We have concluded that any structural and governance reforms that require protections for an important set of users is fundamentally flawed." The T & I Committee passed the bill anyway, with a larger majority than in 2016.

Also complicating the politics of ATC reform in 2017 was the new presidency of Donald Trump. He appointed pro-reform leadership at U.S. DOT and a White House infrastructure advisor (D.J. Gribbin) who was also favorable to ATC reform. The White House held a splashy ATC reform event in June 2017, including principles that did not quite jibe with the carefully worked-out 2017 House bill. The net effect was probably somewhat negative, in that it served to politicize what should have been a bipartisan reform effort, given the Clinton Administration's pioneering efforts two decades before. And despite the support of the controllers' union and several pilots' and flight attendants' unions, a coalition of all the principal federal government employee unions opposed the bill, seeing it as a slippery slope that might open the door to more government functions moving into the private (albeit nonprofit) sector.

A crowded legislative calendar in 2017, and uncertainty by the House GOP leadership about whether there were enough votes to pass Shuster's FAA bill, led to the bill not making it to the House floor in 2017. Early in 2018 the House vote count still looked uncertain, but at a House GOP leadership retreat early that year, which President Trump attended, he agreed to lobby wavering House Republicans to embrace the bill. With that news in hand, Shuster's people passed the word to supporters that the vote would be held in mid-March. But on February 27th, Shuster announced—without explanation—that he would be withdrawing the whole ATC section from the bill when it was brought to the floor. Nobody could figure out why, but a few weeks later *Politico* reported that Trump had reneged on his promise to make calls and twist arms (Gardner 2018). The House subsequently passed the bill, minus the ATC corporation section. As this is written, a Senate FAA bill has not yet made it to the floor, but that seems likely, as does the absence of any ATC reform provisions.

Summary and Conclusions

The 2018 defeat will likely foreclose further attempts at US ATC corporatization for the duration of the reauthorization period, usually about 4 years. With so many topics on its agenda, and very limited floor time, any stand-alone ATC bill apart from the next FAA reauthorization is highly unlikely.

This latest ATC reform effort garnered much greater support than any previous effort. Openly supporting the bill were all the major passenger and cargo airlines, controllers' union NATCA, unions of pilots and flight attendants, six former DOT Secretaries, all three former Chief Operating Officers of the Air Traffic Organization, 13 former senior Clinton Administration officials, transportation experts from a long list of noted think tanks, taxpayer and consumer groups, and the editorial boards of many leading newspapers, including the *Chicago Tribune*, *Miami Herald*, *Orlando Sentinel*, *The Wall Street Journal*, *Washington Post*, and *USA Today*.

Unfortunately, there was never a debate on the substance of the case for corporatization. Instead, a propaganda war largely bankrolled by business jet organization NBAA made untrue allegations and stepped up its opposition efforts after the bill had been revised to reflect legitimate concerns of general aviation, small airports, and rural America. Thus, while the USA retains the world's largest ATC system, it also remains the only developed country that is not charging airspace users for ATC services, one of the few that has failed to separate safety regulation from ATC service provision, and retains an ATC provider that still has difficulty developing and implementing new technology and procedures in a timely and cost-effective manner.

Nevertheless, the debate has moved significantly in the direction of corporatization. In the 1970s and 1980s, it was widely assumed that the provision of air traffic control services was inherently governmental, since this service was provided by national governments in nearly all countries during those decades. The idea of separating aviation safety regulation from the provision of ATC services was unheard of.

Today, the inherent conflict of interest in having the same agency do both is widely understood, is recommended by ICAO, and has become standard practice in more than 60 developed countries.

Second, the importance of a self-supporting model for air traffic control is now widely understood. Prior to the emergence of ATC corporations beginning in 1987, most governments already charged ATC fees, mostly in accord with ICAO charging principles, but the revenues went into the national government's coffers, to be allocated to whatever purposes the national legislative body decided upon. The move toward self-supporting ATC corporations has created a worthwhile customer/provider relationship that replaces the ATC provider's dependence on politically determined funding. The self-supporting model also permits the issuance of revenue bonds to finance long-lived capital modernization efforts, which was not possible prior to self-support, since the ATC user-fee revenues belonged to the national government, not the ATC provider.

Third, we have seen empirical evidence of a changed organizational culture in many of the ATC corporations. They are generally able to hire and retain experienced managers, engineers, and software experts, thereby regaining control of technology development from aerospace companies on whom they were formerly over-dependent. This is leading to reductions in overhead costs, more cost-effective technology improvements, and increases in productivity.

Governance is still a work in progress, with many of the government corporations being dependent on one or two government shareholders. By contrast, the stakeholder board concept has proved workable and effective for more than two decades at Nav Canada, the world's second-largest ATC provider and widely considered one of the best. A governing board representing all the principal aviation stakeholders gives the ATC provider a governance model much like the user cooperative model well-known in the rural utilities sector in the USA. It is a model that may offer governance improvements to many ATC providers currently organized as government corporations.

To sum up, the world of air traffic control has changed markedly in the decades since the corporatization of Airways New Zealand in 1987. The USA is the last major country that stands apart from this reform. It is conceivable that the growing track record of self-supporting ATC corporations will lead to some version of this model being adopted in the USA within the next decade.

Glossary

A4A Airlines for America, formerly known as ATA.

AAAA Alliance for Aviation Across America, a grass-roots group of rural and small-city officials funded largely by NBAA.

ADS-B Automatic Dependent Surveillance-Broadcast, a way to keep track of aircraft position based on GPS signals.

AOPA Aircraft Owners and Pilots Association, an organization representing pilots of small private planes.

ARINC Aeronautical Radio Inc., formerly a nonprofit corporation but today part of a large aerospace company.

ATA Air Transport Association, former name of A4A.

ATC Air traffic control, the system used to keep planes safely separated while in flight.

ATO Air Traffic Organization, the part of the FAA that is responsible for air traffic control.

BRT Business Round Table, a group representing large companies.

CAB Civil Aeronautics Board, a now-defunct federal agency that was the economic regulator of commercial airlines.

CANSO Civil Air Navigation Services Organization, the trade association for ATC providers worldwide.

DOT U.S. Department of Transportation.

FAA Federal Aviation Administration, the agency that regulates aviation safety and operates the ATC system.

FSS Flight Service Stations, FAA facilities that provide services to private pilots.

GAO Government Accountability Office, formerly known as the General Accounting Office.

GBAS Ground-Based Augmentation System, a system that augments GPS signals to guide planes to a safe landing.

GPS Global Positioning System, a global satellite constellation that provides location and timing information to people and vehicles on the ground and in the air.

ICAO International Civil Aviation Organization, the UN agency for coordinating international aviation.

ILS Instrument Landing System, a 1940s technology that guides planes to landings at airports.

KPI Key performance indicators.

NATCA National Air Traffic Controllers Association, the union representing FAA air traffic controllers.

NBAA National Business Aviation Association, the organization representing operators of primarily jet and turboprop aircraft used for business.

OMB Office of Management and Budget, the White House budget office.

PBN Performance-Based Navigation, a system based on self-monitored performance of precision navigation equipment on board the aircraft.

TCAS Threat Collision Avoidance System, a system designed to anticipate mi-air collisions and have the plane take evasive action.

TRACON Terminal Radar Approach Control, an ATC facility that assists planes in transitioning between airspace around an airport and high-altitude airspace.

TRB Transportation Research Board, part of the National Academy of Sciences.

USATS U.S. Air Traffic Services Corporation, a Clinton Administration proposal for a self-supporting ATC corporation.

References

Air Transport Association. (1985, September). *Federal Corporation approach to the management and funding of the air traffic control system*. Washington, DC: Author.

Baliles, G. L., Anderson, B. B., Babbitt, J. R., Barclay, C. M., Daniell, R. F., DeLeon, S. A., … Thomas, G. F. (1993). *Final report: National commission to ensure a strong and competitive airline industry*. Washington, DC: Government Printing Office.

Bond, L., & Poole, R. W., Jr. (2010). Time to separate the ATO from FAA safety regulation. *The Journal of Air Traffic Control, 52*(2), 14–20.

CANSO. (2016). *Global air navigation services performance report 2016*. Figure 4. Hoofddorp, The Netherlands: Civil Air Navigation Services Organization.

Cordle, V., & Poole, R. W., Jr. (2005). *Resolving the crisis in air traffic control funding*. Los Angeles, CA: Reason Foundation.

Eno Center for Transportation. (2016). *NextGen working group final report*. Washington, DC: Author.

Former DOT Officials. (2007). *The need for fundamental reform of air traffic control*. Los Angeles, CA: Reason Foundation. http://reason.org/files/air_traffic_control_experts_statement_2007.pdf

Gardner, L. (2018, April). How ATC got grounded. *Politico*.

General Accounting Office. (1995). *Profiles of existing government corporations. GAO/GGD-96-14*. Washington, DC: Author.

Gilbert, G. A. (1975). *The United States air traffic services corporation* (2 Vols). Alexandria, VA: Glen A. Gilbert Associates.

Goldsborough, P. (1951). *A history of Aeronautical Radio, Inc. from 1929 to 1942*. ARINC. Unpublished (accessed in ARINC headquarters in 1977 by the author).

International Civil Aviation Organization. (2001). *Safety oversight manual*. Doc. 9734, Part A, Paragraph 2.4.9.

International Civil Aviation Organization. (2012). *ICAO's policies on charges for airports and air navigation services*. Doc. 9082.

Kruesi, F. E., Belger, M., Crowell, C. H., Cutter, W. B., Daschle, L., Downey, M. L., … Valentine, B. (1994, May). *Air traffic control corporation study*. Report of the Executive Oversight Committee to the Secretary of Transportation.

MBS Ottawa. (2006, January). *Air traffic control commercialization policy: Has it been effective?* Ottawa, ON, Canada.

Mineta, N. Y., Bacon, W. E., Barclay, C. M., Barker, L. K., Davis, R. A., DeLeon, S. A., … Yohe, D. S. (1997). *Avoiding gridlock & reducing the accident rate*. Washington, DC: Office of the Secretary, U.S. Department of Transportation.

Neiva, R. (2015). *Institutional reform of air navigation service providers*. Northampton, MA: Edward Elgar Publishing.

Office of Inspector General. (2016). *FAA achieved most of the anticipated cost savings from contracting out flight service stations, but needs to determine the future direction of the program. AV-2017-015*. Washington, DC: U.S. Department of Transportation.

Oster, C. V., & Strong, J. S. (2007). *Managing the skies: Public policy, organization, and financing of air traffic management*. Burlington, VT: Ashgate Publishing.

Poole, R. W., Jr. (1983), Privatizing air traffic control. *Transportation Research Record, 912*.

Poole, R. W., Jr. (2007). *The urgent need to reform the FAA's air traffic control system*. Washington, DC: The Heritage Foundation.

Poole, R. W., Jr. (2012a, January). Spain's control tower outsourcing is under way. *ATC Reform News*.

Poole, R. W., Jr. (2012b, November/December). The lessons of 'zombie towers'. *ATC Reform News*.

Poole, R. W., Jr. (2014). *Organization and innovation in air traffic control*. Washington, DC: The Hudson Institute.

Poole, R. W., Jr. (2015, March). Another ATC billing service enters the market. *ATC Reform News*.

Poole, R. W., Jr., & Butler, V. (2001). *How to commercialize air traffic control*. Los Angeles, CA: Reason Foundation.
Robyn, D. (2008). *Air support: Creating a safer and more reliable air traffic control system*. Washington, DC: The Brookings Institution.
Robyn, D. (2017, May). *The need to reform FAA and air traffic control to build a 21st century aviation system for America*. Testimony before the House Committee on Transportation & Infrastructure.
Transportation Research Board. (1991). *Winds of change: Domestic air transport since deregulation* (Special Report 230).
U.S. Special Air Safety Advisory Group. (1975). *Report to the federal aviation administration*. Washington, DC: Federal Aviation Administration.
Van Beek, S. D. (2014, January). *FAA and aviation policy reform: Now is the time*. Washington, DC: FAA Management Advisory Council.

Chapter 6
Public–Private Partnerships (P3s) for Social Infrastructure

Lawrence L. Martin

Abbreviations

AML	American Library Association
ASCE	American Society of Civil Engineers
CBO	Congressional Budget Office
DBF	Design–Build–Finance
DBFM	Design–Build–Finance–Maintain
DBFOM	Design–Build–Finance–Operate–Maintain
DBIA	Design-Build Institute of America
DBM	Design–Build–Maintain
DD	Design–Build
GFOA	Government Finance Officers Association
NCSL	National Council of State Legislatures
NIGP	National Institute of Governmental Purchasing
P3s	Public–Private Partnerships
Sq. ft.	Square feet
USDOT	United States Department of Transportation\
VfM	Value for Money Analysis

Introduction

Much of the discussion surrounding public–private partnerships (P3s) in the US today focuses on their use in transportation. This focus is understandable owing to the age and condition of the nation's transportation infrastructure (ASCE 2017). The use of P3s for social infrastructure receives less attention. While transportation infrastructure is important to the economic and social well-being of states, cities,

L. L. Martin (✉)
University of Central Florida, Orlando, FL, USA
e-mail: martinl@ucf.edu

R. M. Clark, S. Hakim (eds.), *Public Private Partnerships*, Competitive Government: Public Private Partnerships, https://doi.org/10.1007/978-3-030-24600-6_6

and communities, so too is social infrastructure. Social infrastructure has a direct economic impact because it makes areas more or less attractive places to live and work (Knopman et al. 2018). Businesses, and the people who work for them, make decisions about where to locate based on the quality of social infrastructure.

Defining Social Infrastructure

Infrastructure is frequently divided into three categories: *transportation*, *environmental* (e.g., water/wastewater, and landfills), and *social*. No universally recognized definition of social infrastructure exists. However, Spacey (2017) provides a useful working definition:

> Social infrastructure are foundational services and structures that support the quality of life of a nation, region, city or neighborhood. This includes any infrastructure that goes beyond basic economic functions to make a community an appealing place to live.

The definition covers a broad spectrum of social infrastructure types (Table 6.1).

Despite its importance, government spending on social infrastructure in the USA has declined over the last 20 years. The American Institute of Architects (Schneidawind and Ciminio 2016) estimates that the gap between social infrastructure needs and spending is some $100 billion annually.

Social Infrastructure P3s

Social infrastructure P3s are essentially the same as transportation and environmental P3s. Social infrastructure P3s operate on the same principles and utilize the same practices. Rather than using traditional public procurement, contracting, and financing (e.g., taxes and tax-exempt bonds), social infrastructure P3s utilize

Table 6.1 Social infrastructure types

• Schools (elementary and high school)
• Universities (dorms, classrooms)
• Libraries
• Parks and recreation facilities
• Housing
• Conventions centers
• Sports facilities
• Correctional facilities (jails, prisons)
• Museums
• Government buildings (all types)
• Others

non-traditional approaches. In most social infrastructure P3 projects, the government owns the asset.

The financing and funding of social infrastructure P3 is again similar to that of transportation and environmental P3s. The private partner delivers the social infrastructure project and may provide or arrange the financing.

Financing covers the upfront design, construction, and operating costs. *Funding* to pay for the design, construction, and operating costs comes from user fees or availability payments (Inderest 2015). User fees generally take the form of dedicated revenue streams such as (1) admission fees to parks, recreation facilities, museums, art galleries, sports facilities, health care facilities, etc. or (2) utilization fees tied to college and university dorms, housing, etc. Either the public or the private partner may collect the user fee. Availability payments are monthly, quarterly, or yearly payments made by the government to the private partner when the social infrastructure is open and available for use by the public. The source of funding for availability payments frequently comes from the government's general fund. In some instances, funding can involve both user fees and availability payments. For example, user fees may be insufficient to cover the total operating costs of a social infrastructure project (e.g., museum or park), so the government covers the deficit via availability payments.

Similar to transportation and environmental P3s, the length of social infrastructure P3 contacts varies from 20–50 years depending upon the type of project, the use of private sector financing and citizen tolerance for user fees.

State P3 Enabling Legislation and Social Infrastructure

Social infrastructure P3s, like transportation and environmental P3s, present unique procurement and contracting challenges for state and local governments. Social infrastructure P3s are strictly speaking neither construction contracts nor service contracts; they are both. This dual construction/service nature is frequently at odds with the procurement and contracting statutes, ordinances and regulations of many state and local governments. For this reason, the Government Finance Officers Association (GFOA 2015) recommends that states pass P3 enabling legislation. As of September 1, 2018, 37 states had passed some form of P3 enabling legislation (NCSL 2016; USDOT 2017; Martin 2018a). Unfortunately, the majority of this legislation restricts the use of P3s to transportation projects only or makes no specific provisions for social infrastructure. Additionally, the P3 enabling legislation of the states that do provide for social infrastructure frequently restricts their use to specific activities (e.g., university facilities and sports facilities). Consequently, only eight states have P3 enabling legislation that applies broadly to social infrastructure. Table 6.2 identifies these eight states and indicates if the P3 enabling legislation extends to and covers local governments.

Table 6.2 States with specific broad statutory authority for social infrastructure P3s

State	Legislation allows for social infrastructure P3s	Legislation includes local governments
Arkansas	Yes	Yes
California	Yes	Yes
Florida	Yes	Yes
Georgia	Yes	Yes
Indiana	Yes	Yes
New Jersey	Yes	Yes
Oklahoma	Yes	No
Texas	Yes	Yes
Virginia	Yes	Yes

Sources: DBIA (2017); Martin (2018a); Oklahoma Legislature (2017); Gregory (2018); LegiScan (2018)

Local Governments and Social Infrastructure P3s

While state departments and agencies must rely on state enabling legislation in order to use P3s for social infrastructure, local governments have more discretion. Local governments have two sources of authority for the use of social infrastructure P3s. Local governments covered by state P3 enabling legislation can utilize this authority. In the other states, local governments can rely on their home rule authority (Allen and Overy LLP 2009). In either case, local governments can still adopt their own P3 ordinances that provide additional authority for social infrastructure P3s and establish procurement and contracting requirements.

Case Examples

The following case examples illustrate the diversity of social infrastructure P3 projects. The taxonomy proposed by the National Institute of Governmental Purchasing (NIGP 2016) is utilized to identify and classify each of the social infrastructure examples discussed (Table 6.3).

The NIGP taxonomy is based on the component parts of a generic P3 (design, build (construction/rehabilitation), finance, operate, and maintain). The taxonomy is not unique to the NIGP; it has also been used by the Congressional Budget Office (CBO 2012), the US Department of Transportation (USDOT 2016, 2017), and the International City/County Management Association (Martin 2018b).

Table 6.3 P3 types

P3 type	Characteristics
Design–build (DB)	Design (D) and construction (B) are bundled into one procurement and contract
Design–build–finance (DBF)	Design (D) and construction (B) are bundled into one procurement and contract with financing (F) provided by the contractor
Design–build–maintain (DB)	Design (D), construction (B), and maintenance (M) are bundled into one procurement and contract
Design–build–finance–maintain (DBFM)	Design (D), construction (B), and maintenance (M) are bundled into one procurement and contract with financing (F) provided by the contractor
Design–build–finance–operate (DBFO)	Design (D), construction (B), and operations (O) are bundled into one procurement and contract with financing provided by the contractor
Design–build–finance–operate–maintain (DBFOM)	Design (D), construction (B), maintenance (M), and operations (O) are bundled into one procurement and contract with financing provided by the contractor. This P3 type is also called a *concession*

Social Infrastructure P3s for University Facilities

Several years of state funding reductions to public universities have resulted in faculty reductions, fewer course offerings and campus closings (Center on Budget and Policy Priorities 2016). These funding reductions come at a particularly trying time for public universities tasked with doing more in terms of preparing state and community workforces. Social infrastructure P3s are helping public universities deal with these funding reductions by financing and delivering classroom, dorms, and even entire campuses. For example, some 300-student housing projects, with a value of over $9 billion, have been completed at US public and private universities (Baum 2011; Cole 2012). The majority of university social infrastructure P3s are of the DBFOM type and utilize availability payments (Brailsford and Dunlavey 2017). The University of South Florida and the University of California Merced are two examples of the use of social infrastructure P3s for university facilities.

The University of South Florida

The University of South Florida (USF) in Tampa used a DBFOM social infrastructure P3 to upgrade its student housing.

The USF "P3 Residential Village Project" includes over 500,000 sq. ft. of new on-campus space including: five buildings with 2000 resident housing beds, a 400-seat dining facility, a recreation and wellness center, and 6000 sq. ft. of light commercial retail space (USF News 2016; USF 2015; University of South Florida, Housing, and Residential Education 2018).

The total cost of the P3 Residential Village Project is $132 million comprised of $92 million in debt and $40 million in equity provided by the private partner, Capstone Development Partners, and Harrison Street Real Estate Capital (Capstone

Partners 2017). Student rents provide a dedicated revenue stream (user fee) to compensate the private partner. The private partners is "at risk" for all debt as well as student demand and occupancy levels. USF has no financial exposure. The private partner is required to utilize life cycle repair and replacement schedules verified every 5 years by an independent assessment. The first phase of the USF social infrastructure P3 project opened in October 2017; the second and final phase opened in August 2018.

The use of social infrastructure P3s has generated considerable interest on the part of other Florida public universities (e.g., Florida Polytechnic University 2018). In response, the State University System of Florida (2015) has issued guidelines providing direction for the use of social infrastructure P3s covering such topics as project requirements, procurement procedures, and contract terms and reporting requirements.

University of California Merced

The University of California Merced is using a social infrastructure DBFOM P3 to essentially finance and deliver a new campus. The Merced 2020 project is the largest social infrastructure P3 project ever undertaken in the USA. This social infrastructure P3 project calls for financing and delivery of new: academic space, student housing (1600 beds), dining (600 seats), parking (1500 spaces), athletic facilities, and other associated campus operations. The budget for Merced 2020 is $1.3 billion including $590 million contributed by the private partner, Plenary Properties Merced. The project will use preventive maintenance life cycle costing principles. Availability payments compensate the private partner. When completed this social infrastructure P3 project will accommodate upwards of 10,000 students (Merced 2020 2018; NCS Madison 2017; WikiBooks 2018).

The use of social infrastructure P3s by public universities expands the US P3 market. Public university use provides support and legitimacy for social infrastructure P3s and may encourage other state and local governments to consider their use.

Social Infrastructure P3s for Schools

Similar to the situation of public universities, state governments, local governments, and school districts are unable to fund the infrastructure needs of public elementary, middle, and high schools. The funding short fall now approaches $50 billion per year (Schneidawind and Ciminio 2016).

The use of social infrastructure P3s for school facilities is widely used in many countries (e.g., Australia, Canada, and United Kingdom). In the USA, the use of social infrastructure P3s for schools has received some attention but has not caught on as a working concept. Two case examples demonstrate the use of social infrastructure P3s for schools. The first case example comes from Alberta, Canada. The second is from New York City.

Alberta, Canada

Alberta, Canada, has used a DBFO social infrastructure P3 for the financing and delivery of new elementary and middle schools. The social infrastructure P3 project included both public and private schools. The P3 project was implemented in three separate stages with stage 1 commencing in 2008. The entire social infrastructure P3 project involving 40 schools was completed in June 2014. Three separate P3 contracts were used with terms averaging 30 plus years.

Separate *ex-post* value-for-money (VfM) analyses were conducted on all three phases (e.g., Alberta Government 2010a, b, 2013). The VfM analyses concluded that the social infrastructure P3 approach would save the Alberta Government some C$245 million over the terms of the three contracts compared to traditional public procurement approaches. The VfM analyses also concluded that on average all 40 schools came online earlier than would have occurred with traditional procurement approaches. In 2014, when an additional 19 schools were considered for yet another social infrastructure P3, an *ex-anti* VfM analysis (Alberta Government 2014) indicated that the social infrastructure P3 approach would not result in any cost savings compared to traditional public procurement approaches. The report concluded that the local economic situation in Alberta had changed. Where the P3 approach had demonstrated value for money in the past, "tight market conditions" and a lack of competition in 2014 were responsible for the different outcome.

The Alberta example demonstrates that past financial success with social infrastructure P3s for schools, and perhaps for other project types, is not a guarantee of future success owing to the vagaries of local economic conditions.

New York City Department of Education

The New York City Department of Education used a social infrastructure DBF P3 for the financing and delivery of two new schools, PS 59 and the High School of Art & Design. Whole Foods Market is also involved in this P3 social infrastructure project. The $500 million mixed-use project was developed by World Wide Group and covers 1.5 acres. World Wide Group holds a 75-year lease on the property from the New York Department of Education. Whole Foods Market occupies 38,000 square feet of retail space on the ground floor. The two schools include new classrooms, a new gymnasium, and a new auditorium. PS 59 accommodates 730 students, while the High School of Art & Design has room for 1700 students. By most measures, this social infrastructure P3 project is considered successful (DNAinfo 2010; Johnson 2012).

Social Infrastructure P3s for Judicial Facilities

The Long Beach Courthouse is a DBFOM social infrastructure P3. Open and operating since 2013, the Long Beach Courthouse is the first social infrastructure P3 courthouse project in the USA.

The old Long Beach Courthouse was the busiest complex in the California judicial system and seriously out-of-date (Barandiaran 2011). Although badly needed, a new courthouse was not a priority for state funding. By utilizing a social infrastructure P3, the state of California was able to move forward with the design and construction of a new courthouse utilizing private sector financing (Bodek 2016). The Judicial Council of the state of California, Administrative Office of the Courts oversaw this social infrastructure P3 project.

The new 500,000 sq. ft. Long Beach Courthouse complex contains 31 courtrooms as well as office, commercial, and retail space. (Barandiaran 2011). Design and construction costs for the courthouse totaled $492 million. Long Beach Judicial Partners, a consortium of several private sector firms headed by Meridiam Infrastructure, arranged the project financing. The original financing scheme consisted of 10% equity and 90% debt. The term of the P3 contract is for 35 years (Governing n.d.; Martin and Saviak 2014, 2017).

Availability payments are used to compensate the private partner. The Administrative Office of the Courts pays the private sector partner an annual service fee. Payments are tied to specific performance milestones. Upon contract termination, the operations and maintenance of the Long Beach Courthouse reverts to the California Administrative Office of the Courts (Governing n.d.; Barandiaran 2011; Martin and Saviak 2014).

Several other states (e.g., Arizona, Florida, and Maryland) are considering social infrastructure P3s for judicial facilities and infrastructure.

Social Infrastructure P3s for Libraries

Several studies (e.g., ALA 2015; Pitas et al. 2017; Martin and Saviak 2014) document that the majority of America's public libraries continue to suffer from level or decreased public funding.

Some argue that standalone libraries may not be attractive prospects for social infrastructure P3s, but when bundled with other infrastructure projects, they can be. The Washington DC West End Library is a case in point. The West End Library is a DBF P3. The library was constructed at no cost to the DC government as part of a land swap. The new 20,000 sq. ft. library can accommodate 500 persons and includes an auditorium and meeting rooms.

The DC Public Library, EastBank, Inc., and CORE Architecture + design are the private partners. This library social infrastructure P3 project is part of a larger mixed-use development that includes condominiums, rentals, and light commercial. The library opened in December 2017 to positive reviews for its design and amenities (PRWeb 2017; The Georgetowner 2017).

Looking Toward the Future

In the absence of alternative methods to finance and deliver the facility needs of universities, schools, libraries, and government buildings, social infrastructure P3s provide an attractive alternative.

The use of social infrastructure P3s by state and local governments appears poised to expand dramatically. As more projects come online, more interest is generated in social infrastructure P3s. Universities are leading the way. In 2008, only four university social infrastructure projects existed; today the number is over 30 (Renner et al. 2018).

Social infrastructure P3s will also benefit from increased interest on the part of public and private pension funds (Ryan 2014). Pension funds traditionally have a low tolerance for risk. Consequently, pension funds find social infrastructure P3s attractive investment opportunities because of their reliable income streams, limited supply, and stable demand (The Economist 2018). The Canadian Pension Plan Investment Board has invested over $1 billion in US university student housing.

Making Greater Use of Social Infrastructure P3s

State and local governments can take several actions to increase the use of social infrastructure P3s:

- Enact or amend state P3 enabling legislation to specifically authorize social infrastructure projects
- Enact or amend local government P3 ordinances to specifically authorize social infrastructure projects
- Bundle smaller P3 social infrastructure projects into larger single procurements in order to attract private sector investment and reduce contracting transaction costs
- Encourage state and local government pension funds to invest in social infrastructure P3s

Summary and Conclusion

This chapter has defined social infrastructure and explained its importance to states, cities, and communities. A number of case examples demonstrated the wide variety of social infrastructure projects. The NIGP P3 taxonomy was used to differentiate between different social infrastructure P3 types. The topic of public pension funds helping to in finance social infrastructure P3s was discussed. Finally, steps that state and local governments can take to increase the use of social infrastructure P3s were identified.

References

Alberta Government. (2010a). *P3 value for money assessment and project report – Alberta School alternative procurement (ASAP) project phase I*. Retrieved from http://www.infrastructure.alberta.ca/documents/asapip3valueformoneyassessmentandprojectreport.pdf

Alberta Government. (2010b). *P3 value for money assessment and project report – Alberta School alternative procurement (ASAP) project phase II*. Retrieved from https://open.alberta.ca/dataset/3d1a6da9-246e-4f27-9244-679dffeeb426/resource/9d6e1f6b-eae1-4bed-9386-0c339adb3f5d/download/5476377-2010-09-asap-2-value-money-assessment-project-report-.pdf

Alberta Government. (2013). *P3 value for money assessment and project report – Alberta School alternative procurement (ASAP) project phase III*. Retrieved from http://www.infrastructure.alberta.ca/documents/ASAP_III_VfM.PDF

Alberta Government. (2014). *P3 value for money assessment and project report – Building Alberta School construction program phase 1*. Retrieved from http://www.infrastructure.alberta.ca/documents/BASCP-I__final_VFM.pdf

Allen & Overy LLP. (2009). *PPPs and municipal home rule*. Retrieved from http://clientlink.allenovery.com/images/0912-homeRule_SP09.pdf

American Library Association (ALA). (2015). *The state of America's libraries*. Retrieved from http://www.ala.org/news/sites/ala.org.news/files/content/0415_StateAmLib_0.pdf

American Society of Civil Engineers (ASCE). (2017). *2017 report card for America's infrastructure*. Retrieved from http://www.infrastructutreportcard.org

Barandiaran, I. (2011). *Social infrastructure public-private partnerships – Helping government overcome budget constraints to deliver services*. Retrieved January 10, 2018, from https://www.Pillsburylaw.com/en/news-and-insights/social-infrastructure-public-private-partnerhips-helping.html

Baum, G. (2011). *Privatized student housing non-recourse financed projects*. Retrieved from https://www.gkbaum.com/images/pdfs/Tabs_Content/Higher_Ed/PDFs/Privatized_Student_Housing_Database.pdf

Bodek, A. (2016). *Long beach civic center: Lessons learned from a successful public-private partnership. The planning report (July)*. Retrieved from https://www.planningreport.com/2016/07/22/long-beach-civic-center-lessons-learned-successful-public-private-partnership

Brailsford & Dunlavey. (2017). *Higher education public-private partnerships: State of the industry report*. Retrieved from http://p3resourcecenter.com/index.php/2018/03/09/higher-ed-p3-state-of-the-industry-report-download-available/

Capstone Partners. (2017). *Capstone development partners opens first phase of new university on-campus mixed-use student housing village at the University of South Florida*. https://capdevpartners.com/capstone-development-partners-opens-first-phase-of-new-on-ampus-mixed-use-student-housing-village-at-the-university-of-south-florida/

Center on Budget and Policy Priorities. (2016). *Funding down, tuition up – State cutes to higher education threaten quality and affordability at public colleges*. Retrieved from https://www.cbpp.org/research/state-budget-and-tax/funding-down-tuition-up

Cole, B. (2012). *Building social infrastructure through public-private partnerships: The case of student housing in public higher education* (Dissertation, Clemson University). Retrieved from https://tigerprints.clemson.edu/cgi/viewcontent.cgi?referer=https://www.google.com/&httpsredir=1&article=2056&context=all_dissertations

Congressional Budget Office (CBO). (2012). *Using public-private partnerships to carry out highway projects*. Retrieved from https://www.cbo.gov/sites/default/files/112th-congress-2011-2012/reports/01-09-PublicPrivatePartnerships.pdf

Design-Build Institute of America (DBIA). (2017). *State P3 legislation matrix*. Retrieved from https://www.dbia.org/resource-center/p3-resources/Documents/p3_state_statute_report.pdf

DNAinfo. (2010). *Construction begins on Midtown East's new home to PS 59 and whole foods*. Retrieved from https://www.dnainfo.com/20100521/manhattan/midtown-east-construction-begins-on-ps-59s-roomy-new-home/

Florida Polytechnic University. (2018). *Florida Polytechnic University P3 solicitation (RFI #18–004 March 2, 2018). Development & construction of mixed use building on the main campus of Florida Polytechnic University, Lakeland, Florida*. Retrieved from https://floridapoly.edu/wp-content/uploads/18-004-Request-for-Information-for-P3-Solicitation.pdf

Governing. (n.d.). *Guide to financial literary, vol 3: Under the risk & rewards of public-private partnerships*. Retrieved from https://afd34ee8b0806295b5a7-9fbee7de8d51d-b511b5de86d75069107.ssl.cf1.rackcdn.com/GOV16_P3_Guide.pdf

Government Finance Officers Association (GFOA). (2015). *ADVISORY: Public-private partnerships (P3s)*. Retrieved January 11, 2018, from http://www.gfoa.org/public-private-partnerhips-p3

Gregory, P. (2018). *New Jersey expands public-private partnerships to include infrastructure projects (August 14)*. Retrieved from https://whyy.org/articles/new-jersey-expands-public-private-partnerships-to-include-infrastructure-projects/

Inderest, G. (2015). *Social infrastructure investment: Private finance & institutional investors*. Munich Personal RePEc Archive. Retrieved from https://mpra.ub.uni-muenchen.de/69504

Johnson, M. (2012). *High school of art and design kicks off school year in new building*. Retrieved from http://www.dnainfo.com/new-york/20120914/midtown-east/high-school-of-art-design-kicks-off-school-year-new-building/

Knopman, D., Wacsh, M., Miller, B., Davis, S., & Pfrommer, K. (2018). Renewing America's infrastructure: An agenda for federal transportation and water policy. *Public Works Management & Policy, 23*(4), 310–323.

LegiScan. (2018). *State of New Jersey, 218th legislature. Senate no. 865*. Retrieved from https://legiscan.com/NJ/text/S865/2018

Martin, L. L. (2018a). *PPP policy & practice in the United States: One step forward, one step backward*. Paper presented at the 2018 Conference of the International Public-Private Partnerships Scholars Network (IP3SN), Toronto, Ontario, Canada, September 20–21.

Martin, L. L. (2018b). *Public-private partnerships (P3s): What local government managers need to know*. Washington, DC: International City/County Management Association (ICMA). Retrieved January 10, 2018, from https://icma.org/sites/default/files/18-109%20Public-Private%20Partnerships-P3s%20White%20Paper_web%20FINAL.pdf

Martin, L. L. & Saviak, J. (2014). *Contracting & public-private partnerships (P3s): A guide for state & local government officials & administrators*. Jacksonville, FL: Government Services Partnerships Institute. Retrieved January 10, 2018, from https://purchasing.colliergov.net/Vendors/Shared%20Documents/State%20of%Florida%20Guide%20for%20Contracting%20and%20Public%20Private%20Partnerships.pdf

Martin, L. L., & Saviak, J. (2017). *Public-private partnerships for library operations*. Rockville, MD: Library Systems & Services.
Merced 2020. (2018). Retrieved from https://merced2020.ucmerced.edu/
National Conference of State Legislatures (NCSL). (2016). *Public-private partnerships for transportation: Categorization and analysis of state statutes*. Retrieved January 11, 2018, from http://www.ncsl.org/Research/transportation/public-private-partnerships-for-Transportation-categorization-and-analysis-of-state-statutes-January-2016-aspx
National Institute of Governmental Purchasing (NIGP). (2016). *Public-private partnership (P3): Facilities & infrastructure*. Herndon, VA: Author. Retrieved January 11, 2018, from http://engage.nigp.org/acton/attachment/24793/f-00a2/1/-/-/-Public-Private%20Partnership%20%28P3%29%20Facilities%20and%20Infrastructure.pdf
NCS Madison. (2017). *Public-private partnerships impact on U.S. infrastructure*. Retrieved from http://ncsmadison.com/2017/04/11/public-private-partnerships-impact-u-s-infrastructure/
Oklahoma Legislature. (2017). *Senate bill 430- "Oklahoma Public & Private Facilities And Infrastructure Act"*. Retrieved from https://www.sos.ok.gov/documents/legislation/56th/2017/1R/SB/430.pdf
Pitas, N., Barrett, A. G., & Mowen, A. (2017). Trends in local park and recreation department finances and staffing in the early twenty-first century. *Journal of Park & Recreation Administration, 35*(3), 20–34.
PRWeb. (2017). *First DC public library in public-private building venture opens in West End*. Retrieved from https://www.prweb.com/pdfdownload/15012370.pdf
Renner, C., Kline, C., & Pollets, M. (2018). *P3 - Public private partnership trends report*. Retrieved from https://www.huschblackwell.com/~/media/files/news/2018/02/p3_trends_report_open_page_1.pdf
Ryan, J. (2014). *The public pension core funding gap and infrastructure public-private partnerships*. McGraw Hill Financial. Retrieved from http://www.inrecap.com/wp-content/uploads/2017/02/Pension-InfraPPP-MHGFI-synergies-05-14-2014-v3.pdf
Schneidawind, J. & Ciminio, S. (2016). *Rebuilding America's infrastructure starts with thinking locally*. American Institute of Architects. Retrieved from https://www.aia.org/articles/24506-rebuilding-americas-infrastructure-starts-wi:61
Spacey, J. (2017). *9 Examples of social infrastructure*. Simplicable. Retrieved from https://simplicable.com/new/social-infrastructure
State University System of Florida. (2015). *Public-private partnership guidelines*. Retrieved from http://www.flbog.edu/documents_regulations/guidelines/Public-Private%20Partnership%20Guidelines.pdf
The Economist. (2018, May 12). *Higher earnings*. pp. 62–63.
The Georgetowner. (2017). *Glass-encased west end library opens*. Retrieved from https://georgetowner.com/articles/2017/12/11/glass-encased-west-end-library-opens/
U. S. Department of Transportation (USDOT). (2016). *Successful practices for P3s*. Retrieved from https://cms.dot.gov/sites/dot.gov/files/docs/P3_Successful_Practices_Final_BAH.PDF
U. S. Department of Transportation (USDOT). (2017). *Federal Highway Administration (FHWA) center for innovative financing. State P3 legislation*. Retrieved January 11, 2018, from https://www.fhwa.dot.gov/ipd/p3/legislation/
University of South Florida (USF). (2015). *Student success USF P3 residential village project*. Retrieved from http://www.flbog.edu/documents_meetings/0196_0938_7046_02.6%20FAC%20USF%20P3%20Residential%20Village%2011%2001%202015%20V2%20Slides.pdf
University of South Florida, Housing & Residential Education. (2018). *The village*. Retrieved from https://www.usf.edu/student-affairs/housing/about-us/the-village.aspx
USF News. (2016). *Largest campus housing project in USF history unveiled*. Retrieved from http://news.usf.edu/article/templates/?a=7566&z=220
WikiBooks. (2018). *Public-private partnership case book/UC Merced*. Retrieved from https://en.wikibooks.org/wiki/Public-Private_Partnership_Policy_Casebook/UC_Merced

Chapter 7
Public-Private Partnerships for Health Services: Construction, Protection and Rehabilitation of Critical Healthcare Infrastructure in Europe

Stephen Wright, James Barlow, and Jens K. Roehrich

Abbreviations

AAA	Top credit rating, for example bonds from the rating agencies
BOOT	Build–Own–Operate–Transfer, a project financing scheme
DBFO	Design–Build–Finance–Operate, a project financing scheme
DRG	Diagnosis-Related Group, a hospital activity classification system for charging
EPEC	European PPP Expertise Centre, advisory unit based in the EU's European Investment Bank
EU	European Union
EUR	Euro, currency unit used by some EU Member States
FM	Facilities Management, within a concession contract, where "hard" applies to maintenance of space & infrastructure and "soft" to provision of ancillary services
GBP	Great Britain Pound, sterling currency unit
IMF	International Monetary Fund
KfW	(Originally Kreditanstalt für Wiederaufbau), German publicly owned investment and development bank

S. Wright (✉)
Freelance Consultant, Ingleton, UK
e-mail: steve.wright@echaa.eu

J. Barlow
Imperial College Business School, South Kensington Campus, Kensington, London, UK
e-mail: j.barlow@imperial.ac.uk

J. K. Roehrich
HPC Supply Chain Innovation Lab, Information, Decisions and Operations Division, School of Management, University of Bath, Bath, UK
e-mail: j.roehrich@bath.ac.uk

R. M. Clark, S. Hakim (eds.), *Public Private Partnerships*, Competitive Government: Public Private Partnerships, https://doi.org/10.1007/978-3-030-24600-6_7

MVZ	Medizinischen Versorgungszentren, Medical Care Centres offering primary care
NAO	National Audit Office, body which scrutinises public spending for the UK Parliament
NFP	Not for Profit, corporate form not expected to return cash profits to shareholders
NHS	National Health Service, full-population health service financed largely by public taxation
NPV	Net Present Value, an index of the time-discounted value of a project's generated cash flows
PFI	Private Finance Initiative, UK terminology for an infrastructure-only PPP (see below)
PF2	Recent variant of PFI
PPP	Public–Private Partnership
PSPV-PSOE	Partit Socialista del País Valencià-Partido Socialista Obrero Español, left-wing political party in Valencia allied to a similar national party
SHI	Social Health Insurance, full-population health service financed largely by compulsory public or private health insurance
USD	US Dollar, currency unit
VA	United States Department of Veterans Affairs, federal Cabinet-level agency providing healthcare services to eligible military veterans

Introduction

The idea of public–private partnerships (PPPs) is both very old and right up to date. Old because companies have been mandated to provide public services on behalf of the state at least since the creation of the United East India Company in 1602 in the Netherlands, the Canal du Midi in France from 1666 (Button 2016), or Turnpike Trusts in England in the eighteenth century which have been estimated to generate social savings of at least 0.5% of national income in 1800 and 1820 (Bogart 2005). There are many other examples. PPPs are also modern because so many governments, across developed, emerging and frontier economies, are currently exploring their potential use (Barlow et al. 2013).

In the health sector, they represent part of the continuum between pure state provision of services (which is visible nowhere in the world) and purely private or commercial provision (equally invisible)—note that, even concerning *payment* for services, rather than *provision*, there is usually a public–private mix. PPPs are not limited by economic sector, as can be seen from the chapter list of this volume, or by country, by size or by timescale (Barlow et al. 2013; Roehrich et al. 2014). This chapter focuses on healthcare PPPs in Europe, as it constitutes one of the core areas in which PPPs have been deployed to improve patients' experience through new infrastructure and innovative services (Roehrich et al. 2014).

The remainder of this chapter is organised as follows: The section "The Big Picture: The Why, What and Where of PPP" covers the definition of PPP and the size of the market. The third section sets out the interface between the public and private sectors, develops a typology of health PPPs, and draws out characteristics of four archetypal health sector PPP models used in Europe. The fourth section discusses some problematic issues, given the findings on real-world cost and performance, together with the dangers of lack of flexibility or lock-in of parties, and it summarises the various payment mechanisms employed. We also present here a stylised economic case for hospitals, not for its intrinsic interest but rather for the light that it sheds on the four selected PPP models. We note the political difficulties experienced by PPPs as a procurement system. The fifth section reviews some potential and actual issues of healthcare funding in the markets since the beginning of the global financial crisis. Conclusions are drawn in the last section.

The Big Picture: The Why, What and Where of PPP

What Are Public–Private Partnerships and Why Do They Exist

Some descriptions of PPP are wide enough to encompass what is merely an opportunistic short-term cooperation between public and private sectors, which almost loses meaning, whereas other definitions are so limited as to foreclose on valid examples of asset and service partnership. In this Chapter, we take in some respects a restrictive definition of what counts as PPP but in other respects a liberal one, for reasons that will be explained when we discuss the typology of PPP arrangements in more detail below. We draw very largely on European PPP experience, and therefore that of relatively rich countries, and these are also ones where the state controls health policy and healthcare finance and provision (Barlow et al. 2013). This state dominance holds irrespective of whether the country tradition is of a tax-financed national health service (NHS) or of financing from social health insurance (SHI). The differentials in the levels of broad performance between these two health system structures in Europe are relatively insignificant today. However, SHI more or less automatically embeds a purchaser/provider split; healthcare providers are independent, or at least semi-independent, and sometimes private sector, which lessens the apparent place for PPP arrangements. In an NHS structure, the provider is much more likely to be a public institution, and so the role of PPPs as an intermediate contractual structure is much more easily imagined.

With such public domination of service delivery across all healthcare systems in Europe, the answer of using the private sector for certain services is predictable—but the question being asked is not so evident. The reasons for engaging the private sector are usually characterised in terms of two dimensions: (1) provision of private capital in substitution for public finance; and/or (2) acquisition of commercial skills of design, property maintenance, and operational and medical services supplementing or replacing those available within the state (Roehrich et al. 2014; Barlow and Köberle-Gaiser 2009). This work argued that the requirement, certainly in Europe and at a time of very low interest rates, for private finance is less than sometimes perceived, though not zero, and that the evidence for superior private sector management is also decidedly mixed (Barlow et al. 2013). The broad lesson, then, is that the decision to deliver services by private sector actors including PPP should be taken on pragmatic grounds—case by case, when the finance could not otherwise be accessed on acceptable terms or the services could convincingly be better—and not on ideological ones. In a European context, there is thus no inevitability for a stable or increasing role for PPPs and the private sector generally.

Roehrich et al. (2014) enumerate seven conceptualisations of PPPs, and these variously share some but not all common characteristics (e.g. inter-organisational relationship and risk-sharing). For the purposes of this chapter, we bear in mind two of the definitions. The first is by Forrer et al. (2010, p. 476), stating that "[p]ublic-private partnerships are on-going agreements between government and private sector organizations in which the private organization participates in the decision-making and production of a public good or service that has traditionally been provided by the public sector and in which the private sector shares the risk of that production". This captures key features to be discussed, but it seems to allow for relatively short-term arrangements which are probably best seen as outsourcing rather than true PPP, and only hints at the financial commitment. The second definition is from the UK's finance ministry and defines a PPP as "[a]n arrangement between two or more entities that enables them to work cooperatively towards shared or compatible objectives and in which there is some degree of shared authority and responsibility, joint investment of resources, shared risk taking, and mutual benefit" (HM Treasury 1998).

The Health PPP Market in Europe and Beyond

In Europe, the PPP market as a whole, irrespective of sector, peaked just before the global financial crisis in the late 2000s, and has since fallen by more than half, measured by either number or the value of projects (see Fig. 7.1).

This list includes PPPs in a range of sectors, including transport, education, justice and health (see Fig. 7.2). The aggregate drop-off has been caused by political problems and was further compounded by financing difficulties.

Europe dominates in the total number of PPP projects in healthcare, with North America far behind (Figs. 7.3 and 7.4). However, the balance is shifting, as seen by the proportion of projects in "pre-development". While Europe still has the largest share of projects (over one third), North America, Asia and Latin America are all now more prominent than before. For example, in Canada more than 50 PPP hospital projects were completed between 2003 and 2011. There is a view in the USA that this demonstrates the viability of PPP in financing healthcare infrastructure and given the need to curb government spending on the health sector the model may spread in the USA (KAW 2017).

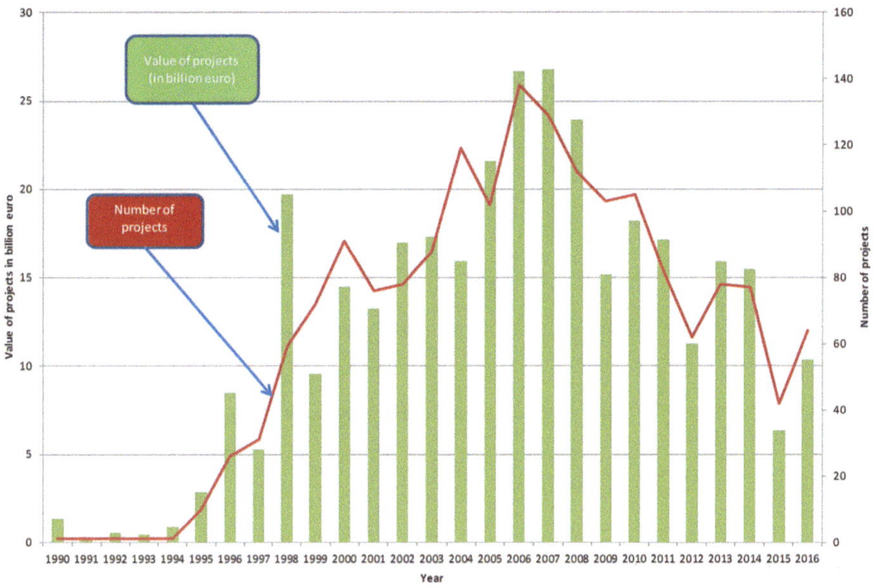

Fig. 7.1 Overview of the EU PPP market from 1990 to 2016 (Source: European Court of Auditors based on information provided by EPEC 2018)

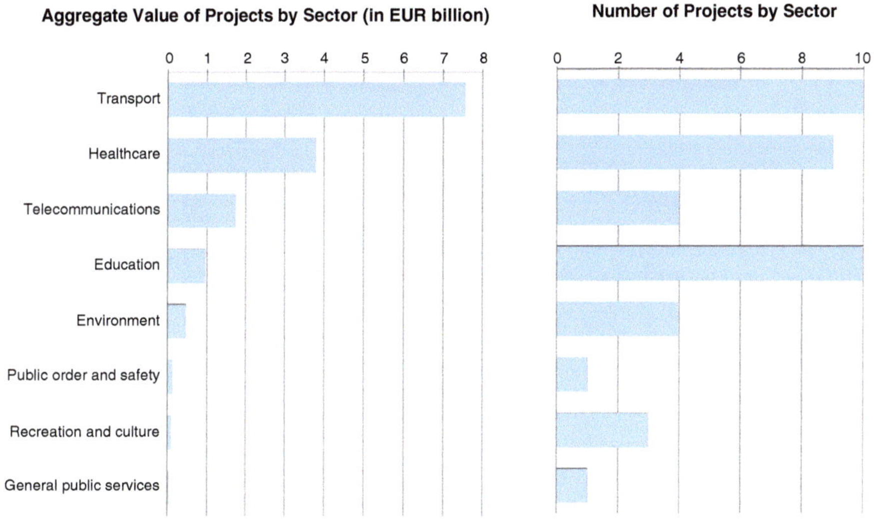

Fig. 7.2 Sector breakdown by value and number of projects in 2017 (Source: EPEC 2018)

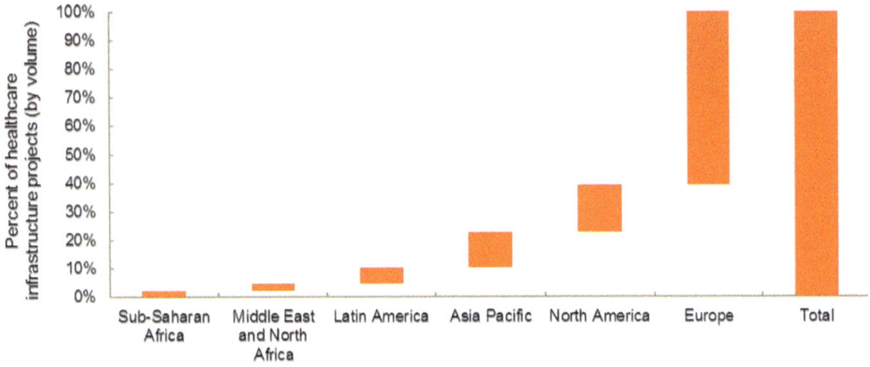

Fig. 7.3 Healthcare PPP infrastructure projects by geographic region (May 2017) (Source: Abuzaineh et al. 2018)

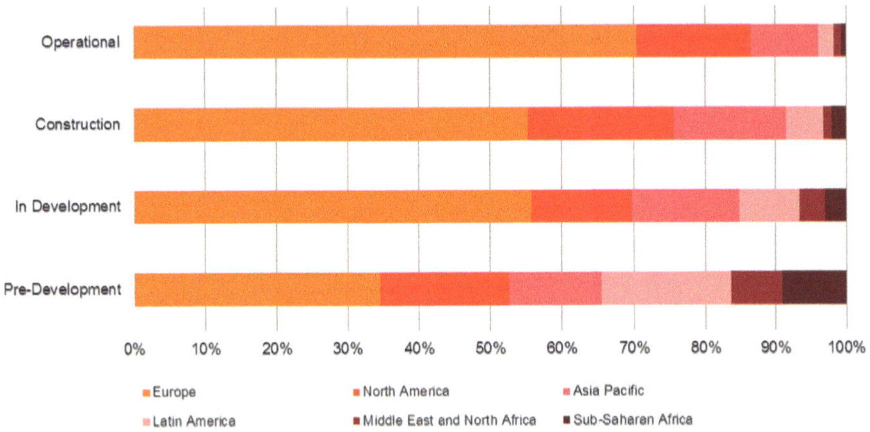

Fig. 7.4 Geographic distribution of healthcare PPP infrastructure projects by project stage (May 2017) (Source: Abuzaineh et al. 2018)

Key Elements of Health Sector Models

An aspect that is at the heart of a PPP relationship in health (or other sectors) is the existence of a scalable, replicable and sustainable business model. Charitable or third sector social activities fit less well into this characterisation, particularly on the grounds of scalability, and this also applies to outsourcing which, as stated above, is in principle largely short-term. This chapter describes what constitutes these potential PPP business models, and the characteristics which allow them to be flexed in size or used repeatedly.

Public or Private Finance

A PPP contracting structure, among other things, turns a public asset (e.g. buildings and/or equipment) into a stream of services over time (e.g. the *use* of a building). Because the services being transferred are still publicly controlled ones, the state usually pays for their provision during the asset's life, inclusive of the capital cost involved (unless there is actual privatisation, which is different from the conceptualisation of PPP which is being used here). This implies that there is a choice for the public sector between, on the one hand, financing up-front a piece of capital stock together with the ongoing through-life operating costs and, on the other hand, allocating the responsibility to a PPP contractor who will raise the finance in the markets and then receive fees for the full cost of the resulting services (Barlow et al. 2010). Either way—public provision or PPP—the public sector, or its agents in the case of highly regulated social insurers[1], one way or another ends up paying 100% of the cost of the healthcare service, and the debt service, across the project life-cycle.

The state can either finance the capital from its own account at the beginning, where the funding at the margin involves issuing public debt such as bonds, or instead can contract out the responsibility for financing the investment to a private or PPP party which raises the funding commercially, and is reimbursed by the state through the life of the contract; again, in principle, these lifetime payments will at the margin be funded via public debt (Barlow et al. 2010). There can and often are attempts to shift PPP borrowing "off (public) balance sheet", but this is usually an accounting exercise. In this picture, in economic as distinct from accounting terms, PPP mainly constitutes public services financed via a different sort of public debt than in the case of conventional procurement. The private sector does not therefore meaningfully "pay" for a PPP.

Another aspect of this concerns the costs of commercial finance. Interest rates worldwide have been extremely low since the global financial crisis started in 2008—even current increases in the USA and elsewhere take them to levels which are modest in historical terms. Some of the blame for the global financial crisis can be ascribed to excessive public sector debt levels (which have not decreased much if at all in the period since 2008, despite government attempts to deleverage), and there has been consequently resistance in the capital markets to the continued extent of state borrowing. However, many countries, in the jargon, do have fiscal space, even if many are still maintaining economic policies of austerity. The IMF (IMF 2018) suggests that many governments have "some" (e.g. USA, Canada, UK and Japan) or "substantial" (e.g. Australia, Sweden, and Germany) leeway to borrow if they wished to do so, for legitimate and economically valuable capital investment. This fiscal space, alongside very low real interest rates, implies that state borrowing to fund economic and social infrastructure would be very feasible for eligible

[1] Note that in many SHI countries (e.g. Germany), the state pays directly for capital costs, and the insurers pay for the operational costs of running the system.

countries. Further, it is almost everywhere true that the state can borrow cheaper than commercial entities within the country concerned; apart from anything else, there is a risk premium attached to non-sovereign borrowing. Private financing issues are discussed below.

In conclusion, the public sector eventually pays the whole bill for a PPP (and the capital markets for state funding should take this into account). Most states can also borrow on their own account, even in current circumstances, and state borrowing is usually cheaper than commercial borrowing.

PPP Typology

Public–private partnerships can be interpreted in two ways: first, as a movement along a spectrum from mostly public to increasingly private provision of care and associated services; second, as a shift along a spectrum which increases the amount of "bundling" of health-related services, including provision of the built infrastructure and medical services, into one contractual framework (Barlow et al. 2013; Roehrich et al. 2013). There is a distinction between these two ideas, even if they are linked. We discuss the "bundling" perspective below.

At one end of the spectrum, most care-related services are provided and often paid for by public sector entities. Private but not-for-profit (NFP) suppliers such as charities, or other organisations which are statutorily required to plough back surpluses into current activity, may also be involved. This model is characteristic of hospitals in many European countries, including charity-owned institutions such as Caritas (a Catholic organisation) in Germany, or the private foundations comprising almost all Dutch non-university hospitals; the state regulates activities in such organisations very tightly. For-Profit provision is at the opposite end of the spectrum; most European countries have an element of this, in a varied landscape running from negligible in the Netherlands to almost a half in Cyprus (Eurofound 2017). The USA is positioned towards the extreme of private sector healthcare provision (though of course there is also a very significant public delivery too, via the VA and other providers). Public–private partnerships sit somewhere between these two extremes.

In sum, PPPs can thus be seen as simply one part of the progression from largely state to largely private provision. The fascination of PPP is that it involves an attempt to reconcile the private interests of stockholders with the wider public concerns of stakeholders.

The second spectrum referred to earlier involves the concept of PPP "bundling": capturing within one envelope an increasing number of services (Roehrich et al. 2013). The bundling spectrum is more general than the public–private one, because a PPP could in fact be an arrangement between purely public firms. It is closely linked to the implications of two other ideas: life-cycle thinking and risk management. Bundling consists of adding extra service responsibilities into a contract. A minimal level of bundling would be, for example, where a contractor has responsibility for a building not just in terms of construction but also its operation throughout its functional (or at least, contractual) life. Life-cycle maintenance—"Hard Facilities Management"—is then an integral part of the contract; the contractor designs, constructs and operates the building for an agreed and lengthy period of time (Barlow et al. 2013). This generates an incentive to minimise costs taken across the whole life-cycle. In such a setting, it would not be prudent for the contractor to skimp on the design or construction phases, because the building will be eventually more expensive to maintain than is desirable, and the burden for paying for that would fall on the contractor. In practice for this "first-stage" bundling mechanism to work, the contractor would take responsibility for *two* sub-contracts beyond that of construction—the FM and the finance (Zheng et al. 2008). It would in principle be possible to develop terms which just impose a contractual obligation on the contractor to operate the building efficiently throughout its life, but by far the simplest route to achieve this is when the contractor has "skin in the game" by raising the finance. The reimbursement over the years to the chosen finance sub-contractors (banks or the capital market) is at risk if the building fails to perform[2].

Inherent in any PPP is the role of risk management—formally, the passing of responsibility for project risks to the party most capable of controlling them. Because the party bearing the risk has an incentive to manage it efficiently, this should theoretically help to achieve cost efficiencies and stimulate innovation. Efficient allocation of risk between public and private sector organisations in a PPP should then ensure that risks are transferred to the party which will require the minimum risk premium, i.e. charge the least to handle it. In fact, the pattern and price of risk transfer almost defines the success or otherwise of a PPP scheme.

Health Sector PPP Models

The authors have previously argued that bundling is the best lens to understand what PPPs achieve, because the nature of a given health sector PPP is determined by the extent of the services which are contracted out to the private sector (Barlow et al. 2013; cf. Iossa and Saussier 2018). Some PPP models place a low level of responsibility in the hands of a non-state partner, and others much more.

There is a variety of PPP models delivering different health-related services. This Chapter deals with four of them, which can be treated as archetypes usefully illustrating the key features. What is described here is not just the usual breakdown of PPP into project categories like DBFO (design, build, finance and operate) and BOOT (build, own, operate and transfer), but rather the broader drivers of PPP model functioning in health.

In the case of a hospital, the first stage of project bundling would actually be some variant of infrastructure DBFO or BOOT: the hospital authorities engage a private contractor to finance and design a building and carry out the relevant Hard

[2] Note that a minority of European PPPs do in fact use government finance.

Facilities Management throughout the contractual life, which would be typically in excess of 25 years (Zheng et al. 2008). The contractor will invariably take the form of a "Special Purpose Vehicle" (SPV) for the venture, and the funding will be mostly via "project finance"—with limited recourse to any substantial balance sheet. This PPP model is effectively a managed real estate lease, in a very granular form because of the ultra-detailed categorisation of the room spaces within the buildings, and it converts the conventional procurement by the authorities of a building asset into the purchase instead of a stream of managed building services. A market in property is created, in a healthcare setting which would be otherwise an almost-fully non-market situation.

This system has been furthest developed in the UK, where it is dubbed the Private Finance Initiative (PFI; or its more recent child "PF2"), and has been used to construct more than a hundred healthcare facilities—with individual projects of up to USD3 billion (Barlow and Köberle-Gaiser 2009; Barlow et al. 2010). The model has been copied in many countries—France, Italy, Portugal, Spain, Sweden in Europe, and Canada and Australia outside Europe, among many others. In Spain, a variant employed a publicly owned but separately constituted SPV, which raised commercial debt. In all these cases, the medical services remain entirely in the hands of public authorities (Barlow et al. 2013). Payment by the public authorities for building services in PFI contracts is tied to "availability" of spaces down to the level of individual rooms, with penalties for lack of "performance" (e.g. quality of service for areas such as cleaning or maintenance).

A more extensive development of this "accommodation-only" model has been used uniquely in Portugal, where a PFI-type long-term hospital building contract is twinned with a separate shorter-term (one third of the length) contract for the medical services (Barlow et al. 2013). Although at the beginning the shareholding parties of the two SPVs are similar, the ownership could in due course drift apart, since the medical services contract will be retendered in the open market at a relatively early stage. The payment mechanism in this twin-SPV model is availability/performance for the estate, and patient throughput for the medical services (with some flat payments for making available, for example, the emergency department).

The linkage between hospital building and medical services is closer when there is a concession structure. In these cases, a company buys the public licence to operate a hospital. This occurs in Germany, where commercial companies operate more than a tenth of the public stock of beds. These hospitals count as public facilities, and therefore because of the contracted private management, can effectively be categorised as PPPs: they are included in the relevant state Hospital Plan, must accept all patients (no "cream-skimming"), are accredited by the social insurers and are paid on the same tariffs as publicly owned hospitals[3]. Such arrangements have often begun with the purchase by a private company of a municipal or regional hospital, but the new owner has invariably wanted neither the site nor the building but rather just the public licence to operate. The payment system here is linked to DRG

[3] Some but not all such hospitals take public capital grants for construction.

activity—i.e. a unitary fee to cover the full operational costs of the medical services delivered.

Finally, there have been PPP concessions where primary care facilities and services as well as hospitals have been included in the contract. The best-known example is the "Alzira Model", based originally on one healthcare area within the Valencia region of Spain (Barlow et al. 2013). Although this started as a hospital-only model, it was quickly reformulated to include primary and community services. There are several Valencia healthcare areas that now use this model, covering around 20% of the region's population. The payment mechanism is unusual in being based on "capitation"—the area is paid a standard sum for each registered resident, and the company has to provide all primary and secondary services within what is in effect a block grant. There are regulatory quality controls, and adaptations of the revenue stream for non-resident patients who access care, or for residents choosing to receive care elsewhere. The politics has, however, turned out to be tortuous.

In summary, working progressively from PFI (accommodation-only) through to the eventual end-point of hospital and primary care, there is increasing bundling of service responsibility, but probably also increasing complexity of the contractual and organisational arrangements—illustratively, Fig. 7.5.

The intention behind such bundling is to align incentives—in economic terms, there is an increasing internalisation of externalities. Economic theory on this point says that this alignment of incentives will improve performance, which would otherwise be degraded by the unintended impact of service activities which are outside of the contract. "Bundling" thus widens the envelope around the project's contract so that more of the externalities—costs or benefits not incorporated and priced in the transaction (Iossa and Martimort 2008, 2012)—are internalised; they will in principle therefore be taken into proper consideration by the contract parties within a PPP. An example of a positive externality is where a building can be designed such

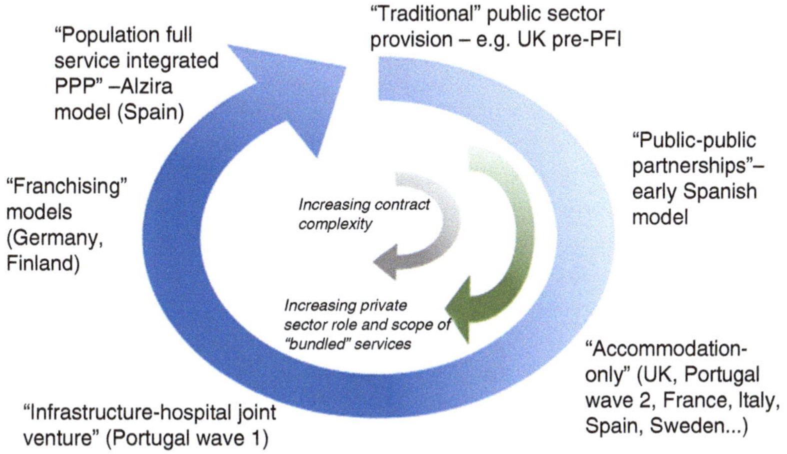

Fig. 7.5 The bundling and public–private progression healthcare (Source: Authors)

that it will incur reducing cost during the operational phase. A negative externality might be an innovation in building design that will cause higher cost in operation but will generate higher quality through the asset's life. In neither case would it be in the interests of a contractual party which is only the project designer or constructor to take such later repercussions into account (Iossa and Martimort 2012).

Governments often stipulate as a condition for agreement to proceed that PPP will secure better value for money than traditional public procurement options: generated by the bundling effects of bringing together the financing, designing, constructing and operating parts (Grimsey and Lewis 2005; Siemiatycki and Farooqi 2012). Proponents of PPP further argue that the efficiency and quality of infrastructure delivery is increased because the payment system can be linked to performance indicators, the achievement of quality targets or the availability of facilities. In the healthcare context, other claimed benefits include the ability to allow healthcare providers to concentrate on clinical services, rather than managing infrastructure, and increased efficiency in project delivery (Barlow et al. 2013; Barlow and Köberle-Gaiser 2009).

Potential Issues with PPP

If the extent of bundling is the key idea describing the way to which theoretical incentive advantages of PPPs can be unlocked, there are clearly some countervailing issues. These tend to be more empirical and behavioural than theoretical.

Costs and Performance

Very many writers have reviewed the performance of PPPs, though not always specific to the health sector. A small sample of this literature is as follows:

- Expert Panel EU on effective ways of investing in health (2014): The panel found that there was no evidence of cost-effectiveness in PPP health projects across Europe, that PFIs should be used only in special cases and that asset ownership should not generally be regarded as a determinant of efficiency;
- Boardman et al. (2016): In a cross-sectoral review, the authors suggest that the clearest advantages of PPP are to politicians who can take credit for new infrastructure while passing future maintenance and operating costs to future politicians, taxpayers and users (by building more infrastructure than might otherwise be justified). Also, costs are just as high as conventional procurement, and there is limited risk transfer ("the government is always the residual risk holder"). In sum, there is no convincing evidence that PPPs add social value[4];

[4] This chapter principally covers the European situation. Healthcare PPP elsewhere in the world

- Torchia et al. (2015): This is a systematic literature review across all sectors, with main findings suggesting that questions about PPP effectiveness, efficiency and convenience remain unanswered;
- Roehrich et al. (2014): This health sector review is neutral about whether PPP should be a social choice. However, it argues for a more coherent research agenda around the significant evidence gaps;
- Vecchi et al. (2010): This study offers insights into the Italian experience with health PPPs, principally focusing on what they assert as excessive rates of return, especially to the equity. They find this unjustifiable, given the low levels of systematic risk actually faced by investors. There is no review of healthcare performance in PPPs;
- Caballer-Tarazona and Vivas-Consuelo (2016): The paper covers the "Alzira" health sector model in Spain, mentioned above. It finds that comparing the PPP areas in Valencia against the state-run ones, the PPP group obtains good results, above the average, but not always better than the best directly managed ones;
- NAO (2018): The National Audit Office's function is to help the UK Parliament to hold government to account, and improve public services. The report looks at all sectors in which PFIs were deployed, and a new but very similar variant of it called PF2 (healthcare was the biggest single user of PPP). NAO suggests that pressures remain to secure capital investments off the (accounting) public sector balance sheet, despite the danger that unquantified benefits will not be adequate to justify the higher cost of private finance over typical project lifetimes. The NAO reports an analysis that the cost of a PFI hospital is 70% higher than the "Public Sector Comparator". The report also points out that "there is still a lack of data available on the benefits of private finance procurement" and that "HM Treasury has not collected any outturn data in order to quantify" the value for money of PPPs compared to projects using public finance.

To summarise, based on extant literature, more often than not the costs of PPP projects are at least as high as conventional procurement. More troublingly, there seems to be little or no evidence that performance is better—though there is no evidence to the contrary, either. Many observers from a health services background do not approve of what is seen as a pseudo-privatisation of the system.

Flexibility and Lock-In

There is a number of interpretations of the meaning of the word "flexibility" in any investment project, including PPPs. The NAO (2018 op. cit.) mentions that government departmental flexibility to use the line budget is compromised by using PFI because the contract prevents changes, once-signed, as a result of the administrative

can be visibly problematic. The new Queen Mamohato Memorial Hospital in Maseru, Lesotho, is apparently absorbing *51%* of the country's health budget (Oxfam Briefing Note 14 2014).

and management fees which will be payable to the commercial partner. All PFI contracts do include variation clauses, but the issue is whether these cover relevant issues and can be activated when reasonably required for the purposes of the particular service. In fact, it seems evident that a public organisation in a PPP structure will not be able to execute process changes in the same way that it would internally. From the commercial partner's perspective, any changes will likely prejudice its ability to manage the asset as cheaply as before. The contract vests the effective ownership in the hands of the party which has invested the most—de facto, the commercial partner—and it will be able to choose which operational changes are allowed and, to a substantial degree, at what cost.

At the start of any service relationship, including a PPP contract, i.e. before the contract is signed, the value of through-life flexibility can be analogised to an option in financial theory. It is worth buying flexibility, but only up to a certain point (the value of the option). It can confidently be expected that most traditionally procured projects will embed too little flexibility at the project design stage as a result of the "rush to certainty", the desire speedily to close the contract. Any such calculus will very likely become even more lost in negotiations to establish a PPP, so the chances are that less flexibility will be contractually guaranteed in the complex negotiations leading to the legal agreement (De Neufville et al. 2008).

One of the issues here is the idea of "contract completeness"—that the parties to a contract can foresee all the contingencies which could impinge on the project throughout its life (Roehrich et al. 2013). The contract should then be written in such a way as to allow for a response to each and every contingency as it arises. This is patently unrealistic, and any contract will always be "incomplete". But, as mentioned earlier, the effective ownership does rest with the commercial partner, and so when unexpected events require a change of operational practice and likely in the assets underlying the practice, this partner will be able to determine whether or not the change is accommodated, and at what price.

A complication in real-world PPPs is that the public authorities for, say, a new or reconstructed hospital project will probably never have negotiated such a project before (Caldwell et al. 2009). The partner on the other side of the table (typically a construction or finance company) will, however, probably have considerable experience of previous similar projects (Roehrich and Lewis 2014). There is an asymmetry of bargaining knowledge, which makes it even more unlikely that change contingencies and flexibility will be adequately catered contracted.

A further real-world issue is that there are systematic differences between factors that can be included in contract and those which cannot. Typically, cost is visible and measurable, so the commercial partner will ensure that it has freedom to control them during the life of the project. Quality is much less contractible; it is much more the concern of the public sector partner, and with a key quality component being the flexibility to adapt to changing healthcare needs over time.

It is well-recognised that renegotiation in PPP contracts will be difficult (Guasch et al. 2014), with a balance to be trod between opportunism, attempts to repair a contract which may have been defective to start with, and legitimate needs to respond to a changing situation. If it is difficult in the transport sector, asset-heavy and service-light and where technology changes little, it is more difficult still in healthcare, which is relatively more service-heavy and asset-light, and where the delivery technology changes rapidly over time (Roehrich and Lewis 2014).

What does the above mean in the healthcare world? The forces described impinge most on contractual structures which are less inclusive: those which, as characterised earlier, have fewer activities bundled into the contract. This is because of the effect of bundling in allowing internalisation of externalities; the more that externalities are outside the contract, the more unknown/unknowable contingencies will exist, and the less likely that the junior owner (the public sector) will be able to ensure future performance. There is therefore a lock-in created at the moment of contract signature, with gaming of the contract possible after that point by the commercial partner.

For PPP models in health, we might expect from theory that the lesser bundling involved in accommodation-only real estate models like the UK's PFI compared with other models would result in poorer outcomes. Whilst direct comparisons between different PPP models have not been carried out, there are certainly criticisms of PFI on account of inflexibility (Black 2015; Barlow and Köberle-Gaiser 2009). This is not surprising: hospital PFI separates the ownership and responsibility for the main capital assets (buildings and equipment) from the ownership and responsibility for the main activity (healthcare provision). Few other process or industrial sectors would want to operate with such arrangements. While they may work at the beginning of the contract, in time significant infrastructure change will be needed, but not incentivised, in most PFI-type contracts. This will have a serious impact on the public–private relationship. Clear governance mechanisms (contracts and trust) need to be in place (Caldwell et al. 2017).

Payment Mechanisms

Payment systems were briefly introduced above in the context of the different PPP models. For an accommodation-only model, the focus is to create a private market which did not exist before. Effectively, since the PFI relates to the building, the payment is analogous to a real estate rent, with performance payments. This should theoretically enable the building to be maintained throughout its life in good technical quality[5]. However, good *technical quality* may not be sufficient for good *medicine* after several years. It is not clear whether actual PFI operating costs are much different from those in conventionally procured projects, because the PFI contractor is paid a "monthly unitary charge" which covers capital as well as operating costs. In general, UK PFI hospital buildings do appear to be well-managed and most contracts are performing satisfactorily or better, and meeting the expectations of hospital trusts (NAO 2010)—even if the penalties for poor performance are actually quite

[5] For an English hospital, the so-called Condition Category B is typically required at contract expiry—"Sound, operationally safe and exhibits only minor deterioration".

low. However, it is unclear so far how well PFI is capable of addressing the need to ensure that the building flexes as new demands are imposed on it (see the section above).

The Portuguese "twin-SPV" model attempts to repair the un-relatedness of healthcare delivery from the infrastructure inherent in the UK PFI model. It does so by adding a medical services contract. However, this is one which has a different term (10 years) from the accommodation (30 years) (Barlow et al. 2013). This brings its own problems in that, after a first retender, the ownership of the two contracts can diverge—and such a strategy removes the possibility of service bundling, the whole point of the incentive power of PPP to start with. Outcomes of this twin-contract mechanism are not yet clear because the hospitals concerned are not old enough for the cycle to have worked through. There is one very positive feature of the medical services contracts in the Portuguese system in the form of the fixed "availability" payment for the emergency department. Given the highly fluctuating demand for emergency facilities, the open-ended nature of many of the commitments, and the strong social case for having adequate capacity on stand-by, it is rather unlikely that relying on a market judgement for these facilities would be adequate. The Portuguese system means that the emergency department is guaranteed as a facility for the population.

The full-service concession model of PPP, used particularly in Germany, aligns medical services and infrastructure services because the concessionaire is responsible for both. There is substantial evidence that in German hospital chains, early investment and re-investment in up-to-date facilities and equipment occur more readily as medical needs change (Dowdeswell 2009). Such investments are achieved even though these hospital chains are paid nominally on the same tariff as purely public hospitals. However, the "envelope" around the project is almost entirely set at the level of the hospital[6]. The interests of the hospital owner/developer are thus to maximise the financial welfare of the hospital, subject to the regulatory constraints and public opinion. Modern healthcare is increasingly moving towards an integrated care approach, where the patient is treated in the appropriate setting, whether home, general practice, hospital, or other facility. Given that the tariff in Germany is hospital-only (primary care is reimbursed separately), there is a danger that the concession hospitals, responding to the hospital tariff alone, will optimise patient treatment within the hospital but not within the wider healthcare system.

For the widest healthcare PPP model discussed in this chapter ("Alzira", Spain), the system covers primary plus secondary (and limited tertiary) care (Barlow et al. 2013). That is, the operator is responsible for primary and community care clinics together with hospitals. The company will attempt—again subject to regulatory constraints—to treat the patient in the appropriate setting. Primary care is clearly

[6] The biggest private for-profit hospital operator in Germany, Helios Kliniken, has set up a substantial number of "Medizinischen Versorgungszentren" (MVZ, Medical Care Centres, https://www.helios-gesundheit.de/unternehmen/wer-wir-sind/unser-angebot/medizinische-versorgungszentren/). These are ambulatory care clinics, but the relationship with most primary care practitioners is still arms-length.

cheaper for most patient contacts, but with limited treatment competence. The operator will aim to keep patients at general practice level unless the problem is severe, or particular interventions are needed. Protocols are in place to handle patients in a typical area who reappear often in the emergency department—a couple of hundred per health area—but who could be dealt with more appropriately if the primary care system were to intercept them (McClellan and Ginés 2015). The tariff for this model is based on capitation (a standard fee per registered resident of the area, escalated annually at a specified inflation index). The impact of capitation has been widely discussed in health policy and services research. The key point in relation to the Alzira-type PPP models is to create a single system tariff which does not create a particular bias to treatment in one setting or another (with the caveats above). The model has therefore been structured to embrace the theoretical advantages of bundling across the relevant healthcare settings, pinned together with an appropriate unitary system tariff. Although the model seems to have functioned well and a range of benefits are claimed (de Rosa Torner 2012; NHS Confederation 2012; Caballer-Tarazona and Vivas-Consuelo 2016), the new Regional Government is progressively dismantling all the PPP concessions.

Economics of Hospital Projects and the Implications for PPP

What should we look out for in designing a health PPP? It is worth stepping back from the detail on different PPP models to review the cost basis of a typical acute hospital. The analysis in this chapter section of such a hospital, based on UK analysis, abstracts from the value created, and focuses just on the identified costs. Typically, at the project appraisal of an investment, the cost stream of a healthcare facility or service will be uncertain in some respects, but in principle measurable. However, metrics around the benefit stream are extremely qualitative, and with highly uncertain links to inputs of the factors of production; we ignore them here.

The cost of a hospital as an investment proposition should be evaluated across the entire life-cycle, even if the notion of what a "hospital" is will evolve over time. For the purpose of analysis, a lifetime in UK public hospital business cases is assumed to be c.60 years, with the recognition that there will be a substantial (possibly almost full) mid-life update. Some sort of discounting is needed to bring the cash flows to a common metric; in the case of the underlying material for the case shown here, the protocol is for a 3.5% real rate of discount for the first 30 years, followed by 3% for remaining 30 years[7]. This generates the full-life costs in net present value (NPV) terms, broken down into capital costs, hard facilities management, other operating costs and clinical plus related costs.

[7] Each and any of the assumptions can be varied, but would not in fact change the broad picture. In particular, using a lower discount rate for the NPV would reduce the weight of capital costs in the calculation.

The exemplar hospital offers full acute services, with a capacity of over 500 beds. Summarising the base case as follows:

- Initial build capital cost ("capex") over 4 years of GBP250 million (~USD415 million at the time), with approximately the same spend assumed after 30 years;
- Full operating costs (maintenance and soft services) of around GBP13 million p.a.;
- Medical services costs—clinical and associated—of around GBP175 million a year.

This results in a full-life NPV of costs of GBP 4,470 million.

It can be seen immediately from these data that the capital cost is small relative to the total life-cycle costs, and so are the costs to run the building services (hard and soft FM). The *only* thing that really matters is the costs of providing the clinical services—this is mostly labour. This is not to say that the building concept and its implementation are unimportant. On the contrary, if the building is not "right", the ability to deliver a quality medical service will be heavily constrained. But, assuming that the design and the construction of the hospital are appropriate, the costs incurred in developing the facility are then relatively immaterial. Equally, the maintenance costs of the hospital are not large—in present value terms, they are a little less than the capital costs. But the medical costs are *ten* times the size of either; this is what the economics of a service-intensive activity look like. An asset like a road would have a very different life-cycle pattern: dominated even in NPV terms by the construction cost.

A useful way of envisaging this is to show the sensitivity of the final economics (the NPV of costs) to given changes in the inputs. Figure 7.6 is a spider chart of the economic model, showing the impact of varying capital costs, operating costs or clinical service costs over a range from 30% below the base case (with its NPV of GBP4.5 billion) to 50% above. Because the present value of capital and operating costs is very similar, the curves on the graph showing variations in these are almost coincident, and have very little impact on project's full-cost NPV. The capex and opex for total lifetime costs of running this facility are essentially unimportant. Clinical services, on the other hand, are all important. Viewed another way, even if a facility is relatively expensive to build, it only has to deliver a small productivity increase in clinical service costs for the expenditure to have been valuable in terms of reducing lifetime cost.

The implication of these findings for PPP is that in cost terms it is vital to get the design right, such that clinical healthcare processes can be delivered efficiently, and then seek to improve the productivity and quality of clinical services over the life of the facility. This might involve through-life flexibility of the buildings, including as services are shifted to new settings outside the hospital facility.

With respect to the PPP models discussed in this chapter, a key finding implied in the chart above is that the space for PFI—a procurement model purposefully oriented to efficiency in the construction and subsequent servicing of the facility—to make any kind of an impact on through-life costs is so limited as to be substantially meaningless. This statement is true as long as PFI does not *systematically*

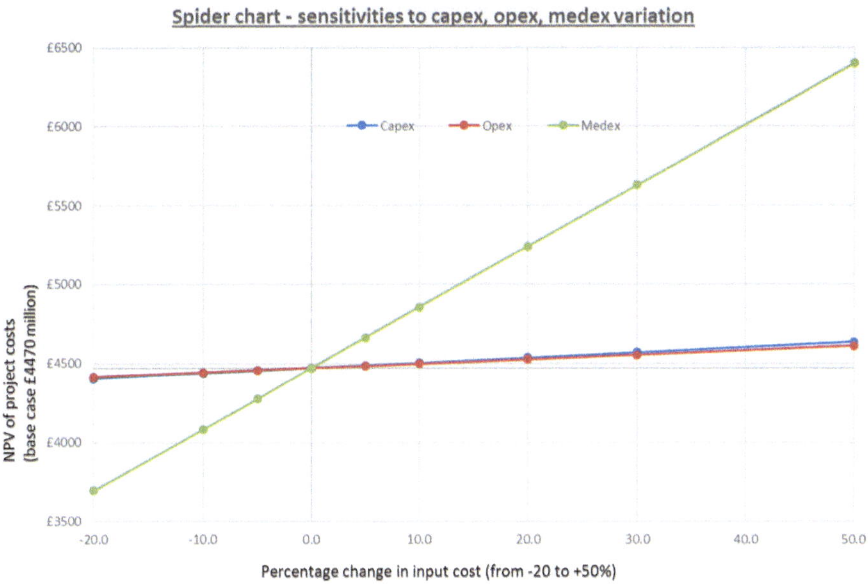

Fig. 7.6 Spider chart of project sensitivities in hospital investment appraisal (Source: authors' calculations, based on a PPP "Outline Business Case" for a mid-size English hospital)

enhance the long-term ability to deliver modern medicine, over and above the results that could be expected from conventional procurement. The evidence on the early PFI hospitals in is that they are not high-performing in relation to design innovation, so there is no reason to expect significant progressive building productivity increases or induced innovation in medical services, either in the UK (Barlow and Köberle-Gaiser 2008) or Spain (Parrado and Reynaers 2018). Excess PFI capital costs, especially in health, have been repetitively criticised over many years (e.g. Pollock and Price 2013; Parrado and Reynaers 2018). We suggest that even if PFI is capital-expensive, which does not say much about whether the hospital full costs are materially expensive. The main criticism of PFI—and the reason not to rely on the accommodation-only model of PPP—should be the separation of the principal capital asset from the process workstream, rendering the facility inflexible and increasingly ill-matched to needs over time, rather than the supposed high capital costs.

The cost analysis also sheds a light on the Portuguese twin-SPV model. It is not surprising that, when the model was being developed, it was stated by the government that the gains would be made in the medical services system, and not in the building. The projects concerned were difficult to finance, because many banks were reluctant to take medical demand risk, but the subsequent retreat to highly financeable PFI for Phase 2 of the Portuguese PPP programme has probably done no favours to the long-term performance of the country's system.

There is an implication as well for the German concession model. It may seem surprising that the companies concerned purchase a hospital for its public operational licence, but not for the site or buildings. They then invest readily and in doing so even often forego public grants in order to speed up development, thus requiring them to fund capital expensively on their balance sheet (it is not generally reimbursed in the operational tariff). This suggests that it is clear to these companies that the capital cost of constructing hospitals is not that relevant to their overall financial performance, which instead depends very largely on continuously maximising process efficiency. They need only aim to be at least slightly more efficient or with slightly higher earnings per patient than competing hospitals, and can then live profitably under the common tariff, whilst municipal hospitals in particular struggle.

Finally, the Spanish hospital and primary concessions in principle achieve the same hospital cost gains as the German ones. They have invested regularly—but the contracts did require this anyway, and the quality regulation by the public authority pushed in the same direction, so it is difficult to be fully sure about the attitude of the company to keeping its capital stock up to date.

The Politics of PPP

Healthcare PPP programmes in Europe, and often elsewhere as well, have proved politically controversial. If the various models had unambiguously proved successful, the controversy would probably have died away and use of PPP would have spread. However, as the analysis above suggests, the evidence is that PPP models have not fully met the original aspirations, either on the basis of cost or quality in healthcare. Plenty of projects have been built when the state would have struggled to achieve this (the massive UK hospital PFI programme is a case in point), costs in the big picture are not out of control, some risks and responsibilities have been transferred away from government or hospital administrators and healthcare is usually being appropriately delivered from at present modern facilities. But this adds up to a qualified acceptance that PPP can sometimes have a place, rather than a ringing commendation for its universal use. The positive messages get lost relative to the claim that PPP represents a privatisation of the European social model. In this context, the advantage for politicians that PPP can deliver social infrastructure off the state's balance sheet, with the pay-back occurring after their term in office, does not now offset the perceived disadvantages.

PFI including in its home country of the UK has had a persistently bad press. Costs, especially for capital, are seen to be high and deliver substantial profits, especially when the original contractors sell the PPP in the secondary markets. There have been some widely publicised maintenance failings. Finally, for ancillary services where the contract allows the SPV to charge, there has been public resistance—since PFI essentially involves no "demand risk" in the main business line of healthcare, almost the only area where the contractor can react to demand is car parking, and the resulting charges cause an inordinate level of public concern. In the October 2018 "Budget" (fiscal statement), the government signalled that it will abolish the use of PFI deals for future capital projects, and establish a centralised capacity to manage better its existing healthcare schemes. In a reversal of previous policy, the Chancellor stated that there was "compelling evidence" that PFI deals do not deliver value for taxpayers or genuinely transfer risk to the private sector (Carding 2018).

The "Alzira" situation is even more notable. The development of the model from its beginnings in the mid-1990s was strongly political. The administration of the right-wing *Partido Popular* used three (two after a failure) state-controlled public banks together with other parties to establish and to fund the project. Only one contractor bid to develop the first of the concession hospitals, and mainly as a financial rather than a medical services entity. The venture collapsed financially, with the government paying a termination fee which was promptly used by the same operator to fund the bid for the second phase, again with only one bidder. Other political parties did not approve. Another of the savings banks in the structure has since collapsed. The contractor has subsequently turned into a healthcare and hospital operator, part-owned by the US group Centene. However, the incoming left-wing PSPV-PSOE is in the process of abrogating the contracts one by one as they reach term.

One clearly successful PPP model—the German concession companies—has not suffered the same level of political attention. Some of this is because the system is not labelled "PPP", in the eyes of most observers. Also, the German Social Health Insurance arrangements embed a purchaser–provider split, with a range of providers across For-Profit, Not-For-Profit, conventional PFI-type PPP, municipal, regional and federal ownerships. Thus, the PPP operators do not stand out, and most patients have little idea, and less concern, about the ownership of their district hospital. There has been some controversy as to whether For-Profit operators can satisfactorily run university hospitals, with their heavy emphasis on research and training, but some tertiary PPP hospitals navigate the situation well. This implies that PPP may be less controversial in SHI countries compared to NHS ones. In the tax-based health systems, extending the PPP model into the delivery of clinical services is likely to be much more problematic than merely building and managing the estate.

It is worth pointing out that many observers make a comparison between an actual PPP and a hypothetical and idealised public service option. Regardless of this, however, the politics is difficult unless the political environment changes. On balance, while PPP activity will continue at a low level in Europe, there is at present no reason to suppose that the market will become more active.

Investment Market Overview

In this section, we discuss issues surrounding the availability of finance for PPPs in the health sector. Broadly, finance for a European project can come from government budget grants, EU grants such as the Structural Funds, private company balance sheet equity, balance sheet or project-recourse debt, and bonds, these either insured ("wrapped") or unwrapped. The debt could be from a commercial bank, one of the European National Promotional Banks such as KfW in Germany, or from the International Financial Institutions (European Investment Bank, European Bank for Reconstruction and Development, Council of Europe Development Bank, World Bank, etc.). Historically, all of these were present, and many were important, but most of the sources ran dry, or at least drier, after the global financial crisis struck.

Projects across Europe have in fact partly blended government grant into PPP funding alongside the commercial partner's resources. Sometimes this was partly hidden, in that the state money went to ancillary expenditures (provision of access roads, etc.), but this was no less important in the development of the projects concerned. Government investment has been curtailed recently. EU grants have only occasionally been used to support a PPP, and virtually never in health: Structural Funds have their own complex rhythm, and attempting to match that against the complexity of PPP project finance has rarely been smooth. For those PPPs carried out by companies with a substantial balance sheet (e.g. the German hospital chains holding concessions), company equity or commercial bank borrowings secured against the parent's balance sheet have been common.

In the case of "project finance", the repayment of the capital spent is largely a function of the cash flow generated by the project itself. It is a commonplace of project finance using thinly capitalised SPVs that this is "*limited* recourse", but very rarely *non*-recourse (i.e. where there is only one source of capital repayment, via the cash flows generated by the project): the financiers will always look for a "second way out" via some kind of credit support from sponsors or third parties (e.g. government), and otherwise the project sub-contractors (which unfortunately are often weakly capitalised themselves).

The structure of an SPV for a PPP, in any sector, will typically involve much debt (treating bonds for the moment as a type of debt) relative to the level of equity or other non-interest-bearing funding. High proportions of debt have the advantage, from the project promoter's viewpoint, of incentivising the lenders to evaluate and monitor the project carefully; and it is cheaper than equity. On the other hand, high debt levels, with fixed repayment schedules, make the project's finances more fragile in the event of a cash shortfall. Given that the debt in a project (especially "senior", i.e. with preferred status) is generally cheaper than either equity or junior/subordinated debt, maximising its share cuts the overall financing cost. PPP bank debt in Europe traditionally came from commercial banks, accentuated by the prominence of banks as a capital source in Europe compared with, for example, the USA where there is a much heavier emphasis on the capital markets issuing bonds. This ended with the financial crisis. The mismatch between banks' assets (long-term lending) and their liabilities (short-term deposits) was very much exposed after 2008. Many European banks remain too weak to use their limited capital base on illiquid PPP loans, and the regulators are not keen on this either.

Although there was the emphasis on commercial bank debt, bond structures were also prominent, particularly in the UK which was by far the most active PPP market; this applied to hospital projects as well. Most of the bond financing achieved the credit ratings required, often because of regulation, by pension fund or life insurer investors, by means of insurance cover via "monoline insurers". These issue unconditional and irrevocable guarantees of timely payment of bond principal and interest, based on maintaining a sufficient capital base to justify their own AAA credit rating. From the mid-1980s, monoline companies expanded from their origin in the US municipal bond market into guaranteeing securities backed by assets such as mortgages and auto loans. They also came to Europe, and entered the PPP market, guaranteeing the bonds funding projects. The non-municipal asset-backed security business of the monolines suffered truly dramatic falls in credit ratings in the financial crisis. The PPP securities which they supported in Europe now trade at a price which reflects the (impaired) rating of the monoline and the (low) underlying rating of the project. This has significantly damaged the wrapped (insured) bond market, effectively taking the route out of play now (Jayasuriya 2016).

This is all a pity because there has been in recent years a growing interest in financing within the capital markets of PPP in substitution for bank debt (Inderst 2013; EIB/EPEC 2010). The sources of finance are principally pension funds, (life) insurers, Sovereign Wealth Funds or other state investment funds, and endowments/family offices. All these providers tend to have a long-term perspective, and most of them have long-term and relatively predictable liabilities which they need to match against long-term assets. A PPP potentially represents exactly such a use of finance; the return to the funders can be structured as inflation plus a modest premium, which many governments are prepared to consider for social infrastructure investments. The problem is often, however, that the bond rating, without an insurance, is too poor (i.e. the risks are judged to be too great). In particular, some bond purchasers are unwilling to take construction risk, therefore requiring early project support from some other source. In general, despite the theoretical match-made-in-heaven, it is not clear that the bond markets will adequately fund PPPs in the foreseeable future.

At present, therefore, PPP finance provision associated with EU funds is complicated; from commercial banks it is unpromising; and bond markets have nowhere near recovered, with the necessary wrapping being problematic. Availability of finance for new PPPs, including the health sector, is by no means assured.

Summary and Conclusions: Will the Real Health PPP Stand Up?

PPPs have been around, under different names, for centuries. Today there is a variety of different definitions, but substantially we are talking about scalable, replicable and sustainable business models. In this chapter, we have focused on Europe—traditionally the most active market for health PPPs, though perhaps prospectively less so.

PPP turns the purchase of an asset into the purchase of a stream of services. In a true PPP (as distinct from real or pseudo-privatisation), the state always pays the full cost of a project, irrespective of whose name appears on the financing package, the contract or above the door. In current economic/fiscal circumstances, governments could invest more on their own account, but both this route to capital investment and PPP have declined with the financial crisis.

In considering PPP, there are two important dimensions—public to private, and lesser to greater degrees of "bundling" services into a contract. Bundling is the key idea to align incentives: progressively through construction, finance, maintenance, hospital clinical services and non-hospital clinical services. In healthcare PPP models, "accommodation-only" (the UK's "Private Finance Initiative" model) is one polar extreme, moving through twin contractual structures offering estate and clinical services, full-service hospitals, and ending with hospital and primary/community care models.

There is a myriad of extant studies on the virtues or otherwise of PPPs across economic sectors including health. The good points are that project delivery is usually to time and to budget, and multiple projects get built when the political system would otherwise struggle. However, there are questions about the cost, true performance differentials relative to public procurement, the extent of future flexibility for changing needs, caution on the asymmetry between the public and private sectors at negotiation and operational stages and difficulties with contracting for quality requirements. Overall, there is a simple lack of evidence one way or another about full health system performance with PPP engaged. The UK's PFI is particularly problematic, in divorcing the main production asset from the main business process.

Payment mechanisms vary, with a hint that capitation systems perform best, perhaps supplemented by flat payments for making capacity available (e.g. for the emergency department). The cost economics of any hospital are absolutely dominated by clinical rather than any other costs. If a modern PPP-provided estate and service provision can enable even a tiny productivity growth component, any raised capital cost at the project start will quickly be washed away. The PFI model—optimised solely on the management of the physical estate—is unlikely to be a good economic choice. Twin accommodation/clinical models could deliver, as could full-service concessions of one form or another.

Politically, PPP has been difficult in Europe. Even PFI, apparently a minimum model, has been controversial, though the profit-gouging criticism is misplaced. In practice, Social Health Insurance national systems, with an in-built purchaser/provider split, have experienced less criticism. It can be observed that, especially in National Health Service (tax-funded) health systems, inclusion of medical services within a PPP contract is close to touching a third rail.

Originally, PPPs in Europe were largely financed by bank debt. A bond market progressively developed, relying on insurance guarantees for credit enhancement offered by monoline companies. These entities promptly blew up in the financial crisis because they had insured financial instruments outside of the US municipal and European PPP markets. It is not clear how any major resurgence of European health PPP would be financed.

In sum, the prospects for PPPs in the European health sector are distinctly shaded—on grounds of cost, performance, funding and political acceptability. Some of these concerns and experience will undoubtedly carry over to different geographies.

References

Abuzaineh, N., Brashers, E., Foong, S., Feachem, R., & Da Rita, P. (2018). PPPs in healthcare: Models, lessons and trends for the future. *Healthcare public-private partnership series, no. 4*. San Francisco, CA: The Global Health Group, Institute for Global Health Sciences, University of California, San Francisco and PwC. Retrieved September 4, 2018, from https://globalhealth-sciences.ucsf.edu/sites/globalhealthsciences.ucsf.edu/files/pub/ppp-report-series-business-model.pdf

Barlow, J., & Köberle-Gaiser, M. (2008). The private finance initiative, project form and design innovation; The UK's hospitals programme. *Research Policy, 37*, 1392–1402.

Barlow, J., & Köberle-Gaiser, M. (2009). Delivering innovation in hospital construction—Contracts and collaboration in the UK's Private Finance Initiative hospitals program. *California Management Review, 51*, 126–143.

Barlow, J., Roehrich, J. K., & Wright, S. (2010). De facto privatisation or a renewed role for the EU? Paying for Europe's healthcare infrastructure in a recession. *Journal of the Royal Society of Medicine, 103*, 51–55.

Barlow, J., Roehrich, J. K., & Wright, S. (2013). Europe sees mixed results from public-private partnerships for building and managing health care facilities and services. *Health Affairs, 32*(1), 146–154.

Black, S. (2015). The real problem with PFI is lack of flexibility. *British Medical Journal, 351*, h4030. Retrieved July 12, 2018, from https://www.bmj.com/content/351/bmj.h4030/rr

Boardman, A. E., Siemiatycki, M., & Vining, A. R. (2016). The theory and evidence concerning public-private partnerships in Canada and elsewhere. *University of Calgary SPP Research Papers, 9*(12), 1–31.

Bogart, D. (2005). Turnpike trusts and the transportation revolution in 18th century England. *Explorations in Economic History, 42*(4), 479–508.

Button, K. J. (2016). Public–private partnerships: A review of economic considerations with particular reference to transportation projects. *Transportation Planning and Technology, 39*(2), 136–161.

Caballer-Tarazona, M., & Vivas-Consuelo, D. A. (2016). A cost and performance comparison of Public Private Partnership and public hospitals in Spain. *Health Economics Review, 6*, 1–7.

Caldwell, N. D., Roehrich, J. K., & Davies, A. C. (2009). Procuring complex performance in construction: London Heathrow Terminal 5 and a Private Finance Initiative Hospital. *Journal of Purchasing and Supply Management, 15*(3), 178–186.

Caldwell, N., Roehrich, J. K., & George, G. (2017). Social value creation and relational coordination in public-private collaborations. *Journal of Management Studies, 54*(6), 906–928.

Carding, N. (2018, October 29). PFI abolished and DHSC to help manage existing deals. *Health Services Journal*. Retrieved from https://www.hsj.co.uk/nick-carding/3007732.bio

De Neufville, R., Lee, Y. S., & Scholtes, S. (2008, March). Using flexibility to improve value-for-money in PFI projects. *MIT Working Paper Series*. Retrieved August 10, 2018, from http://ardent.mit.edu/real_options/Real_opts_papers/Flexibility%20in%20PFI%20projects%20270308.pdf

de Rosa Torner, A. (2012, May 1). *Lessons from Spain: The Alzira model*. The King's Fund International Integrated Care Summit.

Dowdeswell, B. (2009). Rhön-Klinikum Group, Germany. In B. Rechel, J. Erskine, B. Dowdeswell, S. Wright, & M. McKee (Eds.), *Capital investment for health*. Copenhagen, Denmark: European Observatory.

EIB/EPEC. (2010, March). *Capital markets in PPP financing: Where we were and where are we going*? Retrieved August 14, 2018, from http://www.eib.org/attachments/epec/epec_capital_markets _en.pdf

EIB/EPEC. (2018, March). *Market update: Review of the European PPP Market in 2017*. Retrieved September 4, 2018, from http://www.eib.org/en/attachments/epec/epec_market_update_2017_en.pdf

Eurofound/European Foundation for the Improvement of Living and Working Conditions. (2017). *Delivering hospital services: A greater role for the private sector?* Luxembourg: Publications Office of the European Union.

European Court of Auditors. (2018). *Public Private Partnerships in the EU: Widespread shortcomings and limited benefits, Special Report, 09/2018*, 1–79.

Expert Panel on Effective Ways of Investing in Health (EXPH). (2014, February). *Health and economic analysis for an evaluation of the Public-Private Partnerships in Health Care Delivery across Europe*. Retrieved August 28, 2018, from https://ec.europa.eu/health/expert_panel/sites/expertpanel/files/003_assessmentstudyppp_en.pdf

Forrer, J., Kee, J. E., Newcomer, K. E., & Boyer, E. (2010). Public–private partnerships and the public accountability question. *Public Administration Review, 70*, 475–484.

Grimsey, D., & Lewis, M. K. (2005). Are public private partnerships value for money? Evaluating alternative approaches and comparing academic and practitioner views. *Accounting Forum, 29*(4), 345–378.

Guasch, J. L., Benetiz, D., Portabales, I., & Lincoln, F. (2014). The Renegotiation of PPP contracts: An overview of its recent evolution in Latin America. In *International transport forum discussion papers, 2014/18*. Paris, France: OECD Publishing.

Inderst, G. (2013). *Private infrastructure finance and investment in Europe*. EIB Working Papers, 2013/02.

International Monetary Fund – IMF. (2018, June). *Assessing fiscal space: An update and stocktaking*. Policy Paper.

Iossa, E., & Martimort, D. (2008). *The Simple Micro-economics of Public Private Partnerships* (Working Paper No. 08/199). Mimeo Toulouse School of Economics.

Iossa, E., & Martimort, D. (2012). Risk allocation and the costs and benefits of public private partnerships. *RAND Journal of Economics, 43*(3), 442–474.

Iossa, E., & Saussier, S. (2018). Annals of public and cooperative economics. *Annals of Public and Cooperative Economics, 89*, 25–48.

Jayasuriya, D. D. (2016). The rise and fall of the monoline/bond insurers: Icarus of the 21st century. *4th National Business & Management Conference, Ateneo de Davao University*, 22–23 July 2016. Retrieved August 14, 2018, from https://nbmconference.files.wordpress.com/2017/03/648-665.pdf

KAW. (2017, October 26). How public-private partnerships can boost innovation in health care. *Knowledge @ Wharton*. Retrieved from http://knowledge.wharton.upenn.edu/article/public-private-partnership-enabled-innovation-health-care/

McClellan, M. B., & Ginés, E. T. (2015). *Spain: Reinventing chronic care management for the elderly*. Ribera Salud Hospital System, Valencia, Spain; Center for Health Policy at Brookings.

NAO. (2010, June 17). *The performance and management of hospital PFI contracts*. Report by the Comptroller and Auditor General.

NAO. (2018). *HM Treasury PFI and PF2 HC 718 Session 2017–2019 18 January 2018*. https://www.nao.org.uk/wp-content/uploads/2018/01/PFI-and-PF2.pdf (Accessed 22/07/2019).

NHS Confederation. (2012). *The search for low-cost integrated healthcare. The Alzira model—from the region of Valencia*. Brussels: NHS European Office.

Oxfam. (2014). *Dangerous diversion; Will the IFC's flagship health PPP bankrupt Lesotho's Ministry of Health?* (Briefing Note 14, 2014A).

Parrado, S., & Reynaers, A.-M. (2018). Agents never become stewards: Explaining the lack of innovation in public–private partnerships. *International Review of Administrative Science*. https://doi.org/10.1177/0020852318785024

Pollock, A. M., & Price, D. (2013, June). *PFI and the National Health Service in England.* Retrieved August 13, 2018, from https://www.allysonpollock.com/wp-content/uploads/2013/09/AP_2013_Pollock_PFILewisham.pdf

Roehrich, J. K., & Lewis, M. A. (2014). Procuring complex performance: Implications for exchange governance complexity. *International Journal of Operations & Production Management, 32*(2), 221–241.

Roehrich, J. K., Barlow, J., & Wright, S. (2013). Delivering European healthcare infrastructure through public-private partnerships: The theory and practice of contracting and bundling. In T. K. Das (Series Ed.), *Managing public-private strategic alliances, research in strategic alliances* (1st ed.). Charlotte, NC: Information Age Publishing.

Roehrich, J. K., Lewis, M. A., & George, G. (2014). Are public-private partnerships a healthy option? A systematic literature review. *Social Science & Medicine, 113*, 110–119.

Siemiatycki, M., & Farooqi, N. (2012). Value for money and risks in public private partnerships. *Journal of the American Planning Association, 78*(3), 286–299.

Torchia, M., Calabro, A., & Morner, M. (2015). Public-private partnerships in the health care sector: A systematic review of the literature. *Public Management Review, 17*(2), 236–261.

Treasury, H. M. (1998). *Partnerships for prosperity: The Private Finance Initiative*. London, UK: Author.

Vecchi, V., Hellowell, M., & Longo, F. (2010). Are Italian healthcare organizations paying too much for their public-private partnerships? *Public Money & Management, 30*(2), 125–132.

Zheng, J., Roehrich, J. K., & Lewis, M. A. (2008). The dynamics of contractual and relational governance: Evidence from long-term public-private procurement arrangements. *Journal of Purchasing and Supply Management, 14*(1), 43–54.

Chapter 8
Public–Private Partnerships for Fire, Police, and Ambulance Services

Patrick T. I. Lam

Abbreviation

DCLG	Department of communities and local government
EMS	Emergency medical service
ENS	Emergency services network
FRS	Fire and rescue service
GBP	Great Britain Pound
IT	Information technology
Kbs	Kilobytes per second
Kbps	Kilobits per second
NEFRA	North east fire and rescue authorities
PFI	Private finance initiative
PF2	Project finance 2
PPP	Public–private partnership
PSC	Public sector comparator
SAR	Search and rescue
VfM	Value for money

Introduction

As public budgets become increasingly strained in many countries for various reasons, most governments would consider some form of public–private partnerships as an alternative for emergency services. These emergency services include police, fire rescue, and ambulance services. When citizens are in distress and their health or safety is at stake, it is only human nature that they desire immediate assistance to

P. T. I. Lam (✉)
Department of Building and Real Estate, The Hong Kong Polytechnic University, Hung Hom, Hong Kong
e-mail: bsplam@polyu.edu.hk

R. M. Clark, S. Hakim (eds.), *Public Private Partnerships*, Competitive Government: Public Private Partnerships, https://doi.org/10.1007/978-3-030-24600-6_8

relieve them from danger, irrespective of whether such assistance is rendered by public or private means.

In the late 1960s, private guards and investigators numbered hundreds of thousands in the USA, and by 1990, private police grew to account for 75% of all policemen in the country so as to meet the high expectations of business managers (e.g., prevention of department store pilferage), given the tight budgets of public police departments (Savas 2000). Contracting out has always been used to supplement inadequacies in the public disciplinary and emergency-relief forces, in addition to voluntary services offered on humanitarian grounds. However, controversy resulted when governments made it standing policy to outsource the majority of disciplinary and emergency services to the private sector. This chapter will first examine the trend toward outright privatization of such essential services and analyze the pros and cons, before moving on to discuss the more specific forms of public–private partnership which relate to asset provision and management as well as provision of services. Business models of the latter type will be elaborated in relation to contractual mechanisms and risk mitigation measures. Less successful examples from the UK, and to a lesser extent, the USA, are evaluated in order to draw useful lessons, since similar partnerships are being increasingly replicated globally in addition to the two noticeable forerunners of privatization. Despite many similarities in the privatization track, there is one important difference between the USA and the UK which must be remembered as far as emergency services are concerned: in the former, one dials "911" and in the latter, "999."

Revisiting Pros and Cons for Privatizing Emergency Services

It is generally perceived that police, fire protection, rescue, and ambulance services should be provided by public authorities. The possibility of profiteering by private operators, thereby compromising service quality, discourages most privatization initiatives by local authorities, unless outsourcing is accepted as unavoidable. Unlike municipal services such as street cleaning and waste disposal, the efficiency gains, if any, of privatizing emergency services are not easily demonstrated. Worse still, as discussed below, unfortunate incidents of poor performance, which do happen from time to time, by privatized emergency services, create a negative impression in the minds of the people. In reality, however, successful cases abound, especially when the private sector is called in for help during incidents entailing swift responses and provision of special equipment and/or expertise. The dilemma exists in that if the local private sector is not routinely relied upon to provide emergency services on a day-to-day basis, it will not invest in the critical resources necessary to demonstrate an efficiency edge over the public sector. Hence, with few exceptions, success stories usually relate to international firms, which have good geographical spread and hence participation rates enabling efficient deployment, in an emergency setting, of their expertise and resources.

Fortunately, however, paradoxically as it may seem, emergency services may be viewed as manifesting the virtues of heroism and humanitarianism. The common objectives of fighting crime and saving lives are hailed by the general public, and the private sector profit motive may be laid aside, at least temporarily, when tragic events occur or disasters strike. In the latter context, Jerolleman and Kiefer (2015) used the example of Hurricane Katrina as an illustration of the case of the private sector coming to help the government, which by itself was not able to respond effectively to large-scale disasters. The cited benefits of engaging the private sector include supply chain capabilities, quick mobilization, versatile communication knowhow, engineering expertise, and specialized equipment. What is even more pertinent in such cases is the reduced likelihood of political finger pointing, which would worsen the victims' well-being. Disadvantages might include, perhaps, the difficulty for private operators to fulfill their contractual obligations during major disasters, either due to the skyrocketing prices for commodities or resource shortages, or transportation blockages, etc. If privatization was too heavily relied upon by the local authorities, the private sector, too, might not be able to respond. The onus of alleged bribery is always in the mind of officials suspected of favoring particular private companies, as seen in the conviction of a number of officers in New Orleans and Louisiana of the USA after Hurricane Katrina struck. According to Jerolleman and Kiefer (2015), additional costs included the cost of the trials for these officials and the reduction of trust in the government.

In the ordinary course of daily business, however, other advantages of outsourcing may exist for local authorities. For example, it may be used to evade union pressures and lessen the difficulty of dismissing unproductive workers. A reaction may occur, however, against the private sector, when political considerations prevail over the economic and efficiency justifications for outsourcing. A city council in Georgia was forced to scrap a fire protection contract because fire department staff gained community support (Mercer 1983). Economic downturns or a financial crisis (as opposed to natural disasters) may also affect the cash flow of private entities as a systemic risk. What could make matters worse in such situations is that the ownership of private concerns may not be in the hands of entrepreneurs but may be in the hands of financiers. There are many examples of the pros and cons associated with privatizing specific emergency services as discussed in the sections below.

Police Private security patrolling providers used to be hired by commercial concerns, recreational premises, shops, residential compounds, factories, etc. Many universities in the USA employ their own security forces on campuses, having powers similar to those of public police since they obtain certification from the commissioner of public safety. Private patrolling is perceived as being more economical than equivalent public provision, but in a 1981 court case (*Warren vs District of Columbia, 444 A.2d. 1*) it was determined that the public police bore no contractual responsibility to respond to calls for assistance. Controversial issues surrounding private policing include the possible abuse of authority (such as search, arrest, and interrogation) and access to public police records. In the UK, starting with the engagement of an international security firm to undertake backroom roles in

Lincolnshire in 2012, it was claimed that a public saving of GBP 1 billion could be made per annum if all 43 of the country's police forces were privatized (Shaw 2015). Whilst feasibility studies were subsequently made by several local authorities in the East Midlands, distrust was spreading, especially among the Police Federation. Some comments were made that a one-size-fits-all solution should not be applied to varying force structures and systems of accountability, especially if public safety would be compromised. The occasion itself, for which private security is to be provided, also needs to be taken into careful consideration. For example, the Olympics security fiasco (where the shortfall in private security guards led to the call-in of military personnel) in 2012 might reoccur (Beattie 2013). Whilst wide-sweeping reforms such as these are taking place, locally, small teams of retired police officers are protecting homes on a 24-h basis for a unitary charge of GBP 1 per week in Stoke-on-Trent. Apart from patrolling, they help to install burglar alarms to subscribing residences and report suspicious activities to the public police. Resident associations regard this as a deterrent to crime. As a result of this contribution, it was estimated that the local public police would face a budget reduction of around GBP 23 million in 5 years' time (Metro 2015).

Apart from such outright privatization drives, some PPP schemes which have taken place include the funding and operation of custodial facility construction, police stations (some remain unoccupied), and police telecommunications in the form of PFI, which is discussed later in the chapter.

Fire Services In the USA, fire protection service was started by private fire companies. Public service companies took over when the private fire companies did not respond to non-subscribers and fires spread along row houses. Privatization attempts such as those in Rye Brook resulted in nearly US$ 1 million in home losses (Henderson 2014). The approaches attempted with varying degrees of success include subscription-based services and municipal contracts. Much tribute also goes to volunteer firefighting groups and non-profit organizations such as the American Red Cross (for installing smoke detectors in homes). In 1989, an analysis involving the privately operated Scottsdale (Arizona) Fire Department was conducted. In the study a public *vs* private sector fire services comparative performance exercise (in particular cost and quality) was made, with a discussion on how private fire companies achieve cost savings (Guardiano 1992). Such a debate is still going on with increasing pressure being applied to public fire departments to transform themselves (e.g., to embrace emergency medical services rather than to resist) as different forms of privatized fire services (e.g., hybrid) are being considered in the USA (Thompson 2011; Byrne 2015). Despite these impending changes and the reasons for them, tribute needs to be paid to the public firefighters who bravely and selflessly lost their lives in tragedies such as the "9–11" incidents.

Fire services privatization in the UK seems to be taking place at a quicker and more determined pace than in the USA. With seemingly successful privatization models springing up globally, private companies offer competitive annual subscription-based fire protection with innovations. Another "advantage" is that private firefighters normally do not go on strike during busy periods such as Bonfire Nights for fear of losing their customer base (Hayns 2010).

One peculiar feature of firefighting is that not only is the building on fire being worked on by firemen, but its neighbors as well. Hence, subscription-based fire services may be called into question. Those who advocate privatization may like to see the scope being extended to firemen training and the ownership of firefighting appliances. Others support the establishment of independent employee-led mutuals, making firemen shareholders in fire services provision. Firemen do not necessarily welcome this move (e.g., 97% of firemen in Cleveland rejected the proposal of mutualization) (Minister reveals fire service privatization plans 2014). Sometimes, of necessity, firefighters are employed as private specialist crews, e.g., in East Midlands Airport (Hess 2013). In the city of London, the government used the reduced number of fire incidents as a reason for closing down 10 fire stations, making over 500 firemen redundant and cutting 14 fire engines from the budget, saving GBP 45 million in a 2-year period (Gander 2014). Sensational scenes were captured in newspapers of firemen weeping after their last call for service, as they were bid farewell by their supporters and as they departed in civilian clothes.

To take this further, proposals were made by the government to put the control of fire services in the hands of local police and crime commissioners. An "experiment" (dubbed "privatization by the back door" by protesters) put water rescue including diving and confined space operations into a contract package awarded to an international specialist firm for an extended period of 3 years. More recently, privatization is said to be "by attrition" (The London Economic 2017).

Other PPP types of business model have been tried, e.g., PFI fire stations (below) and the building of nine regional control centers, linked by IT, to replace 46 fire and rescue control rooms spread all over the UK. The latter project was terminated, wasting at least GBP 469 million as a result (elaborated below).

Whilst still on the subject of fire protection privatization, the case of Denmark must be mentioned as a successful counter-example. Half of Denmark's 5 million-plus population has been protected from fire by a private (again international) company since 1922 (Guardiano et al. 1992). As part of an insurance business empire, a group of eight integrated-companies provides firefighting, fire loss prevention, road and air rescue and patient transportation, security guard, and surveillance services. Their crew is trained in multiple rescue functions. Danish law requires a public fire chief to be assigned to each private local fire contractor to ensure compliance with all regulations. The other half of the population is served by a municipal firefighting service or a voluntary fire brigade.

Ambulance and Helicopter Rescue Services Much like firefighting, the life-saving functions of ambulance and helicopter services are being privatized. Response time matters a great deal for such services too, hence penalties are usually specified in the contracts for late service. It works well if the cash flow is there, but otherwise things can go wrong.

In New York after the 2008 financial crisis, private equity firms acquired numerous emergency medical service firms (EMS) since cities had problems in paying for public services and banks faced increasingly tight monitoring of their financing activities. The private equity firms aimed at profiteering from emergency calls, but when prices increased and costs had to be cut, patients suffered from increased response times and aggressive billing. Three bankruptcies occurred out of 12 ambulance companies owned by private equity firms, perhaps due to problems predating the acquisitions. Critical medical supplies and even gas to fuel the ambulances ran low. Heart monitors did not function well, as revealed by some past employees (Friese 2016). Then employee wages were delayed. Workers scrambled into the ambulances to rush to get their paychecks cleared, worrying that these would bounce. Subsequent takeovers by other companies enabled new ambulance purchases and salary rises. According to the National Association of State EMS Officials, private companies now provide about 25% of all ambulances in the USA (Ivory et al. 2016).

UK's ambulance services faced a similar set of circumstances. Wages in arrears and liquidations took place among ambulance operators, and their vehicles were seized by bailiffs.

Ambulance workers held demonstrations in Brighton, calling for public re-ownership of patient transport service (Ellis 2016).

To combat great heights and the seas, helicopters are now flown by mountain and sea rescue teams, replacing the British military. A controversial move to privatize this type of service started in 2013, reducing the 12 search-and-rescue (SAR) bases along Britain's coastline to 10. Instead of the fleet of retiring Sea King helicopters, smaller helicopters with shorter ranges were to be used. Concerns were raised as to the possible refusal of private operators to fly in bad weather conditions on rescue missions. Doubts were cast on the future of the 275 military personnel engaged in the rescue service. The Department for Transport assured that the speed of the new helicopters would shorten flight time by 20%. With an incoming Texas-based operator, experienced in flying workers to and from offshore oil rigs (McTague 2013), the commercial contract of 10-year duration, worth GBP 3 billion, starting in 2015, ended the 70-year much valued life-saving service of the Royal Air Force and Navy.

Public–Private Partnerships (PPPs)

Outright privatization or outsourcing, as above, have raised many concerns, especially by public emergency workers, who resent the potential loss of jobs and downgrading of employment conditions. The public fear the possible downgrading of services, particularly when human lives and safety are compromised by profiteering motives. Governments do, however, maintain their roles as the ultimate client, and hence have a monitoring role, when they invite the private sector to contribute its resources and expertise. The efficiency benefits of privatization are supposedly obtainable as long as the private sector is subject to some form of competitive (or even discretionary) selection, and their rights to payment are conditional upon their fulfillment of contractual obligations. The US Department of Transport (2013) defines PPP as "a contractual agreement between a public agency and a private sector entity that allows for greater private sector participation in the delivery and financing of infrastructure projects." The latter typically designs, finances, constructs, and operates a facility or provides a service for a number of years, during which a series of payments are made either by the public agency or by the users to reimburse and reward the private company. Variants exist in any of these components but the essence is that the public agency collaborates with the private company. In the USA, this type of procurement or project delivery approach has been used mainly in the transportation sector since the 1980s due to the shortage of public funds. Since then, the use of PPPs has spread gradually to other infrastructural sectors. In the arena of emergency services, more advances seem to have been made in the UK, where a number of Private Finance Initiatives (PFI—the British name for PPPs whereby the government still acts as the eventual paymaster of public services) thrived. Examples of PFI schemes existing in the respective emergency services, the subjects of this chapter, are described below.

PFI Examples

Police A telecommunication project was launched around the turn of the twenty-first century called the Airwave. A private company was engaged to finance, design, install, and operate the equipment and infrastructure to transmit and receive voice and data signals based on the Terrestrial Trunked Radio (TETRA) system, initially with the police forces throughout the UK. Initial cost was estimated at GBP 1470 million to cover all the emergency services on a national basis. However, the fire services opted for a number of regional telecom systems without the need for encryption and roaming. The Department of Health preferred a national system and rightfully required interoperability with the local police and firefighters. They then participated as potential sharers of the Airwave system, but there were adverse financial repercussions due to various uncertainties. A number of problems occurred because to have only a single bidder created a difficult negotiation position for the responsible government unit. In addition, the varying interests of local police forces and authorities made the procurement process difficult to manage as a national project (NAO 2002). Roll-out of the system commenced in 2001, and as technological development accelerated in the early part of this century, by 2009, there were calls to replace the Airwave system with another Emergency Services Network (ENS) system which allows faster data transfer (7.2 kbs versus 700 kbps available by 2015) (Rockman and Hall 2015). Interoperability between the police, ambulance, and helicopter services would be enhanced with live video images shared between them (McCaskill 2015). This change was estimated at another GBP 1.2 billion to be carried by a British Telecom-owned company (Fiveash 2016). Delays occurred since the police required the "push-to-talk" functionality on smart phones of the traditional walkie talkie, since latency (non-instant connection) was not acceptable for the safety of the force and of the public. It was also important for the police to have preferential use of the bandwidths available vis-à-vis general users during crisis situations. There was also the issue of concurrent use of handheld and vehicle-mounted devices. These take time to resolve even with the 4G technology available to date. Geographical coverage of the ENS also needed improving (70% of the country as in July 2016, compared to Airwave's 97%). As the original Airwave contract came to an end in mid-2016, an extension was sought at a cost of GBP 475 million a year (Fiveash 2016), seemingly expensive due to the mounting maintenance costs of a quickly becoming-obsolete system. By the end of 2016, Airwave was still in use, presumably until the end of 2019, as the ENS is progressively tested to go onstream across the whole of the UK.

Police stations and training centers, as types of built facilities, were also constructed using PFI in the UK. These were procured typically through the granting of 25-year concessions to the private sector to finance, design, build, and maintain the physical buildings. Examples include the Greater Manchester Police Authority stations in Manchester and the Cleveland & Durham Training Center. The former accommodates 3000 police officers from 53 previous stations putting patrol, criminal investigation, and community officers as well as the Crown Prosecution

Service and sun-lit custody suites under one roof, whilst the latter contains classrooms, firearm shooting ranges, an abseil tower, and a skills house.

Fire Services Building of new community stations and improvement of the existing fire stations and associated facilities of the Fire and Rescue Services (FRS) have been procured by PFI in the UK since 1997, through a series of programs including the early Pathfinder scheme. Essentially, like police stations, the award of a contract is undertaken following a rather convoluted process to ensure fair competition and value-for-money (VfM). The process starts with an Expression of Interest, going through a Bidders conference, Prequalification, Submission of Outline Solutions, Submission of Detailed Solutions, Negotiation, Call for Final Tenders, Preferred Bidder Selection, Due Diligence, and then Financial Close. Before proceeding down the PFI route, a Public Sector Comparator (PSC) needs to be evaluated as if it were a traditionally procured project to help assess the value-for-money. For FRS projects, the VfMs were usually a few percentage points above the PSCs at the procurement stage (House of Commons 2011a). Financing was assembled by a private consortium, consisting of equity and loan (the latter often being a higher proportion). Government may partially support the construction cost by granting PFI credits throughout the life time of the projects as an incentive for local authorities to use PFI, but later on these were withdrawn. Design and Build contracts were undertaken by the contractor member in the consortium. Upon completion, a facility management contractor (again part of the consortium) operates (if needed) and maintains the facilities based on an agreed output specification, the satisfactory fulfillment of which (e.g., reaching availability or service standards) would lead to utility payments over the concession period by the local authorities to the consortium, or concession company as it becomes later. The concession company derives an income to compensate its capital and operating expenditures, with a profit element built in.

Upon expiration of the concession period (usually 25 years in the case of FRS), the facilities are to be handed over to the local authorities.

In the following sections, one successful and one unsuccessful example of a PPP are described.

Successful Case Study

An official review of PFI contracts illustrated the achievements made possible by this procurement approach for Fire and Rescue Services. Without using this approach, asset replacement would not otherwise have been possible due to affordability problems. The building quality was high, and use of this approach reduced the uncertainty of facility management costs over a 25-year period (Office of the Deputy Prime Minister 2005).

One such successful series of cases was the Tyne and Wear Fire and Rescue Service, as well as the North East Fire and Rescue Authorities (NEFRA1). The former comprises financing, design, construction, and operation of six community fire stations, one technical services center, and one headquarters complex. The latter is of similar scope to five community fire stations and one headquarters. Capital cost was around GBP30 million. Apart from a slight delay of 2–4 weeks at Tyne and Wear, all construction contracts were completed on time (Office of the Deputy Prime Minister 2005).

The buildings are community orientated and design was focused on the change in emphasis from intervention to prevention (Napper Architects 2006). Facilities include station buildings accommodating fire engines and target response vehicles (with some stations housing an ambulance service), as well as firemen's communal areas (e.g., canteens) and lecture rooms.

Due to the vast volume of documentation involved in the projects, only salient features will be mentioned here. A Project Agreement was executed between the Authorities and the Contractor, dealing with the respective obligations and rights such as site access (alerting any contravention of land title deeds) and guarantees. Although the Contractor submitted detailed proposals to meet the Output Specifications, the Station Requirements prevailed over the Contractor's Proposal in the event of discrepancies arising. Design reviews were stipulated, and no construction could commence before such reviews by the Authorities' Representatives. Procedures were laid down for relief and compensation. An independent certifier was agreed upon to ascertain availability of the allegedly completed facilities. These are all risk mitigation measures.

Other controlling documents include construction contracts, Contractor's parent company guarantee, performance bond, Architect's deed of warranty and consultants' collateral warranties, facility management agreement, interface agreement, land documents, and insurance agreements. As to finance, a loan agreement and shareholders' agreement form the main documents. These are supplemented by a host of corporate and authorities' documents to complete the entire agreement package.

All projects were completed by 2011. Good partnership among the Authorities, the Contractor, and the public ensued. It has been reported that the projects "dramatically improved facilities for the fire and rescue service in the North East", which is facing the challenges of fast and diverse changes—including the management of major emergencies, as well as fostering a safer community in the light of climate change impacts (Liang 2018).

Unsuccessful Case Study

In the UK, emergency calls used to be handled by 46 local FRS control rooms spread over the country, using a range of different technologies. In 2004, a project was launched by the Department of Communities and Local Government (DCLG) to consolidate the control and emergency forces dispatch functions into a network of nine purpose-built regional control centers linked by a national IT system. This project, though not labeled as a PFI, was outsourced to the private sector, and was terminated in December 2010, wasting at least GBP469 million without achieving any of its objectives (House of Commons 2011b).

The saga was highly publicized, and an investigation was conducted by Parliament and the National Audit Office. Major findings are as follows:

1. Despite the novel objective of the project (providing secure, efficient, and resilient modern communication and emergency dispatch facilities to cater for major incidents), preparation works and clarity were lacking.
2. The original estimate was put at GBP120 million in 2004, with completion planned for Oct 2009. A contract was awarded to an air and defense private corporation as late as 2007. By Mar 2011, GBP250 million had been spent but progress was unsatisfactory. Over half of the management team, costing GBP69 million, comprised consultants and temporary contract staff, who were insufficiently clear on the rules and their responsibilities. There was a high turnover of managers and a lack of leadership. Accountability was reportedly loose (House of Commons 2011b).
3. Although the project involved work by local fire brigades, there was no incentive for them to contribute or take ownership of the proposed new system. They were more concerned about the feasibility of fewer staff manning the new system, due to their lack of familiarity with local situations when they answered emergency calls (the new system was said to possess the functionality to identify the callers' addresses). As such, they also worried about liability issues as the frontline fightfighters, since they did not want to be accused of late response to rescue calls. For these reasons, there was no "buy-in" by local fire brigades, who were not obliged to use the new system. In fact, there was minimal engagement with these intended users of the new facilities.

4. The outsourcing contract did not provide interim milestone payments to the contractor, who was paid only when key installation and testing milestones were completed toward the end of the contract period. This belated payment caused tension in the relationships between the contracting parties (NAO 2011).
5. DCLG tried to rectify the situation after June 2010 but with further shortcomings by the contractor, took action to terminate the contract at the end of 2010 to avoid further delay and cost overruns. By that time, the fitting-out works for all nine regional control centers had been completed but were left empty due to the incomplete telecom system, with shell maintenance cost estimated at over GBP400 million by 2035, when their leases expire (NAO 2011).

After contract termination, the task of achieving the original intended objectives remains, whilst trying to attract FRS local units to use the regional centers (London was one). With a further GBP84.8 million spending, DCLG tried to get local FRS collaboration in a new program with defined outputs, clear approval criteria, suitable milestones, and transparent and accountable delivery approaches (House of Commons 2011b).

Summary and Conclusions

It is understandable that many governments try to tap into private sector resources either when the public burden of providing municipal services becomes heavy, or when low efficiency seems to occur. With emergency services, as with all other sectors, varying degrees of success have been seen in the cases presented in this chapter. However, reliability is the central theme that remains at the core of any decision associated with the provision of public emergency services. It stems from the critical need to save human lives, and to reduce casualties in a world full of uncertainties. Because the private sector's motive for contributing toward public services is predominantly and undeniably concerned with profitability, the resource inputs and responsiveness of their commercially oriented actions are often a heated subject of debate from the points of view of sufficiency, efficiency, and efficacy. To ensure success, the public body can only put extra effort into the selection of the contractors, their governance, and their monitoring, once the decision to go down the private path is made. Prior to this, the need to consult and engage the public and concerned stakeholders is greater than ever in the modern social–political atmosphere. More recently, government has been taking a minority equity stake as co-investor (as exemplified by UK's PF2 since the end of the financial crisis in 2012) which seems to better align interests between the contracting parties. Hopefully, no matter who pays, our human nature and values will remain intact. When a survivor is pulled out from tons of debris by emergency workers, claps and applause follow to the satisfaction and joy of all involved.

References

Beattie, J. (2013). *Fire sale: Secret government bid to privatize fire and rescue services revealed.* Mirror.

Byrne, D. (2015). *Privatization is coming to the American Fire Service.* Retrieved October 7, 2017, from www.firehouse.com.

Ellis, M. (2016). *Privatization leaves ambulance crews literally running on empty with vehicles low on fuel and workers left unpaid.* Mirror.

Fiveash, K. (2016). *UK's emergency services shared 4G network plan is very risky, NAO warns.* Retrieved December 20, 2017, from https://arstechnica.com.

Friese, G. (2016). *Private equity struggles to make EMS profitable—is anyone surprised?* New York, NY: New York Times.

Gander, K. (2014). *Firefighters cry as 10 London stations including Clearkenwell close due to cuts.* Independent.

Guardiano, J. R. (1992). *Fire protection privatization: A cost effective approach to public safety.* Retrieved December 23, 2017, from http://reason.org.

Guardiano, J. R., Haarmeyer, D., & Poole, R. W. (1992). *Fire protection privatization: A cost-effective approach to public safety.* Fire Extinction, No. 152, Reason Foundation.

Hayns, N. (2010). *Privatize the fire brigade.* Retrieved October 7, 2017, from https://iea.org.uk/blog/privatise-the-fire-brigade.

Henderson, A. (2014). *6 things that should never be privatized.* Retrieved December 20, 2017, from www.salon.com.

Hess, J. (2013). *MP Chris Leslie warns of fire service privatization.* Retrieved October 7, 2017, from www.bbc.com/news/uk-politics-21524059.

House of Commons. (2011a). *Lessons from PFI and other projects.* London, UK: The Stationery Office.

House of Commons. (2011b). *The failure of the FiReControl project: 50th report of session 2010–12.* London, UK: The Stationery Office.

Ivory, D., Protess, B., & Bennet, K. (2016). *When you dial 911 and wall street answers.* New York, UK: The New York Times.

Jerolleman, A., & Kiefer, J. J. (2015). *The private sector's role in disasters: Leveraging the private sector in emergency management.* New York, UK: CRC Press.

Liang, J. (2018). *John Laing and Shepherd construction are working together to deliver the North East Fire and Rescue Authorities (NEFRA) collaborative PFI project.* Retrieved January 4, 2018, from http://www.laing.com/project_portfolio/6/62/north-east-fire-and-rescue-authorities-nefra.html.

McCaskill, S. (2015). *EE wins £1bn 4G emergency services network contract.* Retrieved December 23, 2017, from http://www.silicon.co.uk.

McTague, T. (2013). *Search and rescue privatization: Government to sell off helicopter service to American firm.* Mirror.

Mercer, J. L. (1983). Growing opportunities in public service contracting. *Harvard Business Review.*

Metro. (2015). *Britain's first private police force charging 1 pound a week to protect local homes.* Retrieved December 20, 2017, from http://metro.co.uk.

Minister Reveals Fire Service Privatization Plans. (2014). Retrieved October 7, 2017, from www.frmjournal.com.

Napper Architects. (2006). *Durham fire service headquarters.* Retrieved May 31, 2018, from https://www.napperarchitects.co.uk/index.php/durham-fire-service-headquarters.

NAO. (2002). *Public private partnerships: Airwave, report by the comptroller and auditor general.* London, UK: National Audit Office.

NAO. (2011). *The failure of the FiReControl project.* London, UK: National Audit Office, The Stationery Office.

Office of the Deputy Prime Minister. (2005). *Report for fire and rescue services directorate: Review of PFI contracts*. London.
Rockman, S., & Hall, K. (2015). *Police radios will be killed soon—yet no one dares say "Huawei"*. Retrieved December 20, 2017, from https://www.theregister.co.uk.
Savas, E. S. (2000). *Privatization and public-private partnerships*. Retrieved December 10, 2017, from www.cesmadrid.es/documentos/Sem200601_MD02_IN.pdf.
Shaw, D. (2015). *Police cuts: G4S says private firms could save forces 1 billion pounds a year*. Retrieved December 15, 2017, from www.bbc.com/news/uk-34864781.
The London Economic. (2017). *Revealed: UK fire brigade slashed by cuts and failed privatization*. Retrieved October 7, 2017, from www.thelondoneconomic.com.
Thompson, J. (2011). Privatization push: Can fire departments survive? *FireRescue News*.
USDOT. (2013). *2013 Status of the Nation's Highways, Bridges, and Transit, Conditions and Performance—Report to Congress*. Washington, DC: United States Department of Transportation.

Chapter 9
How Successful Has the PPP Model Been in Australia?

Tristan P. Gleeson, Darrin Grimsey, and Mervyn K. Lewis

Introduction

This chapter examines the track record of the Public–Private Partnership (PPP) model in Australia from its inception in 2000 to the present. Australia, alongside the UK and Canada, has been at the forefront of PPPs, and there have been around 80 PPP projects over the last 18 years. Nearly every jurisdiction in Australia has developed PPP policies and programmes, and PPPs have been delivered across all infrastructure asset classes for which governments are responsible including roads, water, energy, hospitals, prisons, courts, schools, social housing and convention centres. There has also been a diversity of different models employed ranging from relatively simple property-based projects to more complex whole-of-service PPPs, as well as user pay models (e.g. toll roads), availability-type approaches with a unitary charge levied on the public sector (e.g. public hospitals) and brownfield long-term asset maintenance models (e.g. for outer suburban arterial roads). Some PPP projects are unquestionably mega-projects (US$1 billion or more) of considerable complexity; others are of more modest proportions.

On this basis, there would seem to be considerable enthusiasm for PPPs in Australia. Nevertheless, problems have arisen and it may be timely to take stock, and ask how successful this revolution in infrastructure procurement has been and

T. P. Gleeson (✉)
Infrastructure Advisory, EY, Australia, Abbotsford, VIC, Australia
e-mail: tristan.gleeson@au.ey.com

D. Grimsey
Infrastructure Advisory, EY, Australia, Camberwell, VIC, Australia
e-mail: darrin.grimsey@au.ey.com

M. K. Lewis
FASSA, University of South Australia, Stirling, SA, Australia
e-mail: Mervyn.lewis@unisa.edu.au

R. M. Clark, S. Hakim (eds.), *Public Private Partnerships*, Competitive Government: Public Private Partnerships, https://doi.org/10.1007/978-3-030-24600-6_9

what type of model and size of project and application seems most suited to it? What can a PPP achieve and what can it not do?

Answers can be sought at three levels. First, at a practical level, a PPP potentially can bring private sector efficiency, regulation through competition, economic pricing of services, filter out 'white elephants' and free up public (i.e. 'free') services but cannot bring in additional funding for infrastructure except in the case of 'user pays' tolls and charges, and on this score the Australian experience is very mixed indeed. Hence asset recycling and other funding approaches have been explored, but these are applicable to all infrastructure procurement models. Other than toll roads, nearly all PPP projects in Australia are fully funded by Government out of budget appropriations, i.e. Government pays the quarterly services charge from consolidated revenues (taxes and other incomes), and the service is usually provided free at the point of consumption by the citizen.

A second aspect revolves around the theoretical basis of a PPP. Economic theory suggests that performance differences relative to traditional procurement lie in ownership rights, the bundling of construction and operation into a single contract, and the transfer of risks of design, construction overruns and time delays to the private body. Are these contentions borne out by the Australian experience?

Finally, the third issue examined concerns the criticisms surrounding PPPs. These have been directed at the failed toll roads and the performance of the social infrastructure projects. The latter has concerned late delivery, some cost over runs and poor contractor performance bringing into question whether the PPP is delivering value for money.

With the PPP model being adopted in many countries and currently being investigated in many more, these issues are central to public policy thinking, on which Australia can shed some light.

Australia's Policy Settings

Australia has a long history in using project finance to deliver infrastructure projects. Most infrastructure is carried out by the state governments, and in the early 1990s structured finance was used by some states to fund infrastructure development, although the role of the private sector in service delivery was minimal as was the risk transfer. Effectively, this approach was used by governments 'strapped for cash' as a way of raising funds. The mid 1990s saw large-scale power privatisations in Victoria and then South Australia. Moving onto the new millennium PPPs started to emerge in the public policy environment of most states, most notably in Victoria.

Australia has been one of the leaders of the PPP model and this status has been facilitated by the policy framework. This framework has evolved as the PPP environment has changed. Infrastructure and related services have been procured by governments in each Australian jurisdiction (states and territories) since the 2000s, under separate, but related, policy frameworks.

These developments started in Victoria, the second most populous state, with *Partnerships Victoria* in 2000. The new Bracks Labor Government had won the

1999 election seemingly against the odds against the previous reformist conservative coalition Government led by Jeff Kennett. The Kennett Government had rebuilt the state's finances, having sold off assets such as in electricity, and was embarking on a PPP style programme of its own (though not at that time using the acronym PPP). The incoming Treasurer John Brumby was inspired by the 'Blairite' third way policies delivered in the UK, including the Private Finance Initiative (PFI). He championed the PPP model thereby creating the political leadership needed to convince Labor stakeholders of its veracity. The Bracks Government also learnt from the mistakes of the UK's PFI and set up the PPP policy and guidelines founded on fundamental grounds:

- Value for Money (VfM) was the driver for the policy and the Public Sector Comparator (PSC) test was introduced as its yardstick
- VfM implied a new concept of risk allocation as opposed to the former Kennett Government's hard edge approach to risk transfer. Central to this concept was that risks should be allocated to the party best able to manage them, both in terms of capability and financial capacity
- A Public Interest Test had to be satisfied to demonstrate that the PPP would not negatively impact on equitable access to government services by citizens
- Rules would be developed and administered through a newly formed unit based in the Department of Treasury and Finance (DTF). This was in stark contrast to the early days of the UK's PFI where the mantra had been 'deals not rules', which created inconsistencies in application. Combined with the Blair Government moratorium on capital spending unless projects had been tested against the PFI, an enormous backlog of projects was created, many unsuitable for the model or with teams not equipped to deliver, e.g. some or many hospital PFI in the National Health Service
- The workforce in both the public and private sectors would be trained to give them the skills needed to deliver successful projects. DTF formed a partnership that endures to this day with the University of Melbourne to deliver *Partnerships Victoria* training
- Finally, and recognising that the planning and preparation comes to nothing without action, the Government embarked on pilot projects including the first projects to be completed under *Partnerships Victoria*, Southern Cross Station and Casey Hospital.

Other states and territories quickly followed Victoria's lead and released PPP policies, guidelines and projects of their own. For a while this led to some confusion in the market as governments inevitably took different positions on aspects of the model, most notably in risk allocation. Some of these differences survive today, and even under National guidelines the jurisdictions are able to derogate from risk allocation as each sees fit. Some notable differences that emerged in New South Wales (NSW), the most populous state, are as follows:

- The risk of movements in underlying interest rates was retained. This was in stark contrast to Victoria that had embarked on the practice of transferring this risk, as had the UK Government in its PFI. While hedging products are available in the market, the NSW position may have been more sensible, given the Government's natural hedge with its revenues linked to the economy in much the same way as interest rates move with the economy. Government can also use its borrowing power in the market to issue fixed rate bonds and create its own hedge against interest rate movements, much cheaper than at the individual project level

- Initially, the Carr Labor Government was reluctant to take on its public sector union base and developed a management model whereby the private sector would manage the delivery of services, such as cleaning and porter services in a PPP hospital, and take performance risk on these services, but the staff would remain employees of the government. This led to asymmetric risk transfer where the private sector took on services performance risk but was unable to enforce employment conditions through enterprise bargaining arrangements. In the case of Royal Northshore Hospital, the Government eventually had to take back the responsibility (and risk) of delivering these services. Subsequent conservative Liberal National coalition governments have not been so hamstrung by union relations.

The National PPP Policy Guidelines ('national guidelines') were introduced in November 2008, when they were agreed by the Council of Australian Governments (COAG), comprising the state, territory and federal governments, to provide a consistent approach to PPP procurement and use of best practice approaches across Australia. However, jurisdictional policy takes precedence and the national guidelines allow flexibility for state (and territory) jurisdictions to adopt the national guidelines but implement specific requirements as required. For example, in relation to risk allocation, the national framework provides guidance; however, this does not result in a consistent commercial risk allocation across the jurisdictions. While the jurisdictional policy preference comes first, the national guidelines have still resulted in a more consistent framework, to the benefit of the PPP model.

The national guidelines were updated in 2015, with the changes focusing on assessing modified financing options, optimising risk allocation, improving procurement outcomes and monitoring long-term performance-based contracts. Under the national guidelines there is a requirement to consider PPP delivery as a procurement option for capital expenditure projects over A$50 million.[1]

Australia's PPP Market

All states, plus the Australian Capital Territory (ACT), Northern Territory and the Commonwealth, now have PPP projects underway. Only one jurisdiction, Tasmania, has not delivered a PPP. The 80 PPP projects procured over the past 18 years have a combined capital value of just over A$83 billion.[2]

[1] Department of Infrastructure and Regional Development (2015), National Public Private Partnership Policy Framework, Commonwealth Government of Australia Publication, Canberra.

[2] Inframation Deals, an Acuris Company, https://www.inframationnews.com/deals, accessed 16 April 2018.

Local, state and federal governments have flagged their intention to invest more than A$260 billion[3] over the next 10 years in projects ranging from schools and hospitals, to roads, railways and airports. Not all of this projected spend will be delivered as PPPs. Historically PPPs represent between 10 and 15% of government capital expenditure. That would mean around $40 billion could be delivered in this way and thus the Australian PPP market looks set to continue and possibly even grow.

Victoria and NSW are the major markets for PPP. Victoria currently has 27 PPPs operational and a further three in construction. These projects amount to approximately A$28 billion[4] of capital expenditure. NSW has completed 32 transactions (A$35 billion[5] capex) and currently has five in procurement across a range of sectors including healthcare and education. In Queensland, the state government completed its first PPP, the A$309 million (2006)[6] Southbank TAFE, in 2008. The Brisbane City Council completed the A$2.7 billion (2006)[7] North South Bypass Tunnel project in 2010. The outlook in Queensland should be very good, given the state's economic growth, population increases and the Government's South East Queensland infrastructure plan.

Elsewhere the size of the other jurisdictions in Australia tends to prohibit a pipeline of PPP projects simply because of the lower level of capital expenditure in these jurisdictions. Nevertheless, South Australia, Western Australia, the ACT and the Northern Territory each have adopted PPP policies and delivered at least one project. While the main activity is always going to take place in Victoria, NSW and Queensland, it also seems likely that the smaller jurisdictions will carry on delivering PPPs from time to time. The Commonwealth Department of Defence has also delivered three projects: HQJOC, and single Leap 1 and 2 accommodation for Defence Force personnel.

Australian PPP projects since 2000 have been predominantly in the social and transport sectors. Social projects made up the majority of PPP projects until more recently (2012–2013), when transport projects have been more prominent (Fig. 9.1). The trend has been to use the PPP model for the larger and more complex projects. This is in contrast to other countries such as the UK and Canada which have both

---

[3] The Australian Government has committed over A$75 billion for the next 10 years (Budget 2018–2019), The Victorian Government has committed A$42 billion for the next 4 years (Budget 2018–2019), The NSW Government has committed A$80 billion for the next 4 years (Budget 2017–2018), The Queensland Government has committed A$45 billion for the next 4 years (Budget 2018–2019), The Tasmanian Government has committed A$2 billion for the next 4 years (Budget 2017–2018), The Northern Territory Government has committed A$1.4 billion in 2018–2019 (Budget 2018–2019), The Western Australian Government has committed A$21.5 billion for the next 4 years (Budget 2018–2019) and The Australian Capital Territory Government has committed A$1.7 billion for the next 4 years (Budget 2017–2018).

[4] Inframation Deals, an Acuris Company, https://www.inframationnews.com/deals, accessed 16 April 2018.

[5] Inframation Deals, an Acuris Company, https://www.inframationnews.com/deals, accessed 16 April 2018.

[6] Inframation Deals, an Acuris Company, https://www.inframationnews.com/deals/308731/southbank-tafe-ppp.thtml, accessed 16 April 2018.

[7] Inframation Deals, an Acuris Company, https://www.inframationnews.com/deals/310386/clem-7-tunnel-river-city.thtml, accessed 16 April 2018.

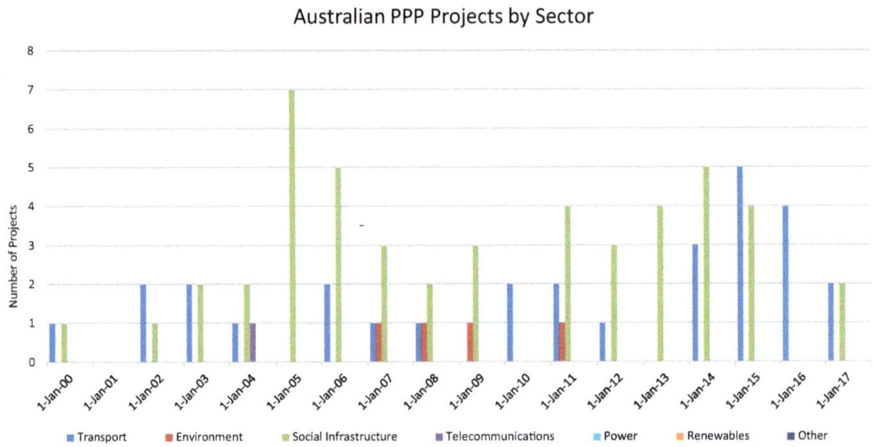

Fig. 9.1 Value of Australian PPP projects. Source: Inframation Deals, an Acuris Company, https://www.inframationnews.com/deals, accessed 16 April 2018

delivered small and large projects. Part of the reason these countries have been able to do this was the early adoption of standard forms of contract that reduced the cost and time of negotiating bespoke contracts. Australia has only just adopted a standard form contract with Victoria releasing its Standard Form Project Deed template in 2017 and using it for the first time to deliver its Western Roads Upgrade PPP (Outer Suburban Arterial Roads (OSARs) PPP) that reached financial close in December 2017.

Before this development, all Australian PPPs developed bespoke contracts drawing on the National guidelines on Commercial Principles. These guidelines were intended to create uniformity across Australia and therefore reduce the cost of bidding and the time taken to negotiate the contracts. As noted, in practice the guidelines permit the jurisdictions to deviate from these principles and did not really achieve the stated aims.

Consequently Australia trended towards using PPPs for the high value and more complex and risky projects. The PPP model is also currently being used or considered to procure a number or large mega transport infrastructure projects (e.g. Melbourne Metro Tunnel, Sydney Metro, Outer Suburban Arterial Roads and North East Link).

The value of PPP projects has increased since the early projects in 2000. While part of this can be explained by escalation and cost increases, Fig. 9.2 shows that the market for PPPs is still strong in Australia and the model is still being used mainly for large (mega) projects.

Most projects have been procured as availability-type PPPs, rather than user charge models, with toll roads accounting for most of the user charge (economic) PPPs between 2000 and 2008. High-profile toll road failures and the Global Financial Crisis (GFC) that constrained capital flows effectively put a stop to

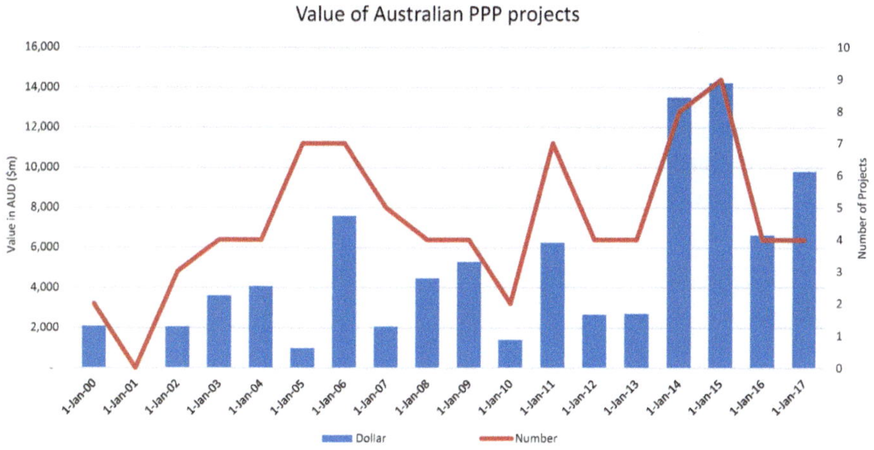

Fig. 9.2 Value of Australian PPP projects (Inframation Deals, an Acuris Company, https://www.inframationnews.com/deals, accessed 16 April 2018)

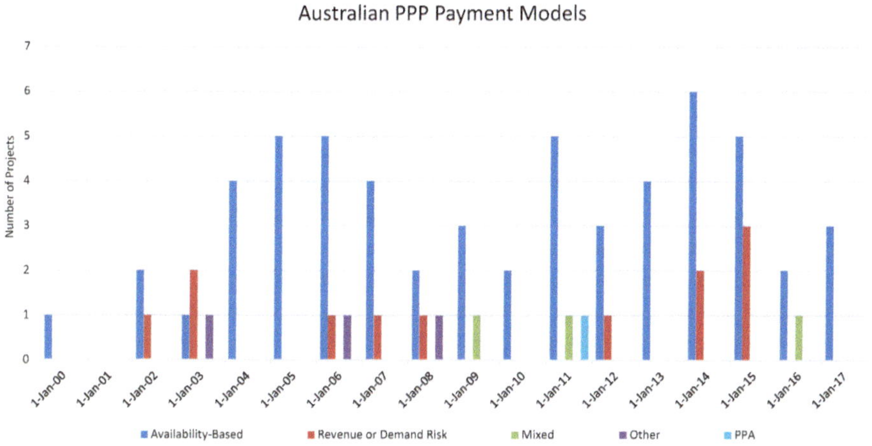

Fig. 9.3 Australian *PPP* payment models. Source: Inframation Deals, an Acuris Company, https://www.inframationnews.com/deals, accessed 16 April 2018

new toll roads in Australia. That persists to date although Victoria and NSW are working on toll road models with more limited risk transfer to the private sector (Fig. 9.3).

Five PPP projects have been cancelled during the period from 2000 to 2017; East West Link, Adelaide Courts Precinct, Adelaide Supreme Court, Airds Bradbury Renewal Project and Cranbourne-Pakenham Rail Corridor. The reasons for these cancellations are varied and in some cases political (i.e. East West Link) but are few in number as compared to the extent of completed projects.

Australian PPP Models

A diversity of different models have been developed to deliver Australian projects. Rather than attempt to cover the large number of asset classes, the following review focuses on hospitals, prisons and roads. These examples illustrate how the different PPP models have been used, and why they were developed.

Hospitals

Hospitals were amongst the first PPP projects delivered in Australia. Casey Hospital was a pilot *Partnerships Victoria* PPP. At only A$118 (2002)[8] million capital cost it is now considered to be on the small side. As a pilot project it was deliberately simple and the scope of services was kept to a minimum.

Very shortly after delivering Casey, Victoria embarked upon the Royal Women's Hospital (A$308 million (2005)[9]) and Royal Children's Hospital (A$894 million (2007)[10]). Together with Casey these three hospitals are very similar in contract structure and risk allocation even though they are different in size, complexity of operations and architectural merit.

All of these projects are what has colloquially been dubbed as 'property-based PPPs'. They are limited in the services to be provided by the private sector. Essentially the private sector is responsible for the delivery of the hospital, the maintenance and life-cycle replacement of the physical assets. The scope of operational service is very limited. All clinical services are delivered by the public sector and ancillary services such as cleaning and portering similarly delivered. The model is akin to a commercial property arrangement whereby a landlord provides the building and the tenant does everything else, ergo property-based PPP.

The A$894 million Royal Children's Hospital PPP involved redevelopment of the original hospital, including construction of a new facility in Parkville, Victoria, Australia. It was considered to be a very large hospital construction but has since been eclipsed by several other hospital PPPs. The redeveloped facility includes 353 beds, of which 85% of the beds are located in single rooms. The winning consortium was responsible for designing, building, financing and maintaining the hospital for a 25-year period. The PPP reached financial close in 2007 and construction was completed in 2011. The PPP model was chosen to deliver the children's hospital to ensure the delivery of outstanding facilities, innovative models of care and

---

[8] Inframation Deals, an Acuris Company, https://www.inframationnews.com/deals/310136/casey-hospital-berwick.thtml, accessed 16 April 2018.

[9] Inframation Deals, an Acuris Company, https://www.inframationnews.com/deals/310096/royal-womens-hospital-redevelopment.thtml, accessed 16 April 2018.

[10] Inframation Deals, an Acuris Company, https://www.inframationnews.com/deals/313401/royal-childrens-hospital-victoria.thtml, accessed 16 April 2018.

leading-edge research and education. At that time, the hospital project was one of the largest undertaken in Australia.[11]

The project objectives for the Royal Children's Hospital were to 'provide a modern hospital facility that supports family-centred care which is culturally and spiritually sensitive, respects the dignity and developmental needs of children of all ages; maximises its design and location in the park to provide a healing environment for patients, families and staff, and the community; is operationally efficient, optimising the use of people and resources; harnesses evidence-based design to create an environment that enhances patient safety and clinical excellence'.[12]

Based on the contractor's (Lend Lease) experience in building hospitals of a similar size in the UK, Lend Lease used prefabrication to expedite the instillation of elements that are usually time consuming and an Occupational Health & Safety risk. Further, the contractor implemented innovative construction techniques that increased production and reduced onsite labour needs. Innovation was also applied to safety, emphasised by the introduction of an innovative approach to ensuring the safety of workers using scaffolds. In addition, the bid also focused on environmental aspects. The Ecologically Sustainable Development (ESD) adopted for the project minimised energy use, reduced greenhouse gas emissions, improved indoor air quality and made a positive impact on water conservation.[13]

Elsewhere, governments explored extending the scope of service delivery. The new Royal Adelaide Hospital (RAH), the flagship of the South Australian (free) public hospital system, most certainly qualifies as a megaproject. At a contracted price of A$1.85 billion, to which has been added A$494 million of state-funded works, making a total cost of A$2.34 billion, it is an expensive building by world standards (Kenny and Booth 2015; Booth and Hutchinson 2016), and the dearest hospital in the world, although this claim needs to be put in perspective. Some iconic and innovative features are relevant to this comparison, namely a vertical integration system, use of robots, a system of 'hot lifts', 40 identical technical suites, 100% single-patient rooms and water harvesting.

The RAH scope of services provided by the private sector are extensive compared to the Victoria hospital PPPs. It includes cleaning, patient support, all portering and logistics (on-time delivery), catering and IT integration of medical and facilities support systems. On the down side, however, actual operation has revealed that the previous Labor government that commissioned the facility and oversaw its construction appears to have made the emergency facilities too small, exacerbated by the fact that demand keeps on expanding when the services are provided free of charge. The

[11] Partnerships Victoria (2008), Partnerships Victoria Project Summary, The new Royal Children's Hospital Project, Melbourne: Department of Treasury and Finance, Victorian Government Publication, Melbourne.

[12] Partnerships Victoria (2008), Partnerships Victoria Project Summary, The new Royal Children's Hospital Project, Melbourne: Department of Treasury and Finance, Victorian Government Publication, Melbourne, 2.

[13] Lend Lease (2013), 2013 Australian Construction Achievement Award, The new Royal Children's Hospital, Melbourne Stage 2: Submission—Technical Paper, Lend Lease Publication, Melbourne.

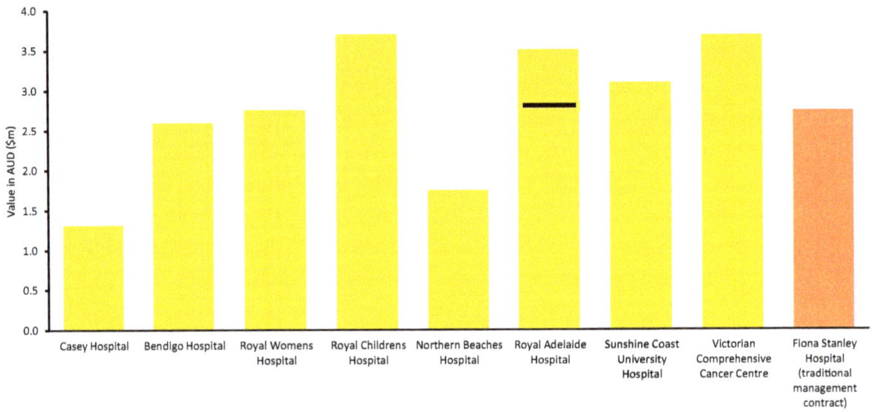

Fig. 9.4 Australian PPP cost per hospital bed. Source: PPP cost per hospital bed has been calculated based on the hospital capex cost sourced from Inframation Deals, an Acuris Company, https://www.inframationnews.com/deals, accessed 16 April 2018, unless stated below. The hospital capex cost has been escalated by the Australian Bureau of Statistics 2018, Consumer Price Index (weighted average for eight capital cities) for Housing, Australia, March 2018, Cat. No. 6401.0, Australian Bureau of Statistics, Canberra, accessed 24 May 2018, to determine the hospital capex cost in 2017 dollars. The capex cost in 2017 dollars has then been divided by the number of hospital beds to determine the cost per hospital bed. The Royal Adelaide Hospital cost per hospital bed has been calculated based on the hospital capex cost sourced from Kenny and Booth (2015) and Booth and Hutchinson (2016) (A$2.34 billion, including contracted price of A$1.85 billion (below the black line) and the state-funded works A$494 million). The Fiona Stanley cost per hospital bed has been calculated based on the hospital capex cost sourced from Western Australian State Budget 2015–16 Paper. This hospital was procured under a traditional management contracting model. Note, the Royal Adelaide Hospital bar graph separates (black line) the cost per hospital bed as a result of the contracted price of A$1.85 billion (below the black line) and the state-funded works A$494 million (above the black line)

result is extensive over-crowding of emergency services, with hospital staff even treating patients in ambulances ramped outside. Also, having only single rooms, and absence of wards, is said to create pressures to release some patients early.

Articles in the leading national conservative-leaning newspaper, *The Australian*, have had a field day pointing out that the new hospital is the world's seventh most expensive building ever (Owen 2018). However, instead of total cost, the cost per hospital bed is a more useful point of comparison. Figure 9.4 provides this analysis and shows that the Royal Adelaide Hospital has amongst the highest cost of the group, but it is below both Royal Children's Hospital and Victorian Comprehensive Cancer Centre in Victoria. Further, the State Works component that is the costs above the black line cover specific site costs. The new hospital is built on former rail yards that were heavily contaminated, and these are environmental clean-up costs that were a liability to the state in any event, regardless of whether it chose to build a hospital on the site. Disregarding these costs and the RAH is comparable, and in fact cheaper, than its contemporaries, noting although that these may also include idiosyncratic site costs.

While the RAH is still at a higher cost per bed than many hospitals in this group, it is a more complex quaternary hospital (some of the others are tertiary level) and the state nominated disaster hospital and cancer centre. It also has some unique features noted above including 100% single occupancy and robotic logistics. Both of these aspects raise the capital costs and also have the potential to improve health outcomes and reduce the costs of running the facility (logistics).

It must be said that hospitals are extraordinarily costly facilities to run, and the annual clinical costs (doctors, nurses and other healthcare professional) vastly outweigh the capital costs. Caution should be exercised in analysing capital costs as between different hospitals when the overall impact on the costs of delivering the services (capital and recurrent), and the savings that may be possible from increased capital investment remain hidden from view. Increased upfront capital cost often generates lower whole-of-life facilities costs and enhanced throughput. This is where the PPP model creates the incentives on the private sector under competition to optimise costs over the life of the infrastructure, and why focusing on one category of cost alone (that is capital) is not an embracing or complete measure of value for money. The economics of healthcare are complicated and extend far beyond the capital cost. For example RAH's single rooms are designed to improve infection control and also provide accommodation for a family member or 'loved one' to stay over and enhance the quality of care. It is hoped that these factors reduce the length of stay and thereby increase throughput, i.e. productivity of the facility and thereby reduce overall healthcare costs. RAH is also the centre piece of a bigger health strategy for South Australia designed to reign in spiralling health costs caused by demographic changes, such as ageing and increased prevalence of obesity. Judging the RAH's performance and value on capital cost alone is far too narrow a measure and unrepresentative of its true economic value, and on that basis it is far too early to tell whether it will deliver on its promises.

By the same token, nevertheless, in this case there may be an element of 'gold-plating' involved in pioneering robotics and eschewing wards completely for hotel-type individual rooms. Notwithstanding, it is important to highlight that these are the Government's specification of the facility. The PPP model did not cause the hospital to be as expensive as it was and in fact it compares quite well against contemporary facilities in Australia, which is generally a high cost construction setting as a result of its industrial relations environment. These costs are largely a function of the Government's specification (as the healthcare operator), which would have also happened under traditional procurement and may well have been more, given the lesser risk transfer. Even so, the delivery of the project was delayed and there have been widely reported problems with the performance of the private sector service providers, which is impacting on patients and understandably raising community concerns over the project. Time will tell whether teething problems can be overcome and how well the new hospital works over time.

Our final hospital considered is NSW's Northern Beaches Hospital. This project harks back to the 1990s when some governments in Australia engaged the private sector to deliver full clinical services to publicly funded patients, e.g. Joondalup in WA, Latrobe Valley in Victoria and Orange in NSW. Northern Beaches includes an integrated private hospital sitting alongside the public facility (i.e. a co-location model). The operator Healthscope is able to provide choice to incoming patients with private health insurance at the point of entry. The government saw this as an opportunity to encourage more patients to use private health cover and thereby reduce the government funding of healthcare in the region where a large proportion of the population hold private cover.

The NSW State Government awarded the contract to design, build, finance, operate and maintain the Northern Beaches Hospital in 2014. The nine-storey hospital contains 488 beds and a helipad. The hospital services to be provided to private patients over a 20-year period include an emergency department, operating theatres and surgical suites, state-of-the-art intensive care and critical care units and an inpatient mental health facility.

Prisons

There is a long history of privately run prisons in Australia predating the PPP policy surge of the 2000s. Victoria had three privately run facilities developed in the 1990s: Fulham, Port Phillip, and the Women's Prison. The State stepped in on the Women's Prison after failures by the private sector operator Custodial Services of Australia. The Victorian Auditor-General's Office noted in its audit that the prison was returned to State control in 2000 as a result of concerns with the prison's management.[14]

Privately financed facilities are also located in NSW, WA and the NT. The New Grafton Correctional Centre reached financial close in 2017 and is for the design, delivery, operations, maintenance and financing of a 1700-bed facility that will service northern NSW, over a 20-year period. The Eastern Goldfields Regional Prison PPP delivered a 350-bed mixed security men's and women's prison, along with a 28-year concession for its operation and maintenance in Western Australia. The NT government procured the Darwin Correctional Precinct through the PPP model, delivering an 800-bed correctional centre, a 30-bed secure mental health and behavioural management facility and a 48-bed centre for community offenders.

Prisons are another sector where the PPP model has taken many forms. Before 2000 most privately run prisons were delivered by the DCMF model in the UK and Australia. America has such a large prison population that private prisons operators invested in new prisons and take full volume risk, relying on 'build it and they will come', which is a commercial response to the very high rates of incarceration seen across the USA. That is not a feature of the DCMF model where the private operator only takes the risk on availability of prison spaces and the performance of the delivery of services that includes custodial and sometimes the delivery of rehabilitation services as well.

[14] Victorian Auditor-General's Office (2018), Safety and Cost Effectiveness of Private Prisons, Independent Assurance Report to Parliament, Victorian Government Printer, Melbourne.

The French mixed management model provides a more limited role for private sector involvement than the DCMF model. Under the mixed management model, the private sector designs, constructs and finances the prisons and manages the provision of a limited range of prison services, but excluding prison operations and custodial services.

This model formed the precedent for the serviced infrastructure model developed under the *Partnerships Victoria* programme in 2001 when, because of dissatisfaction with the operation of private prisons under the previous government, it was decided that all new prisons in Victoria were to be managed and operated by public sector resources. Accordingly, prison services were divided into three categories:

- Core services under public sector control and excluded from the contract, that is, billets (cleaning, laundry, catering), industries and custodial operations.
- Services provided by a private sector partner (infrastructure plus ancillary services), that is, accommodation, security systems, estate management, transport and information systems management.
- Those services with the potential for private sector provision but excluded from the contract at the outset, namely medical, education, works and vocational training.

There are obvious differences between the models in terms of the range of services covered. Another important difference between the serviced infrastructure and the DCMF models relates to the encompassing framework, specifically the extent of the partnering arrangements. Under the DCMF model the contract structure has tended to be rigid and there is therefore limited flexibility for the government to vary its requirements. Under the partnership framework, the serviced infrastructure model can be structured so that flexibility is an inherent feature of the contractual arrangements. For example, contractual mechanisms could provide for upside benefit-sharing where the introduction of new technology results in a reduction in cost of either core services (custodial) or those services provided under the PPP arrangements. There could also be scope for risk-sharing in relation to prison capacity and prisoner mix within defined boundaries. The DCMF or BOOT-type approach can often be more contractual than cooperative.

In the early 2000s the State Labor Government under Premier Steve Bracks took the view that custodial services were core services and developed three PPP prisons under a design, construct, maintain, finance (DCMF) model where the state operates the prisons. These prisons are Metropolitan Remand Centre, Marngoneet Correctional Centre and Hopkins Correctional centre. As an aside, Hopkins is an expansion of the existing Ararat Prison and experienced significant delivery issues that necessitated commercial renegotiations with the project company delivering the project.

In the interim there was a single-term Liberal–National Coalition Government that took the view that custodial services are non-core, and it embarked on the Ravenhall Prison PPP that includes full custodial services in the scope, contracted with GEO Consortium to design, build, finance, operate and maintain a new men's medium-security prison located in Melbourne's west. The incoming Andrews Labor

Government took over this project and has not sought to amend its scope. This chronology of prison PPPs in Victoria serves to illustrate that the question of what service is core and what is non-core is not easily answered and more often than not comes down to a preference of the government of the day.

With Ravenhall, the then State Government of Victoria considered a range of PPP procurement models and determined that a 'full service', which bundled design and construction facilities management, life-cycle responsibility, support services and custodial services in a single PPP contract would best meet the project objectives. The key strengths of the full service model that best met the project objectives were the timeliness and certainty of operational commencement, the greatest opportunity to deliver better operational and service solutions, an optimal risk transfer and competitive bid process. The prison is now operational having been delivered on time and to at the contracted price. It won the Infrastructure Partnerships Australia 2018 project of the year award.

Ravenhall was built to accommodate 1000 prisoners, with a capacity for 1300 in the future. The capex cost of the project was A$648 million (2014).[15] The whole-of-life costs was A$2.5 billion (2014, NPC),[16] which included the design and construction costs, operating costs, maintenance and facilities management over 25 years. A focus of the PPP was providing programmes and services designed to reduce reoffending, such as the establishment of a dedicated forensic mental health (FMH) unit. The prison requires the operator to achieve a 12% reduction in reoffending rates, compared to the Victorian average for public sector prisons. In this respect it can be seen as a benchmark PPP.

Roads

Toll roads appeared in Australia in the 1990s and 2000s. They were mainly used in Victoria (2 toll roads), NSW (6 toll roads) and Queensland (3 toll roads).

The CityLink PPP project was for the build, own, operate and transfer of a toll road in Melbourne, Australia. The capex cost of the project was A$1.9 billion (1996) making it a mega project.[17] The project was an economic PPP with toll revenue funding the project and reached financial close in 1996. CityLink opened to traffic at the end of 2000 and the original concession was for a 34-year period. The concession has subsequently been extended to incorporate a number of road upgrades. The toll road links Melbourne's east, west and north and is 22 kilometres in length.

---

[15] Inframation Deals, an Acuris Company, https://www.inframationnews.com/deals/1036873/ravenhall-prison-ppp.thtml, accessed 16 April 2018.

[16] Partnerships Victoria (2015), Partnerships Victoria Project Summary, Ravenhall Prison Project, Melbourne: Department of Treasury and Finance, Victorian Government Publication, Melbourne.

[17] Inframation Deals, an Acuris Company, https://www.inframationnews.com/deals/914053/citylink-melbourne.thtml, accessed 16 April 2018.

Electronic toll collection systems are now operating in many locations around the world, but in fact were pioneered for Melbourne CityLink PPP. In some automated tolling systems, the cars need to pass through toll plazas, slowing down to 50 kph as they pass through the gates or remain in dedicated lanes (for example, California's State Route 91, SR 91). This was impracticable in the CityLink application, where cars could move between lanes on the freeway system. The problem was thus one of devising a system to 'capture' for tolling purposes cars travelling at 110 kph (or more) and switching from one lane to another and from one route to another at high speeds.

In the event, a system that would do the job, Transroute, was designed by French engineers. The result is a tolling system for the project that is completely automated, so there is no need for motorists to slow down when approaching tolling plazas or to stay in one lane. A transponder in the car registers even high-speed lane changes at tolling points, and payment is transferred from the road user's account by direct debit, according to 'user pays' principles. Overall, the 22 km project includes a 5-km-long tunnel and six toll zones, using automated electronic toll collection.

Three major technologies are employed by CityLink: automatic vehicle identification, automatic vehicle classification and video enforcement. Electronic transactions take place between nodes—transponders[18] and collection points—both tied back to the rest of the financial network. Use of electronic toll collection increases lane or motorway capacity, thereby reducing toll processing time and queue lengths at toll booths. Opening prepayment accounts eliminates the need for patrons to be concerned with having cash ready for each toll booth. Having dedicated electronic collection lanes or whole roads operating on this basis means that transponder-equipped vehicles have no need to slow down or stop when paying tolls, which can reduce noise pollution, air pollution and fuel consumption (Grimsey and Lewis 2004).

Clarke and Hawkins (2006) criticised Melbourne CityLink and other urban road networks because the tolls are for cost recovery and are not efficiency-based, such as being higher at peak periods to reflect higher congestion costs. Nevertheless, CityLink has been acknowledged as a major infrastructure project that helped transform Melbourne and was a benchmark transport PPP project in Australia. The engineering and technical challenges were significant, both during and after the construction period (Odgers 2002). Construction commenced in 1996 and was completed in 2000. Traffic has exceeded forecasts and there have been additional road lane and infrastructure upgrades, which has resulted in extensions to the original concession period.

[18] A transponder is a small battery-powered radio device which is mounted inside the vehicle on the windshield and identifies the customer's prepaid toll account. When travelling through the toll zone, the transponder is read by an overhead antenna, and the posted toll amount is automatically deducted from the customer's account. The transponder can be easily moved from one vehicle to another. In addition, it is possible to add other vehicles to the account even if not equipped with transponders, so long as the licence number is advised to the relevant operator.

Table 9.1 Some failed PPP road infrastructure projects in Australia, 2005–2013

Asset	Daily forecast	Daily actual	Opened	Collapsed
Cross City Tunnel, Sydney	95,000	30,000	2005	2007
Lane Cove Tunnel, Sydney	100,000	55,000	2007	2010
East Link, Melbourne	258,000	134,000	2008	2011
Clem7, Brisbane	60,000	21,000	2010	2011
Airport Link, Brisbane	130,000	77,000	2012	2013

Grimsey and Lewis (2017)

The same cannot be said for other Australian toll roads. In Australia, PPP projects that have collapsed in recent years are the Cross City Tunnel, Sydney (2007), Lane Cove, Sydney (2010), Airport Link, Brisbane (2013), Clem 7 Tunnel, Brisbane (2011), and East Link, Melbourne (2011) (see Table 9.1). In all cases, the proximate cause was gross overestimates of traffic volumes. To some degree this was a result of drivers' reluctance to pay the tolls (even in some cases when lowered to zero to get people to 'try' the tunnel), although the ready availability of finance in the heady pre-crisis years also played its role in allowing projects to go ahead. As with the US subprime crisis, too much money sloshing around the world led to lax lending decisions and overzealous investors. As a result, hundreds of millions of dollars of private finance have been squandered when the project companies that defaulted were later sold at fire-sale prices.

The Cross City Tunnel is one of the failed toll roads. It runs under Sydney's CBD, connecting the eastern side to the western side. The capex cost of the project was A$680 million (2002).[19] The road reached financial close in 2002 and opened to traffic in 2005 after being delivered on-time and on-budget. The toll road consists of two (east and west) 2.1 kilometre tunnels, along with a third service tunnel, and was procured under a 33-year concession period. The objective of the PPP was to reduce traffic congestion, improve environmental amenity in Sydney's CBD and improve east to west traffic flows in the CBD. However, the PPP has been acknowledged as a failure by local media and commentators, largely due to improper allocation of risk, inaccurate traffic forecasting and negative consumer response to changed traffic conditions and road closures which were perceived by the public as attempts to force traffic onto the toll road. The operating company went into receivership less than 2 years after commencing operations (Phibbs 2007).

In the upshot, the failure of the PPP resulted in public anger and questioning of the PPP model for this project. However, the road has since been bought by Transurban Group and traffic revenues have remained stable.

It needs to be emphasised that public procurement is not a one-off or one-shot 'game' in game-theoretic terms, but a repeated one (De Clerk 2015). Losses must be recovered if the contractors are to stay in business, and future bidding behaviour will not remain invariant in response to such experience. The upshot is that it is now virtually impossible to get a privately funded PPP toll road project off the ground in Australia.

[19] The Audit Office of New South Wales (2006), Auditor-General's Report Performance Audit, The Cross City Tunnel Project, New South Wales Government Publication, Sydney.

Nor does it help when the New South Wales premier at the time, Bob Carr (later to become Australia's foreign minister from March 2012 to September 2013), when referring to the Cross City Tunnel, triumphantly pointed out:

> They owned the road, they carried the risk if they miscalculated ... the losses were shifted to the private operators, but that's what the auditor-general told us ought to happen with these public–private partnerships. We settled on a model so perfect in this respect that the entire cost was borne by private-sector bidders – that's required some modification, but there is nothing dishonest about the model in terms of defending the public interest.

Further,

> We got a new toad that threaded traffic under the city, taking thousands of cars a day off the city streets, and the state did not have to put a dollar into it, not a dollar.

To add salt to the wounds, he is reported as making the observation that, during the decade his government was in office, 'the state gained $6 billion in new roads, but the public only contributed $800 million' (Loussikian 2016).

As one commentator put it, 'governments across Australia cruelled the [PPP] market' (Gelber 2014, p. 26). Yet, private sector investors in these projects were hardly blameless. Intense competition for projects, fuelled by easy credit, appeared to alter the nature of the forecasting of demand from hard independent estimates of traffic volumes to calculations of what demand would need to be to make the project work.

Whoever is to blame, the result is the current impasse. Governments want to institute greenfield transport projects, but private firms have backed away from taking on the inherent risks. On this interpretation, it would seem that if governments are to implement infrastructure projects, they have themselves to take on the role of developer, most certainly bearing risk on the revenue side, and perhaps partially as well on the construction side. At the same time, there seems to be no shortage of investors willing to buy 'mature' infrastructure assets. This juxtaposition underpins the idea of 'asset recycling'.

Asset (or capital) recycling enables governments to fund higher-risk projects by selling off assets once they have reached the stage at which risks are lower (Ergas 2014). In a way, the build-own-operate-transfer (BOOT) model PPP is turned on its head. Now it is the government that has to build, own and operate infrastructure before transferring it to the private sector (Gelber 2014). A relatively common method is the government buys, tolls then sells (GBTS) model. Private sector contractors are engaged to design, build and maintain a road, and to install tolling equipment, under public funded contracts. Government retains the tolls collected during the ramp-up period as the project builds some actual traffic history. Once actual traffic levels have been established, the public sector sells the right to levy and collect future tolls to the private sector. With this approach, the government bears traffic risk during the ramp-up period, and the private sector bears traffic risk after ramp-up, when the risk is considerably reduced.

Another way around the impasses is to abandon tolls, as was the case with Victoria's A$873 million Peninsula Link. Peninsula Link is a 27-km four-lane freeway connecting the EastLink freeway and Mornington Peninsula Freeway in Melbourne. The link was not a toll road and was delivered as an availability-type

PPP. Financial close was achieved in 2010 for the design, build, finance, operate and maintenance of the link.

More recently the availability-based PPP has been used on the Western Roads Upgrade implemented to provide a 'whole-of-life' approach to arterial road construction and maintenance under a PPP model. The project represented a significant investment to Melbourne's arterial road network and included the construction of eight capital projects, rehabilitation of other arterial roads (within the maintenance area) and maintenance of approximately 700 lane kilometres of arterial roads and structures. The whole-of-life cost for the project was A$1.8 billion (2017).

Melbourne has experienced high population growth for over a decade and is expected to overtake Sydney in size by 2050. Arterial roads are important connections to efficiently transport people and goods around the city and preserve the amenity and liveability of the suburbs. In light of this situation, the objective of the project was to bring forward a chain of planned upgrades, duplications and new freeway interchanges in Melbourne's west. The Western Roads Upgrade was the first PPP of its kind in Australia. The procurement approach encouraged the private sector to develop innovative design, construction and asset maintenance solutions over the long term, with the objective of delivering better service to the users of the state's arterial road network (within the maintenance area). Construction has commenced and is scheduled to be completed in 2020.

There is also a third way around the impasse left in the wake of the PPP road failures. Obviously, when tolls are levied, those who use the infrastructure services pay for the cost of the provision. With an availability-based system, the cost of provision is borne by the public sector, and the contractor is penalised or charged if facilities are not available on time to the required specified quality standard. Another approach has been developed to augment either user pays or procurer pays. Those who gain from the arrival of infrastructure provided, e.g. those whose houses rise in value, or whose businesses are made more profitable by, say, a new freeway or rail line, contribute to the government's cost of provision via a betterment levy or tax increment financing or infrastructure fund or property development fund. 'Value capture', as it is called, is discussed more fully, along with examples from the UK (Crossrail) and Australia (Gold Coast Rapid Transit light rail), in Grimsey and Lewis (2017, pp. 280–288).

Lessons Learned

There are a number of lessons learned from the Australian experience of PPPs. Successful implementation of a PPP programme relies on five fundamental things:

1. Political support is paramount and must come from the highest positions in government and preferably the Premier and Treasurer
2. PPPs' core purpose is to deliver value for money to the tax payer and this must be evaluated rigorously and include risk pricing such that risk is allocated to the party best able to manage it

3. A core policy statement needs to be supported by clear guidelines that articulate the rules of the game, so to speak, such that both public and private sector participants understand both the government's objectives and also the process
4. Training the workforce is essential and this applies equally to the private sector as it does to the public sector
5. Having a pipeline of projects to support investment in the market place.

If any one of these fundamentals is missing, then it is unlikely that a successful PPP programme will result.

The Australian experience has also shown that not all projects are suited to the PPP model. In general PPPs are best suited to projects that:

- are 'greenfield' projects that involve the construction and operation of new infrastructure rather than the refurbishment of existing assets or so-called 'brownfield' projects;
- do not contain excessive or extreme risk that may translate into uncertainty and therefore cannot be actively managed or competitively priced by the private sector;
- are well-specified in terms of outputs and outcomes that government is seeking to achieve and where there is an existence of reliable data and documentation to support the statement of requirements and risk transfer.

In other words PPPs are most successful where the government has been able to put in a great deal of preparatory work to establish its requirements, understand and document the risks and carefully prepare tender documentation. It is not suited to situations where there are many uncertainties and time is of the essence to design and deliver a capital asset solution to a problem. Ironically, the public sector often thinks that projects with these very characteristics should be delivered as PPPs perhaps in the misguided belief that it is better to transfer large risks and uncertainties to the private sector. The Australian experience in trying to transfer road usage risk under a PPP model is a case in point that illustrates how misplaced this belief can be.

In the early 2000s the debate in Australia centred on whether PPPs or Alliance-based contracts were superior and should be championed for infrastructure delivery. Of course this is a spurious comparison as PPPs are at one end risk transfer and Alliances at the other end where the project sponsor retains most risk, like comparing apples with oranges. This distinction is now clearly understood and rarely in Australia are procurement models still compared in this way. A procurement options approach involves trading off one set of features of a contractual arrangement against those of others in order to choose the contract that best suits the infrastructure services being considered for procurement. Claiming that alliances are superior to PPPs or vice versa clearly misses the point that it is the characteristics of the project that should dictate the procurement model most suited and likely to deliver value for money. One contribution to this debate has been to develop a systematic approach to procurement options analysis based on a decision-making framework to select the most appropriate procurement model and financing mode for a particular project (Grimsey and Lewis 2017).

Building on the lessons outlined above there are a couple of more nuanced points to take away from the Australian experience in relation to capability and rules.

A skilled workforce is not only required to originate and transact on a PPP, it is also a pre-requisite for managing the contract. All too often this is neglected during procurement where the skills are largely focused on winning and negotiating outcomes under competition. The skills needed on both sides to successfully transact are very different to the skills needed to develop a long-term relationship. Contract management is often neglected during the transaction process and relegated to the drafting of complex obligations and processes within the contract. Governments should draw on contract management capability at tender stage and to better consider and specify how it is going to manage the relationship. Bidders also tend to underestimate the size of the task to manage the delivery of the PPP and downplay/underrate these costs at the SPV level. This combination often leads to adversarial relationships at the operating stage of projects.

Our second lesson concerns the rules of the game. Initially Australia adopted a 'bespoke' commercial principles approach that eschewed developing standard form contracts for PPPs. This was in stark contrast to the UK and Canada that both developed standard contracts. Australian PPPs have been criticised for how costly they are to set up and for the private sector to bid on. They also tended to be led by legal considerations when framing the contract. This resulted in the model tending to be used for the most complex and large projects that could afford the investment costs. The legalistic approach created bespoke contracts that are often difficult to navigate and reinvented the wheel on many issues, albeit in slightly different ways and risk allocations.

In contrast the Canadian PPP model adopted standard risk allocations and in some cases standard specifications (e.g. in hospitals) that, while perhaps compromising on idiosyncratic features of projects, has created economies of scale. This enabled the model to be used cost effectively on smaller and more standard projects. It also relegated the legal side to a secondary role and allowed the parties to focus more attention on technical solution, i.e. design. Given that PPPs are all about service delivery, to us this seems to be a much more satisfactory place to focus.

The state of Victoria recently published its standard form PPP contract. The Western Roads PPP is the first Partnerships Victoria project to use the standard form. This marks a significant shift in Australian PPP policy. It remains to be seen if this change will facilitate greater uptake of PPPs and for smaller and less complex projects. But given the Canadian experience this result does seem likely, and it is a welcome development that should reduce bid costs on both sides.

Are Australian PPPS Value for Money?

Achieving value for money (VfM) is the stated prime objective for every government in Australia that has adopted a PPP policy and actively pursued projects. From the outset, the PPP model faced a significant challenge, and had a major hurdle to overcome, in that the public sector can (in most cases) borrow more cheaply from capital markets than can the private sector. This comparison is spurious, given that the PPP model internalises risk pricing under a project finance approach, whereas traditional procurement relying on government borrowing makes use of the government balance sheet and is not a true price for the risk involved to the community (in particular, taxpayers who bear a contingent liability for which they are not remunerated) when investing in the infrastructure project (Grimsey and Lewis 2017, pp. 138–143).

Nevertheless, public perceptions that the PPP model may be an expensive approach forced Australian governments to answer the question on value by comparison with traditional procurement under the Public Sector Comparator (PSC). No other procurement model has had to pass a quantitative test of comparison with alternative models.

The VfM test against the PSC became the benchmark against which projects must be assessed in order to proceed as a PPP. But gradually governments realised that the test is at best hypothetical, and in fact most of the time unreliable. There are many reasons why this is the case and as demonstrated in the paper 'Are Public Private Partnerships Value for Money? Evaluating Alternative Approaches and Comparing Academic and Practitioner Views' (Grimsey and Lewis 2005). In 2013 Victoria recognised the essence of this position and moved away from the PSC as a definitive ('must pass') test of value.

While doing so, it is still recognised that the PSC is valuable as a tool for the public sector to understand its project and to budget accordingly. However, it is less useful as a test of value, which still leaves the vexed question as to how the public sector should decide whether a PPP is the best way to deliver a project. Our view is that this question should be approached by analysing the characteristics of the project including its risk and potential to deliver value as a PPP, along with the extent of the protections built into the contractual framework (such as no commitment to payment until the project is shown to be operable).

Nevertheless, the question as to whether the PPP model is in fact delivering value remains an open one. Unfortunately, retrospective evaluation of projects is not rigorously undertaken by government procuring authorities. On this point, the academic literature does little better. It has tended to focus on comparative studies on the performance of the construction stage of the PPP as compared to other traditional models. These studies are limited by the commercial-in-confidence nature of government capital infrastructure procurement. Also, it is difficult to determine whether it is the model that has failed to deliver or whether it is simply caused by people failing in execution, irrespective of the model.

In 2008, the University of Melbourne published a benchmark study of Australian PPP projects against a representative sample of traditionally procured infrastructure projects on time and cost performance indicators (Duffield et al. 2008). The study sampled 67 projects in social infrastructure, transport, and sustainability and information technology. The research analysed statistically and compared the project data set of traditional and PPP projects. Time and cost parameters were normalised such that projects of differing contractual value and project duration could be benchmarked against each other. Over all time periods considered in this study, PPPs delivered projects for a price that is far closer to the expected cost than had the project been procured in the traditional manner. PPP contracts had an average cost escalation of 4.3% post-contract execution, compared to traditional projects that had an average cost escalation of 18.0% for the same period. During the period prior to project execution, PPP projects were frequently delayed (average 14.8%). However, once PPP projects reached financial close there was only, on average, a further 2.6% delay to these projects. This result suggests that PPP contracts take some time to develop prior to release to market, but changes made after financial close are minimal. Predictions of the duration to reach commissioning are optimistic for traditional projects, with estimates of duration being on average 18.1% early at budget and 19.4% early at contract execution. An average delay of 25.9% occurs during the construction phase of traditional contracts when compared to the actual final outcome.

These findings appear to support the view that PPPs deliver on time and cost more consistently than traditional procurement. However, it must be admitted that the research is somewhat dated, and in particular predates the global financial crisis. Further, the study has also been subject to some criticism, although this appears to relate to traditional, not PPP, procurement. For example, one criticism of the Melbourne study came from the later Productivity Commission (PC) report (2014, pp. 486–487). In addition, the 2012 Victorian Auditor-General's (VAG) report raised some concerns over the quality of the data, although these criticisms relate more to the traditionally delivered projects in the study rather than the PPPs, specifically to the data supplied by one government agency, Major Projects Victoria (MPV). The VAG and by inference the PC consider that the MPV has overstated its own performance in delivering traditional contracts.

A major problem with publicly delivered roads is that they often get caught up in the political budgeting cycle. Governments are often under pressure to develop more roads, and generally do not use tolls (user pays) to fund (or at least fully fund) these investments. In order to achieve this objective there is a great incentive to reduce costs by reducing the quality and durability of the initial construction, and to shift expenditures downstream, perhaps to be dealt with by future governments. Such is a moral hazard of the political process. Private road operators cannot do this, and not just because they know it makes long-term sense to build to a higher life-cycle standard. It is also because these projects carry very high-performance standards (with financial penalties if they do not perform to requirements) that create the incentives on them against closing down roads except at strictly scheduled times for maintenance. This means that typically the private sector builds high quality to mitigate this risk, in order to keep the roads open and free from roadworks, and to achieve whole-of-life savings. By contrast, public roads authorities do not have these same performance standards and freely close down lanes for maintenance without penalty. The net result of traditional procurement is a higher overall net present cost over the life of the asset, and greater congestion and likely inconvenience to road users having to go through more contraflows or road blockages. The Outer Suburban Arterial Roads (OSARs) programme in Victoria referred to earlier is that Government's answer to this issue.

There appears to be a significant gap in the research needed to support the question as to whether the PPP model is delivering superior outcomes on projects in Australia. We would further contend that this issue cannot be solved by comparative studies involving alternative procurement models. Despite previous work along these lines (Grimsey and Lewis 2005, 2007, 2009), it is to some extent a false trail. An alternative is that the many procurement models that have been developed have different drivers of value and merits. Each is appropriate under different circumstances, and VfM is delivered essentially by two things:

1. Critically selecting the right procurement model for the project. Every procurement model has its place. Each is a valid alternative and it is a question of matching the characteristics of the project, the specific risks, and the capacity and capability of both the market and the public sector procuring agency. Effectively, while there is a best procurement model for each project, it is not the only one, and this is why we consider that a strict comparison between models to the detriment of one or another is not the best way to proceed.
2. Recognising that models do not deliver projects, people do. The capacity and capability of the teams in both the public and private sectors are crucial for successful delivery of a project. And the same holds for project selection. Where either capacity or capability of project management is lacking, then inevitably mistakes are made and value may be diminished. It is further contended not only that the skills of the transacting or procurement teams are required but also that the contract managers must forge long-term working (partnering) relationships over the life of a PPP contract if the project is to succeed.

Conclusions

Around 80 PPP projects have been procured in Australia over the last 18 years. This alone stands as a testament to the usefulness of the model; after all it is unlikely that governments would continue to procure PPPs if they were not delivering something positive. Inevitably, however, there have been some failures that have grabbed the media headlines and fuelled the debate on the value of the PPP model and its future use for procuring large and complex infrastructure projects.

Where PPPs have failed, there have invariably been clear decisions made during the procurement phase which have contributed to their failure (e.g. traffic forecasting in toll road PPPs). Further to this observation, it is interesting to note that that a number of failed transport economic PPPs have subsequently been bought in the secondary market and provided a competitive market return to the investor (e.g. Transurban's purchase of the Cross City Tunnel), although considerable value has been lost during this process.

Despite the well-publicised failures, the majority of PPPs have been successful in delivering many of their objectives, as many of examples above reveal. Unfortunately, the PPP success stories do nothing to assuage the appetite of media that sell its product on the salacious and controversial. Public discourse is at best distorted and more often captured by vested interest, political point scoring or ideological predispositions. The 'public good, private bad' debate is well played out in the Australian press, as it is elsewhere.

Continued use alone is not proof that PPPs have been successful in Australia. The hard data measuring its success is few and far between. There have been retrospective studies in Australia and elsewhere that attempt to compare PPPs with more traditional contracting, but these are now dated. They universally fail to take account of the fact that infrastructure projects are all different. A contracting model may well fail to deliver on its promises simply because it is the wrong type of model for the project or that the people delivering the model have not done a good job.

Glossary

Asset recycling Governments build the infrastructure and, after it is tried and tested, sell it to investors wanting to buy 'mature infrastructure assets' and use these funds to re-invest in new assets

Bidder A respondent to a request for expression of interest or an invitation to submit a bid response to a project brief. Typically, a bidder will be a consortium of parties with one lead party responsible for the provision of all contracted services on behalf of the consortium

Build Own Operate Transfer (BOOT) An arrangement whereby a facility is designed, financed, operated and maintained by a concession company. Ownership rests with the concessionaire until the end of the concession period, at which point ownership and operating rights are transferred to the government (normally without charge)

Council of Australian Governments (COAG) The Council of Australian Governments is the peak intergovernmental forum in Australia

Concession Concession-based approaches are the oldest form of public–private partnership, and a variety of arrangements are based on the concept of a fixed-term concession, using various combinations of private sector resources to design, construct, finance, renovate, operate and maintain facilities. Ownership of the facility may remain with government or be transferred to the government upon completion of the construction or at the end of the concession period

Department of Treasury and Finance (DTF), Victoria The Department of Treasury and Finance is a department in the state of Victoria, Australia, that provides economic, financial and resource management advice to the Victorian Government, in delivering its polices. It is a central agency providing treasury and commercial support to spending departments and ordinarily does not itself deliver assets and services to the public

Design, construct, maintain and finance (DCMF) An arrangement whereby a facility is designed, constructed, financed and maintained by a concession company

Funding The revenue sources (for example, taxes, service charges and user payments) tapped, for example by government, to repay the finance raised to pay for the cost of building infrastructure

Global Financial Crisis (GFC) The global financial crisis refers to the crisis of the global economy that is commonly believed to have begun in 2007, with the credit crunch and subprime crisis originating in the US residential market

GBTS Government buys, tolls then sells infrastructure

Megaproject A large-scale complex investment project that typically costs US$1 billion or more

Net Present Cost (NPC) The discounted value of future costs

MPV Major Projects Victoria is a government department in Victoria, Australia, focused on delivering major infrastructure and residential projects

Partnerships Victoria A Policy in the state of Victoria, Australia, giving effect to a commitment to optimise the level of infrastructure spending through a responsible use of the resources of both the public and private sectors. Value for money and the public interest are keynotes of the policy

Private Finance Initiative (PFI) A UK programme encompassing arrangements whereby a consortium of private sector partners comes together to provide an asset-based public service under a contract to a public body. Typically it includes the private financing of the assets

Procurement The component of the commissioning process that deals specifically with purchasing a service from a provider. This occurs once decisions have been taken over what outcomes or outputs are to be secured and involves the negotiation of contracts

Project finance A way of financing capital projects that depends for its security on the expected cash flow of the project itself rather than guarantees from the borrower or third parties

Public Private Partnership (PPP) A risk-sharing relationship based upon a shared aspiration between the public sector and one or more partners from the private and/or voluntary sectors to deliver a publicly agreed outcome and or public service

Public Sector Comparator (PSC) A hypothetically constructed benchmark to assess the value for money of conventionally financed procurement in comparison with a PPP for delivering a publicly funded service or user pays

Risk A situation involves risk if the randomness facing an economic entity can be expressed in terms of specific numerical probabilities (objective or subjective)

Victorian Auditor-General's Office (VAGO) The Victorian Auditor-General's Office is an independent officer of the Victorian Parliament which carries out audits on the spending of departments and other government-owned entities

Value for Money The optimum combination of whole-of-life costs, risks, completion time and quality in order to meet public requirements

References

Booth, M., & Hutchinson, S. (2016, April 6). How Royal Adelaide Hospital's cost blew out (p. 8). *The Australian*.

Clarke, H., & Hawkins, A. (2006). Economic framework for Melbourne traffic planning. *Agenda, 13*(1), 63–80.

de Clerk, D. (2015). *Public-private partnership procurement game-theoretic studies of the tender process* (Dissertation). Doctor in Business Economics, KU Leuven, Faculty of Economics and Business, No. 490.

Department of Infrastructure and Regional Development. (2015). *National public private partnership policy framework*. Canberra, Australia: Commonwealth Government of Australia Publication.

Duffield, C., Raisbeck, P., & Xu, M. (2008). *Report on the performance of PPP projects in Australia when compared with a representative sample of traditionally procured infrastructure projects*. Melbourne, Australia: University of Melbourne.

Ergas, H. (2014, January 13). Wrong way, go back: Mega project funding muddle (p. 10). *The Australian*.

Gelber, F. (2014, May 1). BOOT is on the other foot for infrastructure (p. 26). *The Australian*.

Grimsey, D., & Lewis, M. K. (2004). *Public private partnerships: The worldwide revolution in infrastructure provision and project finance*. Cheltenham, UK: Edward Elgar.

Grimsey, D., & Lewis, M. K. (2005). Are public private partnerships value for money? Evaluating alternative approaches and comparing academic and practitioner views. *Accounting Forum, 29*(4), 345–378.

Grimsey, D., & Lewis, M. K. (2007). Public private partnerships and public procurement. *Agenda A Journal of Policy Analysis and Reform, 14*(2), 171–188.

Grimsey, D., & Lewis, M. K. (2009). Developing a framework for procurement options analysis. In A. Akintoye & M. Beck (Eds.), *Policy, finance and management for public-private partnerships* (pp. 398–413). Oxford, UK: Wiley-Blackwell.

Grimsey, D., & Lewis, M. K. (2017). *Global developments in public infrastructure procurement: Evaluating public private partnerships and other procurement options*. Cheltenham, UK: Edward Elgar.

Kenny, C., & Booth, M. (2015, March 19). Adelaide building costs a world-beater (pp. 1, 2). *The Australian*.

Lease, L. (2013). *2013 Australian construction achievement award, The new Royal Children's Hospital, Melbourne stage 2: Submission—Technical paper*. Melbourne, Australia: Lend Lease Publication.

Loussikian, K. (2016). Public-private road deals take toll on investors. *The Weekend Australian*, 4–5 June, 28.

Odgers, J. F. (2002). *An initial performance review of Melbourne's City link toll road*. Melbourne, Australia: RMIT University.

Owen, M. (2018, April 16). Winter coming, but no cure for hospital (pp. 4–6). *The Australian*.

Partnerships Victoria. (2008). *Partnerships Victoria project summary, the new Royal Children's Hospital project*. Melbourne, Australia: Department of Treasury and Finance, Victorian Government Publication.

Partnerships Victoria. (2015). *Partnerships Victoria project summary, Ravenhall prison project*. Melbourne, Australia: Department of Treasury and Finance, Victorian Government Publication.

Phibbs, P. (2007). *Driving alone – Sydney's cross city tunnel*. Sydney, Australia: University of Western Sydney.

Productivity Commission. (2014). *Public infrastructure inquiry report*. Retrieved June 3, 2015, from www.pc.gov.au/inquiries/completed/infrastructure/report

The Audit Office of New South Wales. (2006). *Auditor-general's report performance audit the cross city tunnel project*. Sydney, Australia: New South Wales Government Publication.

Victorian Auditor-General's Office. (2018). *Safety and cost effectiveness of private prisons, independent assurance report to parliament*. Melbourne, Australia: Victorian Government Printer.

Chapter 10
Public–Private Partnerships for the Development of Port IT Infrastructure

Seung-Kuk Paik

Abbreviations

EDI	Electronic data interchange
GDP	Gross domestic product
IT	Information technology
KL-Net	Korea logistics network
KT-Net	Korea trade network
MOMAF	Ministry of maritime affairs and fisheries
PORT-MIS	Port management information system
PPP	Public–private partnership
TEUs	20-foot equivalent units

Introduction

Countries are faced with huge responsibilities for building and effectively managing their critical transportation infrastructures, such as roads, seaports, and airports because these important infrastructures play a pivotal role in their economic development and growth. Effective development management and administration of these infrastructures involves many parties with different objectives and interests. Because of these complexities, a strong partnership among the stakeholders is essential for the successful development and management of these important transportation infrastructures.

Since the globalization trend is expected to continue, the role of ports will become increasingly important. Thus, building and effectively managing ports has become a national priority. Traditionally, the public sector has owned and operated

S.-K. Paik (✉)
Systems and Operations Management Department, David Nazarian College of Business and Economics, California State University, Northridge, Northridge, CA, USA
e-mail: seungkuk.paik@csun.edu

R. M. Clark, S. Hakim (eds.), *Public Private Partnerships*, Competitive Government: Public Private Partnerships, https://doi.org/10.1007/978-3-030-24600-6_10

ports. However, because of scarce resources, the development, construction, and effective management of ports have been slow and frustrating. In addition, as many participants are involved in port operations, a misalignment of objectives and interests between both public and private sectors has resulted in poor efficiency and performance. A public–private partnership has been considered one of the ways to address such complex issues (Andres et al. 2008; Brinkerhoff and Brinkerhoff 2011; Koppenjan 2005). It enables both public and private sectors to rely on each other and to develop synergistic effects for both parties. It also allows for a successful economic development neither the public nor the private sectors could achieve alone.

Although there have been many cases of PPPs in important infrastructure development, little attention was given to their use in the development of ports, especially in port information technology and system development. The use of information technology (IT) has become widespread in ports, and the advances in IT have been influencing port operations significantly. In addition, little has been reported about who takes responsibility for planning port IT projects and what roles the public and the private sectors should assume for a successful implementation. This chapter will use the case study of the Pusan port in South Korea to examine the major issues and challenges faced by the port and discusses how public–private partnership resolved them. More specifically, this case study looks into the institutional arrangements of both public and private entities and the important steps and actions taken at the Pusan port.

The remainder of this chapter is organized as follows. Section "Public–Private Partnership" briefly explains public–private partnership and its critical success factors. Section "Pusan Port and Its Challenges" describes the challenges and issues faced by the Pusan port, followed in section "Information Technology (IT) Applications in Pusan Port and Its Outcomes" by the steps and actions taken through the public–private partnership. Sections "Guidelines for Successful Public–Private Partnerships" and "Summary and Conclusions" present some guidelines for a successful public–private partnership and include recommendations and conclusions.

Public–Private Partnership

A public–private partnership can be defined as a cooperative agreement between both public and private sectors with the mutual goal of achieving a set of agreed-upon objectives. Through a partnership, the public sector seeks to develop a long-term, broad plan to maintain public accountability and to accomplish public interests by combining the efficiency, expertise, and resources from the private sector. Different types of PPPs have been formed and practiced in infrastructure development in many countries with significantly increased value to the outcomes (Brinkerhoff and Brinkerhoff 2011; Osei-Kyei and Chan 2015; Rosenau 1999; Zhang 2005). On the other hand, a variety of problems, such as delays of projects, and even total failures, have been reported in infrastructure development PPPs as well (Abdel Aziz 2007; Zhang 2005). These problems are not surprising, given the various participants involved, a lack of collaboration between the public and the private sectors, the many uncertainties, and the risks that may arise at different phases in the lifespan of a project. Thus, in order to avoid failures, it is important to identify and understand the critical factors for successful infrastructure development.

The literature has identified the following critical success factors. First, a strong collaboration between public and private sectors is essential for a successful PPP (Bagchi and Paik 2001; Brinkerhoff and Brinkerhoff 2011; Lockwood et al. 2000; Osei-Kyei and Chan 2015). Both parties should foster communication and cooperation and recognize a mutuality of interests. Without this recognition, the partnership results in a waste of time and resources from both parties and fails to achieve the desired outcomes. At the same time, patience from both public and private sectors is necessary for a successful partnership, which requires long-term commitment and perspective. Second, a successful public–private partnership is often based on a strong leadership (Abdel Aziz 2007; Zhang 2005; Zou et al. 2014). A partnership involves many participants from both public and private sectors whose interests and objectives may be different and conflicting. Thus, it is important to have a champion who can lead and facilitate effective coordination among a number of participants throughout the lifespan of a project. The government is usually in a better position than any other party in creating favorable environments where both public and private sectors can work together by providing support and reducing risks associated with a project (Bagchi and Paik 2001; Zhang 2005). Another key to a successful partnership is economic viability. More specifically, there should be sufficient long-term demand for the products/services offered by partnered infrastructure projects. Without this, the private sector may be reluctant to participate (Brinkerhoff and Brinkerhoff 2011; Zhang 2005).

Pusan Port and Its Challenges

Pusan Port

South Korea's economy has been driven by trade. According to the World Bank, in 2016, exports from and imports of goods and services to South Korea accounted for about 42% and 35% of GDP, respectively. Although a few of South Korea's exports and imports are moved by air, sea transportation carries virtually all the rest of South Korea's trade. Among the major ports in South Korea, the Pusan port, which is located in the southeastern region of the country, has played a vital role in the country's economy since its opening in 1876. Pusan has the sixth largest port worldwide with volumes of 19.5 million TEUs (20-foot equivalent units) in 2015, and it accounts for approximately 75% of the total container volume in South Korea. It is also the second busiest transshipment hub in the world (Barnard 2016).

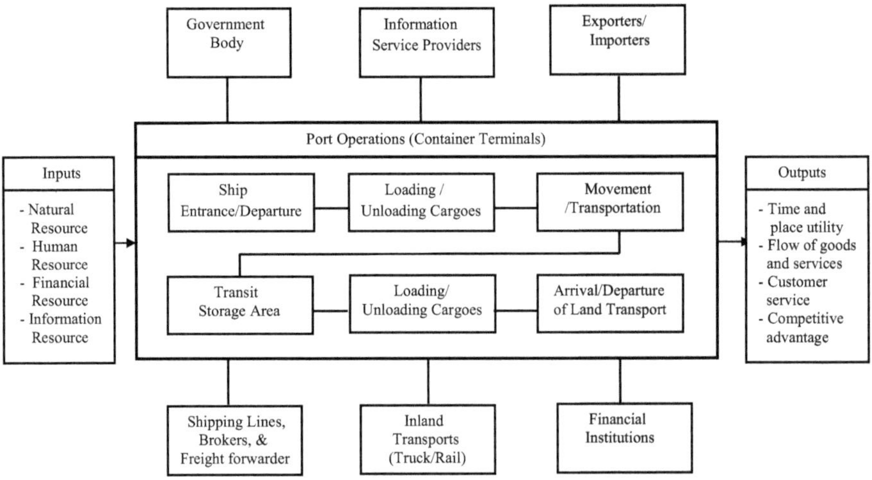

Fig. 10.1 Main actors in the Pusan port supply chain. Adapted from Bagchi and Paik (2001)

Figure 10.1 shows inputs, port operations, outputs, and main users of the Pusan port. Flow of activities at the port is shown in the center of the Figure.

The complete process of moving shipments can be divided into six major activities: ship entrance/departure, loading/unloading shipments, moving shipments to transit areas, storing shipments, loading/unloading shipments, and arrival/departure of land transportation. This set of activities is carried out using the port's several resources, such as land, equipment, human resources, capitals, and information. When properly operated, it can provide time and place utility for consumers, and better customer service for shipping lines and inland transportation, resulting in a competitive advantage for the nation.

Exporters/importers, shipping lines, freight forwarders, inland transportation companies, government agencies, and information service providers play a major role in efficient and effective port operations. Smooth communication and collaboration among these groups ensures unhindered material/information flows in the port supply chain.

Challenges and Issues

In the mid-1990s, large trade volumes, coupled with insufficient port capacity, caused frequent freight and ship congestion at the Pusan port. As shown in Table 10.1, in 1995, the total number of containers handled by the Pusan port was approximately 4.5 million TEUs, while the capacity of the container terminals in the port was only 3.3 million TEUs. As could be expected, the imbalance between capacity and demand at the port caused a significant bottleneck in the supply chain. The number of ships in stand-by and waiting at the port increased to such levels that

Table 10.1 Bottleneck at the Pusan port

	1993	1994	1995
Capacity (million TEUs)	3.3	3.3	3.3
Demand (million TEUs)	3.1	3.8	4.5

Source: Korea Container Terminal Authority (1998)

the transport providers could not offer a fast and flexible response to customer demands. The delay caused by the stand-by and waiting time also resulted in huge amounts of stocks for the channel members in the supply chain, leading to an increased cost of doing business. This performance negatively influenced the logistics costs and weakened the competitiveness of the nation as a whole. Thus, improving port operations became one of the critical elements in boosting South Korea's competitiveness.

In addition to the lack of capacity, excessive government regulations and inefficient procedures for processing exports and imports were another obstacle. A large number of documents, as many as 50–150, were often used for processing one trade transaction. The average time required to complete the whole process from the beginning to the end was as long as 4 weeks. The lack of integration and the practice of personal visits among the parties in the supply chain were cited as the main reasons for delay (KT-Net 1997). The processes and procedures associated with port entry and departure were clearly one of the major causes for poor customer service.

Information Technology (IT) Applications in Pusan Port and Its Outcomes

The use of state-of-the-art information technology and communications is a necessity in today's port operations. Fast and efficient planning, stowage, and tracking of shipments had been the transportation industry's response to the customer's demands (Kim 2014; Parola et al. 2017). Without information technology such as electronic data interchanges (EDI), port operators need to type all the information contained in the bay plan into the port operation system. One port operator mentioned that if he had information for 1500 TEUs, he used to type the information by hand for 12 h (KT-Net 1997). This keying process can cause errors, consume lots of time and costs, and lead to inefficient cargo handling. Therefore, port operators view that the use of information technology is crucial to improve productivity and efficiency. In the midst of a rapidly changing deep-sea transportation industry, managing and controlling the information flow was also considered an essential prerequisite to providing faster and better service to the port users. Realizing these challenges and issues faced by the Pusan port, the South Korean government concluded that an efficient and accurate information flow is the key to achieving material velocity and that the use of information technology can enhance the efficiency of the activities in port operations.

Three main IT applications developed were port-management information system (PORT-MIS), container terminal EDI application, and customs EDI application. PORT-MIS application was designed to electronically exchange the documents between the government, and shipping lines and container terminals for port entry and departure. Terminal EDI application involved the electronic documents transfer between container terminals, and shipping lines and inland transportation. This EDI service enabled the users to reduce time and costs for handling containers, thereby planning and managing their operations effectively. Finally, customs EDI application was intended to facilitate the customs clearance processes for exports and imports. This service allowed the users, such as shipping lines, freight forwarders, brokers, and inland transportation, to handle the customs clearance fast and accurately with very limited amount of paperwork.

Figure 10.2 shows the four major steps in the development of the IT application process.

Development of the EDI applications, which could be traced back to June 1986, began with the selection of the critical processes that could have a significant impact on the performance of port operations, followed by the feasibility study on automating the existing processes with the proposed IT applications. Along with these important steps, a project team was formed. This team was responsible for documenting and studying the existing system to recognize its strengths and weaknesses and to establish baseline data for the proposed system. The identification of key participants and the in-depth understanding of their needs and wants was also one of the important parts of their task. With this understanding, the project team began the redesign of the process and developed the EDI applications. During the implementation stage, the users were given a trial period for pilot testing. Training and education and technical supports were also provided to them. The review of the performance of the initial systems led to further refinement. By April 1996, the EDI applications were fully implemented at the port.

The use of these IT applications led to increased throughputs at the port, improved port operations, and faster customs clearance. After the system was implemented,

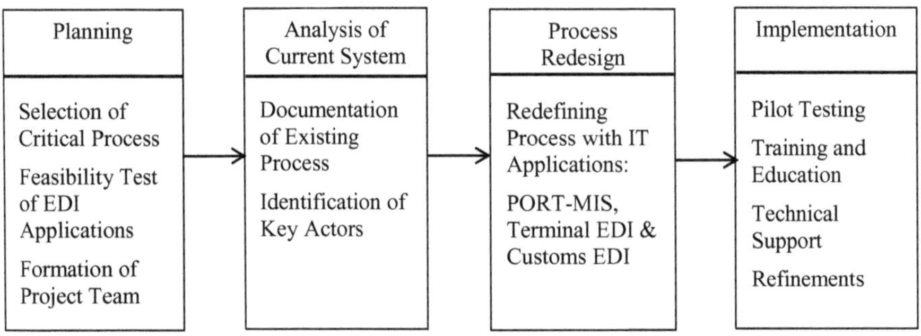

Fig. 10.2 Four steps of EDI development process at Pusan port

the throughput at the Pusan port, expressed in terms of TEUs (20-foot equivalent units), went up 6%, and at the same time the number of ship calls also increased 16% without any significant capacity addition (Bagchi and Paik 2001). The ship turnaround time was also reduced by around 6%. Along with this, the ship-waiting rate of vessels waiting in queue more than 12 h and the stand-by rate with <12 h showed improvements from 10% and 16%, respectively, to around 2% each after the implementation. Just as the use of IT has improved port operations, the customs EDI application allowed the port users to handle the customs clearance within 30 min for imports and only 5 min for exports. In the past, it was reported that around 4 h were required for the same service (Cho et al. 1996). The use of the EDI applications also led to a reduction of paperwork in various government bodies. For example, after the PORT-MIS EDI application, a number of documents used for port entry and departure were reduced from around 75 to only 22, all of which were transferred electronically among the government, shipping lines, and container terminals. Although these IT applications resulted in significant benefits in the Pusan port community, the users still wanted more refinements to the existing systems. For example, the users indicated that they had to send the same electronic documents separately to the Ministry of Maritime Affairs and Fisheries (MOMAF) and the customs administration. This practice was due to the lack of integration among the EDI applications, which resulted from the insufficient coordination among the government parties.

Public–Private Partnership EDI Development and Implementation

The successful development and implementation of information technology and systems at ports largely depends on how well the port actors can address various institutional issues, rather than technology issues. The Pusan port community, as shown in Table 10.2, used various strategies and actions in setting up and implementing its information systems. A successful public and private partnership made it possible.

Table 10.2 Stakeholders of Pusan port IT project

Public sector	Private sector
MOMAF	Container Terminals
Customs Administration	Shipping Lines (Hanjin, Hyundai, etc.)
Quarantine Station	Freight-forwarders (First Express Int'l, etc.)
Korea Container Terminal Authority	In-land Transporters (Global Hanjin, etc.)
Korea Maritime Institute	Information Service Providers (KL-Net and KT-Net)

Proactive Roles of the Government

The South Korean government, including MOMAF and the customs administration, played a critical role in developing and implementing the EDI applications at the Pusan port. Without strong initiative and support of the government, the EDI applications would not have been achieved. In addition to assuming major financial responsibilities, the government mainly initiated and carried out the EDI development and implementation throughout the entire project.

To create dramatic improvements in the Pusan port operations, the government studied its existing operations carefully in order to choose the right approach. As a main project planner, the government concluded that efficient and effective information exchange processes could lead to faster processing time, reduced operational costs and improvements in other important operational parameters. With the help of the government agency that was knowledgeable about the IT applications in port operations, MOMAF set up objectives, articulated needs, and created a thorough plan for the development and implementation of a new system.

Along with the selection of the critical port operation processes, the government also assumed the role of facilitator in the development and implementation stage. In order to solicit inputs from the private sector, the government organized a special task force and several committees that consisted of government officials and users from the private sector. The main purpose of these special groups was to collect various opinions and users' needs on the new systems, to identify and address the possible problems that could arise in the new EDI applications, and to promote the extensive use of the proposed system within the Pusan port community. Through the task force and committees, the government was able to involve the users at the early stage of the IT development and facilitated the acceptance of the systems among them. In addition, the government hosted many information sessions to increase awareness of the new systems among the potential users for a long period of time. These approaches allowed the government to gain trust and build consensus with their clients.

Almost all IT applications at the Pusan port were developed with government funding. Although it was hard to estimate the total government investment in all of these EDI applications, it was believed that the Korean government had spent about eight million dollar just for the design and development of PORT-MIS EDI (Paik and Bagchi 2000). The terminal EDI services, although not developed from direct financial support from the government, were initiated by government influence. This was critical in that the government tried to address risk and uncertainty associated with the IT development and implementation that required large investments. Given the fact that risk and uncertainty are the major sources of the problems in any public–private collaboration, the government recognized the challenges and addressed the thorny issues effectively. Through their financial initiative, the government increased its accountability and at the same time reduced the financial burden of the private sector.

For a successful development and implementation of the new IT applications, the government also took several proactive approaches within the organization and in the Pusan port community. For example, the government used several motivational tools, such as a promise of early promotion and provision of extensive education and training in EDI technology, for the government personnel who were involved in the development and implementation of the EDI applications. Using this approach, the government tried to emphasize the significance of the new system within the government and motivated the people who were involved in establishing the system. Similar approaches were taken to increase the acceptance of the new IT applications among the potential users. The government provided appropriate software and technical support to the users, along with extensive training and education. The government also installed a number of computers with these new IT applications in their office in Pusan so that many small- and medium-sized companies, who could not otherwise afford the whole system, were allowed to use them at no charge.

Along with this soft approach, the government also used coercive actions to force users to use the new system. During a trial period, the users could use either the EDI services or paperwork. However, when the trial period ended, the government accepted EDI only for port entry/departure and customs clearance. In the case of the terminal EDI services, the government urged the container terminals to charge penalties to the users who did not comply with the EDI requirements. Although these somewhat harsh approaches resulted in many complaints from the users at the time, in hindsight, most of them considered the actions one of the success factors.

Participation of the Private Sector

Like the South Korean government with strong commitment to EDI development, the private sector also played key roles in the EDI project and was involved in various task forces and committees throughout the important stages of the IT development process. As a major partner, the private sector provided support to the Pusan port project, which was primarily initiated and executed by the public sector.

Through the task forces and committees, they explained the problems with current practices and systems, suggested users' needs and wants in building a new, user-friendly system, and tried to make sure that the proposed system could be properly developed for improved performance.

Probably, the most important role played by the private sector in the EDI development and implementation was the creation and involvement of the Korea Logistics Network Corporation (KL-Net). This private company was established solely to provide the Pusan port supply chain participants with information services. Among the three EDI applications discussed above, PORT-MIS and the terminal EDI were the main service offerings from this company. Although initiated by MOMAF, several private companies, including several shipping lines, invested in KL-Net. These private companies recognized that better logistics information management capability would help enhance the productivity of their operations. Due to their extensive investment, the private companies involved in the project were willing to cooperate with the development and implementation of the EDI systems, thereby increasing the likelihood of the successful PPP at Pusan port. This institutional arrangement also helped reduce conflicts of interests between both public and private sectors and to mitigate the financial risk of the IT development that required a large capital investment. This nature of the relationship between the private corporations and KL-Net also helped increase the visibility of new EDI applications.

Through educational campaigns from KL-Net, the private sector began to understand the industrial benefits and the advantages to the nation as a whole. These educational campaigns were not limited only to the private sector. Government departments, including quasi-government organization, such as Korea Container Terminal Authority, were also part of the national promotional campaigns. By embracing all the participants involved in the port operations, the government could create widespread awareness of the EDI applications and obtain the cooperation and support from the private sector from the early stages of the project.

Along with these promotional campaigns, KL-Net organized many additional education and training programs. These training programs were usually developed to be aligned with the hierarchy in the customers' organization. For example, the training programs for top managers were designed to build consensus for the use of EDI and to make the transition smooth within the organization, while training programs for the end-users focused on how to run the applications. These education and training programs were also accompanied with the development of manuals and establishment of a help desk for the end-users.

A successful public–private partnership often relies on collaboration and mutuality between the two parties who recognize that each of them has a stake in the success of the other (Lockwood et al. 2000). As mentioned earlier, a special task force and various committees, which were primarily organized by the Korean government, fostered cooperative relationships between both public and private sectors. These special groups consisted of a number of representatives from almost all members of the Pusan port supply chain. After the members of the committees provided valuable input to the new IT systems from the beginning to the end of the project, they returned to their organizations and played a vital role in increasing awareness of the new systems within their organizations and helped their people to better utilize the systems. As a project champion in each of their organizations, they tried to promote its vision and goals and build a trust-based collaborative relationship with the government.

Guidelines for Successful Public–Private Partnerships

The above discussion suggests a list of successful factors for the public–private partnership at the Pusan port. All of these factors have been discussed in the literature (Abdel Aziz 2007; Bagchi and Paik 2001; Bovaird 2004; Brinkerhoff and Brinkerhoff 2011; Lockwood et al. 2000; Osei-Kyei and Chan 2015; Zhang 2005;

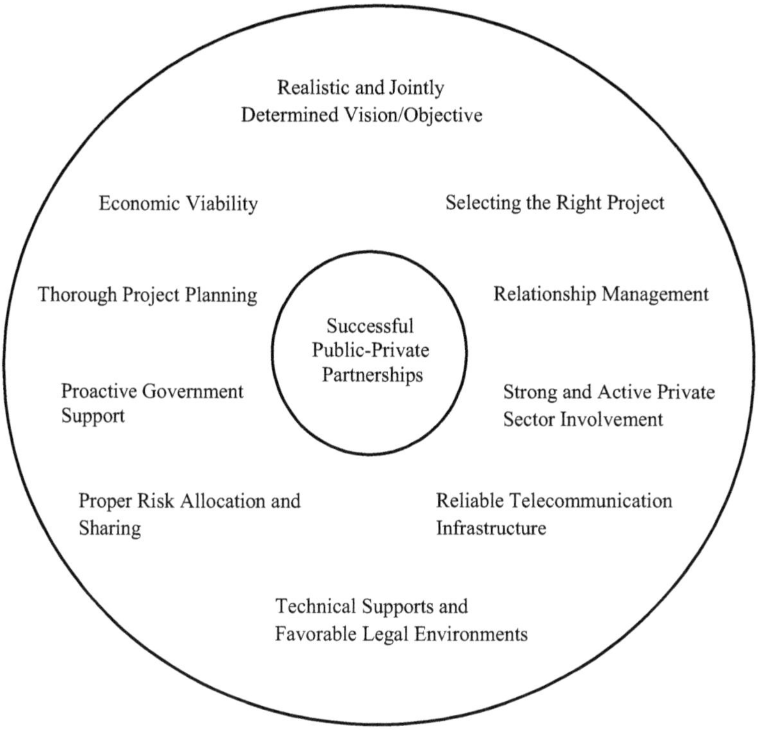

Fig. 10.3 Successful factors for public–private partnership at Pusan port

Zou et al. 2014). Figure 10.3 illustrates these factors. Therefore; the following guidelines are suggested for successful public–private partnerships in the development of port IT infrastructure.

A realistic and jointly determined vision and objective is one of the determinants for a successful PPP. The public sector primarily seeks better customer service as well as increased public interest and social accountability, whereas the private sector often looks for cost savings, increased profitability, and more efficiency and effectiveness. Therefore, the interests of the public and private sectors can converge in the development of a realistic and jointly accepted vision and goals and eventually lead to a successful PPP. Both parties also need to consider long-term economic viability for the potential products/services from a PPP project. Without significant long-term benefit from the project, it would be unreasonable for the public and private sector to form a partnership and develop mutual objectives. Selecting the right project should be based on this long-term economic viability and the mutuality of interests.

Thorough project planning is critical to the success of any kind of IT project. Good plans involve, but are not limited to, developing the scope of the project, determining what must be done and how it will be done, establishing a realistic timetable, managing and controlling resources, monitoring the progress of the project, etc. In doing so, the commitment and responsibilities from both parties are vital. Since ports are often owned and managed by the public sector, it is essential for the public sector to initiate, manage, and control the project. With strong initiative and proactive leadership, the public sector can coordinate and synergize diverse stakeholders in a port supply chain. At the same time, strong and active involvement from the private sector is important. A successful PPP requires early user involvement through open discussions to obtain both private sector and public sector inputs and requires a proper risk allocation and sharing from the private sector through the development of a strong private consortium. The multifaceted nature of a PPP for port operation makes it difficult for a single private company to handle a variety of tasks and issues associated with the project. Thus, a well-structured private sector consortium is desirable.

Relationship management is also important for the success of PPP projects. This can be defined as a set of comprehensive strategies and processes used by project partners to achieve common objectives through developing sustainable relationships (Zou et al. 2014). The complex nature of PPP projects calls for effective relationship management since many stakeholders are often involved. Some of the characteristics of relationship management in PPPs involve open and constant communication among all stakeholders, synergistic networking among project partners, collaborative decision-making, clarifying roles and responsibilities among parties, etc. It should be noted that top management's commitment, developing mutually agreed objectives, and active participation of both parties are critical determinants of effective relationship management in PPPs. Using these success factors and practices, the project partners should be able to build and develop a cooperative business environment, which can lead to the project's success.

Along with these factors, a successful development and implementation of IT in port operations requires a reliable telecommunication infrastructure, the availability of skilled workers, a willingness of potential users to use the IT applications, technical support, including training and education, and a favorable legal environment, such as security and confidentiality of data in port operations. Without these conditions, the development of any IT applications at a port would be difficult to achieve its intended objectives.

Summary and Conclusions

Many ports in developing countries experience similar problems to the one faced by the Pusan port in the late 1980s and early 1990s. The Pusan port case study can provide valuable lessons to decision makers in these nations by highlighting the importance of an effective PPP in the development and implementation of IT applications in port operations. While effective information management can give port managers the means to improve its operations, at the same time, it requires commitment of significant resources, a proper risk sharing, and effective institutional arrangements among many stakeholders. A public–private partnership has been considered one of the solutions to address such complex issues. It allows for a successful development and implementation of complex IT applications neither the public nor the private sectors could achieve alone. The plans and actions of the Pusan port community reported in this chapter is one of the excellent examples of a successful PPP. Strategic vision, strong government leadership, active participation of the private sector, and careful project planning are major ingredients for success of the Pusan port. A trust-based atmosphere in the Pusan port community was noteworthy.

A port is one of the most important transportation infrastructures in a country, connecting the nation to a global marketplace. It facilitates the exchange of raw materials, components, finished products, and relevant information among the countries. The IT system developed at the Pusan port further strengthened the linkage of South Korea's national supply chain to the global marketplace. Port decision makers in other countries should be able to benefit from this case study and a successful example of the use of a PPP for enhancing port operations.

Acknowledgements This chapter is primarily based on the unpublished report entitled "Logistics Information System Using EDI Applications: A Case Study on Pusan Port", which the author completed for the World Bank in 1999.

References

Abdel Aziz, A. M. (2007). Successful delivery of public-private partnerships for infrastructure development. *Journal of Construction Engineering and Management, 133*(12), 918–931.

Andres, L. A., Guasch, J. L., Haven, T., & Foster, V. (2008). *The impact of private sector participation in infrastructure: Lights, shadows, and the road ahead*. Washington, DC: The World Bank.

Bagchi, P. K., & Paik, S.-K. (2001). The role of public-private partnership in port information systems development. *International Journal of Public Sector Management, 14*(6), 482–499.

Barnard, B. (2016). *DP world boosts stake in biggest busan terminal*. Retrieved from https://www.joc.com/port-news/terminal-operators/dp-world/dp-world-boosts-stake-biggest-busan-terminal_20161229.html

Bovaird, T. (2004). Public-private partnerships: From contested concepts to prevalent practice. *Internal Review of Administrative Sciences, 70*(2), 199–215.

Brinkerhoff, D. W., & Brinkerhoff, J. W. (2011). Public-private partnerships: Perspectives on purposes, publicness, and good governance. *Public Administration and Development, 31*(1), 2–14.

Cho, S., Hong, D., & Choi, J. (1996). *Note on one stop information service for exports and imports cargoes*. Seoul, Korea: Korea Maritime Institute.

Kim, J. Y. (2014). Port user typology and representations of port choice behavior: A Q-methodological study. *Maritime Economics & Logistics, 16*(2), 165–187.

Koppenjan, J. (2005). The formation of public-private partnerships: Lessons from nine transport infrastructure projects in the Netherlands. *Public Administration, 83*(1), 135–157.

Korea Container Terminal Authority. (1998, April). *Annual report* (pp. 6, 13). Seoul, South Korea.

KT-Net. (1997). *Manual for automating trade process, KT-Net manual*. Seoul, South Korea.

Lockwood, S., Verma, R., & Schneider, M. (2000). Public-private partnership in toll road development: An overview of global practices. *Transportation Quarterly, 54*(2), 77–91.

Osei-Kyei, R., & Chan, A. P. C. (2015). Review of studies on the critical success factors for public-private partnership (PPP) projects from 1990 to 2013. *International Journal of Project Management, 33*(6), 1335–1346.

Paik, S.-K., & Bagchi, P. K. (2000). Process reengineering in port operations: A case study. *International Journal of Logistics Management, 11*(2), 59–72.

Parola, F., Risitano, M., Ferretti, M., & Panetti, E. (2017). The drivers of port competitiveness: A critical review. *Transportation Review, 37*(1), 116–138.

Rosenau, P. V. (1999). Introduction: The strengths and weaknesses of public-private policy partnership. *American Behavioral Scientists, 43*(1), 10–34.

Zhang, X. (2005). Critical success factors for public-private partnerships in infrastructure development. *Journal of Construction Engineering and Management, 131*(1), 3–14.

Zou, W., Kumaraswamy, M., Chung, J., & Wong, J. (2014). Identifying the critical success factors for relationship management in PPP projects. *International Journal of Project Management, 32*(2), 265–274.

Chapter 11
Public–Private Partnerships for Critical Infrastructure Development: The Hong Kong Experience

Eddie W. L. Cheng

Abbreviations

AA	Airport Authority
AIIB	Asian Infrastructure Investment Bank
APEC	Asia-Pacific Economic Cooperation
AWE	Asia World-Expo
BFA	Boao Forum for Asia
BOO	Build-own-operate
BOOT	Build-own-operate-transfer
BOT	Build-operate-transfer
CWTC	Hong Kong Chemical Waste Treatment Center
DBFO	Design-build-finance-operate
DBO	Design-build-operate
EU	Efficiency unit
FC	Franchises and concessions
JV-WMI	Joint ventures and wider market initiatives
NENT	North East New Territories Landfill
OBOR	One belt one road initiative
PCI	Partnership companies and investments
PFI	Private finance initiatives
PPP	Public–private partnership
PRD	Pearl river delta
PSI	Private sector involvement
SENT	South East New Territories Landfill
WENT	West New Territories Landfill
WKCD	West Kowloon Cultural District
WKR	West Kowloon Reclamation
XRL	Guangzhou-Shenzhen-Hong Kong Express Rail Link

E. W. L. Cheng (✉)
Department of Social Sciences, The Education University of Hong Kong, Tai Po, Hong Kong
e-mail: wlcheng@eduhk.hk

R. M. Clark, S. Hakim (eds.), *Public Private Partnerships*, Competitive Government: Public Private Partnerships, https://doi.org/10.1007/978-3-030-24600-6_11

Introduction

Due to the accumulation of its budget deficit following the Asian financial crisis, the Hong Kong government, inspired by the success of public–private partnerships (PPPs) in the UK and Australia, has introduced PPPs for the delivery of public services and infrastructure (Smith 2004). PPP schemes, as part of the government's Private Sector Involvement (PSI) initiative, are expected to deliver quality infrastructure projects with more involvement from the private sector. Efficiency and effectiveness of an infrastructure project can be expected when strengths from both the public and private sectors are leveraged (Efficiency Unit (EU) 2007).

According to the government's EU (2008), a PPP refers to a contractual arrangement that involves both the public and private sectors to deliver high-quality public services or projects. Under this broad definition, the EU introduced four major PPP forms, each with a unique model of private sector involvement, including private finance initiatives (PFI), franchises and concessions (FC), joint ventures and wider market initiatives (JV-WMI), and partnership companies and investments (PCI). Unlike in traditional methods, such as the design-bid-build method where the private sector is only responsible for the construction stage, a PPP procurement allows the private sector to be involved in designing, building, financing, operating, and maintaining a public service (Federal Highway Administration (FHWA) 2010; Huang et al. 2016). Consequently, the two sectors bring complementary skills to a project, depending on their levels of involvement and responsibility (Smith 2004).

In Hong Kong, the PPP concept has been applied to different kinds of projects, including infrastructure development, hospital services, and tourism-related preservation. Moreover, the PPP concept was first applied in infrastructure development. There are four basic objectives of infrastructure development (Wong 2003): (1) supplying new land for planned developments; (2) designing land structures that offer the basic physical constituents for supporting and accommodating the planned facilities, attaining quality living arrangements for the inhabitants, and sustaining all essential social and/or economical functions; (3) constructing the transportation linkage within and outside the territory for the efficient operation of various functions; and (4) providing hardware facilities associated with the above objectives.

Although there are several successful PPP infrastructure projects in Hong Kong, including the Tsing Ma Control Area, the Chemical Waste Treatment Plant, and the Asia World-Expo (AWE), other projects are known to be quite controversial, such as the Western Harbor Crossing and the West Kowloon Cultural District. As the PPP concept has been applied in Hong Kong for more than 15 years (since the emergence of the term in the UK), it is time to review its past and present applications and analyze the positive and negative aspects to examine potential developments and steer future applications.

This chapter will first present a general background of PPP establishment in Hong Kong. Then, a summative review of the past and present PPP projects will be provided. This review will also identify the trends and lessons learned from these applications. Finally, the chapter will explore the opportunities for expanding PPP services. For example, China's One Belt One Road initiative encourages infrastructure development partnerships along the "new" Silk Roads that cover more than 50 countries. This opportunity helps to leverage Hong Kong's PPP experiences and influences within, as well as beyond, the region. In addition, Hong Kong is now suffering from a shortage of land and housing. This paper will also discuss how the government would increase the use of PPPs to facilitate public housing projects in Hong Kong.

Background of the PPP Concept in Hong Kong

Benefits of PPPs

In Hong Kong, there is a long history of attracting investments from the private sector for public-led projects. Local residents usually think that the application of PPP to public services aims at using private funds in place of capital provided by the government. However, there are other benefits that should not be overlooked. For example, the skills and experience, in terms of innovation, efficiency, and creativity, offered by the private sector may help to remove constraints, including budgetary and borrowing restrictions, faced by the government during public-sector procurement. The private sector is also known to be strong in risk management (Osei-Kyei et al. 2014). Therefore, engaging the private sector in public projects can help transfer part of the project risks that are originally carried by the public sector (Jefferies and McGeorge 2009). Consequently, the primary reason why the local government introduces PPPs is to achieve good value for money. As shown in Table 11.1, the three major stakeholders of a PPP project (i.e., the government, the private sector, and the public) all benefit (Efficiency Unit (EU) 2008).

Despite the benefits for individual stakeholders, PPP proposals must meet certain public interest criteria, such as accountability, transparency, equity, public access, consumer rights, security, and privacy, and preserve the rights of affected individuals and communities (EU 2008). This may lead to unforeseen risks that may offset the PPP benefits (Mouraviev and Kakabadse 2016). More research on this topic is therefore necessary for improving PPP implementations.

Types of PPP Projects

There are many types of PPPs that can be adopted in projects, including build-develop-operate, buy-build-operate, design-build, and design-build-maintain. In Hong Kong, PPPs are most likely to be design-build-finance-operate (DBFO) and

Table 11.1 The benefits of a PPP

Stakeholder	Benefit	Description
The public sector	Lifecycle cost management	Different from conventional procurement methods, an all-inclusive consideration of the design, build, maintenance, and operation of a service by a consortium can achieve cost optimization
	Construction management	As a consortium is not paid for the construction but for the delivery of a service, this provides opportunities to optimize the whole construction work in terms of cost-effectiveness without compromising its quality and durability
	Innovative solutions	With the involvement of the private sector, the design, build, maintenance, and operation of a service can be thought out of the box
	Sharing government assets/facilities with third party users	Cooperation between the public and private sectors can optimize the use of government facilities/assets, such as government-owned land and intellectual property
	Sharing responsibilities with the private sector	The public sector is responsible for identifying public needs and formulating public policies, while the private sector is responsible for meeting the defined service requirements and achieving the desired outcomes
	Saving resources	If there are any savings due to PPP, freed resources can be used by other public services
The private sector	Business opportunities	The private sector can be engaged in the design, construction, operations, and maintenance of a public service as a whole, where some of these components are traditionally performed in-house by public agencies or by multiple private parties
	Export opportunities	New experiences obtained in such projects can increase the strength of the private sector to compete for overseas projects
The wider community	Bond markets	The third party financing associated with PPPs provides an opportunity to strengthen Hong Kong's growing bond market
	Regulation of service provision	The government is no longer a deliverer but a procurer to monitor and regulate the performance of the deliverables in terms of quality
	Job creation	Getting rid of the constraints of the civil service, the private sector is free to create various kinds of jobs when necessary
	Small government	Transferring the responsibility for delivery of some public services to the private sector can help restrain the size of the civil service expected by the local government

Note: Source from EU (2008) with modification

design-build-operate (DBO) (EU 2008). DBFO can be further classified into build-own-operate-transfer (BOOT), build-operate-transfer (BOT), and build-own-operate (BOO). Figure 11.1 illustrates the three typical procurement structures (Forcael et al. 2011).

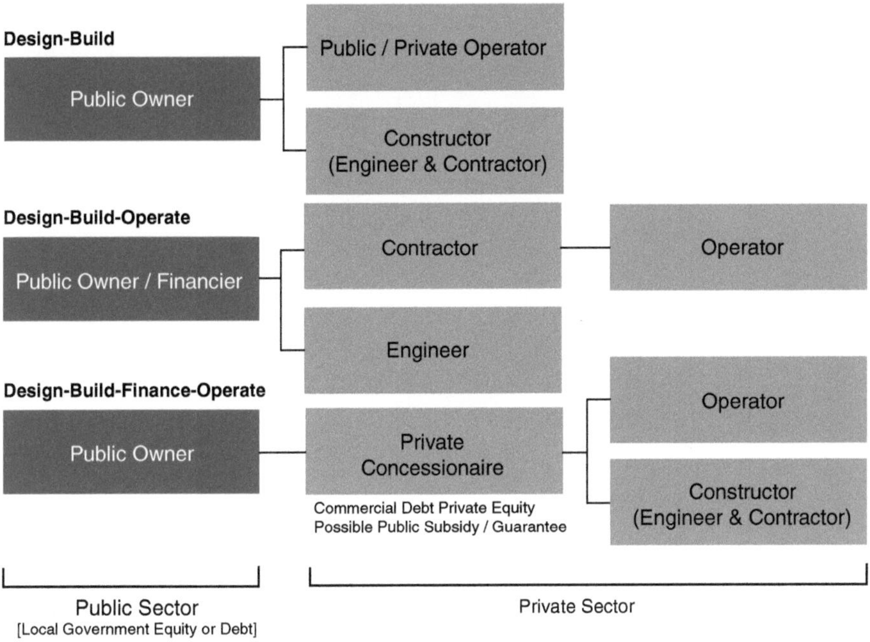

Fig. 11.1 Three typical procurement structures. Note: Source from Forcael et al. (2011) with minor modification

Under DBFO, a concession contract that specifies the outputs required for the PPP facility, details of payment for those outputs, and risk management is signed between the public and private sectors (EU 2008). Figure 11.2 illustrates a more detailed DBFO structure that is being adopted in Hong Kong (EU 2008). In this structure, the private sector assumes the obligation to design, build, operate, maintain, finance, and sometimes own the PPP project. As shown in later sections, the BOT and BOO approaches are commonly used in Hong Kong. Under DBO, a contract that usually involves a much shorter period of private financing is issued by the public sector who agrees to pay the private sector for the cost of designing and constructing facilities upon the commissioning of the facilities. The government retains more risk under a DBO than a DBFO contract.

Unlike the common perception, PPPs are not a novelty to Hong Kong. Hong Kong has a long history of attracting private sector investment and operating skills to deliver public services, most notably major infrastructure facilities, such as cross-harbor and vehicle tunnels developed using the BOT approach, which will be further discussed in later sections.

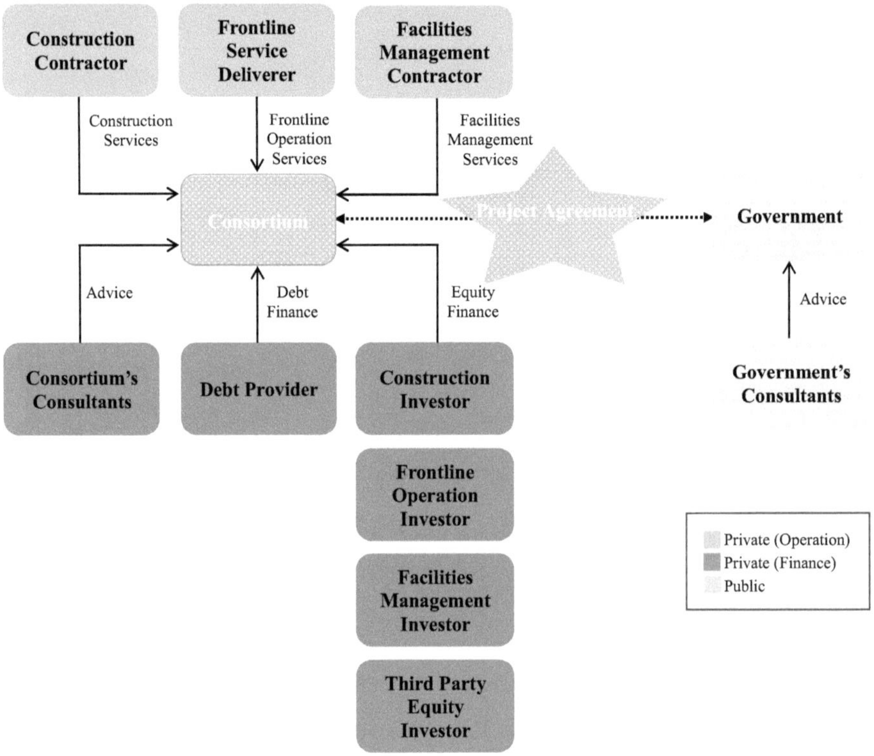

Fig. 11.2 DBFO structure adopted in Hong Kong. Notes: The Frontline Service Deliverer and the Facilities Management Contractor may be the same entity. Source from EU (2008)

Factors Affecting PPPs

The critical success factors (CSFs) of PPPs have been discussed by many researchers around the world (e.g., Bae and Joo 2016; Cheung et al. 2012a; Hwang et al. 2013; Li et al. 2005; Osei-Kyei and Chan 2015; Tang et al. 2013; Zhang 2005). Cheung et al. (2012b), when summarizing the study of the CSFs of PPPs from 17 articles published in various journals between 1994 and 2006, concluded that the 11 most cited factors regarded as critical factors were as follows: project economic viability (cited by 8 articles), competitive and transparent procurement process (7), strong private consortium (7), strong government support (6), available financial market (5), good partner relationship (5), government guarantee (4), stable and transparent political/social situation (4), appropriate project identification (4), clear project brief and client requirement (3), and appropriate risk allocation (3). Another study that ranked 57 CSFs identified in 27 articles published from 1990 to 2013 has indicated that the ten most cited CSFs were as follows (Osei-Kyei and Chan 2015): appropriate risk allocation and sharing (13), strong private consortium (12), political support (9), public/community support (8), transparent procurement (8), favorable legal framework (7), stable macroeconomic condition (7), competitive procurement (6), strong commitment by both parties (6), and clarity of roles and responsibilities among parties (6). Comparing between these two sets of CSFs, it seems that appropriate risk allocation and sharing has been emphasized recently, while some factors are generally more critical, especially strong private consortium, government/ political support, competitive and transparent procurement, and stable political/ social (macroeconomic) environment. As noted by Ke et al. (2010), effective risk allocation strategies can help achieve a more efficient contract negotiation process and reduce the occurrence of disputes during the concession period.

In Hong Kong, the EU (2008) has identified five major success factors (i.e., high level support, project champion, maintaining project momentum, private market interest testing, and stakeholder consultation) and five major obstacles (i.e., problems with land use amendments, lack of confidence and insufficient experience and expertise in the PPP approach, long contract durations, technological changes, and lack of public acceptance on the use of PPPs). Furthermore, there are a few researchers investigating the factors affecting PPP projects in Hong Kong (e.g., Cheung et al. 2012a, b; Ng et al. 2012). For example, Ng et al. (2012), by rating the importance level of a set of factors with a 7-point scale from 1 (the lowest) to 7 (the highest), found that the success of PPP projects relied on such factors as acceptable level of toll/tariff (5.78), the existence of a long-term demand for the proposed services (5.72), availability of strong private consortium (5.72), alignment with government's strategic objectives (5.71), reliable service delivery (5.71), financial interest to private sector (5.67), and more cost effective than traditional procurement methods (5.66). Moreover, Cheung et al. (2012b), using a five-point scale from 1 (least important) to 5 (most important) to rank 18 critical factors, found that the top 10 most important factors were favorable legal framework (4.06), commitment and responsibility of public and private sectors (3.97), strong private consortium (3.91), stable macroeconomic condition (3.85), appropriate risk allocation and risk sharing (3.85), political support (3.76), sound economic policy (3.74), available financial market (3.71), competitive procurement process (3.68), and good governance (3.68). These rankings are quite different from those mentioned above, except for four factors: strong private consortium, appropriate risk allocation and sharing, stable macroeconomic environment, and government/political support. These four major factors are briefly described below:

Strong Private Consortium A consortium equipped with strong technical, operational, and managerial competencies is expected to be more capable of undertaking PPP projects (Zhang 2005). Conversely, a weak and poorly managed consortium fails to address challenges (Osei-Kyei and Chan 2015). Undoubtedly, this should be one of the core assessment items for PPP projects.

Appropriate Risk Allocation and Sharing Risks in the PPP are allocated and shared between the public and private sectors, excluding the end-users (Bing et al. 2005; Hwang et al. 2013). Ke et al. (2010) studied risk allocation and sharing in Hong Kong and compared these practices with those in Australia and the UK. They found that the public sector should retain most political, legal, and social risks, possibly transferring the majority of the meso-level risks (referring to the risks associated with project life cycle, such as late design changes and operational revenue below expectation) to the private sector, while the majority of the micro-level risks (referring to the risks affecting the relationship between the parties involved in a project, such as inadequate distribution of responsibilities among partners and lack of commitment from partners) should be shared equally between the public and private sectors. By knowing the types of risk that should be held by the private and public sectors, a more effective risk management system can be drafted.

Stable Macroeconomic Environment The market is more predictable with a stable macroeconomic environment (Cheung et al. 2012a, b). Fluctuations in financial risks in terms of interest rate, exchange rate, employment rate, and inflation rate would create uncertainties in a project, regarding whether the project costs can be covered and whether the private sector can earn reasonable profits. Different measures must be undertaken to ensure economic viability of the project. These measures include government guarantees, joint investment funding, supplemental periodic service payments, and property development opportunities around the construction site (Cheung et al. 2012a).

Government/Political Support When PPPs are regarded as a public policy, the government must strongly promote it (Li et al. 2005) and must grant financial arrangement for PPP projects (Jacobson and Choi 2008). Full support given to PPP projects would encourage the involvement of the private sector and reduce the political risk that may limit competitions in the tendering process (EU 2008). The Hong Kong government has achieved this balance successfully.

PPP Projects in Hong Kong

As stated earlier, Hong Kong has a long history of cooperation between the public and private sectors. Although researchers have yet to confirm which infrastructures should adopt PPP models (Huang et al. 2016), some Hong Kong experiences can be shared. This section introduces several major categories of projects that have used a form of PPP.

Highway and Tunnel Projects[1]

Traditionally, a government is responsible for the provision of infrastructural facilities to the community. Mak and Mo (2005) have clearly described Hong Kong's transport infrastructure development by using PPP-related approaches.

[1] Description of the highway and tunnel projects in this section was mainly based on Mak and Mo (2005) and Wong (2003).

As early as the late 1960, the first Hong Kong cross-harbor tunnel, namely the Cross Harbor Tunnel, was constructed underwater using the BOT approach. Since then, the BOT approach has been mainly adopted for the construction of other road and tunnel projects. Regardless of the level of involvement of the private sector, the final stage of a BOT project should be the transfer of ownership of the product to the government after the completion of the concession period.

In Hong Kong, an infrastructure project, such as a highway or railway project, normally takes approximately 10 years from inception to completion. According to Mak and Mo (2005), the process for developing an infrastructure project consists of five major stages as follows:

1. Conceptualization and strategic planning—The first stage is to conduct the comprehensive transport study to determine the future transport demands and make the highway or railway network expansion plan to meet the predicted demand, the preferred network configurations and the route alignments, the project priorities, etc.
2. Project definition and detailed planning—The second stage is to clearly set the defined scopes for new highways or railways projects. Key implementation issues are considered to facilitate the selection of the most appropriate implementation method.
3. Project initiation, funding, and authorization—The third stage is to decide the necessary legal, financial, and institutional matters, including environmental impact assessment, public consultation, public exhibition, and objection handling, to enable the authorization of new projects.
4. Design, construction, and commissioning—The fourth stage is to develop the project scheme for the infrastructure. This includes detailed engineering designs, interfacing issues identified and resolved, and the actual construction to be followed by testing and commissioning.
5. Operation, management, and maintenance—The fifth and final stage is to hand over the final infrastructure product to the operating body, which will operate, manage, and maintain the product.

The first category of PPP-related projects presented in this section is tunnel projects. While the government is responsible for operating most of the tunnels, such as the Lion Rock Tunnel and the Aberdeen Tunnel, the private sector is responsible for five tunnels, which were built using the BOT approach. In 1969, the Hong Kong government started considering the BOT approach for building tunnels, especially the construction of tunnels requiring a considerable investment due to unfavorable factors, such as local geological conditions and complicated traffic diversions across urban sites. However, the success of constructing the first tunnel underwater across Victoria Harbor using the BOT approach motivates other tunnel projects to apply this procurement method. Table 11.2 lists the five major BOT projects for constructing highways and tunnels.

Table 11.2 Details of BOT tunnel projects

Name	Year of construction	Client/contractor	Cost (HK$) (approximately)	PPP type	Description
Cross harbor tunnel	1969–1971	Serco Group (HK) Ltd (HK Government)/Scott Wilson Kirkpatrick and Partners—Freeman Fox and Partners JV	N.A.	BOT (30-year franchising period finished at September 1, 1999)	1.86 km long, 2 lanes/2 ways traffic; method of construction: drill and blast
Eastern harbor crossing	1986–1989	Kamaghai led Consortium/ Nishimatsu-Gammon JV	$4.2 billion	BOT (30-year franchising period finished at August 7, 2016)	2.3 km long, submerged twin-tube tunnel with rail and 2 lanes/2 ways traffic
Tate's cairn tunnel	1989–1991	Nishimatsu-Gammon led Consortium/ Nishimatsu-Gammon JV	$2.1 billion	BOT (30-year franchising period to July 11, 2018)	3.6 km long, 2 lanes/2 ways traffic; method of construction: drill and blast
Western harbor crossing	1993–1997	Western Harbor Tunnel Co. Ltd/Mishimatsu-Kumagai JV	$5.7 billion	BOT (30-year franchising period to August 1, 2023)	1.25 km, 3 lanes/2 ways traffic; method of construction: immersed tubes
Tai lam tunnel, route 3	1995–1997	Route 3 (Country Park Section) Co. (Franchise)/Route 3 Contractor's Consortium consisting of Nishimatsu, Dragages, and Gammon	$7.75 billion for the entire route 3 (CP section), tunnel work about $2.5 billion	BOT (30-year franchising period to May 29, 2025)	3.7 km long, 3 lanes/2 ways traffic; method of construction: drill and blast

Note: Source from various publications, including Mak and Mo (2005), Lam and Javed (2016), and Wong (2003)

Among the BOT franchises, the first Cross Harbor Tunnel has completed the 30-year concession period and the operation was "transferred" back to the local government in 1999. This indicated the success of the BOT process, creating a historical milestone for Hong Kong. In 2016, the second cross-harbor tunnel, namely the Eastern Cross Harbor Tunnel, also completed its 30-year franchise period.

Another major category for the application of the PPP approach is highway maintenance. Hong Kong has over 1900 km of roads, highways, roadside slopes, and street furniture, which require more than several hundred million dollars each year to maintain at an acceptable level of safety and serviceability (Mak and Mo 2005).

Traditionally, the engineers of the Highways Department inspect the public roads, plan the maintenance works, and employ contractors to perform such works. They issue numerous maintenance contracts because the maintenance work items are usually very minor and piecemeal. This labor-intensive process, which includes on-site inspection, estimate preparation, checking, approving, work order issuing, work evaluation, interim and final report writing, and payment submittal, consumes a considerable amount of the engineers' time. To drastically reduce their workload, the department uses the new PPP approach to simplify the process by redefining the role of the engineers and maintenance contractors (Mak and Mo 2005).

The new form of the maintenance contracts changes the role of the contractor from a pure work agent to an asset manager (Mak and Mo 2005). That is, most of the maintenance work duties that consume engineers' manpower have been transferred from the engineer to the contractor. The contractor establishes a system of work management to ensure that the works are achieved properly in terms of the cost-effectiveness and performance standards defined by the Highway Department. Moreover, the calculation of the payment made to the contractor is based on the extent to which the performance standards are achieved by the contractor. Therefore, the role of a Highways Department engineer changes to that of an auditor, who evaluates the performance of the contractors and ensures that the contractor performs satisfactorily.

According to Mak and Mo (2005), the first year of operation using this new PPP approach indicated a 90% reduction in the number of work orders issued, resulting in considerable savings of administrative costs and manpower. Due to this performance and experience, the Highways Department has adopted this approach for other maintenance works, including combining contracts to increase the scope of work and extending the contract duration.

Besides short-term projects, long-term maintenance contracts have also been issued under the PPP approach. Two popular examples are Tsing Ma Control Area and Tsing Sha Control Area. Tsing Ma Control Area spans on 17 km of road networks on Tsing Yi Island, Ma Wan, Lantau Island, and Kwai Chung, covering the Tsing Ma Bridge, Kap Shui Mun Bridge, Ma Wan Viaduct, Cheung Tsing Highway, Cheung Tsing Tunnel, etc., excluding the area of rails managed by the MTR Corporation Limited (MTR). The area is currently managed and maintained by Tsing Ma Management Limited. One of its sources of income is the collection of tolls and fees from the Lantau Link at Lantau Toll Plaza. Given the success of Tsing Ma Control Area, the government adopted the same PPP approach for Tsing Sha Control Area, which covers Nam Wan Tunnel, Stonecutters Bridge, Tsing Sha Highway, Eagle's Nest Tunnel, Sha Tin Heights Tunnel, etc. The area is currently managed and maintained by Tsing Sha Management Limited. Its sources of income are tolls and fees from both tunnels at the shared toll plaza situated at the junction of the two tunnels.

Railway Projects[2]

In addition to highways and tunnels, railways are another kind of major infrastructure development in Hong Kong. As a matter of policy for a compact city, public transport has been the prime people mover, carrying people to different parts of Hong Kong. In the recent 10th Asia-Pacific Economic Cooperation (APEC) Transportation Ministerial Meeting, the Secretary for Transport and Housing, Mr. Frank Chan Fan, discussed the employment of PPPs in railway projects in Hong Kong (Chan 2017). As he noted, public transport in Hong Kong accounts for a 90% passenger share, which corresponds to approximately 12 million passenger trips each day. Among other public transport modes, railways are regarded as the backbone of Hong Kong's public transport system and account for over 40% of all passenger trips made on public transport. The railway is the densest transportation network in Hong Kong.

The railways in Hong Kong are owned and operated by the Mass Transit Railway (MTR). According to the MTR's planning vision, the company aims to provide 50% of all passenger trips in Hong Kong through its railway network daily. To achieve this aim, a railway station must be accessible by half of the residential buildings and over three-quarters of the commercial offices within a walking distance of 500 m. For the whole year of 2016, the network provided nearly 2 billion passenger trips, with train services on schedule 99.9% of the time (Chan 2017). Moreover, the MTR is running businesses in Melbourne, Sydney, Stockholm, London, and many cities of the mainland China. In September 2017, the company was ranked by the Fortune Magazine as 33rd among the top 50 companies that "Change the World" (Chan 2017).

Railway projects involve considerable capital investment. To reduce the financial burden of the local government, recent railway projects were initiated through the partnership between the public and private sectors. Two PPP schemes, namely the ownership scheme and the concession scheme, have been used as railway project procurement methods (Chan 2017). Under the ownership scheme, the government is responsible for the initial strategic planning, while the MTR is responsible for the details of project implementation, including funding, design, construction, operation and maintenance, and ultimately ownership of the railway. This is referred to as the BOO approach (Mak and Mo 2005).

To bridge the funding gap, the government offers different kinds of support to the MTR (Chan 2017). For example, the government grants the MTR the property development right, which is called the Rail-plus-Property development model. That is, the MTR can develop residential and/or commercial properties on site, thereby helping the company generate a considerable amount of income to compensate for the spending on the design, construction, and operation of the railways. Additionally, when there is a lack of suitable sites along the railway alignment for property devel-

[2] This section summarized with modification some discussion of PPP for railway projects by Chan (2017) in the 10th APEC Transportation Ministerial Meeting.

opment, a capital grant would be offered to alleviate the amount of private capital investment. In Hong Kong, the railway projects initiated by the MTR are all BOO-type projects. That is, the MTR would finance, build, and own the railways.

Under the concession scheme, the government funds the construction of the railway and shares the operational risk of the project, while the ownership of the railway rests with the government. Upon completion of the railway, the government grants a railway corporation the operating right and receives service concession payments thereafter. This concession scheme has just been adopted for building the Hong Kong Section of the Guangzhou-Shenzhen-Hong Kong Express Rail Link, or XRL in short. This high-speed rail link connects Hong Kong to mainland China's national high-speed rail network. Unlike other local MTR railways, the XRL is a cross-border infrastructure. Ownership of the XRL by the local government helps to facilitate the coordination and resolution of interface issues between the Hong Kong and mainland China counterparts during both the construction and operation phases (Chan 2017).

Other Infrastructure Projects

Previous experience has shown that capital and skills offered by the private sector perform well when they are allowed to implement the entire project cycle of designing, constructing, and managing a facility. As noted by Cheung (2005), PPP, as seen in this context, provides a suitable incentive for new technologies and innovative ideas to enhance productivity, facilitate the transfer of knowledge, and maintain the momentum of infrastructure development without imposing too much fiscal pressure on the government. Due to expanding public expectations for greater efficiency and responsiveness, the PPP concept has expanded into other public facilities. A feasibility study should be conducted to explore the use of a PPP in terms of its business viability and the possible modes of delivery (Cheung 2005). Among other PPP approaches, the BOT model has been a common choice for the provision of other infrastructure projects, such as waste treatment plants and landfill projects. This section summarizes three such projects.

Chemical Waste Treatment Plant Chemical waste in Hong Kong is disposed of at either the landfill site where the chemical waste is generated or at other off-site disposal facilities, including the Hong Kong Chemical Waste Treatment Center (CWTC) on Tsing Yi Island. Regardless of which facility is used, it must be licensed by the Environmental Protection Department. The CWTC has been in operation since 1993 and was developed to accept all hazardous wastes collected in the territory. Under a BOT agreement, the center is being managed and operated by Ecospace Limited (Chan and Cheung 2014). The center offers a permanent destruction solution to limit waste-specific technologies to on-site treatment (Millison 2005).

Strategic Landfills Three strategic landfills, namely the West New Territories Landfill (WENT), South East New Territories Landfill (SENT), and North East New Territories Landfill (NENT), are the key disposal sites in Hong Kong for thousands of tons of garbage to be disposed of daily from the business, industry, and residential sectors. The BOT approach allows the sites, which are owned by the Environmental Protection Department, to be run by the private sector. The BOT contract requires the contractor to carry out the design, construction, operation, restoration, and aftercare of the landfill according to specified performance criteria (Environmental Protection Department (EPD) 2017). Specifically, WENT began operation in November 1993 and is being managed by SITA Waste Services Limited. WENT has an operation cost of approximately HK$303 million per year and possesses an area of 110 hectare to receive municipal and construction wastes. SENT began operation in September 1994 and is being managed by Green Valley Landfill Limited. SENT has an operation cost of approximately HK$227 million per year and possesses an area of 100 hectare to receive only construction waste. NENT began its operation in June 1995 and is being managed by Far East Landfill Technologies Limited. NENT has an operation cost of approximately HK$164 million per year and possesses an area of 61 hectare to receive municipal, construction, and special wastes.

The River Trade Terminal in Tuen Mun Under the terms of the land grant in the BOT contract, the River Trade Terminal Company Limited was given the right to build and operate a terminal in Tuen Mun, while the government provided supporting infrastructure, such as land, access roads, drains, and public services in the port area. This terminal opened in 1998 and was the first purpose-built container terminal for handling river trade cargo in Hong Kong. The terminal lease runs until 2047. The port operator is responsible for consolidating containers and bulk cargo shipped between the port in Hong Kong and ports in the Pearl River Delta (PRD). The company claims that their professional expertise and high-quality services have enabled them to become the foremost logistics hub of the PRD and its hinterland over the past several years. Due to fierce competition with such rival terminals as the China Merchants Port and Chu Kong Shipping-owned Chu Kong River Trade Terminal (Wee 2018), this PPP model has proven to be unprofitable, resulting in the company's forced decision to extend its services to cover containers from other Asian ports to increase income. This extension was argued to breach the original land grant conditions (Kwan 2005). With the overall declining trend in river trade transshipment within the PRD, the container terminal has a consistently low use rate. A government paper indicated that the terminal, on average, operated at only 24% of the total capacity of its 49 berths in 2017 (Zhao 2018). Recently, a task force that advises the government on land supply has discussed the feasibility of developing this underused site for 22,000 new flats to address the city's housing supply issue (Wee 2018; Zhao 2018).

More Generic Projects That Involve Infrastructure Development

In addition to the PPP approaches mentioned above, other government-led projects involving the private sector through other forms of PPPs have been documented (Lee 2005). In these more generic PPP projects that involve infrastructure development, the government acts principally as a joint venture partner, with either the Efficiency Unit as a facilitator or a government department, as in the case of AWE, which was spearheaded by "Invest Hong Kong" and was responsible for attracting foreign direct investment into Hong Kong (Lam and Javed 2016). The following paragraphs in this section, which were written based on Lee (2005) and Lam and Javed (2016), present four of such projects that are well known across Hong Kong.[3]

Tung Chung Cable Car

The Tung Chung Cable Car project in Ngong Ping was a 30-year franchise granted to the MTR in 2002. This is a PFI project, in which the private sector covers the design, finance, construction, operation, and maintenance of the cable car system. The Tung Chung Cable Car Bill provides a legal framework for the grant of the franchise and sets out the rights and obligations of the franchisee during the franchise period. The Bill was enacted on 28 May 2003. The detailed provisions relating to the construction and operation of the cable car system are governed by a Project Agreement signed between the MTR and the government on 19 November 2003. Although the construction of the cable car system and the related developments involve funding by the private sector, the local government was committed to spending HK$235.3 million for the construction of various infrastructure facilities that support the cable car system and related developments in Ngong Ping.

The Cyberport

The Cyberport project, comprising a Cyberport portion and an ancillary residential portion, was undertaken in 1999 by the local government in cooperation with the Pacific Century Group. The Cyberport portion was intended to establish a strategic hub for leading information technology and information services companies and a group of professional information technology/information service talents in Hong Kong, while the residential portion aimed to generate revenue to financially support the project. Under the relevant project agreement, the developer, the Pacific Century Group, was responsible for the provision and procurement of funds to meet all the project expenses. The capital contribution from the government was the surrender

[3]This part described four more generic infrastructure projects, which were based on Lee (2005) and Lam and Javed (2016).

of the value of the land for the residential portion when the development was granted to the developer, who was required to sell the residential units in the open market but was entitled to receive a share of the surplus sale proceeds. However, the developer was required to return the completed Cyberport portion as well as the rental income and any other incomes generated from this portion to the government. Despite a lack of public funding of the design and construction of the Cyberport development, the government provided funds of HK$964 million and HK$231.8 million in May of 1999 and May of 2000, respectively, for the construction of roads, drains, waterworks, and other essential infrastructure to support the Cyberport developments.

The Asia World-Expo

The AWE (formerly known as the International Exhibition Centre) is one of the two major convention and exhibition facilities in Hong Kong. The AWE is situated near the Hong Kong International Airport and is jointly financed and owned by three entities, namely the Hong Kong government, the Airport Authority (AA), and a private sector consortium. While the government and the private sector consortium pay for the construction costs, AA provides the land for the venue. The private sector consortium is also responsible for the design, construction, management, and operation of the AWE. The AWE is currently managed by the AsiaWorld-Expo Management Limited and provides 70,000 m^2 of exhibition space. It opened on 21 December 2005 and has been in full operation since the first quarter of 2006. The construction cost was approximately HK$2.35 billion. While the government funded 85% of the total construction cost up to HK$2 billion, the private sector consortium funded the remaining 15%. This project can be regarded as a JV-WMI because the government, AA, and the private sector consortium (selected through an open tender process) entered into a joint venture agreement for the design, construction, and operation of the AWE.

The West Kowloon Cultural District

The West Kowloon Cultural District (WKCD) is a waterfront site of 40 hectares at the southern tip of the West Kowloon Reclamation (WKR). In October 1998, the former chief executive of the Hong Kong Special Administrative Region, Mr. Donald Tsang Yam-Kuen, announced in his policy address that the government was planning to enact a new, state-of-the-art performance venue in the WKR. In November of 1999, the chief executive mentioned that the southern tip of the WKR could be used to develop a district that integrated world-class artistics, cultural, and entertainment activities. Moreover, the government decided to enlist the help of local and overseas design professionals by holding an open concept competition. However, the competition did not include the eventual development right of the area, and the government was not bound in any way to develop the WKR in accordance with the winning design. In April 2001, the government launched the open concept competition to invite conceptual plans for the development of the WKCD and received a total of 161 entries from local and overseas participants. The first prize was awarded to Foster and Partners (with the competition title of Foster scheme). Additionally, the government launched an Invitation for Proposals for the development of the WKCD in September 2003. The successful proponent was required to plan, design, finance, construct, procure, fit out, and complete the WKCD and subsequently operate, maintain, and manage the core art and cultural facilities for a concessional period. Five submissions were received when the Invitation for Proposals for the development of the WKCD closed on 19 June 2004. Finally, a land grant for the site for a term of 50 years was offered to the successful proponent.

PPPs for the One-Belt-One-Road Initiative

China's President Xi Jinping has proposed the One Belt One Road Initiative (OBOR), which is also known as the Silk Road Economic Belt and the twenty-first century Maritime Silk Road. This initiative has been described as "the most significant and far-reaching initiative that China has ever put forward" (Winter 2016). One of the five main goals is to facilitate connectivity, encouraging infrastructure development partnerships along the "new and old" Silk Roads that cover more than 50 countries. As disclosed in the speech by President Xi Jinping on 29 March 2015 at the Boao Forum for Asia (BFA) annual conference, the Silk Road Fund and the Asian Infrastructure Investment Bank (AIIB) would play key roles in fostering economic connectivity along the Belt and Road by establishing a new type of industrialization that promotes a multilateral trading system and common development of all enclosed countries. In other words, it is expected that the countries involved in OBOR are entitled to and mutually benefit from an equal level of infrastructure development.

As an extension of the infrastructure-driven economic development framework that has sustained the rapid economic growth of China (Oborcon, 2019), investment opportunities in infrastructure connectivity along the OBOR are constantly rising. In November of 2014, in addition to the AIIB that is proposed to have an authorized capital of US$100 billion,[4] China has announced plans to create a US$40 billion development fund, which aims to invest in businesses rather than lend money for projects. The Karot Hydropower Project in Pakistan, started in January of 2016, is the first foreign investment project of the Silk Road Fund. The Chinese government has also promised to offer Pakistan at least US$350 million to finance the hydropower station. Between 2014 and 2016, China's total trade volume in the countries

[4]According to Xinhua Finance Agency (2015), the proposed multilateral bank has an authorized capital of $100 billion, 75% of which comes from Asian and Oceania countries. China is the single largest stakeholder, holding 26% of voting rights. The bank started operation by year end of 2016.

along the Belt and Road exceeded US$3 trillion, created US$1.1 billion in revenue and 180,000 jobs for the countries involved.

Countries with strong skills and experiences in infrastructure development should grasp the opportunities to participate in infrastructure projects along the Belt and Road. Hong Kong is no exception. As a special administrative region of China, Hong Kong should be in a more favorable position than its rivalries, such as Singapore, to connect to the Belt and Road due to its more advantageous geography and status. In the policy address by the former chief executive of the Hong Kong Special Administrative Region, Mr. Leung Chun-Ying, he stressed that Hong Kong should position itself to be the "super-connector" between mainland China and the rest of the world, bringing together parties interested in Belt-and-Road-inspired projects and facilitating their potential collaboration (Leung 2015). Regarding the infrastructure projects, a number of roles, in terms of financing, professional skills, and project procurement, can be played by Hong Kong.

Hong Kong is a rich source of high-achieving professionals in a wide range of services, including accounting, law, construction, engineering, and business management (Yan 2016). According to Leung (2015), Hong Kong can play different roles in the OBOR. For example, major financial players of the OBOR, such as the AIIB and the Silk Road Fund, should make use of Hong Kong's competitive advantage in international financing and asset management. As China's major international financial center and one of the world's well-established financial capital markets, Hong Kong has accumulated the experience, the expertise, and the connections to be able to act as a major fundraising hub for the OBOR. In addition, Hong Kong, as an offshore Renminbi hub with the world's largest Renminbi liquidity pool, is home to the world's busiest air cargo airport and the world's fourth-busiest container port (Yan 2016). Leung (2015) reported that Hong Kong helped China handle approximately 20% of its international trade and further expected that Hong Kong's role as a logistics hub will be enhanced once the OBOR maritime road is in full operation.

In addition to capital investment and financing, resources that are considered to be scarce, such as advanced project development, strategic management, and risk absorption capabilities, are necessary to successfully implement Belt-and-Road-inspired projects, but far exceed what governments can provide. This disparity highlights why PPPs, which are relatively new to Asia, are essential. PPPs contribute not only capital but also innovative ideas, project management experience, and risk control. The private sector, working closely with the public sector, can play leading roles in Belt and Road projects. PPPs are known for leading to the provision of appropriate and innovative designs, cost-efficient and timely construction, and efficient operations.

As mentioned in earlier sections, PPPs have historically played an important role in developing Hong Kong's infrastructure. The opportunity offered by the OBOR helps to leverage Hong Kong's PPP experiences and influences within, as well as beyond, the region. Hong Kong's project practices for infrastructure development, risk control, and financing are unique in Asia in terms of their international business orientation, depth and breadth of services, expertise, and high level of professionalism.

Hong Kong has long functioned as the principal locus of advanced professional capabilities which have served Hong Kong, mainland China, and the region well.

Moreover, key participants for such a great "dream" include public-sector partners, national and local governments, and national and international infrastructure development banks. Among other participants, development banks should play major roles in the larger, more complex PPP projects because of (1) their willingness to accept higher risks than the private sector lenders and investors would accept, (2) the employment of experts who have many years of experience in project procurement and financing in developing countries, (3) their ability in using viable methods for selecting feasible projects, and (4) their understanding of the private sector participants due to their long-term relationships within developing countries (Yan 2016).

The implementation of PPP infrastructure projects, which typically involve multiple parties of different nationalities, is complex and requires special expertise and experience. The "packaging" for such projects, preparing them for the start of construction, is quite difficult and requires dealing with many challenges which must be solved during long project development periods. As public/private partnerships are relatively new to developing Asia, "packaging" them is currently more of an art than a science (Yan 2016).

PPPs for the Public Housing Policy

Hong Kong has been ranked as the world's most expensive property market for seven continuous years. To combat the climbing rents of Hong Kong's private property market, increasing the provision of subsidized homes is a direct and viable means to help local home buyers fulfill their dream of home ownership. Although the government has implemented several policies, such as the Home Ownership Scheme and Hong Kong Property for Hong Kong People Scheme, these policies have yet to solve the housing problem. To address these housing problems, the new chief executive of the Hong Kong Special Administrative Region, Ms. Carrie Lam Cheng Yuet-Ngor (Lam Cheng 2017), has pledged to launch a starter home scheme. While details of the pilot scheme will not be finalized until mid-2018, the development site at Anderson Road in Kwun Tong is envisioned to be the first "Starter Homes" residences project launched by the end of 2018, offering 1000 housing units.

As mentioned by Lam Cheng (2017), "Starter Homes" are intended to build affordable government-subsidized housing units for middle-income families. These units will be constructed using a PPP approach. That is, the government invites private developers instead of the Housing Authority to develop and construct the subsidized homes. The use of PPPs for housing projects has been proposed in other countries. For example, the Thai government has already thought of collaborating with domestic and foreign investors to develop housing projects through a PPP scheme for low-income earners and the lower middle class under the Pracha Rat Home scheme (Theparat 2017).

To truly help average Hong Kong home buyers, the government might have to play a more active role in proposing short-, medium-, and long-term solutions to the severe land shortages faced by the city (Lam Cheng 2017). In addition to possible long-term solutions for building a significant land reserve, such as large-scale reclamation outside Victoria Harbor, implementing a PPP scheme to release the development potential of privately owned land to increase the supply of both private and public housing is regarded as a short- to medium-term solution (Wong et al. 2017).

Theoretically, a PPP allows the sharing of financing risks and expertise of home construction between the public and private sectors, thus improving the quantity and quality of social housing units. However, it is unknown how the private developers will be attracted to these projects if these homes, as described by Wong (2017), are essentially a more upscale version of public housing, permitting ownership but restricting pricing; while the private sector is known for being eager to earn a profit, it often does not attain as much social responsibility as the government does. Therefore, thoughtful planning is required to ensure that co-development housing projects achieve both the noble goal to help local residents acquire their first unit and the business goal to allow the private sector to profit from the projects. Accordingly, local experts have suggested two proposals, which Lam Cheng (2017) summarized as follows.

Attracting Private Developers to Convert Part of Their Land for Social Housing

There is a vast amount of agricultural land owned by major private developers, spanning approximately 1000 hectares. If the land is fully converted into high-rise housing, this area could provide housing for almost 1 million households (3–4 million people), nearly half of Hong Kong's population. Although private developers are known for aiming to build profitable private housing, the land has been left undeveloped because of its remote geographical location and the lack of public amenities. Therefore, an opportunity exists for a public–private collaboration to convert the land for developing social housing.

Given the primary business goal of profit making by private developers, it is expected that private developers would provide certain portions of their land for subsidized homes, and this privately owned land would then be redeveloped. To incentivize private developers to participate into social housing projects, a PPP model is recommended. In such a model, the government compensates the private developers by subsidizing the cost of public infrastructure around the development sites in exchange for private sector commitments to the projects. This partnership model is believed to be favorably received by private developers since the government's investments in infrastructure enable them to monetize illiquid assets by converting hoarded land into profitable housing projects.

Adopting a PPP Model as an Alternative Solution to Sustain Housing Supply

In this PPP model, the government contributes most of the capital and invites private developers to execute the design and construction of the subsidized apartments. As noted by Wong (2017), this practice is common in other large cities, such as London and Paris, where the government could select a winner according to criteria regarding financial capability, the total number of social housing units, and other design elements related to livability and sustainability, instead of those criteria traditionally adopted in land auctions, mainly regarding price. Furthermore, such PPP projects can help unleash the creativity of the private sector, thereby offering potentially higher quality and more inclusive housing solutions, compared to the traditional role of the private sector as a construction partner of the government.

Upon completion, all units will be purchased by the government at an agreed-upon price that generates moderate returns for the developers. While profit margins might not be as attractive as those possible in private housing projects, the risks and capital requirements are significantly lower in these co-development residential projects. By partnering with the government, private developers are assured of a relatively stable return on investment. The PPP model is certainly a well-thought-out alternative solution to sustain the housing supply if managed well.

Lessons Learned from Previous PPP Projects

Many PPP projects in Hong Kong have successful track records and have been operated to the advantage of all stakeholders. Among other factors, the framework agreements are important in leading to the success of a PPP project. Despite no PPP projects being regarded as unsuccessful due to premature termination, several important lessons learned are described hereinafter.

1. The experience in the Cross Harbor Tunnel project clearly demonstrated the advantages of the BOT approach (Mak and Mo 2005). First, the tunnel took only 36 months to build and was 11 months ahead of schedule (Chan et al. 2016). Second, the construction cost could be paid back by the toll revenue collected from the tunnel in approximately three and a half years. The use of tolling schemes on roads in urban areas has been documented (e.g., Albalate et al. 2009). Third, the management of the tunnel has provided a safe and reliable service for the community throughout the franchise period. Fourth, the vision and skill of the private sector has offered innovation in the delivery of a viable infrastructure project, such as the application of the immersed tube technique. Another tunnel, the Tate's Cairn Tunnel, is operating smoothly and is a good example showing how the stakeholders can work together on the issues pertaining to costs, benefits, and risk allocation to better serve themselves (Kwan 2005). However, misconceptions suggested that BOT projects would affect the job security and

career prospects of existing staff. To dispel such misconceptions, clarifications were made to stress that a PPP was merely an alternative procurement method and that there would be neither forced redundancy nor repercussions on the future role of the department (Cheung 2005).

2. Regarding highway maintenance projects, the new form of maintenance contracts has changed the roles of both the contractor and government's engineer (Mak and Mo 2005). Specifically, the contractor has shifted from a pure works agent to an asset manager that fulfills a set of performance standards defined by the government. This shift would not only reduce the workload of the government's engineer by increasing the contractor's involvement in inspection duties but also standardize the contractor's performance quality. The role of the engineer has also shifted to that of an auditor to evaluate the performance of the works contractor on the basis of the performance indicators set by the government and to ensure that the contractor has performed satisfactorily. Moreover, the calculation of the payment to the contractor is changed to be based on the extent to which the performance standards of the works have been achieved by the contractor, instead of the conventional method of paying for the works that have been completed. This greatly improves the value of the payment made to the contractor.
3. Additional investment opportunities for the private financing party of PPP projects have been argued to be insufficient (Carpintero and Petersen 2013). In railway projects, the Rail-plus-Property development model raised by the Hong Kong government has benefited the railway development in several ways (Chan 2017). First, the government offers the MTR the right to develop residential and/or commercial properties along the railway alignment. This not only helps the company generate high incomes but also enhances the topside use of the land for other purposes. Second, the combination of railway and property development helps streamline the interface between stations, depots, and topside developments to facilitate the necessary development of the area. Moreover, harmonizing property and railway development helps to create more convenient accessibility between railway stations and nearby residential and commercial properties, thereby improving the viability of the railway projects.
4. Apart from the above positive lessons, negative experiences are also crucial for future references. One such major lesson was provided by the River Trade Terminal project in Tuen Mun. In this PPP model, the company that operated the terminal faced tough competition with nearby Chinese rivals and was forced to extend its port services for containers from other Asian ports, resulting in the accusation of breaching the BOT contract that allowed the company to only address port-to-port services across the border between Hong Kong and mainland China. This long-standing underused facility and the overall declining trend in river trade trans-shipment within the region have led to the idea of redeveloping the site into a housing development project (Wee 2018). As stated earlier, all involved parties of a PPP should work together to resolve problems that would prevent any parties from obtaining benefits from the project (Kwan 2005). Risk allocation should be fair and reasonable, and litigation should be the last

resort. This case indicates that a successful PPP project must offer the operator a stable income stream spanning the whole concession period (Kwan 2005; Zou et al. 2008).

5. Another lesson was learned from the management experience of the Western Harbor Crossing. The government signed an agreement with the franchisee, indicating that tolls may be raised if the actual net revenue or traffic level falls below projections. The franchisee has then made use of this clause to maintain their revenue stream by continuously increasing the tolls above those of other cross-harbor tunnels. As noted by Rouhani et al. (2016), unlimited profit-maximizing tolls, while raising substantial revenues, would negatively impact the average users. In addition to the criticism made by those who pay more to cross the harbor through the "expensive" tunnel, this profit-maximizing has led to a negative feedback from customers who choose to use alternative routes to avoid higher tolls, causing traffic congestion at less expensive tunnels, especially the Cross Harbor Tunnel. Under the franchise agreement, the government cannot intervene in the franchisee's strategic decision. From a social-welfare perspective, all major stakeholders should benefit under a Pareto improvement concept (Rouhani et al. 2016). The Hong Kong government is, therefore, considering offering subsidies to the franchisee in exchange for lower tolls prior to the end of the franchise period in August of 2023 (Yau and Yeung 2017). To ease chronic traffic jams in Hong Kong, the government is seeking to have a comprehensive policy to manage the traffic distribution of the main tunnels, including the three harbor crossings and other vehicle tunnels. Hence, an effective long-term infrastructure franchise agreement requires more consideration before implementation. Alternatively, a mixed public and private tolling scheme, as suggested by Rouhani et al. (2016), that proposes to return a significant portion of the economic value created by road pricing back to the community and tunnel users may offer a better solution to solve this problem.

Conclusions

This chapter has summarized the PPP backgrounds and experiences in Hong Kong and the comments and opinions from local leaders, academics, columnists, and journalists. As noted earlier, PPPs are not a new procurement concept in Hong Kong, although the term emerged in the UK in the late 1990s. The BOT approach used in the late 1970s for the development of the first cross-harbor tunnel in Hong Kong was a typical joint effort between the public and private sectors. In this chapter, the definition of a PPP, its objectives and benefits, and the factors affecting it have been discussed in regard to Hong Kong. Some infrastructure cases have been described. The experiences gained have indicated that the government has implemented measures to enhance the project procurement and delivery processes. While the lessons learned from the infrastructure projects form a knowledge base for guiding future projects in Hong Kong, such valuable experiences will also be useful to relevant applications in other countries. Moreover, this chapter has discussed the opportunities for expanding PPP services, highlighting the popular topics of the OBOR initiative and the public housing problems in Hong Kong. However, the PPP concept is not the only solution for infrastructure project procurement; rather, a PPP is an alternative viable method when traditional procurement methods are regarded as less appropriate.

Acknowledgements This work was supported by The Education University of Hong Kong under a departmental research grant. The author wishes to thank his research and student assistants for their outstanding assistance on this work.

References

Albalate, D., Bel, G., & Fageda, X. (2009). Privatization and regulatory reform of toll motorways in Europe. *Governance, 22*(2), 295–318.

Bae, Y., & Joo, Y.-M. (2016). Pathways to meet critical success factors for local PPPs: The cases of urban transport infrastructure in Korean cities. *Cities, 53*, 35–42.

Bing, L., Akintoye, A., Edwards, P. J., & Hardcastle, C. (2005). The allocation of risk in PPP/PFI construction projects in the UK. *International Journal of Project Management, 23*, 25–35.

Carpintero, S., & Petersen, O. H. (2013). PPP projects in transport: Evidence from light rail projects in Spain. *Public Money & Management, 34*(1), 43–50.

Chan, A. P. C., & Cheung, E. (2014). *Public-private partnerships in international construction: Learning from case studies*. New York, NY: Routledge.

Chan, A. P. C., Lam, P. T. I., Chan, D. W. M., & Cheung, E. (2016). *Application of public private partnership (PPP) model in procuring infrastructure projects in Hong Kong*. CIB W065/055 commissions: Transformation through construction, Hong Kong.

Chan, F. F. (2017). *Hong Kong's transport infrastructure public-private partnerships*. In Presented at the 10th Asia-Pacific Economic Co-operation (APEC) Transportation Ministerial Meeting, Panel Session on Sustainable Transportation, October 5, Port Moresby, Papua New Guinea.

Cheung, C. (2005). *Permanent secretary for works (acting)'s speech at the 2nd annual public private partnerships Asia summit*, May 25, Hong Kong. Retrieved from https://www.devb.gov.hk/en/publications_and_press_releases/speeches_and_presentations/index_id_4787.html

Cheung, E., Chan, A. P. C., & Kajewski, S. (2012a). Factors contributing to successful public private partnership projects: Comparing Hong Kong with Australia and the United Kingdom. *Journal of Facilities Management, 10*(1), 45–58.

Cheung, E., Chan, A. P. C., Lam, P. T. I., Chan, D. W. M., & Ke, Y. (2012b). A comparative study of critical success factors for public private partnership (PPP) between mainland China and the Hong Kong Special Administrative Region. *Facilities, 30*(13/14), 647–666.

Efficiency Unit (EU). (2007). *Serving the community by using the private sector: Policy and practice* (2nd ed.). Hong Kong: Efficiency Unit, the Government of the Hong Kong Special Administrative Region.

Efficiency Unit (EU). (2008). *Serving the community by using the private sector: An introductory guide to public private partnerships (PPPs)* (2nd ed.). Hong Kong: Efficiency Unit, the Government of the Hong Kong Special Administrative Region.

Environmental Protection Department (EPD). (2017). *Strategic landfills*. Environmental Protection Department, The Government of the Hong Kong Special Administrative Region, Hong Kong. Retrieved from http://www.epd.gov.hk/epd/english/environmentinhk/waste/prob_solutions/msw_strategic.html

Federal Highway Administration (FHWA). (2010). *Public-private partnership concessions for highway projects: A primer*. Washington, DC: Office of Innovative Program Delivery, Federal Highway Administration, U.S. Department of Transportation.

Forcael, E., Ellis, R., & Jaramillo, F. (2011). Design-build-finance in the US: The case of iRox, I-75 road expansion project. *Revista de la Construcción, 10*(1), 24–35.

Huang, Z., Zheng, P., Ma, Y., Li, X., Xu, W., & Zhu, W. (2016). A simulation study of the impact of the public-private partnership strategy on the performance of transport infrastructure. *Springerplus, 5*(1), 958–972.

Hwang, B.-G., Zhao, X., & Gay, M. J. S. (2013). Public private partnership projects in Singapore: Factors, critical risks, and preferred risk allocation from the perspective of contractor. *International Journal of Project Management, 31*, 424–433.

Jacobson, C., & Choi, S. O. (2008). Success factors: Public works and public-private partnerships. *International Journal of Public Sector Management, 21*(6), 637–657.

Jefferies, M., & McGeorge, W. D. (2009). Using public-private partnerships (PPPs) to procure social infrastructure in Australia. *Engineering Construction and Architectural Management, 16*, 415–437.

Ke, Y., Wang, S., & Chan, A. P. (2010). Risk allocation in public-private partnership infrastructure projects: Comparative study. *Journal of Infrastructure Systems, 16*(4), 343–351.

Kwan, J. (2005). Public private partnerships: Public private dialogue. One day conference on public private partnerships – Opportunities and challenges, jointly organized by Civil Division of Department of Civil Engineering, The University of Hong Kong and the Hong Kong Institution of Engineers. Opening address by the President, the Hong Kong Institution of Engineers, February 22, Center for Innovation in Construction & Infrastructure Development, Hong Kong Convention and Exhibition Center, Hong Kong.

Lam Cheng, Y.-N. C. (2017). *The chief executive's 2017 policy address*. The Hong Kong Special Administrative Region of the People's Republic of China.

Lam, T.-I., & Javed, A. A. (2016). Public private partnership in Hong Kong. In A. Akintoye, M. Beck, & M. Kumaraswamy (Eds.), *Public private partnerships: A global review* (pp. 118–131). New York, NY: Routledge.

Lee, V. (2005). *Public private partnerships* (Research report no.: RP03/04-05). Research and Library Services Division, Legislative Council Secretariat, The Hong Kong Special Administrative Region.

Leung, C. Y. (2015). *HK's key role in one belt, one road future*. Published on March 27, 2015. Retrieved December 12, 2017, from http://www.news.gov.hk/en/record/html/2015/03/20150327_190815.shtml

Li, B., Akintoye, A., Edwards, P. J., & Hardcastle, C. (2005). Critical success factors for PPP/PFI projects in the UK construction industry. *Construction Management and Economics, 23*, 459–471.

Mak, C. K., & Mo, S. (2005). *Some aspects of the PPP approach to transport infrastructure development in Hong Kong*. In Paper presented at Conference on *Public Private Partnerships - Opportunities and Challenges*, February 22, jointly organized by Center for Infrastructure and Construction Industry Development, The University of Hong Kong and Civil Division, The Hong Kong Institution of Engineers, Hong Kong.

Millison, D. (2005). Reviving the scorched earth: A snapshot of China's hazardous waste management and cleaner production programs. In K. A. Day (Ed.), *China's environment and the challenge of sustainable development* (pp. 201–232). Armonk, NY: M.E. Sharpe.

Mouraviev, N., & Kakabadse, N. K. (2016). Conceptualising public-private partnerships: A critical appraisal of approaches to meanings and forms. *Society and Business Review, 11*(2), 155–173.

Ng, S. T., Wong, Y. M. W., & Wong, J. M. W. (2012). Factors influencing the success of PPP at feasibility state – A tripartite comparison study in Hong Kong. *Habitat International, 36*(4), 423–432.

Oborcon, (2019). Belt and road initiative. Oborcon Belt and Road Consultancy B.V, Alkmaar NH, The Netherlands. Retrieved from http://oborcon.org/bri.html.

Osei-Kyei, R., & Chan, A. P. C. (2015). Review of studies on the critical success factor for public-private partnership (PPP) projects from 1990 to 2013. *International Journal of Project Management, 33*, 1335–1346.

Osei-Kyei, R., Dansoh, A., & Ofori-Kuragu, J. K. (2014). Reasons for adopting public-private partnership (PPP) for construction projects in Ghana. *International Journal of Construction Management, 14*(4), 227–238.

Rouhani, O. M., Geddes, R. R., Gao, H. O., & Bel, G. (2016). Social welfare analysis of investment public-private partnership approaches for transportation projects. *Transportation Research Part A, 88*, 86–103.

Smith, H. (2004). *Public private partnerships (PPPs) in Hong Kong*. Retrieved August 18, 2017, from http://www.cannonway.com/web/page.php?page=96

Tang, L.-Y., Shen, Q. P., Skitmore, M., & Cheng, E. W. L. (2013). Ranked critical factors in PPP briefings. *Journal of Management in Engineering, 29*(2), 164–171.

Theparat, C. (2017, August 29). Thai government pushes public-private partnership for housing scheme. *South China Morning Post*, Hong Kong.

Wee, V. (2018). *Hong Kong's River Trade Terminal may be redeveloped.* Retrieved April 3, 2018, from http://www.seatrade-maritime.com/news/asia/hong-kong-s-river-trade-terminal-may-be-redeveloped.html

Winter, T. (2016). *One belt, one road, one heritage: Cultural diplomacy and the silk road.* Washington, DC: Diplomat Media Inc..

Wong, M. (2017, April 6). How to make Carrie Lam's "starter homes" truly affordable for Hong Kong people. *South China Morning Post*, Hong Kong.

Wong, R. (2003). *A review on the recent large scale infrastructure projects in Hong Kong*. In Presented in a technical seminar on June 7, organized by the Hong Kong Institute of Surveyors, Hong Kong.

Wong, Y.-C. R., Wong, Y.-S. S., Tsang, W.-H. W., Ip, M-K. R., Chu, T.-H. M., Tong, K.-Y. F., & To, S.-Y. M. (2017). *Housing policy reform to narrow wealth gap: Urgent formation of land to improve people's livelihood* (Land and Housing Policy Research Series 3). Our Hong Kong Foundation, Hong Kong.

Xinhua Finance Agency (2015). *China-led AIIB agreement signed in Beijing*. Published on June 29, 2015. Retrieved on December 22, 2017 from: http://en.xfafinance.com/html/BR/Main_Step/2015/116879.shtml.

Yan, H. (2016). One belt one road – The role of Hong Kong. *City Business Magazine*, Spring, City University of Hong Kong, Hong Kong.

Yau, C., & Yeung, R. (2017, November 14). Tolls at cross-harbor and lion rock tunnels may increase to ease Hong Kong jams. *South China Morning Post*, Hong Kong.

Zhang, X. Q. (2005). Critical success factors for public-private partnerships in infrastructure development. *Journal of Construction Engineering and Management, 131*(1), 3–14.

Zhao, S. (2018, March 6). Hong Kong task force mulls plan to scrap cargo terminal in Tuen Mun to build 22,000 new flats. *South China Morning Post*, Hong Kong.

Zou, P. X. W., Wang, S., & Fang, D. (2008). A life-cycle risk management framework for PPP infrastructure projects. *Journal of Financial Management of Property and Construction, 13*(2), 123–142.

Chapter 12
The "Water-Specific PPP Risk Model": A Case Study in Egypt

I. M. Korayem and S. O. Ogunlana

Abbreviations

ANP	Analytic network process
ASB	Adjusted shadow bid
BOD	Biochemical oxygen demand
COD	Chemical oxygen demand
EGP	Egyptian pound
IFC	International Finance Corporation
IRPI	Idealized risk priorities index
NUCA	New Urban Communities Authority
PPIAF	Public–Private Infrastructure Advisory Facility
PPP	Public–private partnerships
PSC	Public sector comparator
TSS	Total suspended solids
VFM	Value-for-money

Water Public–Private Partnerships

In the early 1990s, market-driven approaches for water resources management started to gain acceptance. Privatization became one of the main reform policies of the major international organizations (World Bank, International Monetary Fund,

I. M. Korayem (✉)
ASTAD Project Management, Doha, Qatar
e-mail: ibrahim@korayem.com

S. O. Ogunlana
Heriot-Watt University, Edinburgh, UK
e-mail: S.O.Ogunlana@hw.ac.uk

R. M. Clark, S. Hakim (eds.), *Public Private Partnerships*, Competitive Government: Public Private Partnerships, https://doi.org/10.1007/978-3-030-24600-6_12

Organization for Economic Cooperation and Development). Water became recognized as an economic good, i.e., a commodity that should be priced at its cost of provision and its true value to society (Ouyahia 2006). The number of people served to some extent by the private sector was 5% of the world's population in 1999, increased to 10% in 2006, and 11% in 2008, and by 2012 reached approximately 14% of the world's population, with around 960 million people being served (Pinsent Masons 2012). The water PPP market includes well-established markets like UK, USA, France, Italy, Spain, and Germany. Emerging markets includes mainly China, Brazil, India, and Russia.

However, the water sector has many characteristics that make it challenging for private sector involvement. One of which is the large fixed cost in its capital investment that has no alternative use (irreversible). Such high fixed cost of water systems leads to economies of scale that contribute to conditions of natural monopoly. Also, given the sensitivity of the water sector to the public, the governments are typically heavily involved in regulating water services, which increases the regulatory and political risks to private companies undertaking this type of investment. Historically, the attraction of water infrastructure for investors was considered to be low when compared to other types of infrastructure.

There has always been a heated debate on the usefulness of private participation in the water sector where the proponents and opponents typically support their claims with figures that should strengthen each party's arguments. The proponents of water privatization have always linked the deficiency in water supply management to poor political governance in some countries, especially in third world countries. This is a very general assumption that ignores the fact that the same political bodies will be responsible in engaging private sector parties in new water PPP projects. On the other side, the opponents have put most of their efforts opposing the concept of water privatization disregarding the currently known operation and management deficiencies under the public scheme.

As of 2005, privatization in water infrastructure attracted only 5% of the investment commitments in developing countries (Izaguirre and Hunt 2005). A severe drop in water PPP investment occurred between 2008 and 2009 with a minor rebound rate since then (Fig. 12.1).

Moreover, the cancelation rate of water PPP projects is about 26% of committed investments compared to 4% in electricity, 3% in telecom, and 13% in natural gas. This has added to the heated debate on private participation in the water sector.

Research dedicated to risk assessment of water public–private partnerships has historically been very limited, typically adopting generic risk lists and considering risk evaluation techniques that are not being used in industry practice. Both academia and industry are lacking the consideration of the interdependency between the risk elements for a given water PPP project, as evident from the extensive literature review undertaken by the authors (Korayem et al. 2015).

In response to such findings, the authors have introduced in previous research, a risk model titled the "*Water-Specific PPP Risk Model*" which, as the name implies, places a special concentration on "Water-Specific" risks in PPPs. It further would

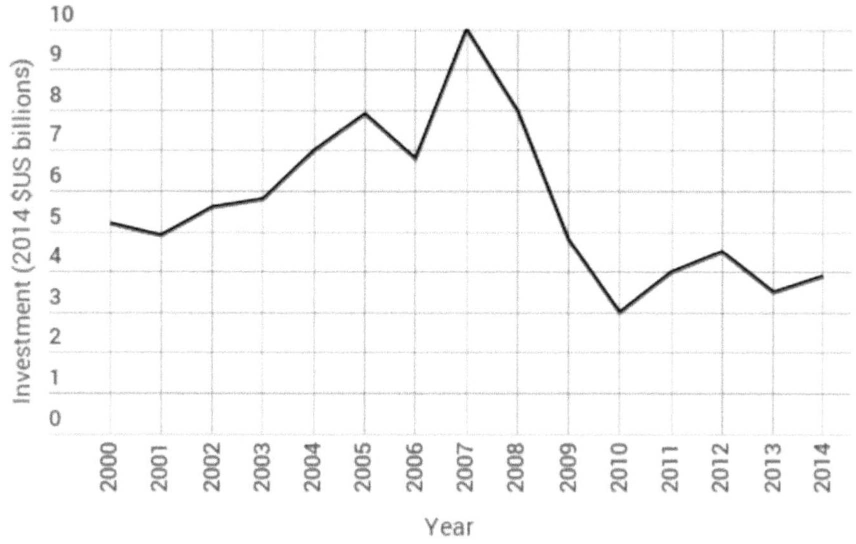

Fig. 12.1 Private participation in water infrastructure between 2000 and 2014 (Source: World Bank Group)

consider the interdependency between such risks by implementing the Analytic Network Process.[1] The research proposed introducing benchmarked risk priority indices, which can be used and further developed so as to enhance the risk assessment process of water PPP projects.

The authors, upon concluding with this earlier research, have acknowledged the model limitations; the most significant one was the lack of real data to validate the model. At the time, and due to confidentiality reasons noted by the respondents, it was not possible to obtain real data from public sector officials or from contractors.

How This Chapter Is Being Structured?

The chapter starts by introducing the background of the project (section "The Egyptian Case"), then introduces the project details (section "The 'New Cairo Wastewater Treatment Plant (WTP)'"), and the socio-political context in Egypt for the period being studied (section "The Egyptian 2011 Revolution"). The

[1] Analytic Network Process: A multi-criteria decision analysis tool that structures a decision problem into a network with a goal, decision criteria, and alternatives. It uses a system of pairwise comparisons to measure the weights of the components of the structure, and finally to rank the alternatives in the decision. The ANP has a unique feature being a tool that considers the interdependency between the elements of the matter, the alternatives, and the decision criteria.

introduction of the authors' previous research and the development of the risk model is presented in section "The 'Water-Specific PPP Risk Model'" and the commentary on the case study and the validation of the model is presented in section "The 'Water-Specific PPP Risk Model' in the Context of the New Cairo WWTP".

The Egyptian Case

In Egypt, the gap between water and sanitation coverage has grown, with access to drinking water reaching 96.6% in 2006 for Egypt overall (99.5% in Greater Cairo and 92.9% in rural areas) and access to sanitation reaching 50.5% (94.7% in Greater Cairo and 24.3% in rural areas). In addition, 27% of wastewater collected in the Greater Cairo area is not treated, and the renovation need is estimated at 50% of the existing network (Salvador et al. 2016). In 2006, the government of Egypt adopted a new policy to increase the involvement of the private sector in economic development so as to expand investment in infrastructure within the country.

In parallel, and in response to the rapid increase in population, the "New Urban Communities Authority (NUCA)" was assigned as the agency in charge of developing new areas and redistributing the population far from the narrow strip of the Nile valley. New Cairo is a city that was created in 2000 in the southeastern part of Cairo, in a former desert area, to ease problems deriving from an overcrowded capital. New Cairo covers an area of about 30,000 hectares with a presumed plan to host a population of five million.

One of the main challenges faced by the new city was the shortage of drinking water. Besides, in absence of the necessary treatment plants, wastewater is typically emptied into the river, which leads to significant negative effects on the river's ecosystem and public health. It was envisaged that the construction for an urban wastewater plant to treat regular urban wastewater in New Cairo would offer the following: (a) improve water treatment; (b) increase freshwater availability since treated water would be used for irrigation purposes instead of freshwater, (c) allow the compost from the wastewater sludge to be used as agricultural fertilizer, and (d) improve the river ecosystem and public health, as an indirect long-term effect.

The Public–Private Infrastructure Advisory Facility (PPIAF) prepared an assessment for the plant procurement method. PPIAF recommended the use of a PPP framework to carry out the project. In 2007, the Government of Egypt appointed the International Finance Corporation (IFC) to structure a PPP transaction for the design, financing, construction, operation, and maintenance of a Wastewater Treatment Plant ("WWTP") in New Cairo under a long-term agreement. At that time, Egypt did not have a specific PPP law. Instead, the public procurement law and its executive regulations were considered for the project.

The "New Cairo Wastewater Treatment Plant (WTP)"

Environmental Impact

The construction of the plant when it is fully operational will have a substantial environmental impact. It is estimated that when working at full capacity the effluent will reduce river pollution as follows: 94 tons of biochemical oxygen demand (BOD), 105 tons of total suspended solids (TSS), and 135 tons of chemical oxygen demand. As of 2016, the plant was operating at one-sixth of capacity. Funding for the project included only the new plant and not the collection system. Before the construction of the plant wastewater was discharged directly into the river which had significant negative effects on the ecosystem and on public health.

Tender Process

The government of Egypt invited companies to participate in a tender to design, finance, build, and operate the wastewater plant within a PPP framework. The International Finance Corporation (IFC) of the World Bank worked as an adviser to the Egyptian government in the process. A number of meetings were held between the contracting authority and the bidders during the prequalification stage to discuss the tender documents and make changes, if deemed necessary.

The procurement method of the New Cairo WWTP was an international open tender with a previous prequalification stage for local and international investors concluding with seven prequalified bidders. The offers were evaluated on a "pass/fail" basis where five bidders "passed" and were invited to the commercial bid opening. A project setup was set as shown in Fig. 12.2.

The Project Special-Purpose Vehicle (SPV)

Orasqualia, the SPV made up of Orascom and Aqualia, was awarded the contract, where each party is holding 50% of the shares.

Aqualia is a water management company within the FCC Group. The group's three main business areas are environmental services, water, and infrastructure. It has presence worldwide serving more than 23.5 million people in 22 countries in Europe, Latin America, the Middle East, and North Africa. Aqualia is the fourth largest private water company in Europe by population served and is among the top ten in the world. Aqualia has significant experience and a track record in the EPC and O&M sectors.

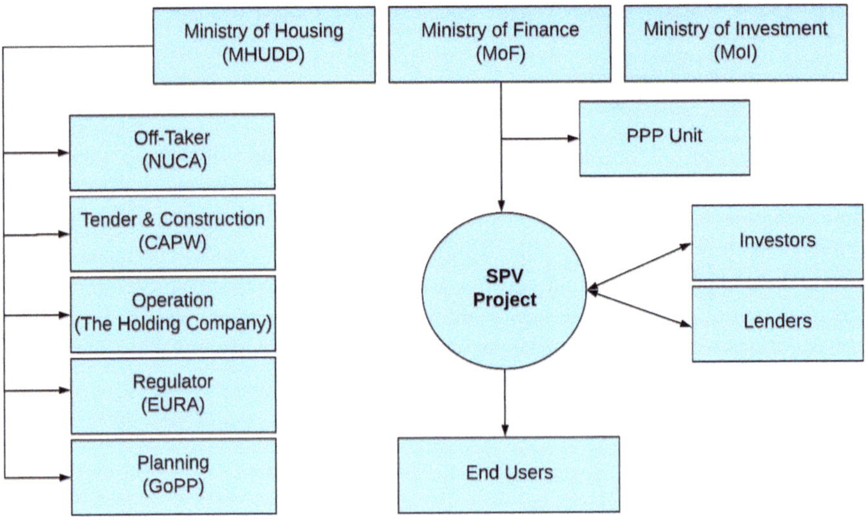

Fig. 12.2 The project setup

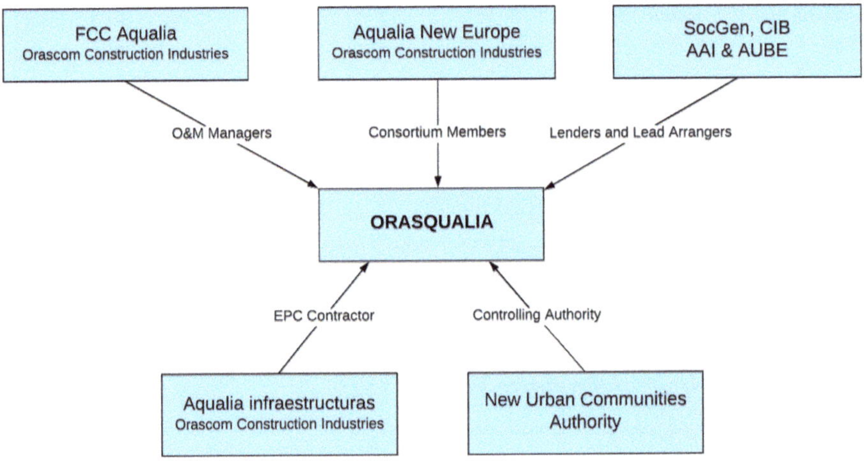

Fig. 12.3 The special-purpose vehicle (SPV) setup

Orascom Construction is an engineering, procurement, and construction (EPC) contractor that was founded in 1950 in Cairo, Egypt. The company was Egypt's first multinational corporation and is one of the core Orascom Group companies. The company focuses on infrastructure, industrial, and high-end commercial projects in the Middle East, North Africa, the USA, and the Pacific Rim for public and private sector clients. The SPV setup is demonstrated in Fig. 12.3.

Payment Mechanism

Orasqualia invoice, the so-called sewage treatment charge, was structured into four different payment parameters (Salvador et al. 2016):

1. Capacity charge—a fixed payment covering:
   (a) Total investments made in the design, construction, and the capital expenditure required during the operational period
   (b) Debt service costs
   (c) Return on equity
   (d) Insurance premium.
2. Fixed operating charge—a fixed payment covering the operating costs that are not volume-related.
3. Variable operating charge—covering variable operating costs with the exception of the electricity consumption cost.
4. Pass-through charge—reimbursement of the full cost of electricity (up to a maximum electricity consumption proposed in the bid by the award-winning consortium).

There were two indexing mechanisms to adjust the price paid by NUCA:

- Adjustment for inflation: Applicable on an annual basis to the fixed operating charge and the variable operating charge but not to the capacity charge. The capacity charge represents the main portion of revenue for the SPV.
- Adjustment for interest rate changes: Applicable every 3 years to reflect changes in Egyptian interest rates on borrowing in Egyptian pounds.

Orasqualia won the bid with the following proposed values (baseline values for 250,000 m^3 per day) (Salvador et al. 2016):

- Capacity charge (EGP[2]/quarter) = 31,272,591.25
- Fixed operating charge (EGP/quarter) = 3,815,625
- Variable operating charge (EGP/m^3) = 0.0355
- Maximum electricity consumption (kWh/quarter) = 5,338,254

Table 12.1 provides a summary of samples invoices made by Orasqualia.

Risks and Risk Mitigation

A fundamental principle is that risks should be allocated to the party that is best able to manage the risk in a cost-effective manner. The risk allocation in PPP projects is fundamentally different to that in traditional projects as the latter include finance

[2] EGP: Egyptian Pound.

Table 12.1 Summary of sampled invoices (quarterly)

	Flow average m³/day	DAYS quarter	Quarterly flow	Variable operating charge	Total × m³	Fixed + variable	% Variable/ total
Dec 13	34,648	120	4,157,760	0.0355	147,600.48	35,235.816	0.42
Dec 14	40,045	120	4,805,400	0.0355	170,591.70	35,258,807	0.48
Dec 15	38,899	120	4,667,880	0.0355	165,709.74	35,235,925	0.47
Jun 16	33,625	120	4,035,000	0.0355	143,242.50	35,231,458	0.41

Table 12.2 Risk register of the New Cairo WWTP

Risk element	Risk owner
Land and space	NUCA
Design and construction	EPC joint venture of Aquila Infrastructure and Orascom
Financing	Orasqualia
Inflation	NUCA/Orasqualia
Interest rates	Orasqualia
Forex	Orasqualia
Creditworthiness	NUCA
Operations and maintenance	O&M joint venture of Aquila Infrastructure and Orascom
Supply of utilities	NUCA
Demand	NUCA
Performance	Orasqualia
Politics	NUCA/Orasqualia

and operational risks to the private party. The literature review showed no evidence of issuing a particular risk assessment by the project sponsors. As such, the work of Salvador et al. (2016), completed with the collaboration of Aqualia, was considered as the basis for observing the risks identified by the project sponsors, as summarized in Table 12.2.

Land and space risk: NUCA obtained the land use concession from the Egyptian army. In addition, a secured area has been allocated for a potential future expansion of the plant.

Design and construction risk: Design is a significant risk in successful project development (Li 2003) where the design deficiency may cause the risk of not meeting the necessary authority approvals or impacting the construction and maintenance costs as noted by Partnership Victoria (Victoria 2001). Design variations may increase project direct cost and time, and may impact the construction schedule leading to additional time and cost overrun (Dawood et al. 2001).

The Engineering, Procurement and Construction (EPC) joint venture composed of Aqualia Infrastructures and Orascom assumed this risk. Aqualia had previous experience of many large wastewater treatment plants, and Orascom had wide experience of big construction projects in Egypt, which makes them the best party to handle this risk.

Financing risk: This was assumed by Orasqualia, which managed to reach financial closing in 7 months.

Inflation risk: The contract included an annual adjustment for inflation. However, this was only allowed for the fixed operating charge and variable operating charge components of the sewage treatment charge, to the main source of revenues for the SPV, the capacity charge. The inflation risk was borne by both agents, Orasqualia & NUCA.

Interest rates risk: The debt was indexed to 3-year certificates of deposit of four "reference" banks every 3 years.

Forex risk: This risk was considered although it was reported that the risk was not perceived as very high in comparison to other developing countries.

Creditworthiness risk: The Egypt's Ministry of Finance was assigned as a grantee of paying the sewage treatment charge if NUCA became in default for more than 30 days of the invoice date.

Operations and maintenance risk: This risk was borne by the O&M joint venture formed by Aqualia and Orascom.

Supply of utilities: The contract included an allowance for a pass-through by NUCA up to a maximum established rate. This has reduced the electricity cost risk.

Demand risk: A small part of the revenues of the SPV was considered dependent on the volume of treated sewage, which means that the risk was mainly borne by the NUCA versus the SPV.

Performance risk: A set of performance indicators was listed in the contract. Quality standards were defined according to Egyptian law and industry standards, and it was agreed to have such KPIs as the basis of future payments. The plant's performance was the responsibility of Orasqualia.

Political risk: This was assumed by NUCA where it was agreed that any risk resulting from the plant's construction or performance would be handled by the political and governmental authorities.

The Egyptian 2011 Revolution

The Egyptian revolution of 2011 took place across all of Egypt. It consisted of demonstrations, marches, occupations of plazas and acts of civil disobedience and strikes. Millions of protesters with various backgrounds demanded the overthrow of the Egyptian President Hosni Mubarak. Violent clashes between security forces and protesters occurred. The Egyptian protesters' grievances focused on legal and political issues, lack of free elections and freedom of speech, corruption, and economic issues including high unemployment, inflation, and low wages.

On February 11, 2011, Mubarak resigned as president and On May 24, 2011, he was ordered to stand trial on charges of premeditated murder of peaceful protesters. After the revolution against Mubarak and a period of rule by the Supreme Council of the Armed Forces, the Muslim Brotherhood took power in Egypt through a series of popular elections, with Egyptians electing Islamist Mohamed Morsi to the presidency in June 2012. On July 3, 2013, Morsi was deposed by the minister of defense, General Abdel Fattah El-Sisi who went on to become Egypt's president in 2014.

The "Water-Specific PPP Risk Model"

The Authors' Previous Research

The authors studied the risk assessment in PPP in general. A systematic process of risk management can be divided into risk identification, risk evaluation, and risk response, where risk response can be further divided into four potential actions: retention, reduction, transfer, and avoidance.

The literature review conducted by the authors showed that risk identification in previous research work has been typically based on literature review, or by applying pre-determined existing lists, or through case studies, or surveys, where the latter has been the most common method. In some cases, a mix between those methods was considered. Risks are typically evaluated through qualitative, semi-quantitative, or quantitative methods. The literature review showed that some researchers categorized risks broadly into general groups (i.e. internal and external), while other researchers classified risks in more details: political risks, financial risks, market risks, intellectual property risks, safety risks, etc. Some research work concentrated on certain categories of risks such as the research conducted on political, financial, commercial, social, and design and construction risks.

The industry practice typically incorporates risk assessment as part of the value-for-money analysis. In order for a governmental agency to proceed with a PPP project, a positive "value-for-money" assessment should be demonstrated. The previous study of a "real-case" assessment of a potential new project showed that the "value-for-money" stage comes after conducting a "Screening Assessment" to determine the potential suitability of the project for PPP delivery. This also occurs after a "Strategic Assessment" that examines not only PPP models but several procurement models that can also be considered.

Specific to risk assessment of water PPP projects, the amount of research work was found to be limited. The critical review of literature showed the potential need for "scope-specific" studies on water infrastructure where "water-specific" risks would be considered rather than depending on generic lists or earlier PPP studies. This observation is also applicable to industry where generic risk lists are generally implemented for the assessment of any PPP project, irrespective of the sector. Finally, the authors observed the subjectivity involved in risk identification with limited survey sampling that is typically being adopted in research and industry applications.

For risk evaluation, the literature review showed that research work mostly varied between adopting over-simplified techniques and over-complex ones. The researchers were of the point of view that adopting an advanced semi-quantitative technique, which considers the interdependency between the various risk elements, would offer a common platform between research and industry and could further develop benchmark values for risks that can be utilized in future assessments.

Development of the Model

Based on findings of the literature review, it was foreseen that adopting an improved risk assessment model would allow for a better evaluation of potential water PPP projects. This would allow governmental agencies in assessing the risks effectively, efficiently, and equitably and in turn develop a more reliable "Value-for-Money" analysis.

The authors' research focused on addressing water-specific PPP risks, which are not effectively covered in previous literature. Further, the model utilizes the Analytical Network Process (ANP) methodology, which contemplates the interdependency between the risk elements.

To achieve the research aim, the following objectives were developed:

- *Objective 1*: To identify and describe the significant risks associated with water PPP projects with respect to cost and to analyze the main reasons for a projects' cancelation
- *Objective 2*: To analyze the interactions among the identified water-specific risks
- *Objective 3*: To assess the severity of the identified water-specific risks
- *Objective 4*: To develop a new model for the assessment of water-specific PPP risks

To achieve objectives 1 and 2, the authors undertook an extensive literature review to identify and analyze the interactions of the risks associated with water PPP. The literature review comprised the coverage of available publications including technical papers, technical and commercial reports, World Bank water sector reports, press releases, and relevant news information. Table 12.3 provides a summary of the main references in literature in which water-specific PPP risks were noted, and summary of those risks is presented in Table 12.4. For a further description of identified risks, the reader is referred to the authors' earlier publication (Korayem et al. 2015).

Following the identification of the set of risks-associated water PPP projects, a questionnaire survey was issued to investigate the severity of each of the identified risks. A total of 53 respondents with previous experience in water PPP provided their responses to the questionnaire survey. The results of the questionnaire survey allowed for listing the risks in order of significance, as seen by the respondents to

Table 12.3 The water-specific PPP risks as identified through the authors' literature review

	Hamilton, Canada	Halifax, Canada	Atlanta, USA	Mali	Gabon/ Gambia/ Chad	Senegal/ Niger	Guainía	Chad	Cochabamba, Bolivia	Manila, Philippines	Buenos Aires, Argentine	Chile	General
Absence of maintenance records	Brubaker (2003e), Buist (1999), Rogers (1999)	Brubaker (2003c)	Segal (2002)										Ameyaw and Chan (2015a), Aisa-Pacific Economic Cooperation (2014), International Bank for Reconstruction and Development/The World Bank (2014)
Absence of environmental data sampling records	Brubaker (2003e), Buist (1999), Rogers (1999), Brubaker (2003b), McGuinness (2001)	Halifax Regional Municipality (2003), Simpson (2003a), Simpson (2003b)											Ameyaw and Chan (2015a), International Bank for Reconstruction and Development/The World Bank (2014)
Uncertainty of value of assets		Brubaker (2003c)	Ippolito (2002)										Ameyaw and Chan (2015a)
Uncertainty of cost of maintenance		Brubaker (2003c)	Ippolito (2002)										Ameyaw and Chan (2015b), Aisa-Pacific Economic Cooperation (2014), International Bank for Reconstruction and Development/The World Bank (2014)
Potential increase in served population			Hardie (1999)			Fall et al. (2009)							Frone and Frone (2013), Ameyaw and Chan (2015a)

	Hamilton, Canada	Halifax, Canada	Atlanta, USA	Mali	Gabon/ Gambia/ Chad	Senegal/ Niger	Guainía	Chad	Cochabamba, Bolivia	Manila, Philippines	Buenos Aires, Argentine	Chile	General
Potential increase in usage			Hardie (1999)										Ameyaw and Chan (2015b), PPP Cell, Department of Economic Affairs, India (2010)
Increase in resources to meet environmental guidelines	McGuinness (2000)		United Water (2002)										Frone and Frone (2013), Carpintero and Helby Petersen (2016), Aisa-Pacific Economic Cooperation (2014), Alfen et al. (2009)
Improper planning of interrelated projects					Fall et al. (2009)		Fall et al. (2009)		Special Unit for South Cooperation (2012)	Brubaker (2003a)			Ameyaw and Chan (2015a), Carpintero and Helby Petersen (2016)
Uncontrolled performance of interrelated projects		Halifax Regional Municipality (2003), Simpson (2003a, b), Brubaker (2003d)											Frone and Frone (2013)
Overly complicated commercial model	Walkerton Inquiry (2001), City of Hamilton (2002)								Special Unit for South Cooperation (2012)				Ameyaw and Chan (2015a)

Table 12.3 (Continued)

	Hamilton, Canada	Halifax, Canada	Atlanta, USA	Mali	Gabon/ Gambia/ Chad	Senegal/ Niger	Guainía	Chad	Cochabamba, Bolivia	Manila, Philippines	Buenos Aires, Argentine	Chile	General
Tariff structure				Fall et al. (2009)			Fall et al. (2009)		Special Unit for South Cooperation (2012)	Cameron et al. (2010), Brubaker (2003a)	Brubaker (2003a)		Frone and Frone (2013), Ameyaw and Chan (2015a), Carpintero and Helby Petersen (2016), Alfen et al. (2009)
Enforcement of right to water resources												Segerfeldt (2005)	Alfen et al. (2009)
Significant change in current billing practice			Segal (2002)			Fall et al. (2009)	Fall et al. (2009)						Frone and Frone (2013), Ameyaw and Chan (2015b)
Potential change in currency exchange rates				Fall et al. (2009)	Fall et al. (2009)	Fall et al. (2009)	Fall et al. (2009)	Fall et al. (2009)		Brubaker (2003b)	Brubaker (2003a)		Ameyaw and Chan (2015a, b), Alfen et al. (2009)
Poor communication with stakeholders	Hamilton-Wentworth Plant Operations Agreement (1994)						Fall et al. (2009)		Special Unit for South Cooperation (2012)	Cameron et al. (2010)	Brubaker (2003a)		Frone and Frone (2013), Ameyaw and Chan (2015a, b)
Potential disruption to current local businesses				Fall et al. (2009)	Fall et al. (2009)	Fall et al. (2009)	Fall et al. (2009)	Fall et al. (2009)	Special Unit for South Cooperation (2012)				
Underperformance of a local partner							Fall et al. (2009)						

Table 12.4 Summary of the water-specific PPP risks identified through authors' literature review

Category	Element
Facility records	Absence of maintenance records
	Absence of environmental data sampling records
Asset condition	Uncertainty of value of assets
	Uncertainty of cost of maintenance
Unsustainable expansion	Potential increase in served population
	Potential increase in usage
	Increase in resources to meet environmental guidelines
Impact from interdependent facilities	Improper planning of interrelated projects
	Uncontrolled performance of interrelated projects
Commercial and/or legal regulations	Overly complicated commercial model
	Potential excessive increase in tariff structure
	Enforcement of right to water resources
	Significant change in current billing practice
	Potential change in currency exchange rates
Mismanagement of stakeholders	Poor communication with stakeholders
	Potential disruption to current local businesses
	Underperformance of a local partner

the survey. Out of 53 respondents to the questionnaire, about 65% of the respondents have 15 years of experience, or more. The majority of the remaining has 5–15 years of experience, with only 4% of the respondents having <5 years of experience. About 64% of the respondents have worked as technical consultants in water industry, 40% of the respondents have worked with a private party, and over 35% of the respondents have worked with the government. Over 75% of the respondents took part in a water management and operation contract. A reasonable mix of expertise between traditional procurement and PPP models was noted. The majority of the respondents (43%) have worked in Africa. Almost a quarter of the respondents have worked in either North America, Europe, or Asia. This would generally indicate the diversity of the expertise of the respondents with respect to geographical areas of professional background.

Following the categorization of identified risks, an Analytical Network Process (ANP) structure was constructed comprising of the project objective, risk categories, and elements. As noted earlier, the implementation of the ANP method allows for the consideration of the interdependency between the various risk elements. Risk categories A, B, C, D, E, and F were considered as primary standards, while sub-variables a1-2, b1-2, c1-3, d1-2, e1-5, and f1-3 were considered as secondary standards. The framework of ANP network process for all risks is shown in Fig. 12.4. As shown in the figure, there is an outer dependency between the different categories and an inner dependency within each member category of risks in the risk prioritization structure. Indirect dominance comparison of variables was carried out according to their influence on project cost.

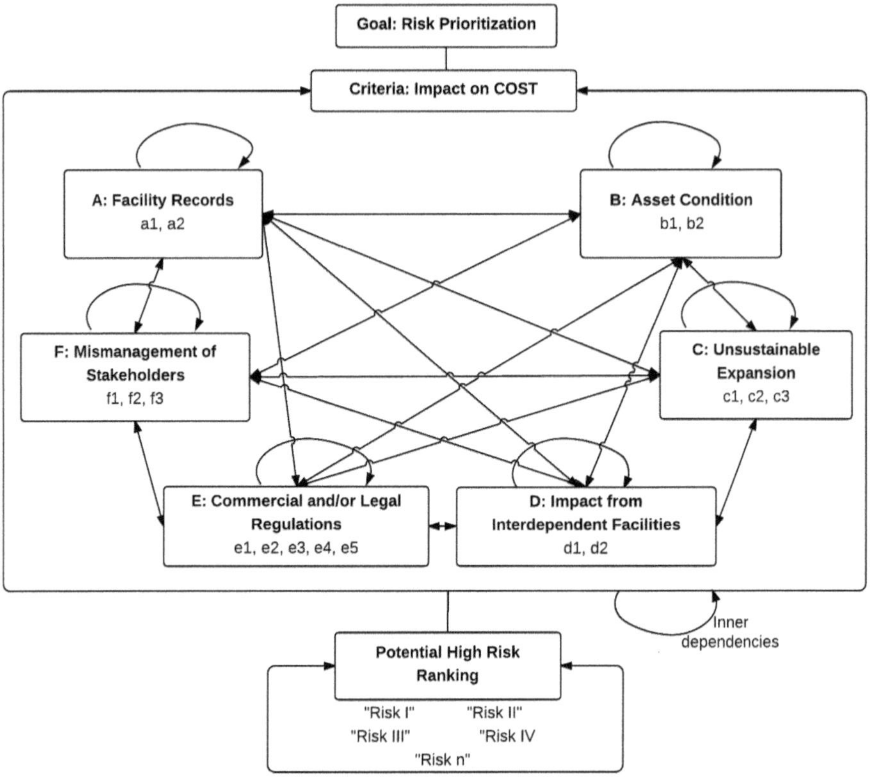

Fig. 12.4 The overall analytic network process structure (Table 12.5)

Once the ANP hierarchy was built, the various elements were evaluated systematically and compared to one another in pairs. In making the comparisons, the rounded mean values derived from the questionnaire survey were used against the ANP fundamental pairwise judgment scale.

After completing the pairwise comparisons, the process requires the developing of the relevant supermatrices, which were computed in three steps. In the first step, the unweighted supermatrix is created directly from all local priorities of the potential risks using the information obtained from the questionnaire survey. Subsequently, in the second step, the weighted supermatrix is calculated by weighing the local priority indices of the unweighted supermatrix with their affiliated priorities for project cost. Finally, the weighted supermatrix is raised to limiting power in order to converge and to obtain a stable set of weights that represents the final priority vector. Stabilization is achieved when all columns in the supermatrix corresponding to any node have the same values.

The risk priorities obtained from the ANP process are subsequently used to list the risks in order of priority adopting the method of "Idealized Risk Priorities Index (IRPI)", where the results can later be evaluated by selecting the appropriate

Table 12.5 Summary of the identified water-specific PPP risks as categorized in the ANP model

Water-specific risk categories		Risk elements	
Code	Category	Code	Element
A	Facility records	a1	Absence of maintenance records
		a2	Absence of environmental data sampling records
B	Asset condition	b1	Uncertainty of value of assets
		b2	Uncertainty of cost of maintenance
C	Unsustainable expansion	c1	Potential increase in served population
		c2	Potential increase in usage
		c3	Increase in resources to meet environmental guidelines
D	Impact from interdependent facilities	d1	Improper planning of interrelated projects
		d2	Uncontrolled performance of interrelated projects
E	Commercial and/or legal regulations	e1	Overly complicated commercial model
		e2	Potential excessive increase in tariff structure
		e3	Enforcement of right to water resources
		e4	Significant change in current billing practice
		e5	Potential change in currency exchange rates
F	Mismanagement of stakeholders	f1	Poor communication with stakeholders
		f2	Potential disruption to current local businesses
		f3	Underperformance of a local partner

"verbal" rating category on their level of impacts on water PPP as Very high (5), High (4), Medium or Moderate (3), Low (2), and Very low (1). The outcome of this process is shown in Table 12.6.

At this point, the development of the water-specific PPP risk model was complete, where the established risk rankings could be considered as benchmarked values (Fig. 12.5).

How to Use the Model?

This section clarifies how to use the model.

- *Step #1: Establish the Project Context and Identify the Risk Assessment Project Team (White in the model)*
  The model is mainly designed to support the "Value-for-Money" analysis, where an estimate of the value of risk is required to assist in developing the associated financial model called the "Adjusted Shadow Bid (ASB)". The model was used to estimate the total project cost if the project is delivered using private sector or public–private partnership. As such, the project manager should carefully establish the project context and identify the risk assessment team who are directly

Table 12.6 Prioritization of the water-specific PPP risks

Risk element	Ranking	IRPI %	Verbal rating
f1: Poor communication with stakeholders	1	100	Very high
d1: Improper planning of interrelated projects	2	99	Very high
a1: Absence of maintenance records	3	99	Very high
b2: Uncertainty of cost of maintenance	4	96	Very high
c2: Potential increase in usage	5	52	High
e5: Potential change in currency exchange rates	6	52	High
e4: Significant change in current billing practice	7	52	High
c1: Potential increase in served population	8	52	High
c3: Increase resources to meet environmental guidelines	9	52	High
b1: Uncertainty of value of assets	10	52	High
f3: Underperformance of a local partner	11	52	High
d2: Uncontrolled performance of interrelated projects	12	52	High
f2: Potential disruption to current local businesses	13	52	High
e1: Overly complicated commercial model	14	51	High
e2: Potential excessive increase in tariff structure	15	51	High
a2: Absence of environmental data sampling records	16	48	High
e3: Enforcement of right to water resources	17	44	High

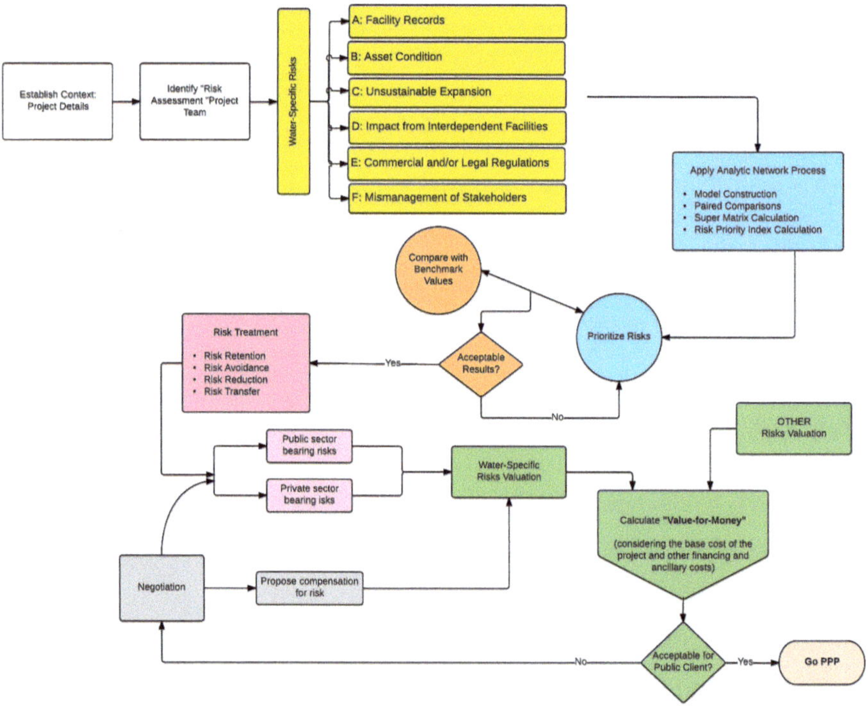

Fig. 12.5 The water-specific PPP risk model

involved in the water sector industry and preferably aware of the project context. Inviting team members who are from the same country (or region) is advisable as it ensures the individual's awareness of the culture and governing laws.

- *Step #2: Risk Identification (Yellow in the model)*
  The model was based on an extensive literature review, which suggested six water-specific PPP risk categories with underlying sub-risks. This would overcome the drawback noted, in research works as well as in industry, where risk assessments are generally based on generic sets of PPP risks with no consideration of the special nature of water projects.

  The use of these risk categories would reduce the exposure to unforeseen project conditions. However, it is important to note that the identified set of risks should not be considered as an exhaustive list. It would however offer a systematic approach for considering additional risks that may be considered applicable by the risk assessment team.
- *Step #3: Risk Prioritization (Blue in the model)*
  The model was based on an extensive literature review that considered risk prioritization. The review of the different methods of risk analysis suggested that the use of the Analytic Network Process (ANP) would overcome the shortcomings observed in other typical risk analysis methods. This is attributed to the ANP capability to take into consideration the interdependency among the identified project risks as oppose to other methods, which in turn would lead to an improved modeling of the identified risks. Besides, the ANP technique is relatively easy to understand and therefore can be easily implemented in industry practice.
- *Step #4: Risk Comparison (Orange in the model)*
  In typical industry practice, the risk assessment team is formed of a limited number of industry experts representing the various stakeholders. This model allows for the opportunity of recognizing previous risk assessments as it offers the priority risk indices, collected from the survey from over 50 industry experts. These values could be used as "benchmarked" values for risk priorities.

  Such comparison with benchmarked values is considered to be unique in this model and offers a way forward for an improvement in risk assessment if the outcome of future risk assessment sessions is consistently being shared and included in the model as priority benchmarked values. The results of previous sessions can be further grouped by country, region, and type of project.

  Obviously, each project would carry its specific unique characteristics and therefore any comparison with the model risks' benchmarks values should be taken with caution. As shown in the model, if the risk assessment team is comfortable with the comparison results, they can move to the next step of risk treatment, otherwise a re-assessment of the identified risks and associated priorities should be considered.
- *Step #5: Risk Treatment (Pink in the model)*
  Looking back at earlier stages, we can see that the risks have been identified, prioritized, and then refined by comparison to benchmark values. The outcome could be considered as a list of risks that have been under a qualitative assessment,

which qualifies per the Project Management Practice, to proceed with the subsequent stage of "Risk Treatment". In this stage, the risk assessment team should consider methods that offer risk reduction, avoidance, retention, and risk transfer. With respect to risk allocation, it should be ensured that the side that owns the risk (public or private) is the party that is best to manage it.

- *Step #6: Calculating the Value-for-Money (VFM) (Green in the model)*
  The estimated cost of the water-specific risks together with the estimated cost of "Other" PPP risks would lead to estimating the "Adjusted Shadow Bid (ASB)", which is the cost estimate if the project is delivered using private sector or public–private partnership. The "Value-for-Money" Analysis can be estimated from the equation below:

$$\frac{\text{Traditional Project Cost under PSC} - \text{Project Cost under ASB}}{\text{Traditional Project Cost under PSC}}$$

  where the "Public Sector Comparator (PSC)" is developed by estimating the total project cost in case the project is delivered by public sector.
- *Step #7: Negotiation (Gray in the model)*
  In case the estimated VFM is not acceptable by the Public Sector, a cycle (or more) of negotiation can take place. The negotiation would include an adjustment to risk allocation, and a compensation for some of the risks undertaken by the private sector. The outcome of this stage should be fed back to the model for re-evaluation of the cost of risks until the VFM becomes satisfactory.
- *Step #8: Go PPP*
  An acceptable VFM is an indication of a feasible PPP project.

The "Water-Specific PPP Risk Model" in the Context of the New Cairo WWTP

The aim of this section is to validate the model by examining the effectiveness and practicality of the model in light of the experience obtained from the New Cairo Wastewater Treatment Plant. To better address this question, it is worth first investigating what has happened in the project from the risk assessment prospective.

What Has Happened?

This section presents a summary of the water-specific PPP risks identified in the model, captured in the project risk register (Table 12.2) and that actually materialized in the project. This is followed by a commentary on the risks materialized in this project.

Table 12.7 Materialization of the water-specific PPP risks in the New Cairo WWTP

Risk element (captured in model)	Captured in project risk register	Risk materialized
f1: Poor communication with stakeholders	NO	YES
d1: Improper planning of interrelated projects	N/A	N/A
a1: Absence of maintenance records	N/A	N/A
b2: Uncertainty of cost of maintenance	N/A	N/A
c2: Potential increase (or decrease) in usage	NO	YES
e5: Potential change in currency exchange rates	YES	YES
e4: Significant change in current billing practice	NO	NO
c1: Potential increase (or decrease) in served population	NO	YES
c3: Increase in resources to meet environmental guidelines	NO	YES
b1: Uncertainty of value of assets	N/A	N/A
f3: Underperformance of a local partner	NO	NO
d2: Uncontrolled performance of interrelated projects	N/A	N/A
f2: Potential disruption to current local businesses	NO	NO
e1: Overly complicated commercial model	NO	NO
e2: Potential excessive increase in tariff structure	NO	NO
a2: Absence of environmental data sampling records	N/A	N/A
e3: Enforcement of right to water resources	N/A	N/A

As indicated in Table 12.7, out of ten applicable risks captured in the model, five risks were materialized in the project and out of which, only one risk was captured in the original project risk register. Before getting further into analyzing the results in relation to the model, it is worth defining the risks noted as “materialized”.

Poor Communication with Stakeholders

There was no evidence of public awareness or consultation during the planning or after the award of the project. Based on industry practice, there would typically be a “Strategic Assessment” analysis, which examines all potential procurement methods covering the traditional and PPP procurement models. The result of this stage is typically published; however, we have no evidence that this stage has taken place in this project.

More importantly, the investigation showed the absence of an evidence of conducting a “Value-for-Money” Analysis, which is an essential deliverable of governmental agencies to justify adopting PPP as a procurement mechanism, if a positive “value-for-money” assessment is demonstrated.

Many political analysts have considered that the absence of transparency of the government at the political and economical levels as one of the main factors that led to the Egyptian revolution. As such, we considered this risk has materialized.

Potential Increase (or Decrease) in Usage and Potential Increase (or Decrease) in Served Population

The PPP agreement is typically set for providing the service assuming a certain design criteria and certain stakeholder requirements. The inability to meet the stakeholders' expectations can draw major negative political implications on the project or affect the project components.

In the Egyptian WWTP project, the plant started its service in October 2013, 16 months after construction finished. However, it was using only one biological treatment line out of the six lines constructed. This is since forecast urban development for New Cairo did not materialize due to several reasons including economic growth moderations and political instability. This has resulted in limiting the sewage water inflows into the plant. From the technical prospective, to keep the plant in the right operating conditions during the whole period at the current levels of inflow, every 4 years Orasqualia would change the line it uses in the treatment process while at the same time it carries out the corresponding preventive maintenance work on all the six lines.

Potential Change in Currency Exchange Rates

Water projects include fixed assets that are considered irreversible. This is typically accompanied with a potential risk of not fully recovering the billing. Even in PPP where the investment program is financed by the partner government, the operator must still finance operating expenses to cover the expatriate staff and imported inputs (chemicals, spare parts, hardware, and software). These costs are in foreign currency, while the operator's revenues are in local currency only.

In Buenos Aires, financial problems plagued privatization, where a private investor won a 30-year water and wastewater concession in 1993. The private investor increased water coverage, billing collection, and operating efficiency. The Argentine financial crisis of early 2002 wreaked havoc on the concession. The peso was "depegged" from the dollar and devalued, and the private investor had trouble servicing its debt, most of which was denominated in US dollars. When the government refused to raise prices to offset the devaluation, the consortium announced its desire to pull out of the agreement, and the matter went into arbitration (Brubaker 2003a).

In the New Cairo WWTP project, Orasqualia assumed the cost of the local currency depreciation. As a result, it has been difficult for the SPV companies to sell Egyptian pounds in the international markets. This is combined with a large depreciation in Egyptian pound as shown in Table 12.8, which was a result of the political instability that occurred following the revolution.

Table 12.8 Depreciation of Egyptian pound

Date	Currency rate (EGP) (EGP equivalent to 1 USD)	Depreciation since March 2009 (%)
March 27, 2009	5.45	N/A
February 5, 2010	5.47	2.91
July 26, 2016	8.68	36.59
November 4, 2016	13.7	63.77
June 4, 2018	17.9	69.55

Increase in Resources to Meet Environmental Guidelines

The private operator is obliged to follow the performance criteria set in the contract. This may require undertaking additional activities that does not form part of the private sector scope of work. The timely implementation of such improvement has been a key factor in success. If not considered in the original private sector planning, the process may be delayed causing problems in the project delivery.

Construction started in March 2010 and lasted for 26 months, until May 2012. The construction period finished with a delay of only 2 months despite the turbulent political situation of 2011. The subsequent delay in the operation period resulted from problems deriving from the quality of the outflow during the commissioning period. During this period, NUCA did not accept, as is the common rule, any discharge of water of a quality outside the parameters established in the contract. This situation forced Orasqualia to construct (at its own cost) a 2-km pipe with a 1.3 m diameter from the New Cairo WWTP to the Hassan Allam Wastewater Treatment Plant for further treatment during the commissioning period. Construction on the pipe lasted from April to June 2013, which meant it was ready when the New Cairo WWTP started to operate in July 2013. The plant managed to achieve the outflow in accordance with legal standards after only 3 months of operations instead of the expected 6 months.

Is the Model Useful?

To offer a systematic approach to the validation, the following set of questions was formulated to examine the model.

1. Is the model useful in identifying risks?
   A shown in Table 12.7, out of ten applicable risks captured in the model, five risks were materialized in the project and out of which, only one risk was captured in the original project risk assessment. This supports the authors' hypothesis that led to the development of the model where it was foreseen that adopting a "Water-Specific" risk register would offer improved risk assessment results. A

careful look at the risks captured under the project risk assessment shows that the only water-specific risks captured in the project risk assessment were the demand risk and the operation and maintenance risks. These general risks are clearly expanded in the model, which would lead to better results when it comes to the assessment of risks of new PPP projects.

2. The model has promoted the use of risk benchmarks. Is that helpful?
   The model promotes the idea of utilizing industry experts' views, which could be utilized toward creating a risk register that may support the industry. The review of the outcome shows that the five of the top six identified risks in the model have materialized in the project. While it is recognized that risks perception and its materialization would change with the change in the location or the specific nature of the project; however, the obtained results can be interpreted that developing benchmark values may offer a valuable support to the risk assessment process of water PPP projects on the long term.
3. How were the model features proven to be effective considering the experience obtained from the case study?

   (a) Risk Treatment
   The model promotes the implementation of risk treatment measures at an early stage of the project. The success of the model in capturing the potential risks associated with the New Cairo WWTP Project encourages undertaking the additional early step of risk treatment measure to reduce, transfer, or eliminate identified project risks.
   (b) ANP and Interdependency
   The model promotes the use of Analytic Network Process to be able to assess the interdependency between the various risks. While there is no possible way to test the effectiveness of this feature, it could be safely assumed that the model's success in identifying the severity of the potential risks impacting the New Cairo WWTP Project is partially attributed to the careful consideration of the interdependency between risks.
   (c) Engagement of experts
   The model promotes the engagement of experts' opinions so as to build on pervious experiences and establish benchmarked values for risks. While there is no feasible way to test the effectiveness of this feature, it could be safely assumed that the model's success in identifying the severity of the potential risks impacting the New Cairo WWTP Project is partially attributed to the consideration given to expanding the pool of experts assessing the water PPP risks.

4. Any proposed modifications to the model?

   (a) Consideration should be given to making the model available for experts so as to continuously obtain their views and update the risk benchmarks accordingly.
   (b) When more data becomes available, splitting between the various WATER project sectors should be considered (water versus waste water, green field

versus expansion, etc.). This would enhance the risk assessment component of the model and enhance the use of the model.
(c) With the engagement of more experts, better results in relation to interdependency of identified risks could be obtained.

Concluding Remarks on the Procurement Process

Reviewing the procurement process, we concluded with the following observations on the process:

(a) There is no evidence of communication with public to discuss the concept of implementing PPP on this project.
(b) For the project feasibility assessment, two stages are typically considered. A “Screening Assessment” stage to determine the potential suitability of the project for PPP delivery which is typically followed with the “Strategic Assessment” stage, which examines not just PPP models, but all potential procurement models. The literature review showed that the International Finance Corporation (IFC) acting as the adviser to the Egyptian government has conducted several meetings during the prequalification phase between the contracting authority (NUCA) and the bidders in order to discuss the tender documents and suggest improvements to the tender design. It has been reported that several suggestions were made by the bidding companies and were accepted and added to the amended tender documents (Salvador et al. 2016). This action would confirm that the “Screening Assessment” stage has taken place. There is no evidence of undertaking a “Strategic Assessment” in the sense described above.
(c) There was no evidence of undertaking a “value-of-money” assessment to demonstrate the cost–benefit analysis justifying the implementation of PPP as a procurement strategy as opposed to a traditional procurement scheme.
(d) NUCA has assumed the cost of electricity, which is to be paid as pass-through cost. This demonstrates a positive approach toward risk allocation, where the risk is allocated to the party that is better able to bear the risk, which is NUCA in this case.
(e) The significant depreciation has impacted the private firm that had to bear the foreign exchange risk. This could limit, in the future, the number of international bidders willing to assume the risk or implement new technologies.

Summary and Conclusions

Private involvement in water sector has been a subject of heated debate where opponents and proponents have been both demonstrating figures supporting their case. The authors’ earlier research resulted in the development of the “Water-Specific PPP Risk Model”. The model offers the decision maker a platform for addressing and analyzing the risk elements associated with water PPP projects considering the interdependency among such risks. The model aims to fill a gap in addressing "Water-Specific" risks in PPP and offers a practical tool for decision makers, approaching new PPP projects, in developing the necessary "Value-for-Money" analysis.

The authors acknowledged the model limitations; the most significant was the lack of real data to validate the model. At the time, and due to confidentiality reasons noted by the respondents, it was impossible to obtain real data from public sector officials or from contractors.

In this chapter, the authors studied the "New Cairo Waste Water Treatment Plant (WWTP)", investigating the impact of the Egyptian 2011 revolution on the project from the social, political, and financial aspects to validate the "Water-Specific PPP Risk Model" and test its capability to enhance the risk assessment process.

In conclusion, the model has proven to be effective in capturing potential water-specific risks in new PPP projects. Out of ten applicable risks captured in the model, five risks materialized in the project and out of which, only one risk was captured in the project's original risk assessment. This also could partially be attributed to the interdependency among risk elements. Further, the model promotes the use of risk benchmarks and implementation of risk treatment measures during planning stages. The case study showed that the utilization of these features in the model would help in addressing and mitigating potential risks in new projects.

It is foreseen that the model could be improved in the future if made open to project experts so as to allow them continuously provide their views and update the risk benchmarks accordingly. When more data become available, splitting between the various water sectors should be considered (i.e., water versus waste water and green field versus expansion), which would further enhance the use of the model.

With regard to the procurement process for the New Cairo WWTP, which is the first PPP project in Egypt, the study has showed some deficiency with regard to the engagement of stakeholders before adopting the PPP procurement scheme. This was observed in the absence of evidence of undertaking and publishing a project "Strategic Assessment" and "Value-for-Money Analysis". These are typically undertaken to evaluate the project and to justify to the public the adoption of the PPP model scheme. A major issue is the significant depreciation of the Egyptian Pound, which impacted the private firm that had to bear the foreign exchange risk. This issue could, in the future, limit the number of international bidders willing to assume the risk or implement new technologies on such projects.

References

Aisa-Pacific Economic Cooperation. (2014). *Infrastructure public-private partnership case studies of APEC member economies*. 2014/FMM/019.

Alfen, H. W., Kalidindi, S. N., Ogunlana, S., Wang, S., Abednego, M. P., Frank-Jungbecker, A., & Zhao, G. (2009). *Public-private partnership in infrastructure development: Case studies from Asia and Europe*. Weimar, Germany: Verlag der Bauhaus-Universität.

Ameyaw, E. E., & Chan, A. P. (2015a). Risk ranking and analysis in PPP water supply infrastructure projects: An international survey of industry experts. *Facilities, 33*(7/8), 428–453.

Ameyaw, E. E., & Chan, A. P. (2015b). Evaluation and ranking of risk factors in public–private partnership water supply projects in developing countries using fuzzy synthetic evaluation approach. *Expert Systems with Applications, 42*(12), 5102–5116.

Brubaker, E. (2003a, October). *Revisiting water and wastewater utility privatization*. Government of Ontario Panel on the Role of Government and presented at "Public Goals, Private Means" Research Colloquium Faculty of Law, University of Toronto.

Brubaker, E. (2003b, October). *Terry O'Neill. Telephone conversation with Elizabeth Brubaker*, January 26, 2001.

Brubaker, E. (2003c, October). *Mike Labrecque. Telephone conversation with Elizabeth Brubaker*, July 18, 2003.

Brubaker, E. (2003d, October). *Labrecque, Ibid. and Gail Lavielle. Telephone conversation with Elizabeth Brubaker*, July 18, 2003.

Brubaker, E. (2003e, October). *Effluent quality data for the period from 1990 through 1999 were provided by Water Quality Manager Mark Stirrup*, April 12, 2000.

Buist, S. (1999, February 2). Ministry investigates Woodward sewage spill. *Hamilton Spectator*.

Cameron, K., Karunananthan, M., & Trew, S. (2010). *Public water for sale: How Canada will privatize our public water systems*. Ottawa, Canada: The Canadian Union of Public Employees and the Council of Canadians.

Carpintero, S., & Helby Petersen, O. (2016). Public–private partnerships (PPPs) in local services: Risk-sharing and private delivery of water services in Spain. *Local Government Studies, 42*(6), 958–979.

City of Hamilton. (2002). *Proposed sale of Azurix North America Corp. to American Water Services, Inc., schedule "D" term sheet* (pp. 15–16)

Dawood, N., Yasuhara, T., Usuda, Y., Matsuda, C., & Sawada, A. (2001, September). Analysis of cost escalation and risk assessment of infrastructure projects: An application in Japanese civil engineering projects. In *Proceedings of the ARCOM 17th annual conference 2001* (pp. 835–844). Salford: ARCOM.

Fall, M., Marin, P., Locussol, A., & Verspyck, R. (2009). *Reforming urban water utilities in Western and Central Africa: Experiences with public-private partnerships*. Water Sector Board Discussion Paper Series, 13.

Frone, S., & Frone, D. F. (2013). Public-private partnerships as mechanisms for risk management in the water sector. *Scientific Papers, 13*(3), 103.

Halifax Regional Municipality. (2003). *News release*, June 20, 2003.

Hamilton-Wentworth Plant Operations Agreement. (1994, December). The region of Hamilton-Wentworth, Philip Utilities Management Corporation, and Philip Environmental. *Plant Operations Agreement, 12*(01), 56–58.

Hardie, A. (1999). City, firm up to their necks in complaints. *Atlanta Journal-Constitution*.

International Bank for Reconstruction and Development/The World Bank. (2014). *WSP report: Running water in India's cities: A review of five recent public-private partnership initiatives*.

Ippolito, M. (2002). Dirty tap water stirs flood of complaints. *Atlanta Journal-Constitution*.

Izaguirre, A. K., & Hunt, C. (2005). *Private water projects: Investments flows up by 36 percent in 2004*. The World Bank Group, note No. 297, public policy for the private sector.

Korayem, I. M., Ogunlana, S. O., & Boateng, P. (2015). Development of the "water-specific P3 risk model: Risks identified". In *CIB proceedings 2015: Going north for sustainability: Leveraging knowledge and innovation for sustainable construction and development* (p. 92). London, UK: IBEA.

Li, B. (2003). *Risk management of construction public-private partnership projects* (Doctoral dissertation). Glasgow Caledonian University

McGuinness, E. (2000). Sewage upgrade tab is $570m. *Hamilton Spectator*.

McGuinness, E. (2001, January 18). Sewage plant firm charged. *The Hamilton Spectator*, p. A1.

Ouyahia, M. A. (2006). *Public-private partnerships for funding municipal drinking water infrastructure: What are the challenges: Discussion paper*. Policy Research Initiative.

Pinsent Masons, L. L. P. (2012). *Pinsent Masons water yearbook 2012-2013*. London, UK: Pinsent Masons LLP.

PPP Cell, Department of Economic Affairs, India. (2010). *Public private partnership projects in India. Compendium of case studies*.

Rogers, W. (1999, October 11). Illegal wastewater dumping triples. *Hamilton Spectator*.

Salvador, J., Trillas, F., Ricart, J., & Planas, M. (2016). *New Cairo wastewater plant, cities case studies. Specialist centre on PPP in smart and sustainable cities*. Geneva, Switzerland: UNECE.

Segal, G. F. (2002). *Atlanta water privatization continues to play out*. Privatization Watch, Reason Public Policy Institute.

Segerfeldt, F. (2005). *Water for sale: How business and the market can resolve the world's water crisis*. Washington, DC: Cato Institute.

Simpson, J. (2003a, June 21). Cleanup contract goes down the drain. *Halifax Herald*.

Simpson, J. (2003b, June 24). City opted for lower-level sewage treatment – consortium. *Halifax Herald*.

Special Unit for South Cooperation. (2012). *Cochabamba, Bolivia, urban water expansion, case study*. United Nations Development Programme.

United Water. (1998, 1999, 2000, 2001, and 2002). *United Water Service Atlanta's drinking water quality report, years 1998/1999/2000/2001/2002*.

Victoria, P. (2001). *Risk allocation and contractual issues*. Melbourne, Australia: Department of Treasury and Finance.

Walkerton Inquiry. (2001, August). *City of Hamilton and Azurix North America. Achieving the vision: The true story of Hamilton and outsourcing* (p. 10). Submission to the Walkerton Inquiry.

Chapter 13
Strategic Management of Public–Private Partnerships: Actors, Aims, and Capabilities

P. O. Achard

Abbreviations

CE	Conformité Européene-European Conformity
ESCAP	Economic and Social Commission for Asia and the Pacific
EU	European Union
ICT	Information communication technology
IGP	Protected geographical indication
MSW	Municipal solid waste
NPM	New public management
PESTEL	Political, economic, social, technological, environmental, legal

Introduction

Public–Private Partnerships (PPPs) are increasingly utilized across the globe. However, this term includes many differentiated modalities of cooperation between companies in the public and private sectors. A PPP has often been intended and applied as a financial instrument aimed at realizing a construction or rehabilitation project, recovering the capital invested through the cash flows generated by the project itself. In this prevailing approach, the focus of a PPP is represented by the structure and articulation of the project, the associated security package, and the elaboration of the economic-financial plan and convention, which specify the modality of investment recovery for the private partner.

The characteristics of PPPs reported in the literature mainly refer to the sharing of final objectives, commitments, and risks (operational and financial) between one or more public entities and one or more private subjects (Hodge et al. 2018;

P. O. Achard (✉)
Department of Industrial and Information Engineering and Economics,
University of L'Aquila, L'Aquila, Italy
e-mail: paolaolimpia.achard@univaq.it

R. M. Clark, S. Hakim (eds.), *Public Private Partnerships*, Competitive Government: Public Private Partnerships, https://doi.org/10.1007/978-3-030-24600-6_13

Thorpe 2018). Typical examples and applications of PPPs in the last 20 years include the construction or rehabilitation of infrastructures all over the world, such as the construction of the tunnel under the English Channel and other important infrastructure in Canada, India, Japan, China, Taiwan, Russia, Brazil, EU, and USA (Bonfim et al. 2018; Carbonara and Pellegrino 2018; Castaldo and Conte 2010; Chou et al. 2015; Kostyak et al. 2017; Robinson et al. 2018; Vinogradov and Shadrina 2018; Yuan et al. 2010). The macro phenomena that have led to the widespread use of PPPs, even though application has been heterogeneous, are related to the globalization of the economy, the financial crises, and the tertiarization and development of the knowledge economy, all of which have profoundly modified the competitive areas, especially in public sectors (Zamanifard et al. 2018).

The globalization of the economy and financial crises have emphasized the socio-economic effects of a competition between companies and country systems no longer based on production (industrial and agricultural), but on knowledge. The tertiarization of the economy and technological development, especially in the ICT sector, has been the catalyst for the collapse of the monopolies of knowledge to which people were accustomed, and has favored the dispersion of knowledge in the most varied territorial and/or sectorial areas.

Research, mobilization, and exploitation of knowledge have become the main competitive factors for companies (Doz et al. 2001). Innovation has become the raw material of the company (Hamel 2007, 2012), the fulcrum of the competition, achieving faster and faster diffusion rates because of the increasing involvement of the clients. The centrality of the public sector promotes development in the knowledge-based economy as the supplier of the entire economic-social system (Zamanifard et al. 2018); therefore, it required a change in the strategic and organizational setup of the public sector.

The diffusion of knowledge, which has become the main factor in economic-global convergence, depends to a large extent on the policies carried out in the field of education and access to training and adequate competences, as well as the institution responsible for these policies (Piketty 2014). Public institutions are particularly complex because they respond to three different models: political, legal, and economic. The search for a dynamic balance between these models is the main criterion for assessing the quality of a public system (e.g., the nation and its territorial articulations, supranational institutions, and international institutes) (Borgonovi et al. 2015).

The introduction of tools, values, and business logic into the public sector, known as New Public Management (NPM), has been applied in diverse ways (breadth, depth, and characteristics). NPM has been differently used in the UK, Canada, Australia, and New Zealand, because of the diversity of the institutional political system and the socio-economic context of reference (Bezes 2018; Gruening 2001; Pollack 2015). However, the common features of these interventions are the promotion of administrative and managerial decentralization, the development of flexible management forms, and governance systems that move toward quasi-market solutions. This has led to an evolution of skills and the role of public management.

NPM does not define a univocal and normative model of management for the public sector, but a set of principles and tools that take on differentiated characteristics according to the political, institutional, social, and economic contexts of implementation and established practices. The vast studies concerning NPM can be articulated according to the perspectives of the investigations and the confluent disciplines. Synthetically, NPM includes four main models in relation to the different degrees of prescriptiveness for the proposed indications and the focus on various managerial tools that can be used for changing the public administration. The first model highlights the need to implement privatistic tools. The second model focuses on the change from centralized and bureaucratic organizational models to structures based on more flexible management systems. The third model highlights the importance of culture in innovation processes, in terms of both the base of the change process and the role of management. The fourth model emphasizes the need to combine privatistic management tools with the mission and values of public services (Ferlie et al. 1996). Several different managerial tools of the rational/mechanistic matrix have been used in the public system, mainly in the 1980s and 1990s. In agreement with the importance assumed by the managerial role in the creation and development of skills, these tools have assumed a humanistic/organic matrix (Bezes 2018; Gruening 2001).

An analysis of the strategic nature of PPPs is the focus of this chapter to underline the importance of strategically appropriate and conscious use of this tool and its repercussions on the system of governance, especially in one of the most relevant sectors of the modern economy, utilities. Utilities are the driving force behind the growth of countries, but by their nature they have a strong social impact, as they directly affect the quality of life of citizens (essential services) (Kostyak et al. 2017; Xie and Thomas Ng 2013; Yuan Sun 2017). A representative example is China, where PPPs are used to develop the internal services but are also to compete in the international market.

An entrepreneurial approach to the provision of services is increasingly requested in the public sector. The social entrepreneurs phenomenon (Kanter 1999) has highlighted the importance of relations with governments and public bodies in order to innovate products, processes, and services. The scientific literature identifies four resources that can be strengthened through the development of relationships with stakeholders: human, technological, reputational, and cultural (Koops et al. 2017; Nederhand and Klijn 2018; Nissen et al. 2014; Surroca et al. 2010).

Strategic partnerships and contractual agreements have become widespread strategic options for business growth (Nucciarelli et al. 2010; Roumboutsos and Chiara 2010). Collaboration strategies can be vertical or horizontal depending on whether the relationship is with suppliers, customers, or competing companies. In PPPs, there is often a network that includes complementors. The motivations behind the collaborative choice are mainly scale-economies, scopes and specialization, the potential expansion of resources and competences, and the often claimed sharing of cost and risk among partners.

Thus, the public service delivery system is governed by horizontal and vertical networks that refer to control mechanisms based on the negotiation of objectives and resources, the implementation of performance evaluation systems (Van der Kolk and Kaufmann 2018), and the traditional hierarchical tools.

The PPP as a Strategic Project

The events and changes described above have had a direct effect of spreading the strategic management perspective in the public system at all its different levels. This perspective is based on a strong motivation for the priority setting and the use of the instruments that are characteristics of planning and control. The main aim is governance of the process of strategy formation, promoting and enhancing the formation of distinctive competences (Eden and Ackermann 2000).

Defining a system of institutional rules that address the activities of managing public companies in order to protect the general interest (Welch and Wilkinson 2004) is important to conjugate the objectives of cost-effectiveness and efficacy for any project with a social nature (Ferraris and Santoro 2014; Purbo et al. 2018). Strategy formulation can be analyzed from both the content perspective and the process perspective. The latter extends the analysis of the peculiarities of companies' strategies to the analysis of strategic methods adopted to transform the available options into competitive responses and implement the possible choices into the organizational system (Mintzberg and Lampel 1999). In such a way, the investigation plan broadens according to two perspectives: (1) a consideration of the wider public decision-making system and its characteristics, and (2) an analysis of the strategy implementation process (Power et al. 2016). Regarding the first perspective, an understanding of the strategic paths of companies cannot ignore the peculiarities of the institutional system and the interrelation of companies with other subjects of the system (both superordinate and not superordinate) that contribute to determining the size and characteristics of the strategic space of decision-makers (Leite and Bengtson 2018; Welch and Wilkinson 2004).

Over the years, regulatory and/or procedural frameworks have been established all over the world at both at the supranational and national levels. In Europe, emphasis has been placed on the design of PPP projects in order to facilitate their application (European Commission 2003). Since the early 2000s, the European Commission has developed an activity for training and providing information on PPP projects, together with the traditional activity of regulating and funding PPP projects (Vinogradov and Shadrina 2018). In the established guidelines, five thematic areas are specified: (1) general characteristics of PPPs, (2) regulatory aspects, (3) financial and economic elements, (4) integration between grant financing and PPP objectives, and (5) planning and implementation phases of PPP projects. The effect of this activity has been the expected adaptation of the modalities of presentation of PPP projects and increasing attention to the main risks that emerged in the applications.

The Economic and Social Commission for Asia and the Pacific (ESCAP), a United Nations agency, has established a guidebook on PPPs in infrastructure that deals with the following topics: (1) main specificities of PPP in infrastructures; (2) elements to be considered before project development; (3) preparatory activities; (4) elements characteristic of process development and key tasks involved; (5) procurement; and (6) management of contracts.

The importance of the role played by the institutions and, especially, the government was recalled effectively in the construction of the Taiwan institutional framework of PPPs aimed at facilitating the subjects interested in investing (Chou et al. 2015). Starting from the awareness that the construction of models and standard practices can only be specific to the country and situation that the country is facing, a framework of analysis of the key stakeholders and their needs is proposed (Nederhand and Klijn 2018), as well as a framework for performance evaluation.

A *managerial* interpretation of the existing documentation highlights the widespread choice to act in line with the strategic planning approach based on the identification of a punctual and formalized strategic planning system. According to this approach, the strategy basically coincides with the strategic plan that must be carried out in a timely and rigorous manner (Anthony et al. 2014).

Although the exigency of regulating PPP projects from both a legal and financial point of view cannot be neglected (Thorpe 2018), the risk of an inversion between *the final aim* and *the way to reach it* must also be considered, though it is rarely considered in the available scientific literature. A consequence of such an inversion is that the virtuous potential circuit generated by the strategic process as a whole, which would be beneficial both publicly and privately, is not activated, though detailed plans are drawn up to finance the project.

The influence of the regulator and, more generally, the institutions must be included within a broader set of internal and external variables (PESTEL analysis) from the involved companies. This set contributes to explaining the characteristics of the strategic paths, as well as the content of the choices (Johnson et al. 2008).

Regarding the second perspective, i.e., analysis of the strategy implementation process, it seems appropriate to underline how the different decision-making levels (EU, ESCAP, nations, regions, etc.) make use of the ideas and proposals from the underlying levels, both in the institutional moments of connection (commissions, project groups, etc.) and the informal situations. This is exactly what happens in terms of corporate strategic planning, which makes use of the informational contributions, competences, proposals, and lines of action emerging from the organizational system. In recent years, such a phenomenon resulted in the application of PPPs to small-scale economic-financial projects of great social importance in several countries, including Italy. An interesting example is the construction of nursery schools in Reggio Emilia in Central Italy, a region considered to be a model of innovation in public utility services. This construction has favored the formation of networks of public–private companies and mixed companies, which act toward common objectives referred to specific territories and/or business. In this situation, the relevance of the project is not related exclusively to the construction of the nursery school, but also to the recovery of an entire suburban area, the enlargement of a central park, the ecological sustainability of the infrastructure, and the provision of new services, all in line with the idea of growth and integrated development.

Analysis of the strategies implies the preliminary definition of the strategic structure, which is the whole of the units of business considering in their specificities and reciprocal interrelationships (Mahoney et al. 2009). Organizations tend to focus their strategic units on core business activities or activities congruent with their own resource base. The need to redistribute critical activities within the organization and/or outsource some of them leads to redefining the supply chain, a useful instrument supporting the evaluation of the company's strategic choices (Grant 2016). Analysis of the supply chain allows strategic interpretation of the organizational system of actors participating in any PPP project and is the starting point for developing fundamental goals, including: (1) identification of the bases of value creation and the definition of strategies of simplification and rationalization of processes; (2) focusing on the core business for the development of core competencies; and (3) analyzing interrelations and defining horizontal strategies (Hamel and Doz 1998). This type of analysis, aimed at building a common strategy in the context of a PPP project, is supposed to include a careful and punctual consideration of the resulting value network. The values network is intended to be a group of companies operating in a specific competitive area, searching opportunities for the creation of value through both cooperation and competition mechanisms.

The examination and definition of the strategic structure of companies must be extended to consider the interdependencies between the various businesses and the definition of horizontal strategies aimed at exploiting possible synergies, not only at the level of the strategic structure of the individual company, but also considering the strategic architecture of partners. Analysis of the interdependencies, which is still poorly explored in PPP projects (Leite and Bengtson 2018), requires knowledge of the technical-economic chains of the various activities in order to grasp the potential for synergies that can be achieved by managing the related relationships (Mahoney et al. 2009).

Assessment of the interdependencies between the value chains of the various business units is a critical element determining the organizational choices of grouping and centralization/decentralization. This explains why many of the studies on PPPs place the organizational modalities and related control mechanisms among the most critical issues (Serrat 2017).

The same conceptual and analytical tools can also be effectively used at higher decision-making levels of the system to define the priority settings, integration mechanisms, and strategic and organizational architectures of public systems. Therefore, formation of the strategy includes the entire process that gradually flows from the deliberate strategies to those realized through the contribution of the flow of actions that spontaneously emerges from the organizational system, pushed by internal and external factors (Mintzberg and Lampel 1999). Strategies are never the result of a completely deliberate process, but arise from the set of intentional and emerging strategies (Mintzberg 1987), following a path that results in organizational learning and the creation of core competencies (Hamel and Prahadal 2010) as the main determinants of the competitive advantage. This is difficult to imitate and, therefore, is defensible over time.

In agreement with the *resource-based theory*, and integrating the *knowledge-based* approach and the *dynamic capabilities* approach, identification and enhancement of the resource assets of companies is a fundamental moment of the strategic process. Nonetheless, it has to be continually renewed according to environmental changes. In this sense, the dynamic capabilities approach may support the importance of relationships among different subjects in identifying the sources of the new knowledge, which is the base of the (dynamic) process of knowledge development. Therefore, in the case of PPPs, the focus of the strategic analysis is not only the business, or the sector, but the value network within which different actors (institutional and non-institutional, partner companies, customers, suppliers, etc.) work together to co-produce value (Ramirez 1999).

In line with the *relational-based* approach, the evaluation of potential relational revenues achievable when the companies involved in an alliance adopt the mechanisms of governance that reduce transaction costs or share their investments in knowledge, resources, and/or capacity is important in all kinds of PPP projects (Dyer et al. 2001). These assumptions are particularly true in the specialization of strategic assets, which is exactly the case in most PPP projects, as private partners are normally the owners of a technical-professional and/or sectorial specialization culture, whereas public partners are the owners of legal and administrative specialization culture.

The strategic network perspective (Lavie 2006) supports understanding and action in the competitive areas that are characterized simultaneously by high uncertainty and high dynamism and strongly affected by the effects of globalization and the rate of technological development. Understanding of the strategic dynamics requires analysis of not only the process of strategy formation, but also the factors that influence this process. These factors can be grouped into the following four macro-areas: the nature of the decision, the characteristics of the decision-makers, the environmental factors, and the internal organizational context.

The nature of decisions in PPP projects flows into a complex decision-making process triggered by both problems and/or crises and opportunities (e.g., the EU policy aimed at funding only certain categories of projects, mainly transportation infrastructure and energy sector) (Pollack 2015). The organizational characteristics of public companies allow a confluence of objectives, values, and needs to push the decision-making processes. These variables activate various logic and decision-making dynamics typical of the various configurations of rationality. Moreover, the organizational action is often activated by a set of cumulative stimuli and factors (internal and external). Partner companies are most likely single-business companies mainly of a technical-specialist nature, which favor more vertical than horizontal sectorial choices.

The second macro-area emphasizes the role of decision-makers, highlighting that the strategic choices mainly reflect the idiosyncrasies of the decision-makers. Therefore, it is important to investigate the influence of the decision-making actor, both as an individual (i.e., preferences, cognitive dynamics, limitations, and cultural and professional orientations) and as a collective (i.e., the formation of decisional coalitions) (Purbo et al. 2018).

The influence of the environment on business strategies can be interpreted according to two different perspectives. First, the decision-making process refers exclusively to adaptation to the opportunities, threats, constraints, and other characteristics of the environment. The role of management is minimized; it is the environment that determines the survival and performance of companies. Second, according to a strategy formation perspective, the influence of the variables can be interpreted by the logic of dialectical interactions between organizational strategies and a series of normative, social, and cultural pressures, which come not only from the institutions but also from the broader and differentiated set of stakeholders.

Given the characteristics of PPP projects and those of the involved actors, the strategic idea is the institution-based view that interprets the strategic analysis as a union between sector analysis, resources used, and institutional framework. In this sense, the institution-based view completes the business and resources analysis. If the environment represents the network of the constraints and strategic opportunities of companies, it is important to consider the way in which individuals interpret and perceive the environment. The same public regulations or environmental factors can be considered by different actors as constraints on decisions or as opportunities to be exploited to increase their strategic options. This is common in the telecommunication sector, initially giving rise only to large-scale projects in metropolitan cities, guaranteeing the partners broad potential for demand and an easy return on investment. Recently, due to the more targeted interventions of utilities and local communities, the sector gave rise to projects in market niches through the exploitation of opportunities and resources that offset the diseconomies derived from the small scale (business innovation) (Gerli et al. 2017).

The environmental context is mediated by the perceptions of decision-makers, by the organizational structures, and by the management systems. The importance of this concept is highlighted by the analysis of three Dutch PPP projects in the transportation sector: the Utrecht Project Central Station, the Amsterdam South Axis, and the Hoog Hage Central Station (Klijn and Teisman 2003). All of these cases demonstrate the difficulty of involving actors at different levels of the public system and the main tensions and problems derived from the different visions of business between the public and private actors (Klijn and Teisman 2003).

Finally, the last macro-area is the internal organizational context, constituting the terrain of collective actions in which strategic choices are transformed into responses to the needs of the area in question. The specific need of PPPs to reconcile economic and efficacy objectives with social goals is met by defining a system of institutional rules that delimit the management action space to protect the general interest. The guiding principle of the strategic choices cannot be represented by the economic result, but has to be represented by the coherence of the choices in the mission of the PPP project. The objectives of the different businesses must be contemplated and aligned with the project objectives (the project as a new business, common to all of the involved partners). The strategic space of the companies is also limited by the conditioning of the plans defined at the national, regional, and local levels, delimiting the strategic corporate development paths.

The institutional setup and influence in the priority setting, the allocation of resources, and general planning and financing cycle of the system outlined above influence the strategic paths in their content and spaces of discretion. The type of business and architecture of the system make the environment highly interconnected relative to the numerous interdependencies linking the network actors. The combination of these two phenomena and need to reduce uncertainty may represent a strong motivation to participate in a PPP project as a strategy aimed to exploit and reinterpret these connections.

The analysis of the macro-structures, formal positions, covered roles, and internal relational dynamics highlights an intolerable and often undervalued risk of PPP project formation, i.e., the lack of a set of organizational and management requirements. This includes, for example, in the case of Dutch maritime industry projects (Keers and van Fenema 2018), employees' lack of preparation, the absence of a performance evaluation system, the poor assignment of responsibility, and an unclear decision-making process.

A differentiated, complex, and variable internal environment characterizes public companies. These characteristics derive, at a strategic level, from the confluence of institutional, social, and economic-managerial purposes and, at an organizational level, from the characteristics of the processes and personnel. An interesting case is represented by health-care processes, which are discontinuous, interconnected, and often fragmented processes characterized by technical and administrative aspects. Analyzing the dynamic relationships between decision-making and organizational processes, a series of influencing factors can be recognized, including (1) the degree of structuring and/or formalization of management policies and systems, (2) the path dependence and/or organizational slacks, (3) the professional management and/or technical coordination tools, and (4) the existence of procedural rules. In Italy, the existence of interconnected units and the need for inter-functionality led to the creation of departmental forms. The departmental organization is based on and simultaneously promotes the inter-functionality of organizational dynamics. In terms of the characteristics of the decision-making processes, this translates into greater decision-making polycentricity and the convergence of information and knowledge (Achard 1999). The presence of departmental forms has solicited various degrees and types of empowerment and influenced the processes of formation of decisional coalitions. An example is the presence of new subjects in the National Health Care system in Italy, the market for which has determined new competitive modality based on dynamic partnerships. This is the case for the H.C. Hospital Consulting S.p.A., which operates in clinical and biomedical engineering, manages 126 healthcare and environmental structures, and has continuously increasing total revenue of approximately 50 million Euros. Recently, this company was acquired by the Austrian VAMED, an international integrated health care provider operating in more than 80 different countries and managing 850 health projects. Notably, in 2017 VAMED realized its 25th PPP project, valorizing the mixture of technical and sectorial competences acquired over the years.

Staff composition in public companies is very different from the composition in other complex organizations because of the stratification of numerous professional categories, with a high intensity of specialized competences, each one permeated with its own professional values. In this sense, the strategic need to exploit interdependencies and organizational need for accountability and responsibility for the project should find a synthesis in contingent organizational arrangements with respect to both internal and external environmental variables, but especially maneuverability and orientation to the objectives, such as through careful evaluation of the centralization/decentralization mix of the organizational units (Bajwa et al. 2017).

Some authors have analyzed the PPP tool using the framework of the I-form (interdependent form), highlighting the organizational role of interdependencies (synergies). In all types of PPPs, the managerial challenges are essentially attributable to the issue of control, mainly focused on resources and competences resulting from collaboration. In this sense, the design of an integrated directional control system can remain detached from the real needs of governance for the entire project if the responsible people are not placed at the center of the system's functioning, combining the economic control needs with the social and temporal needs.

The topic of control in PPP projects is often discussed considering both the technical (project stage) and legal aspects, as contract forms often regulate the partnerships. Moreover, it is frequently discussed from a microeconomic perspective, considering the effects that the verification costs have on project feasibility.

Control System

Governance of the complexity of the management of PPP projects requires a system of controls that is appropriately articulated in relation to the space-time dimensions of the phenomenon to be controlled. In companies of significant complexity, four types of control can be identified: (1) strategic control, (2) organizational control, (3) accounting control, and (4) operational control.

Having defined the role of a PPP as a strategic tool, the strategic control assumes a special relevance. The strategic control concerns both the formulation and implementation of strategic choices, as well as verification of the results of the implemented strategies (Kaplan and Norton 2008). In this sense, the control may operate according to feed-forward mechanisms or feedback. In the first case, the aim of the control is to monitor the environmental variables that played a relevant role in the planning phase, evaluating their impact on the formulated plan in order to perform any required amendments before implementing the plan itself. In the second case, the aim of the control is to achieve the strategic objectives and related intermediate milestones; therefore, it concerns the monitoring of competitiveness factors and the implementation of strategic choices in order to perform any required amendments to the managerial and organizational variables before the strategic choices become economically and/or structurally irreversible (Goold and Quinn 1990).

Strategic choices can be developed within a strategic plan as specific projects, with the relative allocation of resources. In turn, as formalization is one of its constitutive elements, the strategic plan can be seen as a useful tool for the strategic coordination of activities that fall under the responsibility of the project managers, as well as an effective and explicit premise for the formulation of budgets for the involved public partners. The formulation of a strategic plan is more complex in the case of non-profits. In this case, the objectives cannot be measured using only economic-financial indicators due, in part, to the existence of institutional constraints, and of course the trade-off between the targets and scarce resources.

The reporting of management control as part of the strategic control must include not only the short-term economic and financial elements but also the physical and temporal indicators of strategic importance, such as the state of progress of the project and the qualitative and quantitative improvements made during process development. These indicators constitute temporal articulations of the strategic objectives assumed as fundamental to the project's budget.

Organizational control has great importance in PPP projects due to the critical importance that the organizational and behavioral variables assume in order to reach the performance determinants in uncertain and changing environmental contexts. The implementation of effective systems of organizational control appears to be a fundamental step in diffusion of the culture and tools typical of the managerial approach, aiming for improved levels of effectiveness in the management of public utilities. The importance of keeping the processes of organizational change under control is closely connected to the implementation of strategic paths. In this sense, organizational control is an indispensable support for governing the strategic process (Dess and Picken 2000).

The exigency of an adequate control system comes from the need to evaluate the accomplishment of the strategic objectives. With this aim, the organizational control monitors: (1) changes in the organizational structure and operating mechanisms, (2) the evolution of the corporate culture and the prevailing styles of leadership, (3) modifications of the motivational situation, (4) competences, and (5) organizational learning. Therefore, the organizational control is a mechanism of influence and orientation of individual and collective behaviors in relation to the needs of the companies determined by competitive needs and conditioned by the constraints of the base of the resources. This form of control can be considered an aspect of the other control systems and, more generally, the other operating mechanisms, and also an autonomous category of instruments for governing certain management phenomena (Otley 1999).

The mechanisms that directly influence individual and group behaviors constitute the central control system, whereas the mechanisms that exert an indirect influence constitute the factors of the organizational context of control. An important feature of control systems, including the organizational systems, is their extension with respect to the process to be governed. An adequately extended control mechanism tends to control the output variables (i.e., the results) compared to the performance objectives or performance standards (feedback control); the process variables (i.e., the operating methods) compared to the standard operating practices (concomitant control); and the input variables (i.e., the random variables) compared to the needs determined by the functional relationships with the other variables (feedforward control). Emphasis on the whole process or on each of the three classes of variables depends on their measurability in the reference time and on the knowledge of their mutual relationships (Flamholtz 1983).

Input and output control defines a continuum. Every step along this continuum occurs according to the clarity of the causal model, the company size, the degree of differentiation, and the hierarchical level. The organizational control is connected to the other control systems by complementary relationships. The main functions of the control are to influence, address, and ex post verify the performances and organizational behaviors of single individuals and groups. This form of control tends to ensure integration of the divergent objectives of the various organizational subunits through the coordination of activities and maintenance of a system of punctual, selective feedback focused on the relative areas of responsibility (Otley 1999).

The control variables can be input (professionalism or motivation), process (organizational behaviors), or output (performance) variables and have to be considered from both the perspective of influence (ex ante) and the perspective of monitoring their performance for the purpose of governance of management processes. Together with the individual variables, this form of control also monitors the organizational variables (structural, cultural, and others) and related feedback. This feedback influences behavior by either providing information for corrective actions or using the motivational leverage, constituting a source of intrinsic motivation and strengthening the expectation of future rewards. The subjects of organizational control are identifiable among the responsible people of the companies involved in the PPP project at the different levels of the structure, in both their role as supervisors and their role as governmental actors in the other control systems, and among the tools directly aimed at influencing organizational behaviors. From a strategic perspective, these tools mainly include performance evaluation, careers, compensation systems, organizational learning, formation, and changes in the company's culture.

Accounting control is the process by which the objectives and related activity programs are defined and the results and relative determinants are checked, evaluating the deviations and adopting the required corrective actions. The control system tends to include an assessment of the degree of achievement of the objectives (effectiveness control), the use of resources to achieve them (efficiency control), and the relevance of the use of resources with respect to the objectives (pertinent control) (Anthony et al. 2014).

Operational control concerns the process of maintaining efficiency and effectiveness in supporting specific tasks (Anthony et al. 2014). This form of control is based on physical or temporal parameters, rather than economic-financial parameters, using operational programs and progress reports as a reference. The nature of process control implies the use of an immediate feedback system allocated to the areas of responsibility related to the project stages (Berry et al. 2009). Therefore, the related variables are easily controllable in general. A detailed analysis of the criticisms related to the typology of the project is reported by Vinogradov and Shadrina (2018).

The adequacy of any control system depends on the integration of aspects of detection and measurements of present and future events concerning the organizational structures of the areas of responsibility and organizational behavior (Arnaboldi et al. 2015). Thus, the following criteria must be respected: (1) internal organization, (2) timeliness, (3) cheapness, and (4) motivational relevance. In this sense, the adequacy of the information system, the clarity of the hierarchical articulations and contents, and the orientation of corporate culture represent fundamental prerequisites for the feasibility of PPP projects.

ACIAM Case Study

Strategic criticalities in the phases of design, management, and control of projects that include public and private actors can be exemplified presenting the case study of ACIAM Company, a small Italian public–private company, funded not many years ago, which operates in the solid waste management.

ACIAM manages the collection, the transportation, the recovery, and the final disposal of municipal solid waste and industrial non-hazardous solid waste in a large part of Abruzzi Region (central Italy), including the Province of L'Aquila (Fig. 13.1).

The Company operates in the integrated solid waste cycle and, today, has its core business in the management of biological and physical-mechanical treatment plants for Municipal Solid Waste (MSW).

ACIAM is assumed as representative of the strategic complexity of public–private partnership because of several reasons related to the operative sector, the legal-institutional framework, the social composition, the corporative nature, and the activities articulation (Table 13.1).

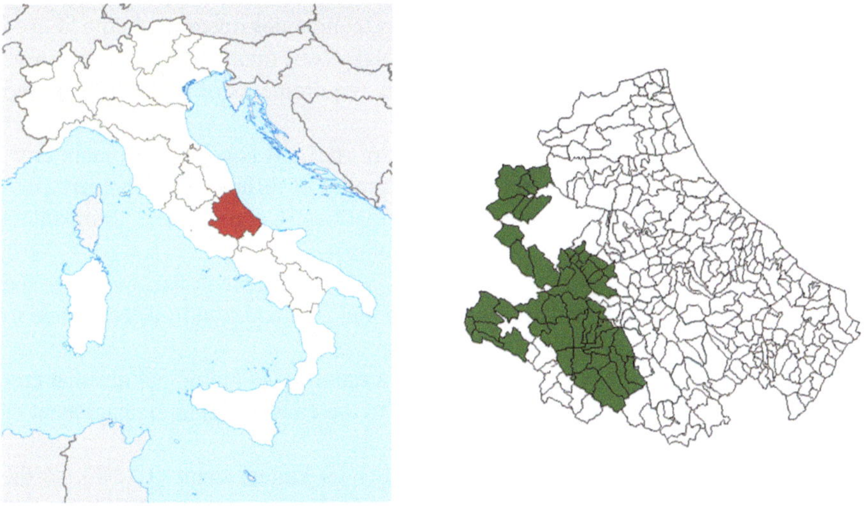

Fig. 13.1 Abuzzi Region and the territory interested by ACIAM activity

Table 13.1 ACIAM in short

Served inhabitants	130,000
Served municipalities	48
Performed activities	commingled waste collection; source-separated waste collection; withe goods collection; management of Aielli MSW sorting plant, including a stabilization phase for the organic fraction; management of Aielli composting plant; management of Avezzano sanitary landfill for the disposal of inert waste; management of five MSW collection centers (Cerchio, Aielli, Pizzoli, Celano, and Lecce dei Marsi)
Employees	125
Revenues	2017: US $18,000,000 2018: US $23,000.000
Technical certificates	UNIENISO 9001: 2000 UNIENISO 14001: 2004 Italian Composting Consortium mark
Management certificates	RINA periodic control on OHSAS 18001 regulations Constant improvement of the company with respect to organizational, environmental, and regulatory standards to safeguard workers' safety and health

Indeed, the analysis of these elements in the framework of the PESTEL set provides many elements of discussion, highlighting existing criticalities.

As said, ACIAM operates in the utility environmental sector, which in Italy is characterized by small- and medium-size companies. Among the first 100 companies of the sector, in fact, only 18 have a total annual revenue higher than 500 million US$. The few of them that have recorded a growth trend in recent years are those diversified into multiple businesses: in most cases the energy business is the only one able to finance the others. Particularly, companies operating in the field of solid waste management have generally very high costs, mainly related to expenses for salaries and wages, and to the continuous requirements of technological and managerial investments.

As far as the legal-institutional framework of ACIAM is concerned, main criticalities arises from the need of managing a plurality of different stakeholders (EU, Central State, Regional Government, Municipalities, Communities, Companies) and their interests, which are not always convergent.

The environmental sector in Italy is subject to several regional, national, and European specific rules (regulatory and sanctioning) in addition to those related to the management of public services.

Furthermore, ACIAM is the expression of a plurality of municipalities that created it originally to satisfy their needs related to the environmental management of the territory (Table 13.2).

The Company has in Avezzano municipality its largest share (12.2%), so the entire strategic process is disaggregated into a multitude of internal and external stakeholders.

Table 13.2 ACIAM strategic history

1990	Foundation of Consortium Marsicano, including 37 municipalities of L'Aquila Province
1997	Conversion to Joint Stock Company Marsia S.p.A. (operated according to the European legislation, with the financial contribution of the Joint stock Company Agac S.p.A. (now Iren S.p.A.)
1999	Participation in the Joint Stock Company Marsia S.p.A. of the Limited Liability Company Tekneko S.r.l
2000	Conversion to Joint Venture Corporation ACIAM S.p.A
2004	Incorporation of the Joint Stock Company Marsia S.p.A
2011	Incorporation of 11 more municipalities and two mountain communities
2014	Disposal of 30% holding in Iren S.p.A 48% of private stock owned by Tekneko S.r.l
2015	Adoption of organizational system prescribed by the new Italian regulation (D.Lgs. 231/2001)

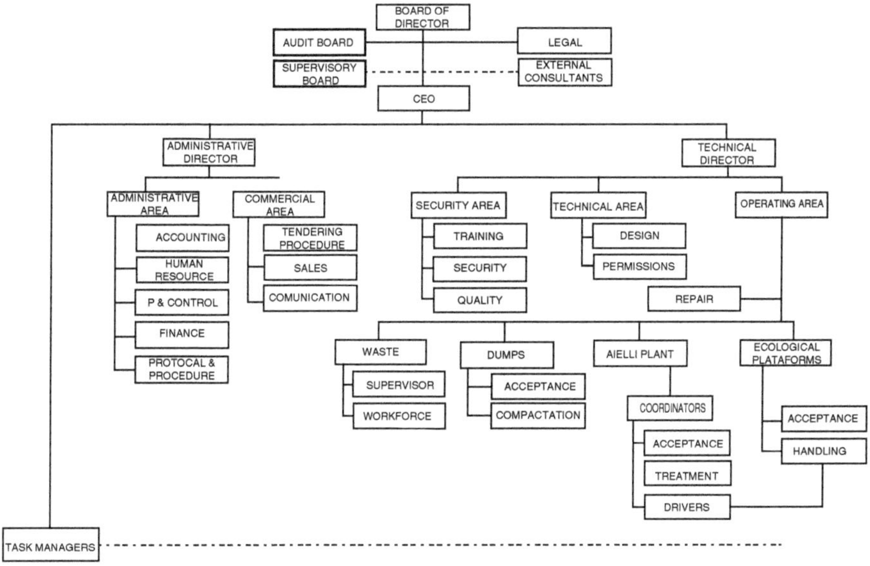

Fig. 13.2 Organizational structure of ACIAM

It is important to highlight that the mayor of a municipality, in Italy, is directly elected by the citizens, and therefore different Mayors may represent shared interests, but different political and institutional approaches.

Internal stakeholders are also private ones, who fundamentally bring capital, technical, professional, and managerial skills.

The multivariate composition of ACIAM also affects the organizational structure of the Company that conceptually embraces both its private and public soul (Fig. 13.2).

It is, in fact, aimed at favoring scale and learning economies, and thus at guaranteeing the efficiency of the entire process of service delivery, but, at the same time, it is subject to its stringent obligations of transparency and responsibility of corporate entities deriving from the full adoption (on a voluntary basis) of the procedures prescribed by the existing legislation (Legislative Decree 231/2001).

The organizational model in this context is a set of rules, procedures, and operating methods that define the organizational, managerial, and control systems within the company, and which aims to prevent or counteract the commission of offenses damaging the security of workers, the environment, the corporates (false corporate communications, improper return of contributions), or the public administration (fraud and corruption). This latter element represents a *trait d'union*, a classic constraint that becomes an opportunity in a country like Italy, scourged by episodes of underworld management, especially in the field of green economy, for the imaginable consequences on health and on socio-cultural aspects of the population. At the same time, in order to mitigate the typical rigidity of these structures and to favor the exploitation of intangible interdependencies (mainly know-how), ACIAM uses integrating roles that work in teams on specific projects.

In terms of articulation of activities, in addition to the recalled characteristics of the sector, it is appropriate to highlight the sharing value not only among municipalities (internal) but also among: (1) customers, represented by the communities to which they belong, playing a key role in the provision of the service; and (2) municipalities and communities not belonging to the consortium, which have entrusted ACIAM, through a tender procedure, to the management of their integrated waste management.

This allows to correctly understand certain aspects of the company's business, such as those related to the correct communication of offered services and performed activities, and those related to the awareness of population (external and internal marketing), carried out during school classes, companies' meetings, and territorial events.

The result of these activities (typically of setup-long term) has led the company to support the achievement of business performances (source-separated waste collection) very rare in the Italian panorama.

The same perspective also allows explaining the technical-managerial consultancy activities that ACIAM provides to the municipalities.

Over the years the strategic architecture of ACIAM has been enriched with business aimed at exploiting the tangible interdependencies typical of waste management, and also of complementary business such as composting, which activates a virtuous circular economy, supplying the nearby farms of the area of Fucino. This area is located in the heart of Marsica, and is known for the high quality of its crops, including the best known carrots and potatoes which have the official and legal trademark of Typical Territorial Product (in Italian IGP), assigned by the Italian regulation.

Overall ACIAM fully represents that the cooperation between public and private actors can be determinant at local level for the improvement of resource, capabilities, and competences improvement.

What is particularly interesting for the specific aim of this work is the activity conducted by ACIAM for the management of the rubble produced by the catastrophic earthquakes, which destroyed many medieval villages of central Italy in 2016.

Indeed, on September 2017 the company signed with the Abruzzi Region a contract for the removal, the transportation, the treatment, the recovery, and the disposal of rubble and other materials deriving from the accidental collapse of buildings caused by the earthquakes occurred between August 24, 2016, and January 18, 2017, together with the management of rubble produced by the demolition of building considered unsafe as consequence of the over-mentioned earthquakes.

In the following months, the company carried out the activities—required in the call for tenders—for the construction of the temporary inter-municipal MSW storage in the Mozzano area (municipality of Capitignano), and purchased the necessary equipment for a new collection center in Montreal, using its own economical resources, or recurring to a leasing procedure.

Overall the Abruzzi Region assigned to ACIAM the removal of about 80,000 rubble tons. In one year, almost one half of them have been collected and managed.

One of the main criticalities of the project is the schedule of the activities, which have to be very rapid, and the number and variety of involved subjects. In fact, the project governance requires the participation of a multitude of subjects, including, for example, the Civil Protection Agency and the Italian Army, which collaborate to the demolition activities.

In addition to the obvious technical, operational, and economical-financial problematic aspects which generally concern management activities, it is representative of the strategic importance of this specific PPP the achievement of the CE mark (in compliance with the EN 13242: 2008 rule) for the recycled aggregate produced by the shredding of the collected rubble, which is reused in civil construction, mainly for the realization of new roads.

The convergence of public–private objectives can be also represented by a picture of June 2018, a few months after the beginning of the project, representing the main square of Campotosto village, a beautiful town of the XIII century particularly affected by the earthquakes, free from ruins, which has been used both for the celebration of religious services and for the events linked to the history of the place, promoting the territory.

Conclusion

The PPP is an articulated and widely used tool adopted worldwide to manage the collaboration between public and private sectors. Its wide and heterogeneous diffusion has also made it a competitive instrument at the national level, as in China.

This chapter dealt with the PPP as a strategic tool for both public and private companies. The instrument must be included in the broadest and most complex strategic business process and oriented toward an adequate analysis, which should not be limited to an evaluation of the balance between costs and benefits related to the project, but has to consider the project in the context of the development of relations with the extended environment (PESTEL) in which the companies are placed. Therefore, this analysis was performed from a business network perspective to highlight the importance that PPPs may assume whenever their strategic advantages are exploited in terms of innovation and learning (shared values).

References

Achard, P. O. (1999). *Economia e organizzazione delle imprese sanitarie*. Milano, Italy: Franco Angeli.

Anthony, R. N., Govindarajan, V., Hartmann, F. G. H., Kraus, K., & Nilsson, G. (2014). *Management control systems: European edition*. New York, NY: McGraw-Hill Education.

Arnaboldi, M., Lapsley, I., & Steccolini, I. (2015). Performance management in the public sector: The ultimate challenge. *Financial Accountability & Management, 31*(1), 1–22.

Bajwa, S. U., Kitchlew, N., Shahzad, K., & Rehman, K. U. (2017). Public-private partnership (PPP) as an interdepend ent form (I-Form) organization. *International Journal of Public Administration, 41*(11), 859–867.

Berry, A. J., Coad, A. F., Harris, E. P., Otley, D. T., & Stringer, C. (2009). Emerging themes in management control: A review of recent literature. *The British Accounting Review, 41*(1), 2–20.

Bezes, P. (2018). Exploring the legacies of new public management in Europe. In *The Palgrave handbook of public administration and management in Europe* (pp. 919–966). London, UK: Palgrave Macmillan.

Bonfim, L. R., Segatto, A. P., & Gonçalves, S. A. (2018). A Conical-Helix Model of technology transfer and public-private partnerships for technological development in Brazilian Public Health. *Technology in Society, 53*, 110–123.

Borgonovi, E., Longo, F., & Fattore, G. (2015). *Management delle Istituzioni Pubbliche* (4th ed.). Milano, Italy: Egea.

Carbonara, N., & Pellegrino, R. (2018). Public-private partnerships for energy efficiency projects: A win-win model to choose the energy performance contracting structure. *Journal of Cleaner Production, 170*, 1064–1075.

Castaldo, A., & Conte, E. (2010). Public-private partnership: Is that the right way to broaden the band in Italy? *Economia e Politica Industriale, 3*, 145–169.

Chou, J. S., Tserng, H. P., Lin, C., & Huang, W. H. (2015). Strategic governance for modeling institutional framework of public-private partnerships. *Cities, 42*, 204–211.

Dess, G. G., & Picken, J. C. (2000). Changing roles: Leadership in the 21st century. *Organizational Dynamics, 28*(3), 18–34.

Doz, Y. L., Santos, J., & Williamson, P. (2001). *How companies win in the knowledge economy*. Boston, MA: Harvard Business School Press.

Dyer, J. H., Kale, P., & Singh, H. (2001). How to make strategic alliances work. *MIT Sloan Management Review, 42*(4), 37.

Eden, C., & Ackermann, F. (2000). Mapping distinctive competencies: A systemic approach. *Journal of the Operational Research Society, 51*(1), 12–20.

European Commission. (2003). *Guidelines for successful public-private partnerships*. DG Regional Policy. Retrieved from http://ec.europa.eu/regionalpolicy/sources/docgener/guides/ppp_en.pdf

Ferlie, E., Pettigrew, A., & Fitzgerald, L. (1996). *The new public management in action*. New York, NY: Oxford University Press.

Ferraris, A., & Santoro, G. (2014). How to develop projects of social innovation in smart city? A Comparative analysis. *Impresa Progetto-Electronic Journal of Management, 4*(1), 1–15.

Flamholtz, E. G. (1983). Accounting, budgeting and control systems in their organizational context: Theoretical and empirical perspectives. *Accounting, Organizations and Society, 8*(2-3), 153–169.

Gerli, P., Van der Wee, M., Verbrugge, S., & Whalley, J. (2017). The involvement of utilities in the development of broadband infrastructure: A comparison of EU case studies. *Telecommunications Policy, 42*, 726–743.

Goold, M., & Quinn, J. J. (1990). The paradox of strategic controls. *Strategic Management Journal, 11*(1), 43–57.

Grant, R. M. (2016). *Contemporary strategy analysis: Text and cases edition*. Hoboken, NJ: Wiley.

Gruening, G. (2001). Origin and theoretical basis of new public management. *International Public Management Journal, 4*(1), 1–25.

Hamel, G. (2007). *The Future of management*. Brighton, MA: Harvard Business School Press.

Hamel, G. (2012). *What matters now: How to win in a world of relentless change, ferocious competition and unstoppable innovation*. San Francisco, CA: Jossey Bass.

Hamel, G., & Doz, Y. L. (1998). *Alliance advantage: The art of creating value through partnering*. Boston, MA: Harvard Business School Press.

Hamel, G., & Prahadal, C. K. (2010). *Strategic intent*. Boston, MA: Harvard Business School Press.

Hodge, G., Greve, C., & Biygautane, M. (2018). Do PPP's work? What and how have we been learning so far? *Public Management Review, 20*(8), 1105–1121.

Johnson, G., Scholes, K., & Whittington, R. (2008). *Exploring corporate strategy: Text & cases*. Harlow, UK: Pearson Education.

Kanter, R. M. (1999). From spare change to real change. The social sector as beta site for business innovation. *Harvard Business Review, 77*(3), 122–132.

Kaplan, R. S., & Norton, D. P. (2008). *The execution premium: Linking strategy to operations for competitive advantage*. Boston, MA: Harvard Business Press.

Keers, B. B. M., & van Fenema, P. C. (2018). Managing risks in public-private partnership formation projects. *International Journal of Project Management, 36*(6), 861–875.

Klijn, E. H., & Teisman, G. R. (2003). Institutional and strategic barriers to public-private partnership: An analysis of Dutch cases. *Public Money and Management, 23*(3), 137–146.

Koops, L., Bosch-Rekveldt, M., Bakker, H., & Hertogh, M. (2017). Exploring the influence of external actors on the cooperation in public-private project organizations for constructing infrastructure. *International Journal of Project Management, 35*(4), 618–632.

Kostyak, L., Shaw, D. M., Elger, B., & Annaheim, B. (2017). A means of improving public health in low- and middle-income countries? Benefits and challenges of international public-private partnerships. *Public Health, 149*, 120–129.

Lavie, D. (2006). The competitive advantage of interconnected firms: An extension of the resource-based view. *Academy of Management Review, 31*(3), 638–658.

Leite, E., & Bengtson, A. (2018). A business network view on value creation and capture in public-private cooperation. *Industrial Marketing Management, 73*, 181–192.

Mahoney, J. T., McGahan, A. M., & Pitelis, C. N. (2009). Perspective-the interdependence of private and public interests. *Organization Science, 20*(6), 1034–1052.

Mintzberg, H. (1987). Crafting strategy. *Harvard Business Review, 65*, 66–75.

Mintzberg, H., & Lampel, J. (1999). Reflecting on the strategy process. *Sloan Management Review, 40*(3), 21.

Nederhand, J., & Klijn, E. H. (2018). Stakeholder involvement in public–private partnerships: Its influence on the innovative character of projects and on project performance. *Administration and Society, 18*, 543–571.

Nissen, H. A., Evald, M. R., & Clarke, A. H. (2014). Knowledge sharing in heterogeneous teams through collaboration and cooperation: Exemplified through public–private-innovation partnerships. *Industrial Marketing Management, 43*(3), 473–482.

Nucciarelli, A., Sadowski, B. M., & Achard, P. O. (2010). Emerging models of public–private interplay for European broadband access: Evidence from the Netherlands and Italy. *Telecommunications Policy, 34*(9), 513–527.

Otley, D. (1999). Performance management: A framework for management control systems research. *Management Accounting Research, 10*(4), 363–382.
Piketty, T. (2014). *Capital in the 21st century*. Cambridge, MA: Harvard University Press.
Pollack, M. A. (2015). *Policy-making in the European Union*. Oxford, UK: Oxford University Press.
Power, G. J., Burris, M., Vadali, S., & Vedenov, D. (2016). Valuation of strategic options in public-private partnerships. *Transportation Research Part A: Policy and Practice, 90*, 50–68.
Purbo, R. K., Smith, C., & Bianchi, R. (2018). ICSSM-71 actor's perception towards motives for adoption of Indonesian PPP programs in the water sector: An email based survey. In *Asia Conference on Engineering and Information* (p. 40).
Ramirez, R. (1999). Value co-production: Intellectual origins and implications for practice and research. *Strategic Management Journal, 20*, 49–65.
Robinson, D., Wells, P., Blandy, S., Ferrari, E., Gore, T., Reeve, K., & Greed, C. (2018). PPP at Ten. *Cities, 11*(3), 165–174.
Roumboutsos, A., & Chiara, N. (2010). A strategic partnering framework analysis methodology for public-private partnerships. *Journal of Financial Management of Property and Construction, 15*(3), 12.
Serrat, O. (2017). Learning in strategic alliances. In *Knowledge solutions* (pp. 639–647). Singapore: Springer.
Surroca, J., Tribó, J. A., & Waddock, S. (2010). Corporate responsibility and financial performance: The role of intangible resources. *Strategic Management Journal, 31*(5), 463–490.
Thorpe, J. (2018). Procedural justice in value chains through public-private partnerships. *World Development, 103*, 162–175.
Van der Kolk, B., & Kaufmann, W. (2018). Performance measurement, cognitive dissonance and coping strategies: exploring individual responses to NPM-inspired output control. *Journal of Management Control, 29*(2), 1–21.
Vinogradov, D., & Shadrina, E. (2018). Public-private partnerships as collaborative projects: Testing the theory on cases from EU and Russia. *International Journal of Public Administration, 41*(4), 1–14. https://doi.org/10.1080/01900692.2018.1426012
Welch, C., & Wilkinson, I. (2004). The political embeddedness of international business networks. *International Marketing Review, 21*(2), 216–231.
Xie, J., & Thomas Ng, S. (2013). Multiobjective Bayesian network model for public-private partnership decision support. *Journal of Construction Engineering and Management, 139*(9), 1069–1081.
Yuan, J. F., Skibniewski, M. J., Li, Q., & Shan, J. (2010). The driving factors of China's public-private partnership projects in metropolitan transportation systems: Public sector's viewpoint. *Journal of Civil Engineering and Management, 16*(1), 5–18.
Yuan Sun, I. (2017). *The next factory of the world: How Chinese investment is reshaping Africa*. Boston, MA: Harvard Business School Press.
Zamanifard, H., Alizadeh, T., & Bosman, C. (2018). Towards a framework of public space governance. *Cities, 78*, 155–165.

Chapter 14
Public–Private Partnerships and Their Application to US Drinking Water Systems

Robert M. Clark and Simon Hakim

Abbreviations

ASCE	American Society of Civil Engineers
CWS	Community water systems
DWSRF	Drinking water state revolving fund
NTNCWS	Non-transient non-community water supply
PPP	Public–private partnerships
PWS	Public water supply
SDWA	Safe drinking water
SRF	State revolving loan fund
TNCWS	Transient non-community water supply
US	United States
USEPA	United States Environmental Protection Agency
WIFIA	Water Infrastructure Finance and Innovation Act
WIN	Water Infrastructure Network

Introduction

It is estimated that there are more than 160,000 public drinking water systems in the US, but most Americans receive their drinking water from one of the nation's over 50,000 community water systems. Three hundred and sixty-one systems serve more than 45% of the total population, or approximately 120 million people. Small- and

R. M. Clark (✉)
Environmental Engineering and Public Health Consultant, Cincinnati, OH, USA

S. Hakim
Center for Competitive Government, Professor of Economics, Temple University, Philadelphia, PA, USA
e-mail: simon.hakim@temple.edu

R. M. Clark, S. Hakim (eds.), *Public Private Partnerships*, Competitive Government: Public Private Partnerships, https://doi.org/10.1007/978-3-030-24600-6_14

medium-sized systems serve the remaining population (Clark 2011). Public drinking water systems in the US are regulated under the Safe Drinking Water Act (SDWA) of 1974 and its amendments. The United States Environmental Protection Agency (USEPA) has promulgated many rules and regulations as a result of the SDWA that require drinking water utilities to meet specific guidelines and numeric standards for water quality. Some of these rules specifically target water quality within the distribution system (Panguluri et al. 2005).

Management and ownership of water utilities can be both public and private, but water supply in the US has a long history of local government control. Water supply systems serving cities and towns are generally administered by city departments or counties or by investor-owned companies. Public systems are predominately owned by local municipal governments, and they serve approximately 78% of the total population that relies on community water systems (CWS). Approximately 82% of urban water systems (those serving more than 50,000 persons) are publicly owned. There are approximately 33,000 privately owned water systems that serve the remaining 22% of people served by CWS. There are also state chartered public corporations, quasi-governmental units, and municipally owned systems that operate differently than traditional public and private systems. These systems include special districts, independent non-political boards, and state chartered corporations (Fujiwara et al. 1994).

The passage of the SDWA has been very effective in protecting the public health of American drinking consumers. It has resulted in the reduction or elimination of exposure from drinking water contaminants ranging from potentially carcinogenic disinfection byproducts to neurotoxic contaminants such as lead. The SDWA provides an outstanding example of the successful collaboration of local authorities (drinking water utilities), state agencies, and the Federal government in protecting the health and welfare of the American public (Allan et al. 2018).

Despite the US success in operating and managing water systems, many organizations have expressed concern over the state of the nation's infrastructure in general and water supply in particular. The American Society of Civil Engineers (ASCE) has graded US drinking water infrastructure at ASCE 2017 Infrastructure Report Card (ASCE 2017). Other organizations including the American Water Works Association (AWWA) and the USEPA have called for increased investment in drinking water infrastructure.

ASCE suggested the use of public–private partnerships (PPPs) to improve drinking water infrastructure. Their argument is that PPPs would facilitate investment in infrastructure. A PPP is a long-term cooperative arrangement between two or more public- and private-sector organizations (Corrigan et al. 2005). An argument frequently expressed for encouraging the privatization of water supply is that private water systems can provide services, at a lower cost, and that PPPs can provide superior access to capital for infrastructure investment. This chapter briefly discusses the nature of water supply systems in the US, and the state of water supply infrastructure. It examines the feasibility of privatizing water systems and/or using public–private partnerships to facilitate infrastructure investment.

Status of the US Water Supply Industry

Water utilities in the USA vary in size, ownership, and type of operation and organizationally have been very stable for many years. The SDWA defines public water systems as consisting of community water supply (CWS) systems, transient non-community water supply (TNCWS) systems, and non-transient, non-community water supply (NTNCWS) systems. CWS systems provide service to year-round residents and range in size from those that serve as few as 25 people to those that serve several million. TNCWS systems serve areas such as campgrounds or gas stations where people do not remain for long periods of time. A NTNCWS system serves primarily non-residential customers but must serve at least 25 of the same people for at least 6 months of the year (such as schools, hospitals, factories that have their own water supply). It is estimated that there are 152,713 water systems in the US which meet the federal definition of a public water system (Clark 2011). Thirty-three (33) percent of these systems are categorized as CWS systems, 55% are categorized as TNCWSs, and 12% are NTNCWS systems. Overall, public water systems (PWSs) serve over 300 million residential and commercial customers. Although the vast majority (82%) of PWSs serve <10,000 people, almost three quarters of all Americans get their water from community water supplies serving more than 10,000 people. Some water systems deliver water to other water supplies, rather than directly to customers. CWS systems are defined as 'consecutive systems' if they receive their water from another community water supply through one or more interconnections (Fujiwara et al. 1994). Table 14.1 summarizes the size and population served by public water systems in the US (Clark 2011).

Distribution system infrastructure is the major asset of most water utilities, even though most of the components are either buried or located inconspicuously. Drinking water distribution systems are designed to deliver water from a source (usually a treatment facility) in the required quantity, quality, and at satisfactory pressure to individual consumers in a utility's service area. Drinking water infrastructure generally consists of storage reservoirs/tanks, and a network of pipes, pumps, valves, and other appurtenances and is collectively referred to as the drinking water distribution system (Clark 2011).

Infrastructure Investment in US Water Supply

The U.S. Environmental Protection Agency's (EPA's) sixth national assessment of public water system infrastructure needs shows a total 20-year capital improvement need of $472.6 billion. The national total comprises the infrastructure investment needs of the nation's community water systems (CWSs), not-for-profit non-community water systems (NPNCWSs), American Indian water systems, and Alaska Native Village water systems. The estimate covers infrastructure needs and

Table 14.1 Public water system inventory data

Type of system, system size, and population served (1)		Very small 500 or less (2)	Small 501–3300 (3)	Medium 3301–10,000 (4)	Large 10,001–100,000 (5)	Very large >100,000 (6)	Total (7)
CWS	# systems	30,417	14,394	4686	3505	361	53,363
	Population served	5,010,834	20,261,508	27,201,137	98,706,485	122,149,436	273,329,400
	% of systems	57%	27%	9%	7%	1%	100%
	% of population	2%	7%	10%	36%	45%	100%
NTNCWS	# systems	16,785	2786	97	16	2	19,686
	Pop. served	2,327,575	2,772,334	506,124	412,463	279,846	6,298,342
	% of systems	85%	14%	0%	0%	0%	100%
	% of pop	37%	44%	8%	7%	4%	100%
TNCWS	# systems	85,366	2657	96	29	4	88,152
	Pop. served	7,315,647	2,602,706	528,624	619,248	12,269,000	23,335,225
	% of systems	97%	3%	0%	0%	0%	100%
	% of pop	31%	11%	2%	3%	53%	100%
	Total # of systems	132,568	19,837	4879	3550	367	161,201

Column 1 in Table 14.1 shows the various categories of water supplies: community water supplies (CWS), non-transient non-community water supplies (NTNCWS), transient non-community water supplies (TNCWS) and the number of systems, the population served, the number of systems, and the percent of population served in each category. Columns 2 through 7 show the categories of water supply considered. For example, very small systems serve 500 or less people. *Source*: Clark (2011)

Table 14.2 US drinking water infrastructure needs

System size/type	Need in billions of $	Population served (millions)
Large community water systems (serving over 100,000 people)	$174.4	174.4
Medium community water systems (serving 3301 to 100,000 people)	$210.6	139.4
Small community water systems (serving 3300 and fewer people)	$74.4	23.4
Not-for-profit non-community water systems	$5.1	

Source: USEPA 2018

includes the installation of new drinking water infrastructure and the rehabilitation, expansion, or replacement of existing infrastructure. The reported projects may be needed to address the existing infrastructure that is deteriorated or undersized, ensure compliance with regulations, provide system resilience, improve energy efficiency, or improve cost effectiveness. Cost estimates reflect comprehensive construction costs including engineering and design, purchase of raw materials and equipment, construction and installation labor, and final inspection (USEPA 2018). Table 14.2 summarizes the cost of US drinking water infrastructure needs by system size.

The findings of the assessment indicate that the need associated directly with Safe Drinking Water Act (SDWA) regulatory compliance remains a relatively small percentage, just over 12% of the total national need. Most water system needs are not directly related to violations of, or compliance with, SDWA regulations. Most needs, such as the replacement or rehabilitation of leaking water mains, are ongoing investments that systems must make to continue delivering safe drinking water to their customers. The assessment includes a total national need of $74.4 billion for small systems. Small systems are defined as serving 3300 or fewer people (USEPA 2018).

The American Water Works Association estimates that here is a need for an investment of $250 billion over the next 30 years in order to meet the need for water supply infrastructure investment. According to the AWWA this would represent the minimum investment needed to make up the difference between needed funds and current underinvestment (Water On Line 2004).

In 2014, Congress authorized a new mechanism to fund primarily large water infrastructure projects over $20 million through the Water Infrastructure Finance and Innovation Act (WIFIA). In 2016 Congress appropriated $17 million in funds for the program. It is estimated that using WIFIA's full financial leveraging ability that a single dollar injected into the program can create $50 dollars for project lending (Water In-frastructure Network n.d.).

PPPs and Their Application to Water Supply Management

Historically, privately owned water utilities were common in Europe, the US, and Latin America in the mid and late nineteenth century. Their importance gradually faded away until the early twentieth century as publicly owned utilities became stronger. In the early 1990s in the aftermath of the Margret Thatcher privatizations in England and Wales, private ownership of water utilities became common. In Scotland, local governments dominated by the Labor Party kept water systems in public hands. The water sector in France has always been characterized by a coexistence of public and private management. The two largest private companies are Veolia Environnement, formerly the Compagnie Générale des Eaux and Vivendi Environnement, formerly Lyonnaise des Eaux. The water supply of Paris was privatized in 1985 when a conservative mayor awarded two lease contracts, each covering one half of the city, but in 2010, a socialist mayor re-municipalized the water system of the French capital (Wikipedia-Water Privatization 2019). However, in the US, private ownership of drinking water utilities is relatively limited, especially for larger systems.

Given the wide use of private water utilities and public–private partnerships throughout the world, it is worthwhile exploring this concept and its potential for application in the US. There is a perception that a PPP might have better access to capital investment funds than municipally owned utilities. There is also a perception that private utilities provide services at a lower cost and then private unities. These issues will be discussed in the following sections.

Do Private Water Utilities Provide Services at Lower Cost?

Frequently privatization offers efficiency gains and has the potential for reducing the costs of providing public services. However, this may not be true in water supply. Some studies have found that private ownership provides cost savings, but other studies have failed to find statistically significant differences in the cost of service between public and private ownership (Bel and Warner 2008). Recent analysis has reported only limited evidence of cost savings. To address this question, a study by Bel and Warner (2008) conducted a meta-regression analysis of 27 empirical studies that compared the costs of private and public water production. The analysis does not show a systematic relationship between cost savings and private production.

In a related study, Bel et al. (2009) conducted a meta-regression analysis of all econometric studies examining privatization for water distribution and solid waste collection services and found no evidence of cost savings resulting from private production. Their results suggest that to ensure cost savings, more attention should be given to the cost characteristics of the service, the transaction costs involved, and the policy environment stimulating competition, rather than to the debate over public versus private delivery of these services. These studies clearly cast doubt on the argument that private water utilities provide drinking water at a lower cost than public utilities.

Is There Adequate Financing Available for Funding Water Supply Infrastructure?

Based on the estimated needs for capital investment to satisfy the demands for water supply, it is reasonable to believe that the lack of capital funding is a major impediment in improving water supply infrastructure. However, historically in the US the quantity of piped water supplied in American cities grew dramatically near the turn of the twentieth century. Most of these systems were owned by local government. According to Cutler and Miller (2005), one of the factors that encouraged this growth were the innovations in local public finance that made it relatively easy for cities to borrow. Therefore, many American cities either purchased or built waterworks, and larger cities that already owned water systems were able to finance massive expansions to previously unserved neighborhoods.

The private sector is already heavily involved in financing water supply infrastructure in the US. This involvement ranges from the engagement of consultants in design, and operation of water utilities to some form of private-sector capital or private-sector financing. A major challenge is the utility's willingness and ability to generate the required necessary funds, and very few water infrastructure challenges are tied to a simple lack of capital. The US water sector has more than adequate with low- and reasonably priced capital from the municipal bond market, banks, and publicly subsidized programs (Hughes and Herndon 2018).

In order to understand the potential for alternative financing models, the University of North Carolina School of Government, in collaboration with USEPA's Water Infrastructure Resiliency and Finance Center, conducted a study in which a sample of communities that employed diverse models using public–private or public–public partnerships was examined (Hughes and Herndon 2018). The project studied the financial implications and risks of different models and approaches. Communities involved were Allentown, PA, the Lehigh County Authority, the City of Allentown PA, Bayonne, NJ, Rialto, CA, the Regina Wastewater Treatment Plant in Saskatchewan, Canada, Davis Woodland Water Supply Project, CA, and the City of Phoenix Water Treatment Plant, in Phoenix Ariz (Hughes and Herndon 2018). They concluded that there are no magic solutions to satisfying the need for funds for drinking water infrastructure investment.

Therefore, it is clear that PPPs do not provide a clear alternative for financing water supply infrastructure because medium to large water utilities can use traditional mechanisms, such as revenue bonds for acquiring capital. But the water supply industry in the US is extremely large and diverse (as illustrated in Table 14.2), and there are thousands of medium to small water utilities that do not have easy access to capital investment markets. It seems reasonable that PPPs could be very effective at the state and regional level for proving private capital for much needed water supply infrastructure investment capital for medium-sized to small utilities. This is an idea consistent with one of the major recommendations of the ASCE Infrastructure Report Card and should be explored thoroughly (ASCE 2017).

Summary and Conclusions

It is estimated that there are more than 160,000 public drinking water systems in the US, but most Americans receive their drinking water from one of the nation's over 50,000 community water systems. One percent (or 361 systems) serve more than 45% of the total population, or approximately 120 million people. Management and ownership of water utilities can be both public and private, but water supply in the US has a long history of local government control. Based on the USEPA's Needs Assessment, the nation's water systems will need to invest $472.6 billion over the next 20 years in order to continue to provide safe drinking water to their consumers (USEPA 2018). The American Society of Civil Engineers and the American Water Works Association have both called for major investment in drinking water infrastructure raising the question as to how this should be accomplished. One approach would be to move toward complete privatization of water system or instituting public–private partnerships in order to provide financing for these investments. However, studies indicate that private water utilities do not provide water services at a lower cost than municipally owned systems, and the water industry has had great success in acquiring capital for larger water utilities (Hughes and Herndon 2018).

It is clear that medium to large water utilities have access to the capital needed for investment in infrastructure. However, there are thousands of medium to small water utilities that do have difficulty in acquiring capital for infrastructure investments. The authors believe that exploring the use of public–private partnerships at the state and regional level and to use state level borrowing authority to assist in acquiring the capital needed to make these investments would be appropriate.

References

Allan, M. A., Clark, R. M., Cotruvo Joseph, A., & Grigg, N. (2018). Drinking water and public health in an era of aging distribution infrastructure. *Public Works Management and Policy, 23*(4), 301–309.

ASCE. (2017). *2017 Infrastructure Report Card. Americas Infrastructure Scores a D+.*

Bel, G., Fageda, X., & Warner, M. E. (2009). *Is private production of public services cheaper than public production? A meta-regression analysis of solid waste and water services* (Working Papers 2009/23) (33 p). Research Institute of Applied Economics.

Bel, G., & Warner, M. (2008). Does privatization of solid waste and water services reduce costs? A review of empirical studies. *Resources, Conservation and Recycling, 52*(12), 1337–1348.

Clark, R. M. (2011). US water and wastewater critical infrastructure. In R. M. Clark, S. Hakim, & A. Ostfeld (Eds.), *Handbook for water and wastewater systems protection* (pp. 135–159). New York, NY: Springer.

Corrigan, M. B., Hambenc, J., Hudnut III, W., Levitt, R. L., Stainback, J., Ward, R., & Witensteinet, N. (2005). *Ten principles for successful public/private partnerships.* Washington, DC: ULI–the Urban Land Institute. Retrieved May 25, 2019, from http://uli.org/wp-content/uploads/2005/01/TP_Partnerships.pdf

Cutler, D., & Miller, G. (2005). *Water, water everywhere: Municipal finance and water supply in American cities. NBER working paper series. Working paper 11096.* National Bureau of Economic Research, Cambridge, MA. Retrieved May 26, 2019, from http://citeseerx.ist.psu.edu/viewdoc/download?doi=10.1.1.610.9066&rep=rep1&type=pdf

Fujiwara, M., Manwaring, J. M., & Clark, R. M. (1994). Drinking water in Japan and the United States: Conference overview. In R. M. Clark & D. A. Clark (Eds.), *Drinking water quality management* (pp. 3–22). Lancaster, PA: Technomics.

Hughes, J., & Herndon, L. K. (2018). Private sector financing: A review of service delivery models in eight communities. *Journal-American Water Works Association, 110*(1), 48–60.

Panguluri, S., Grayman, W. M., & Clark, R. M. (2005, December). *Water distribution system analysis: Field studies, modeling, and management.* Washington, DC: U.S Environmental Protection Agency, Office of Research and Development, National Risk Management Research Laboratory, Water Supply and Water Resources Division. EPA/600/R-06/028.

USEPA. (2018). *Drinking water infrastructure needs survey and assessment: Sixth report to congress.* Office of Water (4606M) EPA 816-K-17-002, March 2018. Accessed May 26, 2019, from https://www.epa.gov/sites/production/files/2018-10/documents/corrected_sixth_drinking_water_infrastructure_needs_survey_and_assessment.pdf

Water In-frastructure Network. (n.d.). *Clean and safe water for the 21st century – A renewed national commitment to water and wastewater.* Retrieved May 26, 2019, from https://www.iatp.org/sites/default/files/Clean_and_Safe_Water_for_the_21st_Century.htm

Water On Line. (2004). *AWWA REPORT underscores value of water.*

Wikipedia-Water Privatization. (2019). Retrieved May 26, 2019, from https://en.wikipedia.org/wiki/Water_privatization

Index

R. M. Clark, S. Hakim (eds.), *Public Private Partnerships*, Competitive Government: Public Private Partnerships, https://doi.org/10.1007/978-3-030-24600-6

D

T